DATE DUE

			PRINTED IN U.S.A.

The Life and Presidency of Franklin Delano Roosevelt

An Annotated Bibliography

Kenneth E. Hendrickson Jr.

Volume 3: Index

The Scarecrow Press, Inc.
Lanham, Maryland • Toronto • Oxford
2005

SCARECROW PRESS, INC.

Published in the United States of America
by Scarecrow Press, Inc.
A wholly owned subsidiary of
The Rowman & Littlefield Publishing Group, Inc.
4501 Forbes Boulevard, Suite 200, Lanham, Maryland 20706
www.scarecrowpress.com

PO Box 317
Oxford
OX2 9RU, UK

British Library Cataloguing in Publication Information Available

Library of Congress Cataloging-in-Publication Data

Hendrickson, Kenneth E.
 The life and presidency of Franklin Delano Roosevelt : an annotated bibliography / Kenneth E. Hendrickson, Jr.
     p. cm.
 Includes bibliographical references and index.
 ISBN 0-8108-5661-1 (hardcover : alk. paper)
 1. Roosevelt, Franklin D. (Franklin Delano), 1882–1945—Bibliography. 2. Presidents—United States—Biography—Bibliography. 3.
United States—Politics and government—1933–1945—Bibliography. I. Title.

 Z8757.29H46 2005
 [E807]
 016.973917'092—dc22

                                                                              2005004305

♾TM The paper used in this publication meets the minimum requirements of
American National Statndard for Information Sciences—Permanence of Paper
for Printed Library Materials, ANSI/NISO Z39.48-1992.
Manufactured in the United States of America.

Contents

Author Index

Aaron, Daniel, 3266, 3267, 3268, 3269, 7173
Aaserud, Finn, 4808
Abbazia, Patrick, 9229, 9230
Abbe, George, 3270
Abbott, Carl, 8101, 8183
Abbott, Frank W., 7174
Abbott, James R. Jr., 6403
Abbott, Mark K., 4631
ABC-Clio Information Services, Comp., 9597
Abell, Aaron L, 4435, 4434
Abell, George, and Evelyn Gerdon, 0033
Abernathy, Elton, 1159
Abraham, Henry J., 6968
Abrahams, Edward, 3608
Abrahams, Paul, 2916
Abramowitz, Mildred W., 0039, 2781
Abrams, Douglas C., 2917, 5290
Abrams, Richard M., 4258
Abrams, Stanley B., 9069
Abrams, Sylvia B. F., 5730
Accinelli, Robert D., 7852, 7962
Acena, Albert A., 6404, 6186
Achenbaum, W. Andrew, 5035, 5106
Acheson, Dean G., 0774, 0775, 2662
Achter, Barbara A.Z., 5107
Ackerman, Bruce A., and William T. Hassler, 1407
Ackley, Stanley W., 2918
Adalan, Farajollah, 7996
Adamic, Louis, 4243
Adams, Arthur B., 1968
Adams, Brooks, 3157
Adams, D. K., 0867, 2663
Adams, David P. Jr., 4809, 8184
Adams, Frederick C., 1947, 2492, 7474
Adams, Gerald M., 1873
Adams, Henry, 3609
Adams, Henry H., 0684, 0974, 7175
Adams, Henry M., 9700
Adams, J.W., 6405

Adams, Jimmie R., 3271
Adams, John A., Jr., 1408
Adams, John C., 1322
Adams, Meredith B., 0650
Adams, Patricia L., 5291
Adams, Paul L., 4181
Adedeji, Moses, 2100
Adelman, Jonathan R., 9464
Adelstein, Richard P., 6981
Adler, Bill, 0030
Adler, Mortimer, 4259
Adler, Selig., 7176, 7711, 7884, 7885, 8992, 8993, 8994, 9070
Adler-Rudel S., 9071
Adorno, Theodor W., 4138
Adubato, Robert A., 5166
Agan, John A., 3030
Agee, James, and Walker Evans, 1309
Agee, Steven C., 1969
Aguilar, Luis E., 7665, 7666
Ahlander, Leslie J., 3610
Ahlgren, Carol, 2919
Ahmed, Hisham H., 8995
Ahola, David J., 6187
Ajay, Abe, 5036
Akers, Stanley W., 9063
Akin, William E., 4810
Akingbade, Harrison, 8662
Al-Nafjan, Fahad M., 7623
Alanen, Arnold, and Joseph A. Edin, 3031
Albertson, Dean, 0665
Albion, Robert G., 4811
Albjerg, Victor, 7886
Albrecht, Donald E. and Steven Murdock, 1409, 1410
Aldcroft, Derek H., 1970
Alder, Les K., and Thomas Paterson, 9465
Aldrich, Mark, 8197
Alexander, Albert, 6880
Alexander, Edward, 9072
Alexander, Jack D., 7351

Alexander, Leslie B., 2101
Alexander, Mary, 0477
Alexander, Robert J., 3517, 6188
Alexander, Ruth Ann, 3272
Alexander, Stanley, 3273
Alexander, Thomas G., 8102
Alexander, Thomas G., and Leonard J. Arrington, 8103
Alexander, William, 3717
Alinsky, Saul, 2438
Alisky, Marvin, 0031
Allan, Donald R., 7260
Allen, Ann, 8198
Allen, Dan C., 7712
Allen, Diane M., 9527
Allen, Edison B., 4108
Allen, Francis J., 9231
Allen, Frederick L., 1651, 2062
Allen, Harry C., 8716
Allen, Howard W., 6406
Allen, Hugh A., 7063
Allen, James B., 8185
Allen, John E., 2102
Allen, Patrick, 4436
Allen, Richard S., 7352
Allen, Robert L., 8251
Allen, Thomas B., 1411
Allen, William R., 0822, 0823, 2048
Alley, Kenneth D., 3718
Allison, David K., 4812
Allred, Kenny, 8968
Allswang, John M., 1652, 4762, 5292
Almaraz, Felix D., Jr., 3189
Almgren, Beverly S., 4139
Alonso, Harriet H., 5913, 7997
Alsaeed, Ibrahim H., 7621
Alsop, Joseph, 0272, 0381
Alston, Lee J., 1323, 1324, 5293, 7064
Alston, Lee J., and Joseph P. Ferrie, 1380
Alston, Lee J., and T. J. Hatton, 1381
Altembaugh, Richard J., 4260
Alter, Robert, 3274
Alteras, Isaac, 7264
Altherr, Thomas L, 4580
Altmeyer, Arthur J., 5037
Alvarez, David J., 7827, 8586
Alworth, E. Paul, 4109
Amann, Peter H., 6365, 6366
Ambrose, Stephen E., 0904, 0905, 0906, 0907, 9232, 9233
Amenta, Edwin, 6407
Amenta, Edwin, and Bruce G. Carruthers, 5038
Amerasia Journal, 8326
American History Illustrated (No author), 2491
Amero, Richard W., 4813
Ames, William E., and Roger Simpson, 2103
Amster, Jeanne E., 4261

Amyx, Clifford, 6136
Andelson, Robert V., 2049
Anders, Leslie, 0920, 3934
Anders, Roger M., 9234
Andersen, Kristi, 6027
Andersen, Kristi, and Stuart J. Thorson, 6028
Anderson, Clifford B., 1325, 1326
Anderson, Dennis M., 6408
Anderson, Elaine, 8186
Anderson, Elizabeth, 5167
Anderson, Herbert L., 4814, 4815
Anderson, Irvine H. Jr., 1744, 7475, 8984
Anderson, James R., 0657
Anderson, Jervis, 5294
Anderson, John T., 1064
Anderson, Karen T., 8199, 8252
Anderson, M. Christine, 1776
Anderson, Michael J., 6800
Anderson, Oscar E. Jr., 4816
Anderson, Paul, 8253
Anderson, Paul G., 4182
Anderson, Terry H., 1412, 9466
Anderson, Walter H., 3275
Anderson, William Cary, 8328
Andidora, Ronald, 9235
Andrade, Ernest Jr., 9236
Andrews, Charles R., 3580
Andrews, Clarence, 8062
Andrews, Faith, and Edward D. Andrews, 3611
Andrews, Pauline, 1578
Anhalt, Walter, and Glen H. Smith, 1327
Anker, Laura, 4140
Ankli, Robert E., 1413, 4817, 4818
Annunziata, Frank A., 0753, 6137, 7065
Ano, Masaharu, 9237
Antler, Joyce, and Daniel M. Fox, 4183
Antognini, Richard, 6409
Antone, George P., 4262
Appel, Benjamin, 9840
Apple, Rima D., 4184
Appleby, Paul H., 6784
Aptheker, Herbert, 5295, 6189
Apthorp, Elaine S., 3141
Archer, Gleason L., 3870
Archer, J. Douglas, 4437
Archibald, Katherine, 8200
Arden, Stuart, 3276
Arendale, Marirose, and Frances Bishop, 8423
Argersinger, Jo Ann E., 2104, 3032, 3033, 5235, 6410
Arguelles, Maria del Pilar, 7702
Armbrester, Margaret E., 6856
Armour, Richard W., 3581
Armstrong, Anne, 8557, 8587
Armstrong, John P., 1262
Armstrong, William D., and John Parascandola, 4185

Arner, Robert D., 3277
Arnold, Frank, 2469
Arnold, Henry H., 0897
Arnold, Joseph L., 3034, 4632, 6411
Arnold, Peri E., 0493
Arnold, Robert W., III, 3035
Arnold, Thurman W., 2782, 7023
Aronsen, Lawrence, 8885
Aronson, Lawrence, and Martin Kitchen, 9467
Arrambide, Pedro M., 7353
Arrington, Leonard J., 1328, 1414, 1568, 1579, 2664, 2665,
    2920, 4674, 8329
Arrington, Leonard J., and Lowell Dittmer, 1415
Arlington, Melvis S. Jr., 5674
Arroyo, Luis L., 2105, 2106
Arthur, Thomas H., 3719, 6412, 4263
Aruga, Natsuki, 8254
Asante, S.K.B., 5296
Asbell, Bernard, 0273
Ashburn, Frank D., 0021
Ashbym, John B., 6969
Ashenfelter, Orley, and John H. Pencavel, 2108
Asher, Robert, 2108
Ashkenas, Bruce F., 6367
Ashmore, Harry S., 0712, 5297
Ashton, Leonora S., 0240
Aslion, Pauol, 9202
Asprey, Robert B., 0965
Astorino, Samuel J., 6413
Astro, Richard, 3278
Athans, Mary C., 4438, 4439
Atkins, George P., 7675
Atkins, Leah Rawls, 6415
Atkinson, Carroll, 7066
Atkinson, Williams E., 6415
Auerbach, Arnold J., 5298
Auerbach, Jerold S., 1252, 1329, 2109, 2110, 5731, 6029,
    6190, 7067, 9701
Auberbach, Jerold S., and Eugene Bardach, 1580
August, Jack, 5712
Ausems, Andre, 9238
Austin, David M., 1581
Austin, Judith, 2921
Austin, Mary, 2111
Austin, Michael J., and Neil Betten, 4633
Autrey, Dorthy A., 5299
Avella, Steven M., 4440
Avery, Inda, 2922
Avery, Laurence, 3279
Awalt, Francis G., 1582
Ayer, Hugh M., 2112

Baack, Ben, and Edward John Ray, 4186
Babcock, John G. C., 1416
Babson, Steve, 2113

Bacha, J. E., 3573
Badash, Lawrence, Elizabeth Hodes, and Adolph Tiddens,
    4819
Bader, Ernest B., 7713
Bader, Robert S., 4745
Badger, Anthony J., 1160, 2923, 2924
Baer, John W., 4110
Baggaley, Philip A., 8588
Bagguley, John, 9468
Bagley, John F., 8589
Bahmer, Robert H., 0541
Bahou, Vistor S., 3190
Baigell, Matthew, 3612
Baigell, Matthew, and Julia Williams, 3142
Bailes, Sue, 6416
Bailey, Garrick, and Roberta G. Garrick, 5808
Bailey, Gary L., 2114
Bailey, John A., 8794
Bailey, Kenneth K., 4441
Bailey, Kristin S., 1777
Bailey, Percival R., 6138
Bailey, Robert J., 1121, 1122
Bailey, Thomas A., 0274, 0382, 0494
Bailey, Thomas A., and Paul B. Ryan, 7265
Bain, George W., 5646
Bain, Reginald F., 3191
Bain, Trevor, 2115
Baines, John M., 7625
Baird, Nancy D., 9239
Baker, Gladys L., 0670
Baker, James F., 7714
Baker, Leonard, 7476
Baker, Melva J., 8201
Baker, Samuel B., 1583
Baker, Susan S., 9702
Balboni, Alan R., 7865
Balderrama, Francisco E., 1653
Baldridge, Kenneth W., 2925, 2926
Baldwin, Carl R., 3613
Baldwin, Hanson W., 8558
Baldwin, John T. Jr., 6417
Baldwin, Roger E., 1821, 6191
Baldwin, Sidney, 1330, 1331
Balfour, Michael, 8590
Ball, Harry P., 4820
Ballantine, Arthur A., 1584
Ballard, Jack S., 9528
Ballenger, Grady W., 3280
Ballowe, James C., 3281
Balog, Cyril E., 0726
Baltensperger, Bradley H., 1382
Baltzell, E. Digby, and Howard G. Schneiderman, 0383
Ban, Joseph D., 9073
Bander, Carol J., 3282
Banfield, Edward C., 1332, 1333

Banks, Anne, 5108, 5039, 5809

Banks, Dean, 5732, 6368

Banks, Larry, 4821

Banner, Lois W., 5914

Banta, Brady M., 1745

Bantell, John F., 9451

Bantly, Trisha, 8330

Baptiste, Fitzroy, A., 7717, 9045

Baram, Phillip J., 8969

Baratta, Joseph P., 9529

Barbeau, Arthur E., 8331, 8332

Barber, Clarence L., 1585

Barber, Henry E., 1929, 5915

Barber, James D., 0275

Barber, William J., 1948, 2025

Barbera, Jack, 3720

Barbour, George Edward, 5300

Barclay, Glen St. John, 8666, 8960

Barde, Robert E., 3084, 9240

Bardolph, Richard, 5301

Barer, Bertram, 3192

Barger, Bob, 6815

Barghoorn, Frederick C., 6192

Barie, Robert W., 0517

Barkin, Steve M., 3935

Barkley, Alben W., 1111

Barlett, Merrill, and Robert William Love Jr., 8717

Barlow, William B., 3518

Barnaby, Marianne G., 4793

Barnard, Harry V., and John H. Best, 4264

Barnard, John, 2116

Barnard, William D., 6418, 6419

Barnes, Catherine A., 5302

Barnes, Harry E., 7716

Barnes, Merritt, 4696

Barnes, William R., 1778, 1779, 1780

Barnes, William R., and A. W. Littlefield, 6947

Barnett, Vincent M., 7041

Barnhart, Edward N., 8333, 8334

Barnhill, John H., 6139

Barnouw, Erik, 3871

Baron, James N., Frank R. Dobbin, and P. Devereaux Jennings, 8104

Baron, Lawrence, 9074

Barone, Louis A., 6030, 6114, 7068

Barrese, Edward F., 9633

Barrese, Pauline N., 5711

Barrett, Glen, 1417, 1853, 1854

Barrett, John W., 8791

Barrick, Nancy D., and Ernest O. Brown, 5303

Barro, Robert J., 2026

Barron, Gloria J., 0384, 0385

Barry, Donald J., 7251

Barry, Michael G., 3283

Barry, Richard, 1334

Barryman, Sol, 0040

Barsh, Russell Lawrence, 5810

Bartels, Andrew H., 1971, 8105

Barthell, Daniel W., 4265

Bartlett, Bruce R., 7477

Bartlett, Peggy M., 9703

Bartley, Numan V., and Hugh Davis Graham, 6420

Barton, Betty L., 7998

Barton, Keith M., 9452

Bartter, Martha T., 3284

Baruch, Bernard, 0724

Bashaw, Carolyn T., 4266

Baskerville, Stephen W., 7006

Baskin, Alex, 2117, 4267

Bass, Bernard M., and George Dunteman, 9241

Bass, Harold F. Jr., 6771

Bassett, Margaret, 0099

Bastert, Russell H., 0824

Bastiste, Joseph C., 8445

Bataille, Gretchen M., and Charles L. P. Silet, 5811

Batchelder, Robert C., 4822

Bateman, Herman E., 0211, 6801

Bates, John L., 0254, 8591

Bates, Sandford, 4697

Batie, Sandra S., 1418

Batman, Richard, 3721

Battenhouse, Paul F., 4442

Battersby, Martin, 3614

Batz, William G., 7999

Batzler, Louis R., 7409

Baudot, Marcel, 7177

Bauer, Boyd H., 8886

Bauer, Gene, 1875

Bauer, Harry C., 3936

Bauer, John I. H., 3615

Bauer, K. Jack, 8106

Bauer, Patrick B., 6421

Bauer, Wolfred, 7266

Baughman, James L., 2050, 2118, 3937

Baum, Christopher F., and Clifford F. Thies, 1972

Bauman, John F., 1781, 1782, 1783, 5304, 5305

Bauman, John F., and Thomas F. Coode, 0685, 0686

Bauman, Mark, 5733

Baxandall, Rosalyn, 5916

Baylis, John, 8719

Baym, Nina, 3582

Bayor, Ronald H., 5734, 5735

Bazelon, David T., 0569 6031

Beal, Fred E., 6193

Beale, Howard K., 9704

Bealle, Morris A., 6194, 7069

Beam, John C., 8682

Bean, Barton, 6868

Bean, Philip A., 6369

Bean, Philip G., 6422

Beard, Charles A., 7178, 7717, 7718, 9705
Beard, Charles A., and George H. E. Smith, 2666
Beard, Earl S., 7070
Bearden, Russell, 8335, 8336
Beardsly, E. H., 4187, 5306
Beasley, Maurine H., 0042, 0043, 0044, 0616, 0617, 0618
Beasley, Maurine H., and Paul Belgrade, 0041
Beatty, David P., 8672
Bebel, Sandra K, 8063
Bechtol, Paul T., Jr., 4141
Beck, Alfred M., 7267
Beck, Kent, 6195
Beck, Robert T., 7626
Beck, Rochelle, 4675
Becker, Harry, 2667
Becker, Joseph M., 1973
Becker, Samuel L., 0130
Becker, Susan D., 5917
Becker, William H., 6196
Beckett, Grace L., 1822, 1823
Beckham, Stephen Dow, 9706
Beckham, Sue B., 5168, 5273
Beckstead, Robert W., 1586
Becnel, Thomas A., 6423
Beddow, James B., 1824, 3938
Bedelow, James B., 1335
Beecher, Lloyd Jr., 8663
Beechert, Edward D., 2119
Beeler, Anne B., 2063
Beesley, David, 2120
Beezer, Bruce G., 5307, 5236
Begley, Adam C., 3285
Beik, Mildred A., 2064
Beiswinger, George L., 3939
Beito, David T., 1587, 1654
Beitzell, Robert E., 8592, 8649
Belgum, Donald T., 6900
Belin, George L., 4143
Belknap, Michael R., 6197, 6901, 7007
Bell, Leland V., 6370, 6371, 6372
Bell, Roger, 8667
Bell, Samuel R., 9707
Bell, Wendell, and Ernest M. Willis, 5308
Belles, A. Gilbert, 5309
Bellow, Saul, 4142
Bellush, Bernard, 0265, 0266, 0276
Bellush, Bernard, and Jewel Bellush, 6198
Bellush, Jewel, 0748, 0749, 6424, 6425
Belz, Herman, 9469
Ben-Moshe, Tuvia, 8720
Ben-Zvi, Abraham, 7478
Benco, Nancy L., 0495
Bender, Jay, 6426
Bendiner, Robert, 3940
Benedict, Blaine E., 8807

Benedict, M. R., 1336, 1337
Benes, Edward, 8804
Benham, R. Leon, 2668
Benigni, Helen, 3286
Benjamin, Jules R., 7627, 7667, 7668
Bennett, David H., 2121, 6816
Bennett, Edward M., 7179, 7410, 7411, 7828
Bennett, James D., 0766, 3085
Bennett, Sheila K., and Glen H. Elder Jr., 5918
Bennett, William E., 2669
Benson, Elmer A., 6427
Benson, Frederick R., 7354
Benson, Jack A., 9242
Benson, Jackson J., and Anne Loftis, 3287
Benson, Paul R., 6902
Benson, Robert A., 3158
Benson, Thomas W., 0131, 0518
Benston, George J., 1588, 2783
Bentinck-Smith, William, 3616
Bentley, H. Blair, 4268
Benze, James G., Jr., 0277
Berber, Milton, 2493
Berberet, William G., 1419
Berck, Peter, 1383
Berens, John F., 6869
Berg, Gordon, 0658
Berg, Meredith W., 7829, 9243
Berg, Roland H., 0212
Berg, S. Carol, 5812
Bergamini, David, 7479
Berger, Henry W., 2122, 7686
Berger, Jason, 0045
Berger, Morroe, 3519
Bergman, Andrew, 3722
Berkes, Ross N., 8887
Berkman, Dave, 3872
Berkowitz, Edward D., and Kim McQuaid, 4190
Berkowitz, Edward D., and Monroe Berkowitz, 4188
Berkowitz, Edward D., 2784, 4189
Berle, Adolph A., 1935
Berlin, Isaiah, 0001
Berlin, Robert H., 0908
Berman, Aaron, 9076
Berman, Daniel M., 6972, 6973
Berman, Gerald S., 9077
Berman, Greta, 5237, 5238
Berman, Hyman, 5736
Berman, Larry, 0496
Berman, Paul, 6199
Bernabe, Rafel A., 7703
Bernanke, Ben S., and Martin Parkinson, 1949
Bernanke, Ben S., 1589, 1590
Bernhardt, Debra, 2123
Berninger, Dieter, 6373
Bernstein, Alison R., 5813, 5814

Bernstein, Barton J., 4823, 6032, 7268, 7719, 8107, 8108, 8559, 9244, 9245, 9470, 9471, 9708
Bernstein, Irving, 2124, 2125
Bernstein, Matthew H., 3723
Bernstein, Michael A., 1591, 1974, 2494
Berry, Mrs. John, 1420
Berry, Robert, 8681
Berstein, Irving, 2065
Beschloss, Michael R., 0855
Bessie, Alvah, and Albert Prago, 7355
Best, Gary D., 7071, 7072, 7073, 7887, 7963
Beth, Loren P., 6903
Bethge, Renate, 9078
Bethune, Beverly M., 6885
Betten, Neil, 2126, 2127, 2128, 2129, 3941, 4443, 4444, 4445
Betten, Neil, and Raymond A. Mohl, 4144, 5310, 5675
Beyer, Barry K., 6033, 6428
Beyer, William C., 3942
Bhana, Surendra, 6429, 7704
Bibler, Thomas E., 3943
Bicha, Karel Denis, 6140
Bicker, Robert J., 6200
Bickerstaff, Joyce, and Wilbur C. Rich, 0046
Bickford, Charles B., 9634
Biddle, Anthony J. D., 0778
Biebel, Charles D., 3036, 4269, 4270
Biegel, Alan I., 6904
Biella, Arnold, 3193
Bierbrier, Doreen, 9079
Bigelow, William, and Norman Diamond, 2130
Bilderback, Willima, 6201
Biles, Roger, 1784, 2131, 3037, 3038, 5647, 5648, 6430, 6431
Biles, William R., 6432
Billinger, Robert D. Jr., 8447, 8446
Billings, Alan G., 5109
Billings, Eldin E., 7180
Billings, Victoria C., 2495
Billington, Monroe, 0999, 1000, 1001, 1073, 1074, 4111, 5311
Billington, Monroe, and Cal Clark, 4446–4452
Bilotta, James D., 5312
Bina, Clarence A., 3944
Bindas, Kenneth J., 5110, 5169
Binkley, John C., 6870
Binkley, Wilfred E., 0519
Binning, William C., 2496
Bird, William L., 3873
Birdsall, William F., 9635, 9636
Birdwell, Christine R., 3194
Birdwhistell, Terry L., 3874
Bishop, Donald G., 7412
Bishop, Jim, 0278
Bishop, Robert L., 6034, 8488, 9246
Bishop, Robert L., and Lamar S. MacKay, 8489
Biskupski, M. B., 9472
Bisson, Thomas A., 7480

Bittker, Anne S., 4191
Bjerk, Roger, C. W., 0856
Bjork, Lennart, 3288
Bjorn, Lars, 5313
Black, Allida M., 0047
Black, Earl, and Merle Black., 6433
Black, Gregory D., 3724, 3725, 8782
Black, Gregory D., and Clayton R. Coppes, 3726, 3727
Black, Henry W., 0785
Black, John D., 1936
Black, Michael R., 2497
Black, Ruby, 0048
Black, Stanley W., 1950
Black, Theodore M., 6785
Black, Wilfred W., 1951
Blackburn, Bob L., 4698
Blackburn, George M., 8109
Blackman, Paul H., 6905
Blackorby, Edward C., 1221, 6817
Blackwelder, Julia K., 3945, 5919, 5920, 5921
Blackwell, Barbara G., 5314
Blackwood, George D., 2132
Blackwood, James R., 4824
Blaine, Peter Sr., 5815, 5816
Blair, Clay, 9247
Blair, John L., 6742
Blair, Leon B., 8560, 8665, 8683
Blaisdell, Thomas C., Jr., and Peter Sels, 4112
Blake, Fay M., and Morton H. Newman, 6434
Blakely, George T., 1338, 2927, 2928
Blaker, Michael, 7481
Blakey, George T., 5170
Blanchard, Margaret A., 3946, 3947, 3948, 3949
Bland, Larry I., 0739, 0944
Bland, Randall W., 5315
Blank, Helen L., 4192
Blantz, Thomas E., 0738, 2066, 2133, 4453
Blasier, Cole, 9035
Blassingame, John W., 5316
Blayney, Michael S., 2785
Blejwas, Stanislaus A., 4763
Blend, Benay, 5817
Blendon, Edith M., 7708
Blesh, Rudi, 3617
Blet, Pierre S. J., Angelo Martini, and Burkhart Schneider, 9637
Blicksilver, Edith, 8337
Bloch, Herman D., 5317, 5318
Block, Alan A., 4699
Block, Marvin W., 1235
Blodgett, Geoffrey, 3159
Bloom, Alexander, 4794
Bloom, Lynn Z., 8255
Bloom, Samuel, 8256
Bloomberg, Marty, and Hans Weber, 9622

Bloor, Ella R., 6202
Bluestein, Gene, 3289
Blum, Albert A., 4825, 4826, 8257, 8258, 8259, 8260, 8261
Blum, Albert A., and J. Douglas Smyth, 2134, 2135
Blum, Albert A., and Ira Spar, 2136
Blum, D. Steven, 7074
Blum, John M., 0279, 0280, 0651, 0652, 0653, 8064, 8065
Blumberg, Barbara M., 2786, 3039
Blumell, Bruce D., 1592, 2471
Blumenson, Martin, 0952, 0953, 4827, 8684, 9709
Blumenthal, Michael D., 7628
Board, John C., 1238
Boddy, Julie M., 5111
Boderick, Frances L., 5323
Bodnar, John, 2137, 9841
Boe, Jonathan E., 2498, 9530
Boettiger, John R., 0114
Bogart, Charles H., 4828
Bogle, Kathryn H., and Rick Harmon, 5320
Bogle, Kathryn H., 5319
Bohlen, C. E., 7413
Bohman, Eric J., 4829
Bohn, Thomas W., and Lawrence W. Lichty, 3875
Boles, Frank, 2458
Boles, John B., 9710
Bolger, Daniel P., 9248
Bolin, Winifred D. W., 1593, 5922, 5923
Boling, David, 2138
Boll, Michael M., 8802
Boller, Paul F. Jr., 0049, 3950, 4454, 7414
Bolles, Blair, 7720
Boll, Michael M., 8803
Bolner, James J., 7061, 7062
Bolt, Christine, 5818
Bolt, Ernest C. Jr., 8000
Bolt, Robert, 0281
Bonacich, Edna, 5321
Bond, Constance, 4581
Bone, Hugh, 6435
Bone, Robert A., 3290, 3618
Boney, F. N., 1201
Bongas, Pamela J., 3195
Bonnell, John S., 0241
Bonnell, Raymond, 3619
Bonner, Helen L. W., 1239
Bonner, Thomas N., 4271
Bonnifield, Paul, 1421
Bonora, Diane C., 3291
Bonthius, Andrew, 2139
Boorstin, Daniel J., 0455
Booth, Larry, 3621
Booth, Larry, and Jane Booth, 3620
Boothe, Leon E., 7482, 7483
Borchard, E. M., and W. P. Lage, 7888
Bordeau, Edward J., 6818

Borden, Neil H., 3713
Borg, Dorothy, 7721, 7853
Borg, Dorothy, and Shumpei Okamoto, 7484
Borie, Marsha, 0282
Boris, Eileen, 2787
Bormann, Ernest G., 1161
Bornemann, Alfred H., 2027
Bornet, Vaugh D., 9831
Borning, Bernard C., 9711
Borton, Hugh, 9531
Boryczk, Ray, 2140, 2141
Boskin, Joseph, 7075
Boss, George P., 0132
Boswell, George T., 0786
Bosworth, Allan R., 8338
Both, Douglas E., 6203
Boudin, Leonard, 2142
Boulard, Garry, 1267, 3040
Boulware, Marcus H., 5649
Bourgeois, Christie L., 1075
Bouton, Michael W., 7076
Bowen, Adelphia D. Jr., 7181
Bowers, C. A., 3951, 4272
Bowers, Claude G., 7356
Bowers, Robert E., 0825, 7415, 7722
Bowers, Thomas A., 3952
Bowie, Chester W., 5171
Bowles, Dorothy, 3953
Bowman, Robert A., 0542
Bowman, Ruth Fisk, 4700
Boxer, Andrea S., 1655
Boxerman, Burton A.,1242, 5737, 5738, 5739
Boyd, Carl, 9249, 9638
Boyden, Richard P., 2067
Boydstun. Q.B., 5172
Boyea, Earl, 4455
Boyens, Charles W., 5040
Boylan, James R., 6035
Boyland, Bernard L., 9250
Boyle, Anne M., 3292
Boyle, John H., 7485
Boyle, Kevin, 2143, 2459
Boyle, Michael, 9532
Boynton, Elwood D., 2499
Bozik, Daniel S., 8339
Brach, Paul, 3622
Brack, Harold A., 4456
Brackman, Harold, 9712
Braddick, Henderson B., 7337, 7338
Braden, Spruille, 0783
Braden, Waldo W., 0133, 0259
Braden, Waldo W., and Earnest Brandenburg, 0134
Bradley, Charles A., 4457
Bradley, Frank G., 3196
Bradley, John P., 6036

Bradley, Omar N., 0899
Bradley, Robert B., 3041
Bradshaw, Nancy, 4193
Bradshaw, Ralph, 6819
Bradshaw, Susan, 7459
Brady, David W., 6037, 6038
Brady, Erika, 7460
Brady, Patrick G., 9533
Braeman, John, 1286, 2670, 6906, 9713, 9714, 9715
Bragdon, Earl, 1746
Brain, Charles M., 6857
Brainerd, John G., 4830
Braisted, William R., 0255
Bramwell, Anna C., 9080
Branan, Herbert L., 6436
Brand, Donald R., 2788
Brandeie, Elizabeth, 2144
Brandenburg, Earnest, 0136, 0137
Brandenburg, Earnest, and Waldo W. Braden, 0135
Brandenburg, Walter O., 2500
Brandes, Joseph, 2145
Brandes, Stuart D., 9811
Brandon, Tom, 3728
Brandt, Irving, 1422
Brannen, Ralph N., 1086
Branscome, James, 2671
Bratzel, John F., and Leslie B. Rout Jr., 6894, 7723
Brauer, Ralph A., 3729
Brax, Ralph S., 8001
Bray, Robert, 3293
Brayman, Walter W., 3143
Brazelton, W. Robert, 2028
Brebner, John B., 7252
Breitman, Richard, and Alan M. Kraut, 9081
Bremer, Howard F., 0138
Bremer, William W., 2789
Bremner, Robert H., 2646
Brennan, John A., 1975, 2672
Brenner, Steven R., 1825
Brent, Robert A., 7609
Brents, Barbara G., 2673
Breslin, James E., B., 3583
Breslin, Thomas A., 4458, 7486
Brewer, James H., 5650
Brewer, John C., 7724
Brewer, Nicholas R., 0100
Brewer, Pat B., 3294
Brichta, Vivian, 3623
Brick, Howard, 6204
Bridenstine, Ellenore M., 6437
Bridgforth, Lucie R., 4194
Bridsell, Dale, 9251
Brienes, Marvin, 1423
Bright, Charles D., 1876
Bright, Philip L, 7077

Brill, James A., 8976
Brinker, William J., 0878
Brinkley, Alan, 1162, 1163, 2674, 6141
Brinkley, David, 8066
Brisbane, Robert H., 5322
Bristol, Horace, 3295
Brito, Patricia, 5924
Brock, William R., 2675
Brockel, Harry C., 9252
Brockie, Melvin D., 1594
Brockway, Ronald S., Jr., 0995
Broderick, Francis L., 4459, 4460
Brody, David, 2146, 2147, 3730, 9082, 9716
Bromert, Linda K., 5819
Bromert, Roger, 5820, 5821
Bronder, Saul E., 4461
Bronner, Edwin B., 6438
Brookhouser, Frank, 4244
Brooks, Cleanth, 3296
Brooks, Cleanth, and Robert Penn Warren, 3954
Brooks, Juanita, and Janet G. Butler, 5925
Brooks, Russell, 8685
Broun, Elizabeth, 3624
Broussard, Albert S., 5324, 5651
Browder, Robert P., 7416, 7417, 7725
Brower, Charles F. IV, 8561
Brown, Charles H., and John R. Skates, Jr., 0901
Brown, Courtney, 6733
Brown, D. Clayton, 1088, 1089, 1728, 2790, 2929, 3086, 9639
Brown, David E., 6205
Brown, Dorothy M., 6439, 6440
Brown, E. Carey, 1976
Brown, Francis C., 8888
Brown, Hurbert O., 8424
Brown, James S., 9842
Brown, Kenneth J., 3297
Brown, Linda K., 2676
Brown, Lorraine, 5112, 5113
Brown, Philip C., 1877
Brown, Richard C., 7078
Brown, Richard J., 6820
Brown, Richard P., 3197
Brown, Robert J., 7253
Brown, Sharon A., 6441
Brown, Sheldon, 4273
Brown, Theodore M., 4195
Brown, William A., Jr., 1977
Brown, William L., 0570
Brown, William R., 3584, 3585, 4113
Browne, Blaine T., 5713
Browning, Edward K., 2791
Brownstein, Ronald, 3955
Bruccoli, Matthew J., 3298
Bruchy, Stuart, 7854

Bruenn, Howard C., 0213
Brugioni, Dino A., 9253
Brume, Lester H., 0826, 2148, 8593
Brunner, Edmond, 1339
Bruns, Roger, and Bryan Kennedy, 4831
Bryan, Alice I., 8202
Bryan, Frank M., and Kenneth Bruno, 6442
Bryan, Violet Harrington, 5325
Bryant, Arthur, 9254
Bryant, Cedric G., 3299
Bryant, Jerry H., 6206
Bryant, Keith L., 6443
Bryniarski, Joan L., 7726
Bryson, Norris C., 1595
Bryson, Thomas A., 8970
Buch, Peter, 4196
Buch, Richard P., 4274
Buchanan, William, 4275
Buchannan, Bruce, 0497
Bucher, Glenn R., 4462
Buckley, Gary J., 9473
Buckley, Thomas H., and Edwin B. Strong Jr., 4832
Buckley, Thomas H., 7830
Bucksar, Richard G., 1854
Buddy, Fred W., 4276
Buell, Thomas B., 0970
Buenger, Walter L., 0703
Buerki, Robert A., 4277, 5173
Buffa, Dudley W., 2149
Bugos, Glen E., 4833
Buhite, Russell D., 0922, 0923, 0924, 7831, 8594, 8889, 9474
Buhle, Paul M., 6207
Bukoff, Ronald N., 3520
Bulkeley, Peter B., 3042, 6444, 7079
Bulkin, Eleanor, 6208
Bullitt, Orville H., 7418
Bullock, Alan, 9213
Bullock, Henry A., 5326
Bulosan, Carlos, 2150
Bumel, Judith Taylor, 9075
Bunche, Ralph J., 5652
Bund, McGeorge, 7889
Bunk, William K., 7890
Bunnell, Helen E., 4676
Bunzel, John H., 2501
Burbank, Lyman B., 4278
Burch, Philip H., Jr., 2502
Burden, Florence Canfield, 5041
Burdette, Franklin L., 6445
Burford, Roger L., 1340, 1384
Burgchardt, Carl R., 6209
Burk, James, 2792, 4834
Burk, Robert F., 9812
Burke, Robert E., 0139, 0283, 1004, 1005, 1065
Burke, Robert L., 7727

Burke, Victor L., 2793
Burkes, Glenn, 5239
Burner, David, 6039
Burns, Arthur R., 2503
Burns, Augustus M., 5327, 5633
Burns, Helen M., 2504
Burns, James M., 0214, 0284, 0285, 0286, 0287, 2151
Burns, Philip J., 7080
Burns, Richard D., 0827, 7488, 7832, 9255, 9256
Burns, Richard D., and Edward M. Bennett, 7487
Burns, Richard D., and W. Addams Dixon, 7855
Burran, James A., 3043, 5328, 5329
Burrows, John H., 5330
Burrows, Robert D., 0727
Burstein, Paul, 2677
Burt, Nathaniel, 0034
Burtness, Paul S., and Warren U. Ober, 7489
Burton, Dennis A., 9832
Burton, Robert E., 6446
Busbice, E. Hollace, 1656
Busch, Frank J., 1729
Busch, Jane, 4835
Busco, Ralph A., and Douglas D. Alder, 8448
Bushnell, David, 7662
Bushnell, Eleanore, 6040
Bussel, Alan, 3956
Bustami, Zaha B., 8996
Butcher, Harry C., 0909
Butcher, M. E., 0967
Butcher, Philip, 5331
Butler, James R. M., 7321
Butler, Joseph T. Jr., 8449
Butler, Michael A., 7182
Butow, R. J. C., 7491, 7490, 7492, 7493, 4836, 9534
Buttenwieser, Ann L., 1785
Buttita, Tony, and Barry Witham, 5114
Buyce, Robert, 3160
Buzzell, Rolfe G., 7339
Byers, Cathrine P., 3957
Byrd, Martha, H., 8067
Byrge, Duane P., 3731
Byrne, Michael W., 7891
Byrnes, James F., 1134
Bystryn, Marcia N., 5042

Cable, John N., 1268, 9475
Cadenhead, Ivie E., Jr., 4114
Cahan, Cathy, and Richard Cahan, 3044
Cahn, Susan M., 4582
Cahn, Louis, and George Neumann, 9535
Cain, Louis P., 2505
Cain, Marvin R., 0919
Cain, William E., 3300
Calabria, Frank M., 3521
Caldeira, Gregory A., 6948

Caldwell, Ellen M., 3301
Caldwell, Oliver J., 8890
California Historical Quarterly, 3606
Caliguirrie, Joseph A. Jr., 4279
Callahan, Raymond, 9181
Callicott, J. Baird, 5822
Calonne, David S., 3302
Calvocoressi, Peter, and Guy Wint, 8562
Cameron, Turner C., 0386
Campbell, Ann M., 3045
Campbell, Christina M., 1341
Campbell, D'Ann M., 5926, 8203, 8204, 8262
Campbell, David, and David Coombs, 3046
Campbell, Debra, 4463, 4464, 4465
Campbell, Edward D. C., Jr., 3198, 5174
Campbell, James E., 5043, 6041
Campbell, John C., 8819
Campbell, Karen E., 4764
Campbell, Rita R., 2794
Campbell, Russell D., 3732
Campbell, Thomas M., 9453, 9454, 9536
Campman, M. Sue, 3303
Canary, Robert H., 3304
Cann, Marvin L., 2930, 6447, 6448
Cannistraro, Philip V., and Theodore P. Kovaleff, 7081
Cannistraro, Philip V., 6210, 6374
Cannon, Alfred O., 7035
Cannon, Brian Q., 1310
Cannon, James P., 6211
Canon, David T., 6042
Cantelon, Philip L., 0543, 6212
Cantor, Louis, 2152
Cantril, Hadley, 6858, 8659
Cantril, Hadley, and Mildred Strunk, eds., 5044
Cantwell, Frank, 6859
Caody, Joseph W., 0256
Capeci, Domini J. Jr., 1786, 4701, 5332, 5333, 5334, 5335, 5336, 5337, 5740, 6449, 6450
Capps, F. Herbert, 7892, 7893
Capshew, James H. and Aledjandra C. Laszle, 8205
Caraley, Demetrois, 4837
Carbone, Peter F. Jr., 4280
Cardashian, Vahan, 7405
Carew, Harold D., 2931
Carey, James C., 7082, 7083
Carey, James C., and V. R. Easterling, 6451
Carleton, Mark T., 6452
Carleton, William G., 0441, 1424, 6043,7894, 8650
Carlisle, John C., 3625
Carlisle, Rodney P., 3958, 3959, 3960, 7084
Carlson, Earland I., 0267, 0268
Carlson, Elizabeth B., 3161
Carlson, G. Bert, 6213
Carlson, Julia L., 3305
Carlson, Lewis H., 0520

Carlson, Paul H., 1425
Carlson, Paul H., and Steve Porter, 6453
Carlson, Robert, 2932
Carmichael, Arnold S., 0140
Carmichael, Donald S., 0185, 0186
Carney, George O., 6454
Carolia, Betty B., 0050
Carosso, Vincent P., 2795, 3522
Carpenter, JoAnn D., 6455
Carpenter, Joel A., 4466, 4467
Carpenter, Keith C., 1978
Carpenter, Ronald H., 7494
Carr, Joe D., 2153
Carr, Mother Eleanor M., 5115
Carraro, Betty F., 3626
Carringer, Robert L., 3733
Carroll, Bernice A. J., 7269
Carroll, Eugene T., 2933
Carroll, Evelyn C., 4281
Carroll, Rosemary F., 1596
Carrott, Montgomery B. Jr., 6871
Carson, S. L., 5741
Carsten, Oliver M., 2068
Carstensen, Vernon, 4282
Cart, Theodore W., 1426
Cartagenova, Gonzalo C., 6907
Carter, Carolle J., 8776
Carter, Hodding, 3306
Carter, Paul A., 4468, 4469
Carter, Robert F., 6456
Carty, Winthrop P., 7629
Caruso, Samuel T., 8340
Carver, Joan S., 5927
Cary, Lorin L., 2154, 2428
Carynnyk, Marco, 3961
Casciato, Arthur D., 6214
Case, H. C. M., 1342
Casebeer, Kenneth M., 2678
Casey, John T., and James Bowles, 0626
Casey, R. G., 8668
Cash, Rosalind, 5338
Cashier, Philip G., 8187
Casillas, Rex J., 8988
Cassese, Sabino, 1952
Cassity, Michael J., 1164
Castle, Alfred L., 7895
Casty, Alan H., 3199
Cater, Dan T., 4702
Catton, William R., 7728
Cauffman, R. Scott, 2840
Cavanagh, R.L., 4838
Cavanah, Frances, 0002, 0187
Cavanah, Frances, and Elizabeth L. Crandall, 0288
Cave Brown, Anthony, 9257
Caves, Roger W., 1787

Cavnes, Max P., 8068
Cazden, Robert E., 4145
Cebula, James A., 6044
Cecchette, Stephen G., 1979
Cerami, Joseph R., 4839
Cerf, Bennett A., 4115
Ceruzzi, Paul E., 4840
Cervone, Barbara T., 4283
Chabot, C. Barry, 3307
Chacon, Ramon D., 2155
Chadwin, Mark L., 7964, 8490
Chafe, William H., 3047
Chaffee, Mary Law, 5339
Chalberg, John C., 8820
Chalk, Frank R., 8188
Chalmers, David M., 6400
Chalmers, Leonard, 6457, 6458
Chamberlain, William H., 0478, 7729
Chambers, Clark A., 1569, 4634, 5742, 9717
Chambers, Gurney, 4284
Chambers, John W., 7055
Champagne, Anthony, 1090, 1091, 1092, 6949
Champagne, Richard A. Jr., 5340
Champion, Thomas, 1225
Champlin, Ardath I., 4285
Chan, Loren B., 6459
Chandler, Harriette L., 0740, 8821, 8822
Chapin, Seymour L., 4841
Chaplin, Charles, 3734
Chaplin, Ralph, 6215
Chapman, Charles C., 2506
Chapman, Richard N., 0289, 2679
Charles, Cleophus, 5341
Charles, Searle F., 0687, 0688
Charney, Wayne M., 3162
Charny, Robert W., 6460
Chase, Francis I., Jr., 3876
Chase, John L., 8595, 8596
Chase, Richard, 3308
Chase, Stuart, 2507, 2680
Chasteen, Edgar, 5342
Chatelain, Verne, 2796
Chatfield, Charles, 7965, 8002, 8003, 8004
Chatfield, Earl C. Jr., 8005
Cheape, Charles, 7270
Chennault, Claire L., 8891
Chenoweth, Richard R., 1216
Chepaitis, Joseph B., 2681
Cheriack, Martin, 2508
Chermol, Brian H., 9258
Cheslik, Helen E., 8425
Chessman, G. Wallace, 2509
Chester, Ronald, 5928
Chestnut, E. F., 2934
Cheston, Stephen T., 7419

Cheyfitz, Eric, 3309
Chiang, Cyrus S., 8263
Chiang, Kai-Shek, 9218
Chiasson, Lloyd E., 8341
Chien, Hou Tsung, 8892
Chilcoat, George W., 5045, 8491
Child, Frank C., 7183
Child, John, 7630, 9259
Childs, Marquis W., 7085
Childs, William R., 1858, 1859
Chiles, Frederic C., 2156, 2157
Chmel, Patrick J., 3200
Choate, Jean, 2935
Choi, Pae-Kun, 2158
Chou, Michaelyn, 1249
Chowdhry, Carol, 7730
Christensen, Bonnie Jean, 0141
Christensen, Terry, 3735
Christensen, William E., 3962
Christgau, John, 8342, 8343
Christian, Henry A., 3310, 6142
Christie, Jean, 1427, 2797, 2798
Christman, Calvin L., 8110, 8111
Chu, Power, 1826
Chukumba, Stephen U., 7184
Chun-Hoon, Lowell, 5671
Church, Verne V., 2799
Churchill, Allen, 0115
Churchill, Winston S., 9182–9190
Ciechanowski, Jan, 8808
Citron, Atay, 3201
Clapp, Thomas C., 2159, 3048, 3849, 3850
Clark, Blue, 5175
Clark, Danae A., 3736
Clark, Daniel J., 2160
Clark, David G., 3877
Clark, David L., 3878
Clark, Dorothy R., 5116
Clark, Eric C., 6461, 6462
Clark, James C., 6463
Clark, James E., 7086
Clark, John G., 1747
Clark, Kenneth B., 5343
Clark, Paul C. Jr., 7679
Clark, Penny, 8450
Clark, Ronald, 9260
Clark, Susan C., 6375
Clark, William B., 3963
Clark, William L., 4746
Clark-Hazlett, Christopher, 1343
Clarke, Mary W., 3311
Clarke, Sally H., 1344, 1385
Clash, Thomas W., 9050
Clausen, Meredith L., 3163
Clauss, Errol MacGregor, 7731

Clavadetscher, Carl J. Jr., 7966
Clawson, Augusta, 8264
Clawson, Marion, 2800, 4635
Clay, Donald A., 1428
Clayton, Dorthy H., 3087
Clayton, Ronnie W., 2936, 5176
Cleary, Robert E., 7732
Cleath, Robert L., 6216
Clegg, Ambrose A. Jr., 4470
Clegg, Brenda F., 5344
Clement, Priscilla F., 2937
Clements, Joyce M., 2161
Clements, Robert B., 3964, 3965
Clemmer, Richard O., 5823
Clepper, Irene, 2162
Cleveland, Hugh G., 9718
Cleveland, Les, 8677
Clifford, J. Garry, 1040, 7733, 8006
Clifford, J. Garry, and Robert Griffiths, 7896
Clifford, John G., 4842, 4843, 7271
Clifford, Nicholas R., 7495
Clifton, James A., 5824
Clinansmith, Michael S., 6401
Cline, Paul C., 8007
Cline, Ray S., 9261
Cline, Ray S., and Maurice Matloff, 9537
Clive, Alan G., 8069, 8113, 8114, 8206
Clive, Alan, and J. P. McCarthy, 8112
Clodfelter, Mark A., 9262
Clough, Shepard B., 8070
Clow, Richmond L., 5825, 5826, 5827
Clurman, Harold, 3202
Clyde, Paul H., 7185
Clymer, Kenton J., 8935, 8936
Coakley, Robert W., 8823
Coate, Charles E., 1730
Cobb, Gerry, 5046
Cobb, James C., 1145, 1208, 3088
Cobb, James C., and Michael V. Namorato, 3089
Cobb, William H., 4286, 4287
Cobb, William H., and Donald H. Grubbs, 6217
Coburn, Mark D., 4583
Coch, Raymond L., 3066
Cochran, Alexander S. Jr., 9263, 9719
Cochran, Alfred W., 3523
Cochrane, Willard W., 1281
Coe, David T., 7087
Coen, Robert M., 1657
Coffet, William E., 7088
Coffey, John W., 6143
Coffey, Thomas M., 4747
Coffey, William E., 2163
Coffman, Edward M., and Paul H. Hass, 0930
Coggeshall, John M., 3312
Cohen, Avi J., 2510

Cohen, Henry, 5743
Cohen, Jacob, 9720
Cohen, Lizabeth A., 2069
Cohen, Marilyn A., 3313
Cohen, Michael J., 8721
Cohen, Paul, 3524
Cohen, Robert P., 1658
Cohen, Sheldon S., 4584
Cohen, Sol, 9721
Cohen, W. I., 7461
Cohen, Warren I., 7897, 9476
Cohen, Wilbur J., 2682, 2801, 5047
Coiner, Constance, 6218
Coker, William S., 1151
Colbourn, Andrea M., 4844
Cole, Arthur H., 1937
Cole, Babalola, 7186
Cole, Dermot, 1878
Cole, Dwayne C., 1597
Cole, Jeffrey I., 3879
Cole, John Y., 5117
Cole, Mary S., 1788
Cole, Merle T., 8265
Cole, Olen Jr., 5345
Cole, Terrence, 8115
Cole, Wayne S., 1041, 1053, 7898, 7899, 7900, 7901, 7967, 9722, 9723
Coleman, George C., 7687
Coleta, Paolo E., 0257
Colgan, Christine Ann, 3737
Colignon, Richard A., 2683
Colin, Scipio A.J., 5346
Colley, Charles C., 1003
Collie, Mary M. P., 6045
Collier, Basil, 9264, 9265
Collier, Thomas W., 4845
Collins, Amy Fine, 3627
Collins, Donald E., 8344
Collins, Ernest M., 5653
Collins, George E., and Adolf K. Placzek, 3164
Collins, Herbert, and David B. Weaver, 0215
Collins, Herbert R., 1860, 1861
Collins, John J., 9266
Collins, Keith E., 5347
Collins, Lois A., 1748
Collins, Robert M., 1598, 2029
Colman, Gould P., 2938, 9843
Colodny, Robert G., 7357
Colorado Heritage, 3156, 8327
Colville, John, 9477
Comerford, Robert J., 6821
Commager, Henry S., 2684, 3314
Comnenos, Caroline J., 2511
Compton, Gail W., 9598
Compton, James V., 7272

Comstock, Rudolph S., 0387
Conant, James B., 4846
Condict, Alden S., 0188
Condit, Celeste Michelle, 5348
Condon, G.A., 4471
Condon, Richard H., 2164
Conference on Research on the Second World War,
    Washington D. C., 1971, 9640
Congressional Quarterly, 6734
Conkin, Paul K., 2685, 2686, 2802, 3051, 4636, 5048
Conn, Stetson, 4848, 8345
Conn, Stetson and Bryon Fairchild, 4847
Conn, Stetson, Rose C. Engleman, and Byron Fairchild, 9267
Connally, Tom, 1142
Connell, Brian, 3738
Connelly, Thomas, 7089
Connor, Celeste, 3628
Connor, R. D. W., 0290
Conrad, David E., 2687
Conrad, James H., 4197
Conrad, Rebecca A., 1429
Conrat, Maisie, and Richard Conrat, 8346
Conroy, Hilary, 7496
Constant, Edward W., II, 1749
Constigliola, Frank, 7902
Contreras, Belisario R., 5049
Controneo, Ross R., and Jack Doizer, 5828
Converse, Elliott V. III, 9538
Conway, John S., 0887, 8492
Conway, Maurice B., 9478
Conwill, Joseph D., 1430
Coode, Thomas H., 1071, 1072, 2688, 6464, 6465, 6466, 6786
Coode, Thomas H., and John D. Petrarulo, 4472
Coode, Thomas H., and John F. Bauman, 0619
Coode, Thomas H., and Dennis E. Fabbri, 3052
Cook, Bernard, 2647
Cook, Charles O. Jr., 4849, 9268
Cook, Fred J., 0003
Cook, James F. Jr., 1209, 8426, 9641
Cook, Paul B., 4288
Cook, Philip L., 2512
Cook, Sylvia J., 1659
Cook, Virginia, 2803
Cooke, Alistair, 7090
Cooke, Morris, 2689
Cooke, Robert J., 0051
Cookingham, Mary E., 4289
Cooley, John A., 7693
Cooling, Benjamin F., III, 4850, 4851
Coombs, Frank A., 1048
Cooney, Terry A., 3966, 6219
Cooper, John Milton, Jr., 0981
Cooper, Stephen, Jr., 3315
Cooper, Wayne F., 3316
Cooper, William G., 1827

Coox, Alvin D., 7497, 9724
Copeland, Gary W., 0521
Copp, Nelson G., 4146
Coppes, Clayton R., 1760, 2709
Corbett, Katharine T., 5929
Corbett, Katharine T., and Mary E. Seematter, 5349
Corbett, P. Scott, 8949
Corcoran, David H., 1259
Corey, Albert B., 0189
Corey, Esther, 6220
Corkern, Wilton C., Jr., 3165
Corley, Florence F., 1789
Corley, Roger W., 6908
Corn, Joseph J., 5930
Cornell, Cecilia S., 0815
Cornwell, Elmer E., 0456, 0457
Cortada, James W., 7358
Cortner, Richard C., 6909
Coser, Lewis A., 4147
Cosgrove, Stuart, 4703
Costello, John E., 4198, 7498
Costi, Robert L., 7340
Costin, Lela B., 4199, 5931
Cotham, Harry C., 0689
Cotner, Robert C., 2939
Cotroneo, Ross R., 1910
Cottman, Richard N., 1841, 1842
Cottrell, Debbie M., 2648
Cottrell, Robert C., 3967, 4473, 9599
Coulter, Matthew, 0522
Covington, James W., 5829
Cowan, Richard O., 4474
Cowan, Ruth Schwartz, 4852
Cowherd, Raymond G., 7734
Cowing, Cedric, 7091
Cowley, Malcolm, 3317, 6221, 6222, 6223
Cowperthwaite, L. L., 0142, 0143
Cox, Charles L., 8680
Cox, James A., 4585
Cox, James M., 6467
Cox, Merlin G., 6468
Cox, Richard W., 3629
Cox, Susan J. B., 7042
Cox, Thomas R., 1431
Coy, Harold, and Mildred Coy, 4290
Coyle, David C., 2804
Crabb, Cecil V. Jr., and Kevin V. Mulcahy, 7735
Cracroft, Richard H., 3318
Craig, Douglas B. S., 6144
Craig, E. Quita, 5050
Craig, Gordon A., 7406
Craig, Gordon A., and Felix G., 7187, 7833
Cramer, Hilton, 3666
Cramer, Victor A., 4015
Crane, Conrad C., 9269, 9270

Crane, Katherine E., 7834
Crane, Robert I., 8937
Cranston, Pat, 3880
Craut, Alan M.; Richard Breitman, and Thomas Imhoof, 4164
Craven, Wesley F., and James L. Cates, 9271
Cravens, Hamilton, 4853
Crenshaw, James T., 0600
Crepeau, Richard C., 4586, 4587
Crew, Spencer R., 5350
Crimmins, Carolyn C., 4795
Cripe, Nicholas M., 0144
Cripps, Thomas, 3740, 5351
Cripps, Thomas, and David Culbert, 3739
Crispell, Kenneth, and Carlos F. Gomez, 0216
Crispin, George A., 4291
Critchlow, Donald T., 0523, 2070, 7092
Critser, Greg, 3319
Cronin, Thomas E., 0291
Cronin, Thomas E., and William R. Hochman, 0292
Cronon, E. David, 0794, 0795, 0796, 4475, 7669
Crosby, Donald F., 7359
Crosby, Earl W., 5352
Crosby, Percy L., 0293, 7093
Cross, Stephen J., and William R. Albury, 4854
Cross, Whitney R., 0294
Crouch, Barry A., 6950
Crouse, Joan M., 1660, 2649, 2650, 2651
Crow, Michael M., and Gregory L. Hager, 4855
Crowder, Daniel B., 2165
Crowe, David M. Jr., 7736, 9083
Crowell, Laura, 0022, 0145, 0146, 0147, 0148
Crowley, James B., 7499
Crownover, A. B., 6781
Crownover, Donald A., 7903
Crozier, Andrew, 7273
Crum, Steven J., 5051, 5830, 5831, 5832
Cruman, Marie W., 0637
Crunden, Robert M., 6115
Cruse, Harold, 5353
Cuff, Robert, 8116, 8245
Culbert, Daivd H., 3881, 3882, 3883, 3884, 5177
Cullen, Countee, 3595
Culley, John J., 8347, 8348
Culley, John J., and Peter L. Peterson, 5118
Culp, Mary Beth, 3586
Cumming, Adelaide F. H., 3885
Cummings, Geraldine D., 0217
Cummings, Tom, 7904
Cummins, Roger W., 5354
Cunningham, Constance A., 5355
Cunningham, Frank D., 8266
Cupper, Dan, 1862
Curlee, Joan E., 5052
Current, Richard N., 0881, 0882
Currie, Lauchlin B., 1980

Curry, Lawrence H. Jr., 6046
Curti, Merle, 4796
Curtin, Mary T., 6469
Curtis, James C., 3630
Curtis, James C., and Shelia Grannen, 3631
Curtis, Peter H., 9084
Cushman, Helen C., 3320
Cushman, M. S., 1165
Cushman, Robert, 6910
Cutler, Phobe, 2805
Cutlip, Scott M., 4200
Cutrer, Thomas W., 3321, 3322, 4292
Cutter, Charles R., 5178, 9064
Cyr, Paul A., 5179
Cywinski, Raymond J., 3741
Czitrom, Daniel, 7360

D'Ambrosio, Charles A., 1911
Daab, Ford G., 9038
Dabney, Virginius, 3968
Dahl, Patrick, 2806
Dahlheimer, Harry, 7188
Dahmen, David S., 7688
Dalfiume, Richard M., 5356, 5606, 5607, 5608
Dalgaard, Bruce R., 1981, 1982
Dalin, David G., 9085
Dall, Curtis B., 0004
Dallas, Jerry W., 1531
Dallek, Robert, 0807, 0808, 7737, 7738, 7835
Dallin, Alexander, 9222
Dalrymple, Dana G., 2513
Dalstrom, Harl A., 1067, 6470, 6471
Dalton, Glen P., 8117
Daly, Gerald, 1790
Daniel, Cletus E., 2166, 2940
Daniel, Edward O., 1093
Daniel James C., 2941
Daniel, Pete, 1345, 1346, 1347, 2690, 8118
Daniel, Robert L., 7401
Daniel, Walter C., 5357, 5358, 5359
Daniels, Elizabeth A., Anne Constantinople, and Marque Miringoff, 5932
Daniels, Jonathan, 0190, 00258, 0458, 0459, 1938, 5933
Daniels, Josephus, 0797
Daniels, Roger, 2096, 4293, 4766, 8350, 8351, 8352, 8353, 9086
Daniels, Roger, Sandra C. Taylor, and Harry L. Kitano, 8349
Danovitch, Sylvia E., 8354
Daoust, Norm LaSalle, 5654
Darby, Michael R., 2472
Dardis, Thomas A., 3323
Darilek, Richard E., 7189, 7856
Darling, Frank C., 8961
Darling, Jay N., 4116
Dauer, Manning J., 6047

Dause, Charles A., 6951
David, Goode B., 3634
David, Leroy Jr., 4294
Davidson, David, 4704
Davidson, Jo, 3632
Davidson, Judith A., 4588
Davidson, Margaret, 0052
Davidson, Mary V., 3324
Davidson, Sue, 5714
Davies, David L., 3053
Davies, John P., Jr., 0388
Davies, Joseph E., 8824
Davies, Richard O., 7094
Davies, Thomas M., 7689
Davin, Eric Leif, and Staughton Lynd, 6472
Davis, Cheryl S., 3325
Davis, David Brion, 9272
Davis, Donald F., 3633
Davis, Everett H., 2942
Davis, Florence H., 4476
Davis, Forrest, 1166
Davis, Gerard H., 6473
Davis, Horace B., 2071
Davis, James R., 2030, 2045, 2046
Davis, James W., 0295, 6048
Davis, Jerome, 0005
Davis, Kenneth S., 0006, 0053, 0054, 0101, 0242, 0269,
    0296, 3090, 4705, 8563
Davis, Kenneth W., 4117
Davis, Lynn E., 8797
Davis, Merle, 2652
Davis, Paul C., 5609
Davis, Polly A., 1112, 1113, 1114
Davis, R. G., 3525
Davis, Richard A., 7095
Davis, Richard G., 9273
Davis, Robert L, 6145
Davis, Shelby C., 1939
Davis, Steve, 1983
Davis, Thadious M., 3326, 3327
Davis, Vernon E., 4856, 4857
Davison, Dexter R. Jr., 4295
Davison, Kenneth E., 9600
Dawidowicz, Lucy S., 9087, 9088
Dawson, Nelson L., 6224, 6982, 6983
Dawson, Oliver B., 5240
Dawson, Raymond H., 8825
Day, Barbara T., 1750
Day, Billie A., 3969
Day, David, 8722
Day, Donald, 0149
Day, Greg, and Jack Delano, 2943
Day, Jane, 3328
Day, Mar, 5676
Day, Richard H., 1432

Day, William R., 3329
Dayananda, Y. James, 6225, 6226
De Groot, Peter T., 8893
De Jongh, James L., 3587
De La Vina, Lynda Y., 8207
Deac, Wilfred P. 7274
Dean, Howard, 7096
deBedts, Ralph F., 0857, 2807
DeBenedetti, Charles, 8008
Debevoise, E. W., 9539
DeBoe, David C., 7739
deBorhegyi-Forrest, Suzanne S., 2944
DeCaaux, Len, 2167
DeChenne, David L., 2072
DeCola, Thomas G., 7740
DeConde, Alexander, 7190, 7905
Dedmon, Donald D., 6049
DeGaulle, Charles, 9203
Degler, Carl N., 2691, 4245, 6474
DeJanes, R. Benneson, 7097
Delano, Daniel W., Jr., 0116
Dellums, Ronald B., 1984
DeLong, J. Bradford, 2047
DeLong, J. Bradford, and Lawrence H. Summers, 1985
Deloria, Vine Jr., 5833
DeMarco, Joseph P., 5360
DeMaria, M., and A. Russo, 4858
Dembo, Jonathan, 1599, 2168, 2169, 2170, 2171, 2172
DeMille, George E., 4477
Demonds, Anthony O., 4590
Deneroff, Harvey R., 2173, 2174
Denisoff, R. Serge, 3526, 3527
Dennett, Raymond, and Joseph E. Johnson, 8826
Dennett, Tyler, 7500
Denning, Dennis F., 3203
Dennis, Paul M., 4859
DeNovo, John A., 8971
Derber, Milton, 8267
Derber, Milton, and Edwin Young, 2073
Derthick, Martha, 5119
DeSanti, Louis A., 7341
DeSantis, Hugh S., 8827, 8828
DeSeversky, Alexander P., 3742, 8493
Dethloff, Henry C., 1167, 1168, 2945, 5241
Detwiler, Donald S., and Charles B. Burdick, 9642
Detzer, Dorothy, 8009
Deutsch, Cynthia, 8208
Deutsch, Harold C., 9274, 9275
Deutsch, Phyllis, 5744
Deutscher, Isaac, 9223
DeVeaux, Scott K., 3528
Devine, James N., 1600, 1601
Devore, Richard O., 3529
DeVore, Donald E., 5361
Dewberry, Jonathan, 3202

Dewey, Donald, 1986
Dewey, Donald O., 3970, 6475
Dewitt, Howard, 2175
Dewitt, John H., Jr., 3886
DeWitt, Howard A., 0767, 1006, 1007
Dexter, B., 9623
Deyo, Jerome V., 0150
Diamond, Sander A., 5745, 6376
Diamond, Sigmund, 4296
Dick, Wesley A., 1731
Dickman, Howard, 2176
DiClerico, Robert E., 0389
Dieckmann, E. L., 3971
Dieckmann, Katherine, 3635
Diener, Jacqulyn M., 5120
Dienstfrey, Sherri R., 3530
Dieterich, Herbert R., 5180
Dieterich, Herbert R., and Jacqueline Petravage, 5181
Diggins, John P., 6227, 6377, 6378, 6379, 7342
DiGianni, John, 3887
DiLeva, Frank D., 1532, 4706, 6476
Dilks, David, 9191
Dill, Clarence C., 1732
Dilling, Elizabeth, 7098
Dillon, Richard, 4860
Dillsaver, Joe D., 3531
Dilsaver, Larry M., 1433
DiMaggio, Paul, 3636
Dimino, Andrea, 3330, 3331
Dingman, Roger, 7501
Dinneen, Joseph f., 6477
Dinnerstein, Leonard, 5746, 5747, 9089
DiNolfo, Ennio, 9479
Dinwoodie, David H., 1434, 4148, 5677
Dion, Susan, 8010
DiPeso, Charles C., 3637
Dippie, Brian W., 5834
Divine, Robert A., 4149, 6735, 7191, 7192, 7741, 7742, 7968, 7969
Dixler, Elsa J., 6228
Dixon-Stowell, Brenda M., 3532
Dizikes, John, 7322
Dobbins, Charles, 6478
Dobbs, Charles M., 3743
Dobney, Frederick J., 1828, 9540
Dobson, Alan P., 8723
Dodd, James W., 1533
Dodd, Walter F., 6911
Dodd, William E., 0809
Dodds, Gordon B., 9601
Doeden, Daniel L., 3888
Doenecke, Justus D., 6116, 7906, 7907, 7908, 7909, 7910, 7911, 7912, 9541, 9725, 9726, 9727
Doerr, Arthur H., 1435
Doherty, Anthony N., 2514

Doherty, Richard P., 1879
Doherty, Thomas, 4861
Dohse, Michael A., 8997
Doler, Thurston E., 1123
Domanski, Robert P., 4589
Dominguez, Jorge I., 7670
Donaghy, Linda, and Maraha L. McCabe, 5182
Donahoe, Bernard. F., 0452, 6787, 8829
Donahoe, Myrna C., 2177
Donahue, Jim, 1436
Donald, David H., 3332
Donald, Ralph R., 8494
Donaldson, Gary A., 2946
Donalson, Melvin B., 3744
Donohew, Lewis, 3972
Donohue, James T., 8998
Donovan, Frank P., 1912, 9455
Donovan, John C., 6050, 7857
Donovan, Timothy P., 3533
Dooley, Patricia L., 8119
Doran, John G., 7099
Dorgan, Howard, 1169
Dorman, Morgan J., 6822
Dorman, Robert L., 6479
Dorn, David R., 8246
Dorn, F., 0956
Dorn, Harold, 7420
Dorn, Jacob H., 1791, 4478, 4637
Dorn, Walter L., 9542
Dorsett, Lyle W., 0601, 6480, 6481, 6482, 6483
Dorwart, Jeffery M., 7836, 9276
Doti, Lynne Pierson, 2515
Doty, C. Stewart, 5121
Dougherty, James J., 8686
Douglas, Donald G., 0828, 7610
Douglas, George H., 3973
Douglas, Krystan V., 3205
Douglas, Mary C., 5242
Douglas, Paul H., 0750
Douglas, Roy, 8651
Douglas, William O., 6995, 6996, 6997
Dower, J. W., 7502
Downing, Marvin L., 0891
Dows, Olin, 5053
Doyle, Frederick J., 8451
Doyle, Judith K., 1083, 1084
Doyle, Michael K., 4862, 4863, 4864
Dozer, Donald M., 7913
Dozier, Richard, 3206
Drache, Hiram, 1437
Drachman, Edward R., 7743
Drago, Edmund J., 5362
Drake, Richard, 4479
Drake, St. Clair, 5363
Draper, Theodore, 6229

Dratch, Howard, 4677
Draves, David D., 2947
Dreier, John A., 7914
Dreier, John C, 7631
Dreifort, John E., 7261, 7262, 9204
Dreiser, Theodore, and H. L. Mencken, 3333
Dressler, James B., 8597
Dreves, Vivien E., 5934
Drewal, Margaret T., 3534
Drewry, Elizabeth B., 9813
Drexel, Constance, 0023
Drier, John A, 7970
Drinnon, Richard, 8355
Driscoll, Barbara A., 1913
Droker, Howard A., 5364
Droze, Wilmon H., 1438, 3091, 3092
Druks, Herbert, 7915
Drummond, Donald F., 0829, 7916
Drury, Allen, 6051
Dubay, Robert W., 5365, 6484, 7100
Dubofsky, Melvyn, and Warren VanTine, 2415, 2439
DuBois, Philip H., 4297
Dubro, Alec, and David E. Kaplan, 4707
Dubrovsky, Gertrude W., 5748, 5749
Ducato, Theresa, 5054
Dudar, Helen, 3745
Dudley, Julius W., 5366
Duerksen, Menno, 1661
Dufault, David V., 7611
Duffy, Bernard K., 6823, 8495
Duffy, Bernard K., and Susan Duffy, 2516
Duffy, John, 0218
Dugger, Ronnie, 4298
Duis, Perry R., 2178, 8071
Duke, Escal, 1206
Dulaney, W. Marvin, 5367
Dulles, Allen W., 9543
Dulles, Foster R., 8268, 8830
Dulles, Foster R., and Gerald Ridinger, 9544
Dumett, Raymond, 8660
Dunagan, J. Conrad, 1751
Dunaway, David K., 3535
Dunbar, Robert G., 1439
Dundes, Alan, 4118
Dunfree, Charles D., 3054
Dunlap, Leslie W., 0563
Dunlap, Thomas R., 1440, 1441
Dunn, James W., 2692
Dunn, Joe P., 8269
Dunn, Larry W., 5655
Dunn, Voorhees E. Jr., 6485
Dunn, Walter S. Jr., 8270, 9277
Dunne, Gerald T., 6974
Dunnigan, Kate, and Richard Quinney, 2179
Dur, Philip F., 0789, 0790

Dura, Juan, 7361
Duram, James C., 3974, 3975, 3976, 6117, 6230, 6231, 6912, 6952, 6953
Durand, Arthur A., 8271
Durant, John, and Alice Durant, 0102
Durden, Robert F., 4299
Durfee, Mary H., 7503
Duron, Clementina, 2180
Durr, Willima T., 1792
Durrence, James L., 8894
Dursoselle, J. B., 7744
Duryea, Polly, 3638
Dusterberg, Richard B., 0297
Duus, Masayo, 8496
Dwan, John E. II, 7745
Dwyer, Thomas R., 8777, 8778
Dye, Scott A., 7917
Dyer, George C., 9278
Dyer, Stanford P., 1076
Dyke, Samuel E., 8120
Dyson, Lowell K., 1311, 1386, 1534, 1535, 1536, 6232, 9602
Dzierba, Timothy R., 2074
Dziuban, Stanley W., 8673

Eagle, Joanna, 3639
Eagles, Charles W., 5368, 5369
Eagles, Keith D., 0801
Earle, Edward M., 7193
Early, Stephen J., 7045
East, Charles, 1170
Eastman, James N. Jr., 1880, 4865
Easton, Carol, 6486
Eaton, William E., 4300
Eatwell, Roger, 7194
Eby, Cecil D., 3334, 7362
Eccles, Marriner S., 2517
Echols, James P., 6487
Eckert, J. Preper, 4866
Eckes, Alfred E. Jr., 2518, 8121
Eckey, Lorelei F., 3207
Eckhardt, William, 8497
Edel, Wilbur, 9456, 9545
Edelman, Eric S., 8783
Edelman, Milton T., 8272
Eden, Anthony, 8724, 8725
Eden, Joseph A., and Arnold R. Alanen, 4638
Eden, Robert, 6052
Edgerton, F. Van, 6233
Edmonds, Robin, 8598
Edmunds, Sterling E., 7101
Edwards, G. Thomas, 9279
Edwards, Jerome E., 1015, 6488, 7918
Edwards, John C., 8498
Edwards, John C., and Joseph H. Kitchens Jr., 5370

Edwards, Rhoda D., 8122
Egan, Clifford L., and Alexander W. Knott, 7195
Egan, Eileen M., 8011
Egan, Ferol, and W. H. Hutchinson, 4119
Egbert, Arch O., 2519
Egger, John B., 2031
Egolf, Jeremy R., 2181
Ehrenreich, Dixie L. W., 7919
Ehrenreich, John H., 2653
Ehrhart, Robert C., 0479
Ehrlich, Walter, 2182, 2183
Eichengreen, Barry, 1602, 1603
Eichengreen, Barry, and Jeffery Sachs, 1953
Eidevall, Gunnar, 3335
Eilers, John A., 9457
Einaudi, Mario, 5055
Einstein, Frank H., 3336
Eisen, George, 0810
Eisen, Margaret B., 3640
Eisenhour, Jerry D., 3208
Eisenhower, David., 0910
Eisenhower, Dwight D., 0911, 0912, 0913
Eisenhower Foundation, 9280
Eisenhower, John S. D., 8726
Eisenhower, John S. D., 0914
Eismeier, Dana L., 7504
Ekirch, Arthur A. Jr., 5056, 6234, 8012, 8013, 9728
El Ayoubi, Mohamad A., 8999
Elam, Harry J., Jr., 3209
Eldersveld, Samuel J., 6489
Eldot, Paula, 6490
Eldredge, David S., 8123
Eliasberg, W. G., 0219
Elkin, Jerrold F., 8831
Eller, Cynthia, 8014
Eller, Ronald D., 9729
Elliot, Charles F., 4867
Elliot, Peter, 8727
Elliott, Mark R., 8832, 9480
Ellis, Ann W., 5371, 5372, 8072
Ellis, William E., 4120, 4480, 4708, 6491
Ellsworth, Lincoln, 4868
Elsasser, Edward C., 7654
Elsey, George M., 0371
Elshtain, Gean B., 0055
Elston, James M., 7363
Ely, Melvin P., 3889
Emerson, Horton W., Jr., 2184
Emerson, Thomas I., 5373
Emerson, William, 0480
Emery, Michael C., 3890
Emmerich, Lisa E., 5835
Emmerson, James T., 7275
Emmerson, John, 0814, 9062
Emmons, William M., III, 1733

Enders, Calvin W., 1106
Endleman, Gary E., 2468
Engelbourg, Saul, 5750
Engelbrecht, Helmuth C., and Frank C. Hanighen, 1042
Engelman, Larry D., 2185
England, J. Merton, 4869
Enser, A. G. S., 9624
Eppard, Philip B., 2520
Epstein, Joseph, 4121
Epstein, Julius, 8599
Epstein, Leon D., 6998
Epstein, Melch, 6235
Epstein, Samuel, and Beryl Epstein, 0103
Erb, Claude C., 9010
Erdmann, James M., 9281
Erenberg, Lewis A., 4748
Ericksen, Eugene P., 6860
Erickson, Erling A., 1312
Erickson, Herman, 3055
Erickson, Nels, 1250
Erickson, Steve, 3746
Erie, Steven P., 6824
Erikson, Joan M., 0056
Erikson, Robert S., and Kent L. Tedin, 5057
Erlebacher, Albert, 6492
Ernst, Morris L., 0298
Errico, Charles J. Jr., 6053, 6788
Esbitt, Milton, 2521
Espeseth, Carolyn, 4678
Esposito, David M., and Jackie R. Esposito, 6493
Estabrook, Susan A., 2522
Estes, Donald H., 5715, 5716
Esthus, Raymond A., 8728
Etzold, Thomas H., 7276, 7277, 7278, 9090
Eubank, Keith, 8600
Eubanks, Richard K., 8833
Eulau, Heinz, 2693, 4639
Evangela, Sister M., 8812
Evans, Art, 5374
Evans, Paul, 8124
Evans, Timothy K., 6494
Evans, Walter, 3747
Evans, William B., 1023
Evearitt, Daniel J., 5751
Evens, Richard, 4301
Everest, A. S., 0654
Everett, Dianna, 3641
Everett, James A., Jr., 3658
Everman, Henry E., 7102
Eversole, Theodore W., 5375
Evins, Joe L., 0830
Evjen, Henry O., 6789, 6790
Ewen, Frederick, 3210
Eyre, James K., Jr., 0931
Eyster, Warren, 3337

Ezekial, Mordecai, 0571
Ezickson, Aaron J., 0104

Faber, Doris, 0007, 0035, 0620
Fabre, Michel, 3588
Fabricant, Noah D., 0220, 0221, 0222
Fabricant, Solomon, 2523
Fabyanic, Thomas A., 9282
Fadely, James Philip 6772
Fagan, George V., 0481, 7323
Fagette, Paul H. Jr., 5122
Fagin, Vernon A., 6782
Fahey, John, 2524
Fahrney, Delmar S., 4870
Fahy, Charles, 7024
Failing, Patricia, 5243
Fair, Daryl R., 4302
Fairbanks, Robert B., 1793, 1794, 3056
Fairchild, Byron, and Jonathan Grossman, 8273
Fairfield, John D., 4640
Falk, Gerhard, 0390
Falkenberg, Pamela, 3748
Fang, Irving E., 3891
Fanning, Richard W., 7196
Fanton, Jonathan F., 8499
Farago, Ladislas, 7505
Farber, Milton L. J., 2186
Farley, James A., 0627, 0628
Farley, Mary, 1442
Farmer, Patrick A., 3211
Farnsworth, Beatrice, 7421
Farnsworth, David, and James W. McKinney, 7694
Faroqui, Hossain S., 9481
Farr, Finis, 0299
Farran, Don, 5183, 5184
Farrell, Kathleen L., 3338
Farren, Eldon, 8274
Farrington, John P., 0300
Fass, Paula, 4303
Faue, Elizabeth B., 2187
Faulkner, Ronnie W., 7279
Fausel, Robert W., 7671
Fausold, Martin L., 7103, 7104
Faust, Wolfgang M., and R. Baird Shman, 3977
Feagin, Joe R., and Kelly Riddell, 8125
Fearis, Donald F., 1387
Fearon, Peter, 1940
Feder, Bernard, 2188
Feder, Donald, 6380
Feder, Ernest, 1348
Fedyszyn, Thomas R., 8500
Fee, Elizabeth, 4201
Fehrenbach, T. R., 7746
Feiling, Keith, 9180
Fein, Richard J., 3589

Feinberg, Barbara S., 0008
Feingold, Henry L., 5752, 5753, 9091, 9092, 9093, 9094, 9095, 9096
Feingold, Miriam, 6236
Feinman, Ronald L., 0982, 6743
Feis, Herbert, 0223, 1954, 2032, 7364, 7506, 7507, 7837, 8652, 8729, 8834, 8895, 9730
Fejes, Fred, 7632
Feldman, Frances T., 3642
Feldman, Martin I., 0757
Felsenthal, Edward, 1191
Felt, Jeremy P., 4679
Fenno, Richard F., 0704, 8601
Fensterwald, Bernard, 7920
Ferdon, Nona S., 0036
Fergunson, Yale H., 7633
Ferguson, Robert Benjamin, 4481
Ferguson, Robert C., 3892
Ferguson, Thomas, 1604
Ferkiss, Victor C., 6381
Fernandes, Marjorie Matthews, 5717
Fernandez, Raul, 5836
Ferrara, Peter J., 2808
Ferrell, Henry C., 0664
Ferrell, John R., 3093
Ferrell, Robert H., 7197, 7634
Ferrill, Martha J. W., 1443
Ferris, William, 3339
Fetner, Gerald, 1795
Fetter, Theodore J., 8501
Fetzer, James A., 8896
Feuer, Leon I., 5754, 5755
Feuer, Lewis S., 7422
Feurer, Rosemary, 2525
Fichter, Joseph H., 5376
Ficken, Robert E., 2526, 6799, 8502
Fickle, James E., 3094
Fiedler, Leslie A., 3340
Field, Alexander J., 1605
Field, Betty M., 1171
Field, Gregory B., 3095
Field, Roger W., 4482
Fields, Alonzo, 0372
Fields, Kathleen R., 4483
Fields, William G., and William C. West, 3749
Filippelli, Ronald L., 2189, 2190
Filler, Louis, 3341
Finberg, Walter, 4304
Finch, Glenn, 1115
Fincher, Jack, 1881
Findlay, James F., 2191
Fine, David M., 3342
Fine, Herbert A., 8962
Fine, Janis B., 4202
Fine, Joyce, 9097

Fine, Lenore, and Jesse A. Remington, 4871
Fine, Robert S., 0151
Fine, Sidney, 2192, 2193, 2194, 2195, 2196, 2197, 2440, 2809, 2810, 7025, 7026, 7027, 7028
Finegold, Kenneth, 2811
Finger, John R., 6496
Finison, Lorenz J., 2198, 2473, 2474, 4305
Fink, Deborah, and Dorothy Schwieder, 5935
Fink, Gary M., 2199, 6146
Fink, Gary M., and James W. Hilty, 0602
Finkelstein, Lawrence S., 8792
Finkelstein, Leo, Jr., 0152
Finkelstein, Marvin S., 2200
Finkle, Lee, 5377, 5378, 5610
Finlay, Mark R., and Don F. Hadwiger, 8126
Fisch, Dov., 5756
Fischer, Adam J., 3343
Fischer, Claude S., 4872
Fischer, George, 8835
Fischer, LeRoy H., and Robert E. Smith, 4873
Fischer, Louis, 0057, 7423, 8836
Fischhoff, Baruch, 6913
Fish, Hamilton, 7747
Fish, Peter Graham, 4709, 6914
Fishbein, Leslie, 3750, 3751, 3752
Fishbein, Morris, 4203
Fishel, Leslie H. Jr., 5379
Fishel, Wesley R., 8564
Fisher, Gideon L., 1444
Fisher, Richard B., 6237
Fishman, Jack, 9192
Fishwick, Marshall W., 7105, 9643
Fitch, Nancy Elizabeth, 9603
Fitch, Noel, 3344
Fite, Gilbert C., 0711, 1445, 1446, 1537, 1538, 1561, 2812, 2813, 2814
Fitz-Simmons, Daniel W., 0572
Fitzgerald, Deborah K., 1282
Fitzpatrick, John J., III, 1008
Fitzpatrick, Vincent, 3345
Fitzsimons, M. A., 3978
Flaccus, Elmer W., 4591, 5837
Flack, Bruce C., 5058
Flanagan, Barney L., 2948
Flanders, Jane, 3346
Flannery, Christopher, 7424
Flannery, Richard F., 8837
Fleener, Nickieann, 5380
Fleischer, Lowell R., 7921
Fleischer, Nat, 4592
Fleischhauer, Carl, and Beverly W. Brannon, 3643
Fleischhauer, Carl, Beverly W. Brannan, and Claudine Weatherford, 5244
Fleischman, Charles W., 8503
Fleisig, Heywood, 7198

Fleming, Denna F., 7971
Fleming, Douglas, L., 3057, 3058
Fleming, Robert E., 3347
Flemming, George M., 2075
Flezenberg, Alvin S., 6495
Fligstein, Neil, 4150
Flinn, Carol A., 3753
Flint, Sam H., 1914
Floyd, Barbara, 4306
Floyd, James R., 5059
Floyd, John E., and Allan Hynes, 1941
Flynn, Edward J., 0736
Flynn, George Q., 0921, 4484, 4485, 4874, 5611, 8275, 8276, 9644
Flynn, John T., 0690, 7106, 7107
Flynt, Wayne, 6497
Fogelson, Nancy, 4875
Folsom, Carlton, 8427
Foner, Philip S., 5381
Fones-Wolf, Elizabeth, 2201, 8127
Forbes, Gerald, 1752
Forbes, Joseph, 0932
Ford, Thomas K., 8813
Forderhase, Nancy K. K., 7247
Fore, Steven J., 8504
Fornari, Harry D., 1349
Forrestal, James V., 0816
Forsythe, James L., 1219
Fosdick, Roger B., 8277
Fossett, Roy E., 2949
Fossey, W. Richard, 1662, 6498
Foster, Alan J., 8730
Foster, Clifton Dale, 9645
Foster, Jack R., 2202, 2203
Foster, Jim, 2815
Foster, Mamie M. B., 5382, 9604
Foster, Mark S., 2527
Foster, Richard H. Jr., 8189
Foster, Robert B., 3212
Foster-Hayes, Carrie A., 8015
Fothergill, Garland W., 3979
Fowler, Dorothy, 6054
Fowler, John G., Jr., 0945
Fowler, William E., 4204
Fowles, Brian D., 4876
Fox, Annette B., 8653
Fox, Cheryl A., 2528
Fox, Daniel M., 4877, 5123
Fox, Frank W., 8505
Fox, Kel M., 4710
Fox, Richard, 6147
Fox, Stephen C., 0902
Fox, William T. R., 9283
Foxworth, Elleanor W., 1207
Foy, David A., 8278

Fraas, Elizabeth M., 6499
Fraden, Rena, 5383
Fradkin, Philip L., 8674
Fraenkel, Osmond K., 6915
Fragnoli, Raymond R., 6500
Fram, Leon, 5757
France, Richard, 5124
Francis, Lynn, 3166
Francis, M. J., 9025
Franco, Jere, 5838, 5839, 5840
Frank, Carrolyle M., 6501, 6502, 6503
Frank, Catherine, 0544
Frank, Felicia N. L., 3980
Frank, Forest, 6504
Frank, Gary, 9026
Frank, Larry J., 9284
Frank, Mary E. V., 8209
Frank, Miriam, Marilyn Ziebarth, and Connie Field, 8210
Frank, Robert L, 4486
Frank, Sam, 3754
Frank, Sid, and Arden D. Melick, 0301
Frankfurter, Felix, 7008, 7009, 7010, 7011, 7056
Franklin D. Roosevelt Library, 9646
Franklin D. Roosevelt Warm Springs Memorial
    Commission, 0105
Franklin D. Roosevelt Memorial Commission, 0545
Franklin, Jimmie L., 4749
Franklin, John Hope, 5384, 5612
Franklin, V. P., 3981, 5385
Franklin, Willard C. Jr., 7365
Franklin, William M., 8602, 9546
Fraser, David, 8731
Fraser, Steve, 2431, 2432
Fraticelli, Carlos R., 7705
Frazer, Heather T., and John O'Sullivan, 8211
Frederick, Richard G., 6148
Fredricksen, Mary K., 5936, 8452
Fredette, Raymond H., 7922
Fredrikkson, Kristine G., 4593
Freedland, Michael, 3536, 7012
Freeman, Elsie T., Walter Bodle, and Wynell Burroughs,
    0058
Freeman, John L., 5841
Freeman, Joshua B., 2204, 8128
Freidel, Frank, 0024, 0037, 0117, 0238, 0302, 0303, 2694,
    5060, 5274, 6744, 7280, 7508, 9605, 9731, 9814
Freidus, Anne, 4307
Fremling, Gertrude M., 1955, 1956
French, Michael, 2529
French, Warren G., 3213 3348, 3349, 3350, 3351
Fretz, Lewis A., 6505
Freund, Paul A., 6984
Freund, William C., 1829
Frey, Richard C., 7108
Frick, Margaret J. B., 3352

Fricke, Earnest B., 1606, 2530
Frieberg, Anne, 3982
Friedberger, Mark, 1388
Friedlander, E. J., 8356
Friedlander, Henry, 9098
Friedlander, Jay, 8357
Friedlander, Peter J., 2205
Friedlander, Robert A., 7343, 7366
Friedman, Arthur L., 8129
Friedman, Donald J., 7923
Friedman, Leon, 6802
Friedman, Martin F., 5125
Friedman, Philip, 9625
Friedman, Saul S., 9099
Friedrich, Gerhard, 3353
Friedrich, K. Marlin, 7509
Friend, Theodore W., 7612, 8958, 8959
Frisch, Michael, 9844
Frisch, Morton J., 0304, 2695, 6149, 8603
Frisch, Morton J. and Martin Diamond, 6055
Frisch, Otto R., 9285
Friske, Leo J., 5245
Frost, Harlan M., 4487, 4488
Fruehauf, Erich, 1313
Fry, Joseph A., 2206, 6506, 6507
Frye, Alton, 9065
Fuchs, Lawrence H., 5758
Fujimoto, Isao, 8358
Fulgham, Ouida J., 2816
Fulkerson, William M., 1070
Fuller, Hoyt, 5386
Fuller, John F., 6508
Fuller, Mary 5246
Fulmer, John L., 2817
Fulton, Tom, 2818
Fultz, Michael, 5387
Funigiello, Philip J., 1734, 1735, 2696, 3096, 5126, 8190
Funk, Arthur L., 8565, 8604, 8687, 8688, 8689, 9205, 9286,
    9606
Furdell, William J., 0831
Furlong, William B., 4594
Furlow, John W. Jr., 5937, 6509
Furman, Bess, 0373
Furmanovsky, Michael, 2207
Furniss, Edgar S., 9011
Fusfeld, Daniel R., 0243, 0713, 5061
Fusonie, Alan E., 1562
Fyne, Robert J., 8506

Gabel, Christopher R., 4878, 9287, 9626
Gabin, Nancy F., 2208
Gabriel, Juerg M., 7866
Gaddis, John L., 8838, 9482, 9483
Gail, Gilbert J., 2209
Gaines, Janes M., 3755

Gal, Allon, 6985, 7622

Galambos, Louis, 2532, 2533

Galambos, Louis, and Barbara B. Spence, 2531

Galbraith, John Kenneth, 0305, 0306, 1957

Galenson, Walter, 2210, 2211

Galentine, Shane N., 6510

Galey, John, 2534

Galindez, Jesus de, 7635

Gall, Gilbert J., 2212, 2416

Gallagher, Brain T., 9732

Gallagher, Hugh G., 0224

Gallagher, Kevin J., 0191

Gallaway, Lowell, 2213

Galliher, John F., and Allyn Walker 5062

Gallo, Franklin W., 8605

Galloway, J. M., 0806, 1069

Gamboa, Erasmo, 5678, 8279, 8280, 8281

Gambrell, Jamey, 3644

Gamer, Robert E., 7867

Gandolfi, Arthur E., 1987

Gandolfi, Arthur E., and James R. Lothian, 1988

Ganger, David W., 2697

Gannon, Robert I., 4489

Ganz, A. Harding, 0964

Ganzel, Bill, 1287, 1663

Garcia, Juan R., 5680

Garcia, Mario T., 5681, 5682

Garcia, Richard A., 5683, 5684

Garcia y Griego, Larry M., 5679

Gardner, Bruce L., 8130

Gardner, Gerald, 3756

Gardner, Greg H., 0768

Gardner, Lloyd C., 7199, 7200, 7748, 9484

Gardner, Martin A., 3214

Gardner, Robert W., 6954

Garland, Claude M., 7109

Garlid, George W., 6511, 7972

Garlock, Peter D., 8938

Garrand, Timothy P., 3757

Garraty, John A., 1607, 1958, 2475, 6056

Garrett, Crister S., and Stephen A. Garrett, 8839

Garrett, John V., 9485

Garrison, Bruce M., 3983

Garrison, Joseph Y., 2423

Garson, Robert A., 6057, 8654

Garvey, Gerald, 6955

Garvey, Timothy J., 1796

Gaskin, Thomas M., 6512

Gaskins, Avery F., 4711

Gaster, Patricia, 3984

Gatell, Frank Otto, 7706

Gates, John, 6238

Gatewood, William B., Jr., 1447

Gatrell, A. Steven, 6513, 6514, 6515

Gatten, Jeffery N., 9607

Gavins, Raymond, 5388

Gay, James Thomas, 2950

Gay, Peter, 9100

Gaydowski, J. D., 7110

Gaylor, Sylvia K., 7749

Gazell, James A., 1269

Geary, Edward A., 5938

Gebhard, David, 3167

Geduld, Carolyn, and Harry Geduld, 3758

Gehl, Jurgen, 7281

Gehring, Wes D., 3759

Geisler, Richard A., 9012

Geist, Sidney, 5127

Gelber, Steven M., 5185, 5186

Gelfand, Lawrence E., 2698

Gelfand, Lawrence E., and Robert J. Neymeyer, 9733

Gelfand, Mark I., 0714, 2699

Gellman, Irwin F., 7636, 7663, 7672, 7673, 9101

Gellott, Laura, 4205

General Jewish Council, 5759

Genevro, Rosalie, 1797

Genizi, Haim, 3985, 5389, 9102, 9103

Gens, Stephen M ., 6239

Gentile, Nancy J., 8359

Gentry, Robert W., 3354

Genung, Albert B., 1350

George, Cynthia, 3760

George, Elsie L., 5939

George, James H., 9547

Gerassi, John, 7367

Gerber, James B., 4308

Gerber, Larry G., 6150

Gerber, Philip L., 3355

Gerlach, Horst, 9104

Gerlinger, Irene H., 0059

German, Kathleen M., 8507

"German Prisons of War in Alaska: The POW Camp
      Excursion Inlet.", 8443

Gerson, Louis L., 7868

Gerstle, Gary L., 2214, 2215, 2216

Gersuny, Carl, and Gladis Kaufman, 2217

Gersuny, Carl, and John J. Poggie, Jr., 3059

Gertz, Elmer, 0307

Geselbracht, Raymond, 9815

Gesenway, Deborah, and Mindy Roseman, 8360

Getz, Lynne M., 4309

Ghirardo, Diane Y., 3168

Giangreco, D. M., 8690

Gibbs, Norman, 7324

Gibson, Chester, 1210

Gibson, Robert C., 3986

Giduz, Roland, 0308

Giebelhaus, August W., 1753

Gieve, Eggert W., 9548

Gifford, Bernard R., 6151

Gilbert, Jess, and Steve Brown, 1539
Gilbert, Martin, 9193
Gilette, Howard, Jr., 1798
Gilkey, Royal C., 7013
Gill, George J., 0888
Gill, Gerald R., 5390
Gill, Robert, L., 5391
Gill, Sadiq A., 8957
Gillespie, Angus K., 3144
Gillette, Howard, 3761
Gillette, Michael L., 1172, 5392, 5393, 5634
Gilley, Leonard, 3356
Gilmore, Al-Tony, 4595
Gimbel, John, 9288
Ginell, Cary, 3537
Ginger, Ann Fagan, 6240
Gingerich, Melvin, 6382, 8016
Girdner, Andrie, and Anne Loftis, 8361
Giroux, Vincent A., Jr., 1124
Girrard, Charlotte S., 8691
Gitlow, Benjamin, 6241
Givens, Larry D., 9013
Glaberman, Martin, and George P. Rawick, 3987
Glaberson, Eric A., 4797
Glad, Betty, 1054
Gladwin, Lee A., 4641
Glaser, Martha, 6383
Glass, William R., 9105
Glasser, Kurt, 9734
Glazer, Penina M., 3988, 8017
Gleason, Philip, 4246, 4490, 8428
Glen, John M., 4310, 8282
Glenn, Robert W., 3357
Glennon, John P., 8566
Glennon, Robert J., 0678
Glicksber, Charles I., 6242
Glover, James M., 1448, 1449
Gluck, Sherna B., 8212, 8213
Glyn, Thomas, 3538
Gobel, Thomas, 2218
Goc, Michael J., 1450
Godfrey, Anthony, 5842
Godfried, Nathan, 7619
Godson, Susan H., 9289, 9290
Goerner, Fred G., 1882
Goggin, Jacqueline A., 5394, 9735
Going, William T., 3358
Gold, Bela, 1351
Gold, Isodore J., 7624
Goldberg, Joseph P., 0659, 2219
Goldberg, Joyce S., 1062
Goldberg, Richard T., 0225
Goldfield, Michael, 2819
Goldman, Eliot, 6999
Goldman, Eric F., 2700

Goldsmith, Adolph O., 1173
Goldsmith, Betty L., 6916
Goldsmith, Harry S., 0226
Goldstein, Donald M., 0963
Goldstein, Harold M., 1989, 3097
Goldstein, Judith, 1830, 1831
Goldsworthy, Harry E., 0741
Goldway, David, 3989
Golembe, Carter H., 2820
Golembe, John C., 6956
Golembeski, Dean J., 4879
Goll, Eugene W., 7111
Gomery, Douglas, 3762, 3763
Gomolak, Louis S., 1077
Gonzales, Gilbert C., 5685
Gonzales, Phillip B., 5686
Goode, Thomas H., 6516
Goode, Thomas H., and Agnew M. Riggs, 7112
Goodenow, Ronald K., 4311, 5613
Goodhard, Philip, 8732
Goodman, Grant K., 7613
Goodman, James E., 5395, 5396
Goodman, Leonard, 6917
Goodman, Melvin A., 7425
Goodman, Walter, 0524, 2441
Goodno, Floyd R., 1220
Goodpasture, H. McKennie, 4491
Goodson, Martia G., 5397
Goodstein, Judith, 4312
Goodwyn, Larry, 4596
Gopinath, Aruna, 7614
Goralski, Robert, and Russell W. Freeburg, 1754
Gordon, Arthur, 7282
Gordon, Bernard K., 8678
Gordon, Ernest, 4492
Gordon, Felice D., 5940
Gordon, Lawrence, 5398
Gordon, Leonard, 9291
Gordon, Lester I., 1234
Gordon, Max, 6243, 6244, 6245
Gordon, Philip, 3359
Gordon, Rita W., 5656
Gordon, Robert J., 8131
Gorman, Thomas R., 3215
Gormley, Daniel J., 8606
Gorni, Yosef, 5760
Gosnell, Harold F., 0260, 0261
Gossett, William T., 7050
Gottlieb, Moshe R., 5761, 5762, 5763, 7283, 9106, 9107, 9108, 9109
Gottlieb, Peter, 2220
Gottsacker, Sister Mary H., 7284
Gough, Paul A., 1608
Gould, Jean, 0227
Gourevitch, Peter A., 1959, 1960

Gower, Calvin W., 2820a, 2821, 2822, 2951, 2952, 3060, 5399
Gowing, Margaret, 9292
Grabavoy, Leann, 3990
Grabill, Joseph L., 4493
Grable, Stephen W., 1799
Grace, Richard J., 7510, 7511
Graebner, Norman A., 6736, 7512
Graebner, William, 4712
Graff, Frank W., 0890
Graff, Robert D., and Robert E. Ginna, 0106
Grafton, Carl, 6517
Graham, Charles J., 6058
Graham, D. L., 2701, 4642
Graham, Fred C., 2535
Graham, Hugh D., 0060, 1174
Graham, Jeanne, 6518
Graham, Mary E., 3360
Graham, Otis L. Jr., 0309, 6059, 6060, 6152, 9486, 9736, 9737
Graham, Otis P., 2702
Graham, Robert A., 4494
Graig, Ian C., 9293
Gramm, William P., 1609
Grant, Barry K., 3539
Grant, H. Roger, 1451
Grant, H. Roger, and L. Edward Purcell, 1664, 2953
Grant, Marilyn, 1755
Grant, Nancy L., 5400
Grant, Philip A. Jr., 0603, 1026, 1116, 1266, 2823, 2954, 6061, 6519, 6520, 6521, 6749, 6773, 6748, 6746, 6745, 6747, 6791, 7924, 9458
Grant, Robert B., 5401
Grantham, Dewey W. Jr., 1610, 6522
Gratton, Brian, 3061, 4680
Gratton, Brian, Arturo F. Rosales, and Hans Debano, 5687
Graves, Gregory R., 1314
Graves, Thomas J., 8132
Gravlee, Grady J., 0153, 0154, 0732
Gray, James, 2221
Gray, Leslie, and Wynell Burroughs, 4313
Gray, R. J., 3361
Gray, Robert C., 8840
Gray, Wendy, and Robert Knight Barney, 7285
Graybar, Lloyd J., 9294
Grayson, A. G., 0604
Grayson, Carmen B., 2051
Grayson, George W. Jr., 7201
Grebstein, Sheldon, 3362
Greco, John F., 7973
Grede, John F., 3098
Green, A. Wigfall, 1125
Green, Anna B., 8214, 8283
Green, Archie, 3540
Green, David, 7637
Green, David E., 9014
Green, David L., 6062

Green, Fletcher M., 6523
Green, George N., 6118, 6524
Green, Harry A., 1800
Green, James R., 2222, 2223, 6246, 9608, 9738
Green, Joe L., 1175
Green, Martin B., 3363
Green, Michael S., 1016
Green, Murray, 4880
Green, Philip E., 9487
Green, Thomas L., 0624
Greenbaum, Fred, 0996, 1009, 6063
Greenberg, Daniel S., 8733
Greenberg, Gershon, 9110
Greenberg, Irwin F., 6525
Greenberg, Karen J., 4151, 8429
Greene, Fred, 4881
Greene, James "Joe", and John Holway, 4597
Greene, Larry A., 1665
Greene, Lorenzo J., 1666, 1667
Greene, Murray, 4882
Greene, Rebecca S., 8284, 9739
Greene, Thomas R., 4495, 4681
Greenfield, Kent R., 8567, 8568, 9647
Greenstein, Fred I., 0391
Greenstein, Fred I., Larry Berman and Alvin S. Felzerberg, 9609
Greenwald, Richard A., 4206
Greenwalt, Bruce S., 7462
Greenwell, Scott L., 3364
Greer, T., 9833
Greet, Robert L., 4314
Grefrath, Richard W., 8508
Gregg, Richard B., 1270
Gregory, Chester W., 8285
Gregory, James N., 1288, 1668
Gregory, Ross, 8073
Grenier, Judson, 6526
Gressley, Jene M., 1049, 2536
Gressman, Eugene, 7029
Grew, Joseph C., 7513, 7514
Grey, Michael R., 2824
Grieb, Kenneth J., 7678, 7680
Grieder, Calvin, 5128
Grier, Peter, 9295
Grieve, William G., 8897
Griffin, Charles C., 7638
Griffin, Donald W., 7657
Griffin, Frederick C., 6247
Griffin, James B., 4883
Griffin, Walter R., 8018
Griffith, Robert K. Jr., 4884, 4885
Grigg, John, 8569
Grimes, Mary C., 2224
Grimm, Charlie, with Ed Prell, 4598
Grimsrud, Theodore G., 8286

Grimwood, Michael, 3365
Grinde, Gerald S., 1117
Grinnell-Milne, Duncan, 9206
Grisso, Karl M., 4315
Griswold, Erwin N., 7057
Grob, Gerald N., 8287
Grobman, Alex, 9111
Grodzins, Morton, 8362
Grogan, Susan F., 7000
Grollman, Catherine A., 0832
Groom, A. J. R., 9296
Groover, Robert L., 3366
Gross, Charles J., 9297
Gross, James A., 2225, 2226
Grossman, James, 7014
Groth, Michael, 4152
Grothaus, Larry, 0605, 5635
Grove, Stephen B., 6527
Grover, Wayne, 9648
Groves, Frank W., 1540
Groves, Leslie R., 4886, 9298
Grow, Earl S., Jr., 3893
Grow, Michael R., 1214, 7701, 9015
Grubbs, Donald H., 1352, 1541
Gruber, Carol S., 4887
Grunfeld, Adalbert T., 7869
Grupenhoff, Richard L., 3216
Gueerin-Gonzales, Camille, 5688
Guerrant, Edward O., 7750
Guffey, Joseph F., 0262
Gugeler, Russell A., 0946
Gugin, Linda C., 5941
Guillame, Bernice F., 3367
Guinsburg, Thomas N., 1027, 7925
Gunns, Albert F., 5402
Gunther, John, 0310
Gunther, Lenworth A., III, 5403
Gurney, Jene, and Clare Gurney, 0118
Gurney, Ramsdell Jr., 7426
Gustafson, Merlin, 9816
Gustafson, Merlin, and Jerry Rosenberg, 0244
Gustafson, Milton O., 0546, 9549
Gustafson, Richard, 3764
Gustafson, Robert W., 3765
Guth, James L., 1542
Gutin, Myre G., 0061
Gutman, Yisrael, and Efraim Zuroff, 9112
Guttman, Allen, 3368, 3590, 5764, 7368
Guzda, Henry P., 0660
Guzman, Raul P. de, 7615
Gyant, LaVerne, 5404
Gysel, Libra J.C., 5063

Haag, William G., 5275
Haas, Edward F., 4122, 6528

Haber, Paul, 0119
Hachey, Thomas E., 7202, 8734, 8735, 8736, 8737, 8738, 8739, 8740, 9299
Hacker, Barton C., 4888
Hackett, Alice P., 3369
Hadley, Worth, 4316
Haessly, Gaile, A., 3645
Hafer, R. W., 1990
Hagan, Monys A., 4599
Hagerty, Donald J.,5247
Haggard, Stephan, 1832
Haggard-Gilson, Nancy J., 4767
Haglund, David G., 0947, 7254, 7639, 7640, 7664, 7751
Haid, Stephen E., 1801
Haight, David J., and George H. Curtis, 9649
Haight, John M. Jr., 0155, 7752, 7753, 7754, 7974, 8692, 8693, 8694, 8695, 8696
Hailey, Robert C., 3217
Haines, Gerald K., 7203, 7515, 9016, 9300, 9740
Haining, Hazel E., 2537
Hairgrove, Kenneth D., 1094
Haislip, Harvey, 8607, 8610
Halasz, N., 0311
Halasz, Piri, 3646
Haldstead, Charles R., 7369, 7370
Hale, F. Sheffield, 1202
Hale, William H., 0802
Haley, Charles T., 1669
Halila nee El Agrebi, Souad, 0788
Hall, Alvin L., 1131, 6529
Hall, Christopher, 9301
Hall, Clarence, 8247
Hall, Fred R., and Mabel Park Hall, 1452, 1915
Hall, Jacquelyn D., 2538, 4713, 5942, 5943
Hall, Robert N., 1078
Halle, Louis J., 7838
Hallgreen, Mauritz A., 7113, 7926
Halliday, Ernest M., 3591
Halperin, Edward C., 5765
Halperin, Samuel, 5766
Halperin, Samuel, and Irvin Oder, 9000
Halprin, Lee S., 8430
Halsey, William F., and Joseph Bryan, 0968
Halsey, William F., 4496
Halsted, James A., 0228
Halsy, Ashley, 0954
Halt, Charles E., 6530
Halter, Ernest J., 9610, 9611
Haltom, Margaret S., 7204
Ham, F. Gerald, 9612
Hamblem, Abigail Ann, 3370
Hamburger, Eric, 3371
Hamburger, Robert L., 7755
Hamby, Alonzo L., 0312, 2703, 5064, 6153
Hamel, April L., 5248

Hamilton, Charles, 0192
Hamilton, David E., 1315, 1611
Hamilton, Dona Cooper, 5405, 5406
Hamilton, Donald E., 2955
Hamilton, Marty, 1010
Hamilton, Virginia V., 6975
Hamilton, Walton, 1612
Hammack, Rudolph C., 2956
Hamme, Nancy S., 3647
Hammen, Oscar J., 8608
Hammer, Ellen, 8697
Hammer, Richard, 4714
Hammersmith, Jack L., 6803, 8809
Hammon, Stratton, 0915, 1453, 3169, 8288, 9302
Hammond, Mary K., 7927
Hammond, Mason, 9303
Hammouda, Abdul-Aziz A., 5065
Hamovitch, Mitzi B., 3372, 3991
Hanchett, Thomas W., 5407
Hancock, John, 2825, 4643
Hand, Samuel B., 0755, 0756, 7114, 9650
Hand, Samuel B., and Gregory D. Sanford, 6531, 6532
Hand, Wayland D., 1916
Handen, Ella F., 7756
Handy, Robert T., 4497, 4498
Hane, Mikiso, 8363
Hanin, Eric M., 8509
Hankey, Lord, 8570
Hankin, Mary A., 4317
Hankins, Barry G., 4499
Hanlon, Edward R., 6064
Hanna, Phil T., 4889
Hannan, Michael T., and John Freeman, 2227
Hanscom, James H., 9741
Hansen, Arthur A., 8364, 8365
Hansen, Harold, John G. Herndon, and William B.
    Langsdorf, 9651
Hansen, John M., 1353
Hanson, Betty C., 7427
Hanson, David E., 4318, 8431
Hanson, James A., 3099, 9652
Hanson, Sam, 0918, 3992
Haralovich, Mary B., 3766
Harap, Louis, 4319
Harbaugh, William H., 6119
Harbottle, Jeanne, 1883
Harbutt, Fraser J., 9488
Hardeman, D. B., and Donald C. Bacon, 1095
Hardeman, Nicholas P., 4890
Hardin, Charles M., 2826
Hardin, William H., 5944
Hardman, J. B. S., 2442
Hardy, Bruce A., 6533
Hardy, Cynthia G., 4320
Hare, Raymond A., 8972

Hareven, Tamara K., 0062
Hargreaves, Mary W. M., 1454, 5945
Harmon, Florence, 1670
Harmon, Mont J., 0631, 0632
Harms, Richard H., 3648
Harney, Andy Leon, 5129
Harper, Donna/Akiba S., 5408
Harper, R. Eugene, 2539
Harpham, Edward J., 2827
Harrell, James A., 5657
Harrell, Mary E., 5249
Harrelson, Elmer H., 0482
Harriman, W. Averell, 8841
Harriman, W. Averell, and E. Able, 0742
Harrington, Daniel F., 9304
Harrington, Jerry, 1251
Harrington, Michael, 2228, 6248
Harris, Brice Jr., 7344
Harris, Charles W., 9550
Harris, Charlotte D., 3541
Harris, Dennis E., 8842
Harris, Irving D., 0025
Harris, Jannette H., 5409
Harris, Michael W., 5410
Harris, Natalie, 3373
Harris, Ruth R., 7516, 8843
Harris, Sally A., 7641
Harris, Ted C., 5946
Harris, William H., 2229, 5411, 5412
Harrison, Barbara G., 4500
Harrison, Dennis I., 5947
Harrison, Donald F., 9051
Harrison, Gordan A., 9305
Harrison, John A., 9306
Harrison, Lowell H., 5130, 5187
Harrison, Patricia G., 8289
Harrison, Richard A., 7757, 7758, 7759, 8019
Harrison, Robert D., 6970, 6918
Harrison, Stanley L., 7428
Harrison, William J., 5413
Harrity, Richard, and Ralph G. Martin, 0063, 0107
Harrod, Frederick S., 5614, 5615
Harrod, R. F., 2033
Hart, Eric H., 7205
Hart, Jeffery, 3374, 4891
Hart, Vivien, 5948
Harten, Lucille B., 5949, 8290
Hartley, Marsden, 3649
Hartman, Susan M., 5950, 5951, 5952
Hartsough, Denise, 2230
Hartz, Louis, 6154
Harvey, Mark W. T., 1455
Harvey, Mose L., 8844
Harwell, Richard B., 3375
Harwood, Edwin, 6861

Harwood, Jonathan, 4892
Hasan, Khurshid, 8609
Hasan, Saiyid Z., 5131
Hasbany, Richard L., 3218, 3542
Hasdorff, James C., 5616
Hasenfus, William A., 1231
Haslam, Gerald, 1671
Hasse, Larry J., 5843
Hassett, William D., 0498
Hassler, William W., 4893
Hastie, William H., 5414
Hastings, Martin F., 8796
Hastings, Max, 9307
Hatch, Alden, 0009, 1132, 9207
Hatch, Fred J., 8675, 9308
Hatcher, John H., 6534
Hatchey, Thomas E., 7206
Hatfield, Eugene A., 1672
Hathway, Robert, 8741
Haunes, Jane I., 3377
Hauptman, Jerzy, 8510
Hauptman, Laurence M., 1013, 5844, 5845, 5846, 5847,
    5848, 5849
Hauptman, Laurence M., and Jack Campisi, 5132
Haury, David A., 8742
Hausdorff, Don M., 3993, 3994, 3995, 3996
Hauser, John D., 1833
Havas, Lasio, 9214
Havig, Alan R., 0460, 4123, 4124
Hawes, Beth Lomax, 3376
Hawkes, James H., 8020
Hawkes, James R., 8845
Hawkins, Helen S., 5066
Hawkins, Robert B., 6862
Hawks, Joanne V., 5953
Hawley, Ellis W., 1942, 2540, 2541
Hawthorn, Billy B., 6535
Hayden, John R., 7616
Haydon, Frederick, 4894
Hayes, Carlton J. H., 8793
Hayes, Grace P., 0499, 9309
Hayes, Jack I., 2957
Hayes, Otis E. Jr., 9310
Hayes, Robert E. Jr., 6536, 6537, 9311
Haymann, Jeanne L., 5133
Haynes, John E., 2231, 2958, 6249, 6250
Hays, Otis E. Jr., 8846
Haywood, Harry, 6251
Hazlet, Raymond L., 0313
Heacock, Walter J., 1068
Head, William P., 8898
Healey, Maryanne F., 0734
Healy, Diana D., 0064
Heard, Doreen B., 5067
Hearndon, Patrick J., 7286, 7839

Hearst, James, 1673
Heaster, Brenda L., 6804
Heath, Jim F., 8133, 8134, 9742
Heath, Vergil, and John C. Hunt, 2959
Hecht, Robert A., 5850
Hecker, David A., 3378
Heckscher, William S., 4321
Hedlund, Richard, 8743, 9551
Heffley, John T., 3997, 8021
Heidt, Raymond J., 8022
Height, John McVickar Jr., 7870
Heilbut, Anthony, 9113
Heilman, Grant, 1389
Heilman, Lawrence C., 9036
Heim, Robert H., 4322
Heimark, J. V., 9312
Heimdahl, William, and Geraldine Phillips, 7517
Hein, Virginia H., and Joseph O. Baylen, 6252
Heinemann, Ronald L., 1133, 2960, 2961, 2962, 9743
Heinl, Robert D., and Nancy Gordon Heinl, 7681
Heinrichs, Waldo H. Jr., 0818, 7458, 7760, 7871, 8899
Heinz, Catherine, 5954
Heitmann, John A., 1884, 8135
Helden, Karl, 0500
Heleniak, Roman, 1613
Helfand, W. H., H. B. Woodruff, K. M. H. Coleman, and D.
    L. Cowen, 8136
Helicher, Karl, 0026, 0027
Heller, Rita R., 4323
Hellerstein, Alice, 4600
Hellerstein, Jerome R., 1991
Helmbold, Lois R., 5955, 5956, 5957
Helmer, William J., 4715
Helmreich, Jonathan A., 9313
Helms, Douglas, 2828, 3100, 9817
Hemenway, Robert, 5188
Hemingway, Ernest, 7371
Hemminger, Carol, 4153
Henderson, Alexa B., 5415
Henderson, F. P., 0229
Henderson, Jeff, 5416
Henderson, Larry L., 1456
Henderson, Richard B., 1085
Hendrick, Irving J., 4324
Hendricks, Ricky L., 1457
Hendrickson, Gordon O., 1458, 5189
Hendrickson, John P., 6750
Hendrickson, Kenneth E., Jr., 1614, 2453, 2963, 2964, 2965,
    3767, 5190, 5191, 5193, 5192, 5194, 6538
Hendrickson, Kent., 5689
Hendrixson, Joe M., 2654
Henegar, Lucielle, 8453
Hennesey, James, 4501
Hennessey, Gregg R., 4502
Henningson, Berton E., 8655

Henrikson, Alan K., 9489, 9552
Henry, Annie B., 4325
Henry, John M., 3650, 4125
Henry, Laurin L., 0671
Henry, Linda J., 5958
Hensley, John R., 1459
Henson, Edward L., 7840
Henstell, Bruce, 6539
Hentoff, Nat, and Albert J. McCarthy, 3543
Henwood, James N. J., 6540, 2966
Hepting, George H., 1460
Herberg, Will, 2232
Herberling, Lynn O., 8291
Herbert, Vernon, and Attilio Bisil, 4895
Herbst, Josephine, and John Nelson, 7287
Herder, John H., 7761
Herman, Alan, 6541
Herman, Douglas E., 4503
Hermann, George B., 3998
Herndon, James S., and Joseph O. Baylen, 8847
Herndon, Jane W., 6542
Hernningson, Bertone E., 1834
Hero, Alfred O. Jr., 7975
Herr, Allen, 7372
Herreshoff, David, 3999
Herring, E. Pendleton, 0392
Herring, George C. Jr., 8656, 8848, 9553, 9490
Herring, Neill, and Sue Thrasher, 2233
Herrmann, Richard E., 4504
Hersh, Seymour H., 0156
Herst, Herman J., 0193
Hertz, Howard L., 6253
Herwig, Holger H., 7288, 7289
Herz, Martin F., 8511
Herzberg, James R., 7518
Herzig, John A., 9314
Herzog, James H., 7519, 7520, 7521
Herzstein, Robert E., 8512
Heslop, David A., 0393
Hess, Gary R., 4154, 8883, 9554, 9744
Hess, Stephen, and Milton Kaplan, 4126
Hessler, Marilyn S., 5417
Heston, Thomas J., 2542
Heuterman, Thomas H., 4000
Hevener, John W., 2234, 3062
Hewes, Leslie, 1289
Hewins, Dana C., 2829
Hewitt, H. Kent, 9315
Hewitt, William L., 8292
Hewlett, Richard G., 4896
Hewlett Richard G., and O.E. Anderson, 4897
Hibbert, Christopher, 9221
Hibdon, James E., 3101
Hibel, Franklin, 0900
Hickock, Lorena, 0065, 0621

Hicks, Alexander M., 2655
Hicks, Floyd W., and C. Roger Lambert, 2967
Hicks, John D., 2704
Hield, Melissa, 5959
Higgins, Trumbull, 8744, 9194, 9745
Higgs, Robert, 0394, 4155
High, Leslie C., Jr., 3768
Higham, John, 9746
Higham, Robin, 9627
Higham, Robin, and Donald J. Mrozek, 9613
Highsaw, Carol A., 5068
Hightower, Paul ,3651
Highwater, Jamake, 3652
Higonnet, Margaret R., James Jenson, Sonja Michel, and
    Margaret C. Weiz, 8215
Hiking, James W., 9316
Hilbert, Alfred G., 8454, 8455
Hill, Edmund R., 1961
Hill, Edwin C., 1674
Hill, John S., 3379
Hill, Norman, 7522
Hill, Thomas M., 0525, 1271
Hill, William S. Jr., 8137
Hilliard, Elbert R., 6543
Hilton, Ronald J., 4326
Hilton, Stanley E., 1835, 7658, 7762, 9039
Hilty, James W., 6065
Himelstein, Morgan Y., 3219
Himmelberg, Robert F., 2830
Hinchey, Mary H., 0395
Hinckley, Ted C., 1675
Hindman, Anne A., 3220
Hine, Darlene C., 5658, 5659, 5660
Hines, Barbara A.B., 4327
Hines, Calvin W., 9046, 9049
Hinton, Wayne K., 2968, 4505
Hirsch, Harry N., 7015
Hirsch, James B., 4328
Hirsch, Jerrold, 5069
Hirsch, Jerrold, and Tom E. Terrill, 5276
Hirschmann, Ira A., 9114, 9115
Hirschorn, Bernard, 0526
Hirshfield, Deborah A., 8216
Hiss, Alger, 7841
Hitchcock, Henry R., 3170
Hixson, Walter L., 0850, 1118
Hobbie, Peter H., 4506
Hobby, Robert M., 1802
Hobson, Archie, and Bill Stott, 2969
Hochwald, Jack, 9116
Hockett, Jeffrey D., 7043
Hodes, Elizabeth, 4898
Hodess, Annette M., 5250
Hodge, Robert W., 7642
Hodges, James A., 2235, 3102, 4001

Hodgkinson, Anthony W., 3769
Hody, Cynthia A., 1836
Hoehling, A. A., 7523
Hoff, Samuel B., 6066
Hoffer, Peter C., 7524
Hoffman, Abraham, 2236, 4156, 4157, 4158, 5690, 5691
Hoffman, Benjamin G., 6254
Hoffman, Edwin D., 5418
Hoffman, James L., 2237
Hoffman, Joan, 1615
Hoffman, Leonore, 5419
Hofsommer, Donovan L., 1917
Hofstadter, Richard, 0314
Hogan, David W. Jr., 9317
Hogan, Lawrence, 4002
Hogan, Robert, 5070
Hoglund, A. William, 1354, 1543
Hohner, Robert A., 4750
Holand, Bill and John B. Holway, 4601
Holbo, Paul S., 6544
Holborn, Hajo, 8679
Holborn, Louise, 8571
Holbrook, Francis X., 1885, 4899, 4900
Holcomb, Josephine C., 8217
Holcomb, Michael, 0883
Holcomb, Robert, 5251
Holdbrook, Francis X., 5960
Holden, Jonathan, 3380
Holder, Alan, 3381
Holl, Richard E., 8456
Holland, Carolsue, 7290
Holland, Donald, 2970
Holland, Henry M., 6992
Holland, John J., Jr., 1616, 2543
Holland, Reid A., 2971, 3063
Holland, Royce Q., 1676
Holley, Donald, 1355, 1461, 2705, 2972, 3064, 5420, 6545
Holley, I. B. Jr., 8138, 8139
Hollingsworth, Harold M., and William F. Holmes, 2706, 6957
Holloway, Halbert A., 2238
Holly, Daniel A., 9017
Holm, K. C., 0194
Holm, Tom, 5851
Holman, C. Hugh, 4003
Holmes, Jack E., and Robert E. Elder, Jr., 0442
Holmes, James H., 8698
Holmes, Michael S., 2973, 5421, 5422
Holmes, W. J., 9318, 9319
Holmes, William F., eds., 5071
Holsinger, M. Paul, 7048, 7255
Holt, Roberta D., 4207
Holter, Darryl, 2239, 2240, 2241
Holtoan, Orley I., 3221
Holton, Gerald, 4159
Holton, Richard H., 2544

Holtz, Alice, 2435
Holtzclaw, Harold W., 8023
Holway, John B., 4602
Hom-Kim, Lillian Lee, 5672
Homan, Gerlof D., 8953
Homel, Michael W., 5636, 5637
Hone, Thomas C., 4901, 4902, 4903, 7525, 9320
Honey, Maureen E., 5961, 5962, 8513, 8514, 8515
Honey, Michael K., 2242, 5423
Honhart, Frederick L. III., 9747
Honor, Leo, 9117
Hook, Sidney, 4004, 6255, 6384
Hooker, Nancy H., 0871
Hooks, Gregory M., 8140
Hoole, W. Stanley, 8457
Hooper, Paul F., 7842
Hoopes, Roy, 4005
Hoover, Herbert, and Hugh Gibson, 9555
Hoover, Herbert C., 4644, 7115, 7928, 7929
Hoover, Irwin H., 0374
Hoover, John G., 3770
Hoover, Roy O., 8141
Hope, Ashley G., 8939
Hope, Clifford R. Jr., 1617, 6546
Hopkins, George E., 2243, 9321
Hopkins, Harry L., 2831
Hopkins, Kenneth N., 5852
Hopkirk, John W., 7001, 7002
Horak, Jan-Christopher, 3771
Horan, James D., 0108
Horan, John F., Jr., 1462
Hornbein, Marjorie, 4682, 5963, 6547
Horne, Gerald C., 5424
Horowitz, Daniel, 1677
Horowitz, David A., 2545
Horowitz, Irving L., 6067
Horowitz, Roger, 2244
Horowitz, Ruth L., 2245
Horton, Myles, and Mary Frederickson, 4329
Horwitz, Dawn L., 3145
Hosley, David H., 3894
Hosoya, Chihiro, 7526, 7527, 7528, 7529
Hostetler, James M., 4330
Hotaling, Burton J., 1176
Hounshell, David A., and John Kenly Smith Jr., 4904
House, Jonathan M., 4905
Houseman, John, 3222, 5252
Housley, Donald D., 1316
Hovey, Graham, 1678
Howard, Beth 5134
Howard, Donald S., 2832
Howard, J. Woodford Jr., 7033, 7032, 7031, 7030
Howard, Michael, 8572
Howard, Patricia E. B., 8218
Howard, Perry H., 6548

Howard, Richard P., 1679
Howard, Walter T., 4716, 4717, 4718, 4719
Howard, Woodford, and Cornelius Bushoven, 5425
Howard, William L., 3382
Howard-Pitney, David M., 5426
Howe, George F., 9322
Howe, Irving, 6155, 6257
Howe, Irving, and B. J. Widick, 2246
Howe, Irving, and Lewis Coser, 6256
Howe, Quincy, 9556
Howell, Bing P., 9061
Howell, Elmo, 3383
Howell, Robert T., 8516
Howland, Nina D., 0892
Howlett, Charles F., 4331, 8024, 8025
Hoxie, R. Gordon, 0483
Hoyt, Edwin P., 3223
Hoyt, Frederick B., 4006, 7463
Hoyt, Morgan H., 0245
Hoyt, Ross G., 4906, 4907
Hritsko, Rosemary F., 2546
Hubbard, Carol A.C., 5072
Hubbard, Preston J., 3103, 3104
Huber, Karen, 4908
Hubert, Sister Mary G., 0848
Hudgins, Maxwell W., Jr., 1992
Hudson, Geoffrey, 8611, 8612
Hudson, James J., 2247
Hudson, Robert V., 8026
Huertas, Thomas F., and Joan L. Silverman, 2547
Huffman, Laurie, 5073
Huffman, Roy E., 2974
Hufft, Jane W., and Anne Nevins Loftis, 1317
Hughes, C. Alvin, 5427
Hughes, Cicero A., 5428, 5429
Hughes, Robert L., 3895
Hughes, Robert S., 3384
Hughes, William 8517
Hull, Cordell, 0833, 7843
Hulse, J. F., 6549
Humes, Dollena J., 6156
Hummel, William W., 3653
Humphreys, Hubert, 2975, 2976
Humphries, Jane, 5964
Hundley, Norris, 9052
Hundley, Patrick D., 3772
Hunnicut, Benjamin K., 2076, 2077, 2078
Hunt, James D., 4507
Hunt, James L., 6550
Hunt, John J., 9323
Hunt, Michael H., 3385
Hunter, Andrea G., 5430
Hunter, Barbara, J., 4332
Hunter, Gary J., 5431
Hunter, Helen M., 2548

Hunter, John O., 3544
Hunter, Lee M., 4333
Hunter, Leslie G., 5195
Hunter, Robert F., 3105
Hunter, Sam, 3654
Huntley, Horace, 2248
Hurd, Rick, 2249
Hurley, Forrest J., 2833
Hurley, Patrick J., and Alvin R. Sunseri, 9845
Hurstfield, Julian G., 8699
Hurt, Douglas R., 1290, 2834, 1463, 1464, 1465, 1680
Hus, Immanuel C. Y., 7530
Huston, James A., 8142
Hutchinson, John, 2443
Hutchinson, W. H., 3655
Hutchison, Janet A., 1803
Huthmacher, J. Joseph, 1278, 1279
Hy, Ronald, 6551
Hyde, H. Montgomery, 9324
Hyman, Collette A., 3224
Hyman, Harold M., 2079

Iannaccone, Laurence, and David K. Wiles, 6552
Ichioak, Yuji, 5718
Ickes, Harold L., 0633, 0634
Iijima, Kazu, Glenn Omatsu, interviewer, 5719
Iiyama, Patty, 8366
Ikenberry, G. John, and Theda Skocpol, 2835
Iles, William P., 7531
Iltis, Roger S., 1177
Ilyashov, Anatoli, 2457
Imler, Joseph A., 6068
Ingalls, Robert P ., 0751, 4720, 4721, 4722, 4723, 6553, 6554
Inge, M. Thomas, 4127
Ingram, Earl, 2977
Inouye, Arlene, and Charles Sussking, 4909
Irey, Elmer L, 4724
Irish, Marion D., 6555
Iriye, Akira, 7532, 7533, 7534
Irons, Janet C., 2250
Irons, Peter H., 8368, 8367, 9491, 9492
Irvin, Thomas C., 7207
Isenberg, Michael T., 3773, 3774
Isenberg, Nancy G., 0066
Isern, Thomas D., 1466
Ishii, Osamu, 1837
Isley, Bliss, 0315
Israel, Fred L., 0157, 1055, 1056, 1057, 9325
Israel, Jerry, 8900
Israelsen, L. Dwight, 0677
Issel, William H., 1544, 2549
Isserman, Abraham J., 2251
Isserman, Maurice H., 6258
Iverson, Peter, 5853, 5854
Ivie, Robert L., 0158

Iwata, Masakuzu, 5720
Izdebski, Christy I., 4334
Izek, Hersch, 7763

Jablon, Howard, 0834, 0835, 0836, 7373, 7764
Jack, Homer A., 4508
Jackes, Frederick D., 6863
Jacklin, Thomas M., 4509
Jackman, Francis V., 7643
Jackman, Jarrell C., 4160
Jackman, Jarrell C., and Carla M. Borden, 9118
Jackson, Carlton, 0316
Jackson, Charles O., 2836, 4208
Jackson, Charles O., and Charles W. Johnson, 4910, 4911
Jackson, Frances, 9326
Jackson, Kathy M., 3775
Jackson, Kenneth T., 1804, 1805
Jackson, Miles M. Jr., 5432
Jackson, Susan M., 3386
Jackson, Thomas S., 3225
Jacob, C., 2707
Jacob, Sir Ian, 8745
Jacobs, Herbert, 2252
Jacobs, Lea, 3776
Jacobs, Leonard J., 0573
Jacobs, Lewis, 3777
Jacobs, Mark L., 0635
Jacobs, Travis B., 0159, 7765
Jacobs, William A., 9327, 9328
Jacobsen, Hans, 9748
Jacobsen, Hans-Adolf, and Arthur L. Smith Jr., 9653
Jacobson, Joanne, 3656
Jacoby, R. L., 0160
Jacoby, Sanford M., 2253, 2254
Jaffe, Dan, 3592
Jaffe, Irma B., 3657
Jaffe, Joseph L. Jr., 7930
Jaffe, Louis L., 7016
Jaffe, Philip J., 6259, 9493
Jakeman, Robert J., 5617
Jakoubek, Robert E., 7116
James, Clayton D., 9329
James, D. Clayton, 0933, 0934, 0935
James, D. Clayton, and Anne S. Wells, 0896
James, Henry T., 8369
James, J. C., 9818
James, Ralph C., 2255
James, Robert R., 9195
James, Thomas, 5855, 8370, 8371, 8372
Jameson, John R., 1467, 9749
Janeway, Eliot, 4912
Janick, Herbert, 4335, 8027
Janowitz, Morris, 6385
Jay, Martin, 6260
Jaynes, Gerald D., and Robin M. Williams Jr., 5433

Jayroe, Linuel D., 5638
Jeansonne, Cynthia, 4336
Jeansonne, Glen, 1178, 1179, 4510, 5767, 6556, 7117, 7118
Jeffrey, Harry P. Jr., 6069, 8518
Jeffries, John W., 6157, 6557, 8519
Jeffries, Ona G., 0375
Jellison, Charles A., 1681
Jellison, Katherine, 5965, 5966
Jemison, Marie Stokes, 5967
Jenkins, J. Craig, and Barbara G. Brents, 5074
Jenkins, Philip, 6386
Jenkins, Roy, 0606
Jennings, Edward J., 2256, 8143
Jennings, Frances S., and James Gilbert, 4337
Jensen, James R., 4007
Jensen, Joan M., 1390, 5968, 8028
Jensen, Katherine, 5856
Jensen, Richard J., 2476, 6792
Jervey, Edward D., 4008
Jervey, William H., 2550
Jesperson, Shirley D., 4338
Jessner, Sabine, and Peter J. Sehlinger, 0780
Jessup, Philip C., 7872
Jewel, Richard B., 3778
Jewell, Fred R., 8746
Jiang, Arnold X., 8901
Jo, Yung-Hwan, 7535
Johansen, Harley E., and Glenn V. Fugquitt, 2551
Johnpoll, Bernard K., 6261
Johnsen, William T., 8747
Johnson, Abby A., and Ronald W. Johnson, 4009
Johnson, Alvin P., 0120
Johnson, Ann R., 5969
Johnson, Charles W., 2837, 5434
Johnson, Claudius O., 0983
Johnson, Clyde, 2257
Johnson, Dolores D., 5970
Johnson, Donald B., 0769, 6737
Johnson, Donald L., 3171
Johnson, Ethel M., 0893
Johnson, Evalyn C. and Donna Beardsley, 4339
Johnson, Evamarii A., 5253
Johnson, Evans C., 1110
Johnson, Frederick K., 2978
Johnson, Frederick L., 6558
Johnson, Gerald W., 0317
Johnson, Glen M., 3387
Johnson, Hugh S., 2708
Johnson, James P., 2258, 2259, 2552, 2838
Johnson, James R., 7931, 7932
Johnson, Jerah, 5196
Johnson, Judith R., 8293
Johnson, K. I., 3226
Johnson, Loretta L., 4010
Johnson, Louise, 5971

Johnson, Lyndon B., 1079, 1080
Johnson, M. Glen, 0396
Johnson, Mary, 3779
Johnson, Oakley C., 4340
Johnson, Paul, 0318
Johnson, Robert E., 4913
Johnson, Ronald W., 6387
Johnson, Walter, 0397, 4011, 9557
Johnson, William R., 1468, 2839, 2979
Johnson, William S., 4914
Johnston, Louise, 4341
Johnston, Patricia A., 3659
Joliet, Paul V. II., 8700
Jonas, Manfred, 7291, 7766, 7933, 7934, 7935, 9119
Jonassen, Christen, 4161
Jones, Adrienne L., 5435
Jones, Alfred H., 0319, 0398, 3388, 3896
Jones, Bessie Z., 4162
Jones, Beverly W., 5972, 5973
Jones, Byrd L., 0547, 2034, 2035, 2036
Jones, Calvin P., 7046
Jones, Carolyn C., 8219
Jones, Charles V., Philip C. Enros, and Henry S. Tropp, 4342
Jones, Daniel C., 7119
Jones, David Lloyd, 8520, 8521, 8522
Jones, Elias F., 5436
Jones, Gene D., 4209, 6559, 6560
Jones, James P., 3389
Jones, Joel M., 3390
Jones, John F., 1682
Jones, Joseph M., Jr., 1838
Jones, Kathleen W., 4210
Jones, Kenneth M., 4915
Jones, Kenneth P., 7844, 7845
Jones, Linda R.W. 4645
Jones, Margaret C., 3391
Jones, Mary H., 4511
Jones, Michael O., 2553
Jones, Terry L., 0629
Jones, Winfield, 6751
Jordan, Layton, 7345
Jordy, William H., 3172
Jorgensen, Arthur W. Sr., 4343
Joselit, Jenna W., 5768, 5769
Josephson, H., 7976
Josephson, Matthew, 2433, 2554, 3392
Josephson, Matthew, and Hannah Josephson, 0758
Joslin, Theodore G., 7120
Joy, Neill R., 3393
Joyner, Charles W., 3394
Judd, Richard M., 2980
Juergensen, Hans, 9120
Juhnke, James C., 4512
Juhnke, Roger, 8029
Julian, Thomas A., 8849

Jumonville, Neil T., 6262
Jungk, Robert, 4916
Jungmyer, Roger L., 9053
Jurkovic, Lynne D., 0812
Justus, James H., 3395

Kagel, John, 2260
Kahan, Mitchell D., 3660
Kahn, David M., 5254, 9330, 9331
Kahn, Gilbert N., 0527, 6825, 7767
Kahn, Herman, 9819, 9820
Kahn, Lawrence M., 2261
Kalin, Berkely, 0501
Kalinoski, Lynda L., 5857
Kalish, Richard J., 4646
Kalmar, Karen L., 5437
Kaltenborn, H. V., 7768
Kamen, Martin D., 4917
Kampleman, Max M., 6263
Kanawada, Leo V. Jr., 4768, 4769
Kane, Joseph H., 0320
Kaner, Norman J., 1226
Kang, Joon-Mann, 3897
Kann, Kenneth, 6264
Kanter, Kenneth Aaron, 5770
Kantor, J. R. K., 9654
Kantowicz, Edward, 6561
Kaplan, Charles, 3227
Kaplan, George, 6562
Kappel, Tim, 3396
Karamanski, Theodore J., 9332
Karger, Howard Jacob, 5438
Kargon, Robert, and Elizabeth Hodes, 4918
Karimi, Amir M., 3780
Karl, Barny D., 0548, 0549, 2555
Karlstrom, Paul J., 3661
Karman, Thomas, 2262
Karmarkovic, Alex, 0889
Karnes, David, 3781
Karolevitz, Robert F., 8191
Karpf, Stephen L., 3782
Karpik, Steven, 1469
Karr, Albert S., 7121
Karr, Rodney D., 1318
Karsh, Bernard, and Garman L. Phillips, 6265
Karwin, Harry W., 4211
Kase, Toshikazu, 7536
Kass, D.A., 4603
Kasurak, Peter C., 7256, 7257
Kateb, George, 0851
Katterjohn, Monte, 0230
Katz, Barry M., 9333
Katz, Norman D., 4012
Katzman, David M., 1618
Kauffman, Christopher J., 4513, 4514

Kaufman, Andrew L., 6993
Kaufman, Jacob J., 8144
Kaufman, Menahem, 9001
Kaufman, Robert G., 7537
Kaufmann, Stephen R., 4344
Kavanagh, Jack, 4604
Kawabe, Nubo, 1839
Kazacoff, George, 5075
Kazin, Alfred, 3397
Kearful, Frank G., 3398
Kearnes, John, 4751
Kearney, James R., 0067
Keathley, Clarence R., 1619
Keating, John S., 8985
Keck, Daniel N., 9558
Kecskemeti, Paul, 9334
Keefe, Thomas M., 4515
Keefer, Louis E., 8432, 8458
Keenan, Hugh T., 5255
Keeran, Roger R., 2263, 2264, 2265, 2266
Kefoot, Glenn, 1886
Kehl, James A., and Samuel J. Astorino, 6563
Keilor, Steven J., 6564
Keim, Albert N., 4516
Keiser, Norman, 0550
Keister, Stephen D., 4345
Kell, James A., 4128
Kelleher, Daniel T., 5639
Keller, Lynn, 3662
Keller, Morton, 7122
Keller, Richard C., 2981, 2982, 6565
Keller, Robert R., 1620
Kelley, Leo, 9335
Kelley, Robin D.G., 5439
Kellogg, Peter J., 5440, 6158
Kelly, David H., 2267
Kelly, Karen K., 1203
Kelly, Kathleen, 4519
Kelly, Lawrence C., 0636, 5858, 5859, 5860, 5861
Kelly, Maurice, 6120
Kelly, Paul M., 7292
Kelly, Robin D. G., 6266
Kelly, Thomas C., 1756
Kelly, William B., Jr., 1840
Kelly, William R., 2983
Kelman, Sidney, 2460, 9121
Kemler, Edger, 7123
Kemmerer, Donald L., 1993
Kemp, Arthur, 8613
Kemp, Kathryn W., 0231
Kennan, George F., 7429, 7430, 7846
Kenneally, James J., , 6566, 6958
Kennedy, David M., 4212
Kennedy, Donald, 2268
Kennedy, Gerald J., 4919

Kennedy, Joseph P., 0399
Kennedy, Ludovic, 4725
Kennedy, Susan E., 2556, 2557, 2558, 8220
Kennedy, Thomas C., 7936, 7937, 7938, 7939, 9750
Kennett, Lee, 8074
Kenney, Ann R., 5974
Kenney, William H., III, 3545
Kent, Alan E., 1253
Kent, Frank R., 3898
Kepner, William E., and John H. Scrivner, Jr., 1887
Kerber, Stephen, 6567
Kerig, Dorthy P., 1470
Kerr, Harry P., 6826
Kerr, Thomas J., IV, 2841
Kerr, William A, 4520
Kersey, Harry A. Jr., 5862, 5863, 5864, 5865
Kertesz, Stephen D., 7431
Kerz, Louise, 3783
Kesler, Jon C., 7644
Kessel, Ruben, 2842
Kesselman, Amy V., 8221
Kesselman, Jonathan R., and N. E. Savin, 2477
Kesselman, Steven, 6159, 9751
Kessler, Lauren, 8373
Kessler, Peter, 7540
Kessler-Harris, Alice, 5975, 8222
Ketchum, Richard M., 7940
Keubler, Edward J., 5640
Kevles, Daniel J., 9559, 9560
Kevlin, Arleen, 0109
Key, Donald, 3663
Key, Jack B., 1105
Keynes, John Maynard, 2037
Keyserling, Leon H., 1280, 2038
Khair, Mohammed A., 8940
Kieffer, William A., 4213
Kiely, Edward S., 0551
Kiem, Albert N., 4517, 4518
Kiester, Edwain, Jr., 4214
Kifer, Allen F., 5441
Kildahl, Earling E., 1888, 1918
Killgrew, John W., 4920
Kilpatrick, E., 0798
Kim, Ki-Ae, 3228
Kim, Richard C.C., 4521
Kim, Sam G., 5442
Kimball, Warren F., 7769, 7771, 8614, 8615, 8748, 8749, 8750, 9196, 9494
Kimball, Warren F., and Bruce Bartlett, 7770
Kimbell, Warren F., 7293
Kimberly, Charles M., 6568, 6569
Kimche, Jon, 9336
Kimmel, Husband E., 0969
Kimmett, Leo, 3065
Kimpel, Ben D., and T. C. Duncan Eaves, 1962

Kincheloe, Teresa Scott, 4346
Kincher, Joe, 1471
Kindelberger, Charles P., 1621
King, Ernest J., and Walter M. Whitehall, 0971
King, Francine M., 5443
King, Frank, 8616
King, Richard H., 4163
King, Robert G., 0574
King, Wayne, 5076
Kingsland, Susan F., 4647
Kingston-McLoughry, E.J., 8573
Kinnamon, Kenneth, 3399
Kinney, John W., 5444
Kinsella, Dorthy C., 6864
Kinsella, William E. Jr., 7772, 7773
Kirby, Jack T., 1391, 1392, 3106
Kirby, John B., 5445, 5446, 5447, 5448
Kirby, Linda K., 6267
Kirchhoff, Mark J., 2559, 2560
Kirk, Grayson L., 7617
Kirkendall, Richard S., 0575, 0576, 0577, 0578, 0579, 0607,
    0608, 0728, 1356, 1472, 1563, 1564, 1565, 2052, 2053,
    2984, 9752, 9753, 9754, 9755, 9821
Kirker, Harold, and Burleigh Taylor Wilkins, 7432
Kirkland, Mary, 3546
Kirschke, Amy, 3664
Kirschner, Don S., 0580
Kirstein, Barbara F., 0679
Kirstein, Peter N., 1919, 5692
Kirwin, Harry W., 6570
Kiser, George C., 5693
Kiser, George C., and David Silverman, 5694
Kissane, Leedice, 6571
Kissh, Bela, 1757
Kivisto, Peter, 4770, 4771
Kizer, George A., 4347
Klapthor, Margaret B., 0068, 0069
Klare, Karl E., 6919
Klass, Bernard, 1319, 1357
Kleeman, Rita H., 0028, 0038
Klehr, Harvey, 2269, 6268
Kleiler, Frank M., 8145
Klein, David H., 7538
Klein, Herbert S., 1758
Klein, Walter E., 5771
Klick, John R., 8294
Klimmer, Richard, 6160
Klimow, Matthew S., 9337
Kline, Geraldine, 4013
Kling, Joseph M., 6269
Klingbeil, Kurt A., 4522
Klingberg, Frank L., 7208
Klingman, Peter D., 6572
Klingman, William K., 8075
Klinkenborg, Verlyn, 3665

Klischke, Elmer, 7793
Klotter, James C., and John W. Muir, 6573
Knapp, Margraert M., 3229
Knapton, Ernest J., 8701
Knee, Stuart E., 5772, 5773, 9002
Kneebone, John T., 6865
Knepper, Alvin, 6574
Knight, Edgar W., 4348
Knight, Oliver, 3107
Knock, Thomas J., 3784
Knoth, Bernard P., 4349
Knotts, Alice, 5976
Knowles, Kenneth, 9338
Knudson, David L. T., 1759
Kobler, John, 7124
Koch, John C., 5277
Koch, Raymond L., 6575
Kodachi, Zuigaku, and Jan Heikkala, 8374
Koenig, Louis W., 0691
Koeniger, Alfred C., 1146, 1147, 1148, 6576
Koerner, J. D., 3400
Koginos, Manny T., 7539
Kohler, John H. III., 7125
Kohler, Robert E. Jr., 4921, 4922
Kohn, Walter S. G., 6577
Koistinen, Paul A.C., 4923, 8146, 8295, 9296
Koliopoulos, John S., 7334, 8771
Kolko, Gabriel, 7294, 8574
Kollmorgen, Walter M., 1473
Kollock, Will, 7126
Kolsky, Thomas A., 5774
Kommers, Donald P., 4014
Konovitch, Barry J., 9122
Koontz, Elizabeth Duncan, 5977
Koppes, Clayton R., 1474, 5866
Koppes, Clayton R., and Gregory D. Black, 3785, 8523, 8524
Koprowski-Kraut, Gayle, 1683
Korbrin, Solomon, 4726
Korgan, Julius, 1545
Korman, Gerd, 9756
Korn, Marjorie S., 5135
Kornbluh, Joyce L., 2843, 4350
Kornweibel, Theodore Jr., 8525
Korrol, Virginia Sanchez, 5978
Korstad, Robert R., and Nelson Lichtenstein, 5449
Korstad, Robert R., 2270
Korth, Philip A., 2271
Kosberg, Roberta L. 0161
Koskoff, David, 0858
Kotlanger, Michael J., 6578
Kottman, Richard N., 7258
Koury, Phil A., 1684
Kraditor, Aileen S., 6270
Kraig, Beth, 5136
Kramer, Hilton, 3401

Kramer, Randall A., 2710
Kramer, Randall A., and Sandra S. Batie, 2711
Kramer, William M., 5775
Krammer, Arnold P., 8076, 8459, 8460, 8461
Kramp, Robert S., 1622
Kraus, Theresa L., 9040
Krause, Fayette F., 6579
Kreader, J Lee, 4648
Kreider, Robert, 8030
Kreizenbeck, Alan D., 5077
Kriegel, Leonard, 5776, 6271
Krikun, David, 0400
Krislov, Sam, 6920
Kritzberg, Bary, 2272
Krock, Arthur, 0321, 0322
Kroll, Morton, 0162
Krome, Frederic, 7127
Krompak, Frank J., 5137
Krough, Peter F., 7674
Krueger, Thomas A., 4649, 9757
Kshirsagar, Shiwaram K., 8941
Kublin, Michael B., 8902
Kuczun, Sam, 4016
Kuehl, Marshall R., 0847
Kuehl, Warren F., 4017
Kuhn, Cliff, 2656
Kuklick, Bruce R.,0401, 0837, 7209, 9561
Kuklick, Henrika, 4351
Kulevsky, Shirley G., 7374
Kumamoto, Bob, 6886
Kunert, Dirk T., 7210
Kunetka, James W., 9339
Kunitz, Stanley, and Howard Haycraft, 3402
Kunitz, Stephen J., 5867
Kunkel, Joseph A., 6272
Kunzelman, Charles J., 9340
Kurihara, Kenneth K., 2039
Kuroiwa, Wallace H. R., 8375
Kurrey, Cecil B., 0929
Kursrud, Carl J., 9655
Kurtz, Michael L., 6580
Kurzman, Paul A., 0692, 0693
Kutulas, Judy A., 6273, 6274
Kuykendall, James R., 4247
Kuznets, Simon, 2019
Kuznick, Peter J., 4924, 4925, 4926
Kvasnicka, Robert M., and Herman J. Viola, eds., 5868
Kwong, Peter C., 2273
Kybal, Vlastimil, 0246
Kynerd, Tom, 0443
Kyvig, David E., 0402, 4752, 4753, 6070, 6921

Lacey, Ralph, 9341
Lacy, Alex B., 0376
Lacy, James F., 7645

Ladd, Everett C. Jr., and Charles D. Hadley, 6071
Ladd, Everett C. Jr., 6161
Ladenburg, Thomas, 1570
LaFeber, Walter, 7541, 8946
Lafferty, Jim, Sr., 3667
Lafferty, William C., 4927
Laffey, Robert M., 8987
Lafore, Laurence D., 7211
LaForte, Robert S., and Richard Himmel, 6581
Lages, John D., 2274
LaGumina, Salvatore J., 1227, 1228
Laing, Edward A., 8617
Laing, Vernon, 3592
Laird, William E., and James R. Rinehart, 1623
Lake, David A., 1843
Lal, Malashri, 7375
Lally, Kathleen A., 5138
Lam, Julie Shuk-Yee, 4018
Lamb, David, 4129
Lamb, Karl, 6959
Lambert, C. Roger, 2844, 2845, 2846, 2847, 2985, 2986,
    3067, 3108, 7128
Lambert, Walter K., 1994
Lambrakis, George B., 8983
Lammers, William W., 0461
Lamont, Corliss, 6872
Lamoreaux, David, and Gerson Eisenberg, 1624
Lamson, Peggy, 5450
Landau, Zbigniew, 7212
Landess, Thomas H., 3403
Landis, James M., 2712, 6986
Landon, Brooks, 3404
Landy, Marc, 0323
Lane, James B., 0502
Lane, Janet A., 7690
Lane, Peter B., 8798
Langenberg, William H., 7774
Langer, John D., 7433, 8850
Langer, Walter C., and Sanford Gifford, 7259
Langer, William L., 7213, 8702, 8851, 9758
Langer, William L., and Everett S. Gleason, 7941, 7942
Langford, Walter, 4605
Langley, Harold D., 7434
Langley, Lester D., 7695, 7696, 7697, 7698
Langlois, Janet L., 5451
Langsam, Walter C., 9656
Lanier, James C., 4650
Lanouette, William, 9342
Lansky, Lewis, 4651
Lantz, Herman R., 5278
LaPlante, John B., 9343
Lapomarda, Vincent A., 0764, 6582, 6583
Lapping, Mark B., 1806
Laqueur, Walter J., 9123, 9124
Larabee, Eric, 0484

Larence, Michael A., and Jerry M. Guess, 5453
Larkin, Oliver W., 3668
Larrowe, Charles P., 2420
Larsen, Charles E., 6584
Larsen, Lawrence H., 1256, 4352, 6585, 7943, 9344
Larsen, Lawrence H., and Barbara J. Cottrell, 1625
Larson, Bethene W., 0324
Larson, Bruce L., 1393, 7542
Larson, Edward J., 6586
Larson, T. A., 2987
Lash, Joseph P., 0070, 0071, 0072, 0073, 0074, 0075, 0076,
     2713, 7017, 7775
Lashbrook, Lawrence G., 2988
Lasky, Melvin J., 0655
Lasser, William, 6922
Latham, Earl, 1920, 6873
Latta, Maurice R., 1291, 1626
Lauber, Patricia, 1292
Lauderbaugh, Richard A., 2561, 2562, 8147
Lauderdale, William B., 4353
Laue, Theodore H. Von, 7435
Launius, Roger D., 4928, 8903
LaVere, David, 1685
Lawford, Valentine, 0195
Lawler, Patricia M., 0638, 3405
Lawren, William, 4929
Lawrence, Charles R., 5452
Lawrence, David, and Richard Fleisher, 6072
Lawrence, Happy J., 5197
Lawrence, James R., 2275
Lawrence, Ken, 9846
Lawrence, William B., 4523
Lawson, Richard A., 6162
Layton, Edwin T., 7543
Lazalier, James H., 7776
Lazin, Frederick A., 5777, 5778
Lea, Florence B. M., 3230
Lea, James, 3406
Leab, Daniel J., 1686, 2276, 2277, 2278, 3786
Leach, Charles B., 3068
Leader, Leonard J., 1627, 6587
Leader, Stefan H., 7847
Leaf, VaDonna Jean, 1687
Leahy, John A., 4354
Leahy, Stephen M., 7325
Leahy, William D., 8618, 8703
Lear, Linda J., 0639, 0640, 1475
Learn, Elmer W., 1358
Lears, T. J. Jackson, 4019
Leary, John J., III, 3787
Leary, William M. Jr., 0936, 4930, 7464, 8526
Leavy, Robert J., 3669
Lebeau, John J., 9345
Lebowitz, Neil H., 8148
LeBrun, John L., 2279

LeCompte, Mary Lou, 4606
Ledeboer, Suzanne G., 6388
Lee, Alfred McClung, 4931
Lee, Bradford A., 0325
Lee, Chang, 2657
Lee, David D., 3788, 6588
Lee, Douglas W., 8904
Lee, Frederic S., 1995, 2054, 2055
Lee, Jeon, 3109
Lee, Joseph E., 1103
Lee, Lawrence B., 1476
Lee, Raymond E., 7326
Lee, Sang-Chul, 4020
Lee, Susan, and Peter Passel, 1628
Lee, U-Gene, 8950
Leeder, Elaine J., 2456
Leemhuis, Roger P., 1156
Lees, Lorraine M., 8077, 8814
Leff, Leonard J., 3789
Leff, Mark H., 1996, 2848, 2849, 8149
Leffall, Dolores C., and Janet L. Sims, 5454
Leffler, Melvyn P., 9495
Legislative Reference Service, Library of Congress, 0492
Lehe, Robert E., 4607
Lehman, Arnold, 3173
Lehman, Orin, 2714
Lehman, Paul, 5455
Lehman, Timothy J., 1477
Lehmann, Herbert, 9346
Leigh, Michael, 9496
Leighinger, Leslie H., 4216
Leighton, Dorthea C., 5869
Leighton, George R., 9759
Leighton, Isabel, 0326
Leighton, Richard M., 8078, 8619, 8704, 9347
Leistner, Charley A., 1119
Leiter, William M., 6589, 2715
Leivy, James, 4215
Lekachman, Robert, 2040
Leland, Waldo G., 9760, 9822
Lemieux, Christina M., 5779
Lemke-Santangelo, Gretchen, 8031
Lempke, Duane A., 0955
Lenburg, LeRoy J., 2280
Leng, Shao-Chaun, 7544
Lensen, George, 8852
Lent, Tina O., 3790
Lentz, Charles M., 2563
Leonard, Brother E. A., 7058
Leonard, Charles, 7059
Leonard, Kevin Allen, 8376
Leonard, Neil, 3547
Leonard, Robert J., 1043
Leonard, Stephen J., 8150
Leonard, Thomas M., 7545, 7699, 9761

Leopold, Richard M., 4355, 9657

Leotta, Louis, 2281, 4217

Lepawsky, Albert, 2056, 4652, 4653

Leslie, James P., 6590

Leslie, Stuart W., 2564

Lester, Robert L., 0528

Letts, Laurence A., 6275

Leuchtenburg, William E., 0327, 0328, 0403, 0404, 1571, 2716, 3110, 6591, 6923, 6976

Leupold, Robert J., 6592, 8954

Leuschen-Seppel, Rose-Marie, Nina Morris-Farber, and Henry Friedlander, 9125

Leutze, James R., 4932, 7327, 8751

Levenstein, Harvey, 6276

Leverett, William E. Jr., 4654

Levering, Patricia W., and Ralph B. Levering, 4218

Levering, Ralph B., 8853, 8854

Levi, Steven C., 4130

Levin, James, 6752

Levin, Linda L., 4021

Levine, Alan J., 9497

Levine, Lawrence W., 6924

Levine, Rhonda F., 2717

Levinson, L. Harold, 6593

Levinson, Mark, and Brian Morton, 2444

Levitan, Sar A., and Dvid Marwick, 4219

Levite, Ariel, 7546

Levitt, Theodore, 8297

Levy, Lester S., 2282

Lewandowski, Richard B., 8805

LeWarne, Charles P., 4524

Lewin, Ronald, 9348, 9349

Lewinson, Paul, and Morris Rieger, 9658

Lewis, David L., 2565, 4933

Lewis, Earl, 5456

Lewis, James A., 1997

Lewis, John E., 4754

Lewis, John M., 8620

Lewis, Michael E., 1478

Lewis, Ronald L., 5457

Lewis, Thomas A., 1889

Leyerzapf, James W., 0683

Liang, Chin-tung, 8905

Libbey, James K., 7436, 6163

Libby, Justin H., 1058, 7547, 7858

Libecap, Gary D., 1761

Licht, Walter, and Barron Hal Seth, 2417

Lichtenstein, Nelson N., 2283, 2284, 8079, 8298, 8299

Lichtman, Sheila T., 8223

Lichty, Lawrence W., and Malachi C. Ropping, 3900

Lichty, Lawrence W., and Thomas W. Bohn, 3899

Liddel Hart, Basil H., 8752

Lidman, Russell, and D. Lee Bawden, 1479

Lieberman, Robbie, 3548

Liebovich, Louis, 9498

Liggio, Leonard P., and James J. Martin, 7214

Liker, Jeffrey K., and Glen H. Elder, Jr., 1688

Lilienthal, David E., 3111, 4934

Lind, Andrew, 8377

Lindbergh, Charles A., 7944, 7945

Lindblad, Richard G., 4655

Lindenbaum, Regina, 1481

Linder, Leo J., 2718

Lindley, Christopher, 7777

Lindley, Ernest K., 0247, 0329, 2719

Lindley, James T., 1998

Lindley, William R., 1629, 8621

Lindmark, Sture, 4772

Lindsay, David S., 6074

Lingman, Richard R., 8080

Link, Eugene P., 4525

Linneman, William R., 4131

Linsenmeyer, William S., 8784

Linton, Thomas L., 2285

Liotti, Anthony E., 4935

Lipari, Joseph A., 3593

Lipman, Sue, and Norton B. Stern, 5780

Lippmann, Theo, Jr., 0461

Lipscomb, Lena E., 5078

Lipstadt, Deborah E., 4022, 9126, 9127

Lisles, Granville, 1480

Liss, Samuel, 8151, 8152, 8153

Litchtman, Allan Jr., 6073

Litsky, Elliot B., 8705

Littell, Norman M., 0503

Little, Douglas J., 0781, 7376, 7377, 7378, 7437

Little, Dwayne L., 1096, 1097

Littlefield, Douglas R., 1482

Littlefield, Roy E., III, 4023

Liu, Daniel J. J., 7548, 7549

Lively, Bruce R., 9350

Livermore, Charles H., 2455

Livingston, Jeffrey C., 6121

Livingston, Mary W., 8942, 9823

Lizza, Richard W., 3670

Lloyd, Charles D., 8527

Lloyd, David D., 0163

Lloyd, F.R., 4608

Lloyd, Marcia L., 4356

Lobdell, George H., 0862

Loebs, Bruce D., 0164

Loewenheim, Francis L., 7946, 9762

Loftin, Bernadette K., 0729, 6594

Loftis, Anne, 2430, 3407, 3408, 4024

Lofton, Paul S. Jr., 5458, 6595

Logan, Logna B., 0077

Logue, Cal M., 4025

Lohbeck, Don, 0925

Lomawaima, Kimberly T., 5870, 5871

Lomax, Michael L., 3594

Lombardo, Peter J., 1630
LoMonaco, Martha S., 3231
Long, Breckinridge, 0706
Long, David, 3069
Long, Diana E., 4936
Long, Durward, 1631
Long, Fred H., 2989
Long, Huey, 1180
Long, Irma J., 1689
Long, Jesse R., 0232
Long, Norton, 6164
Long, Robert E., 6277
Long, Terry L., 6278
Longin, Thomas C., 2566
Longley, Lawrence, 0552
Longstaff, S. A., 4026, 6165
Longstreet, Stephen, 3409
Looker, Earle, 0010
Lookstein, Haskel, 9128
Loomis, Charles P., 4526
Looper, Robert B., 8753
Loosli, Alden, 4357
Lopata, Roy H., 7129
Lopez, Consuelo, 6279
Lopez, Enrique M., 5695
Lopez, Ronald W., 5696
Lora, Ronald G., 6122
Lorant, Stefan, 0110
Lord, Russell, 0581
Lord, Walter, 7550
Lorell, Mark A., 7295
Lorence, James J., 1215
Lorentz, Sister Mary R., 1261
Lotchin, Roger W., 4937, 4938, 4939, 6596
Lothrop, Gloria Ricci, 4527
Lothrop. Gloria R., 4773
Lott, Davis N., 0165
Lottich, Kenneth V., 8754
Louchheim, Katie, 0672, 2720, 9562
Love, Robert W. Jr., 0972, 8575
Loveland, Anne C., 5459
Loveland, William A., 8706
Lovin, Hugh T., 2286, 2287, 6280, 6597, 6598, 6827, 6828,
    6829, 6830, 6831
Low, Ann M., 1293
Lowe, Harry J., 9563
Lowe, R. L., 3671
Lowe, Thomas E., 1890
Lowenheim, F. L., M. Jonas, and H. D. Langley, 9197
Lowenstein, Sharon R., 9129
Lowenthal, Mark M., 8576, 9198
Lowitt, Richard, 0582, 1028, 1029, 1030, 1031, 1032, 1033,
    1483, 1484, 3112, 6960
Lowrie, Walter E., 0248
Lowry, Charles B., 2567

Loy, Jane M., 3791
Loyd, Laura J., 4940
Lu, David, 7551
Lubeck, Sister M. Evangela, 8806
Lubell, Samuel, 6738
Lubick, George M., 6832
Lubove, Roy, 1807, 4220
Lucas, John A., 4609
Ludwig, E. Jeffrey, 6753
Ludwig, Emil, 0111
Lujan, Joe R., 0994
Lukas, Richard C., 8810, 8811, 8855, 8856, 8857, 8858
Lundberg, David, 3410
Lunt, Richard D., 0872
Lurie, Melvin, 2288
Lurie, Nancy O., 5872
Luthin, Reinhard, 7130
Lutton, Wayne C., 9351
Lydon, Cindy A., 7620
Lyle, John D., 1149
Lyles, Leon, 1485
Lyman, Stanford M., 3792
Lynch, James J., 4358
Lynd, Staughton, 2289, 6281
Lynn, Kenneth S., 4359, 4360, 9763
Lyon, Bruce W., 5139
Lyon, Edwin A., II, 5279
Lyons, Paul H., 6282
Lytle, Mark H., 8977

Maas, Jim, 1891
Mabon, David W., 2290
MacArthur, Douglas, 0937
MacCarthy, Esther, 8032
MacDonal, J. Fred, 3901
MacDonald, Callum P ., 7215
MacDonald, Charles B., 9352
MacDonald, Dwight, 4027
MacDonald, Fred J., 8528
Maceda, Laura, 8378
MacGregor, David, 4941
Macinko, George, 1486
MacIsaac, David, 9353, 9354, 9355
MacKay, Lamar S., 8529
MacKay, Robert E., 2568
Mackey, Warren C., 9764
MacKinnon, Stephen R., and Ottis Friesen, 8906
Mackintosh, Barry, 0641
MacLean, Elizabeth K., 0803, 0804
MacLeod, Glen, 3596
MacMillian, Harold, 8755
MacMillian, Michael E., 5807
MacNaughton, Mary D., 3672
MacNeil, Neil, 0330
Madan, B. K., 9564

Maddala, G.S., 4942

Madden, David, 3411, 3412, 3413

Madden, Ray J., 8300

Maddock, Mary D. C., 3232

Maddox, Robert Franklin, 1157, 1158, 4943, 6599

Maddox, Robert J., 0984, 6166, 7778, 9765

Maddux, Thomas R., 4028, 6389, 7438, 7439, 8859, 8860, 8861

Madison, Charles A., 2434, 2437, 2461, 6977

Madyun, Gail., 5460

Maga, Timothy P., 0078, 0791, 0792. 7296, 7471, 9130, 9131, 9132

Magden, Ronald, 4029

Magee, James J., 6978

Magnuson, Landis K., 3233

Magnussson, Tor, 3549

Magrass, Yale R., 4798

Mahler, Kenneth E., 4610

Mahoney, Leo J., 9356

Mahoney, Thomas, 0196, 0197

Maines, Rachel P., 8192

Maines, Shelia G., 4165

Major, John, 0975, 2721, 7977

Major, Mark, 7407

Majors, William R., 6600, 6601

Makowsky, Veronica, 3414

Maland, Charles J., 3793, 3794

Mallin, Jay, 0198

Mallman, Sharon M., 0793

Maloff, Saul, 1690

Malone, Michael P., 2990, 6602, 6603, 6604, 6605

Malsberger, John W., 6075, 6076

Mamot, Patricio R., 0866

Manchester, William, 0938

Mandel, Richard, 9357

Maness, Lonnie E., 8081

Maney, Patrick J., 1254

Manfred, Frederick, 6606

Mangione, Jerre G., 5140

Mangusso, Mary C., 6607

Mankin, Lawrence D., 5079

Manley, John H., 4944

Mann, Kenneth E., 5461

Mannard, Joseph G., 5462

Manning, Clarence, 8622

Manning, Donald J., 7440

Manser, Richard L., 8907

Mansfield, Don L., 9499

Manson, Elizabeth, and Louis M. Starr, 9847

Manson, Janet M., 7297

Manwaring, David R., 6925

Marabell, George P., 8033

Maranell, Gary M., 0444

Maranell, Gary M., and Richard A. Doddler, 0405

Marburg, Theodore F., 2569

Marcello, Ronald E., 0694, 2991, 6608, 6609

March, Michael S., 2850

Marchand, Roland , 2570

Marchs, Stephen, 3415

Marcus, Alan I., and Erik Lokensgard, 4361

Marcus, Sheldon, 4030

Marcuse, Peter, 1808

Marden, David, 5873

Mardis, Robert F., 5198

Marger, Martin, 6610

Margo, Robert A., 5463, 5641

Margolis, Joel P., 6123

Marion, Carol J., 8862

Mark, Eduard M., 7441, 9500, 9501

Mark, Edward M., 8863

Mark, Gregory Y., 5673

Mark, Steven M., 0863

Markey, Gregory T., 8908

Markoe, Arnold, 2851

Markowitz, Gerald, and David Rosner, 1691

Markowitz, Gerald, and Marlene Park, 5199

Markowitz, Norman D., 0583

Marks, Frederick W. III., 7552, 7779, 7780, 7781

Markusen, Eric P., 9133

Marling, Karal Ann, 3673, 5080, 5141

Marling, William, 3416

Marmorstein, Gary, 3550

Marquardt, Virginia H., 3674

Marquart, Frank, 2291

Marquez, Benjamin, 5697

Marquis, Alice G., 4248

Mars, David, 6994

Marsh, Richard R., 4362

Marsh, Robert, 8154

Marshall, George C., 0948

Marshall, George C., H. H. Arnold, and Ernest J. King, 8577

Marshall, Schuyler, 4031

Marshall, Thomas R., 6926

Martel, Leon C., 9502

Marten, James, 2992

Martenson, Katherine A., 4528

Martin, Boyd, 6805

Martin, Charles H., 2292, 5464, 5465, 5661, 6284, 6390

Martin, Dorris B., 5979

Martin, Douglas D., 4727

Martin, G., 0661

Martin, James V. Jr., 8963

Martin, Jay 4363

Martin, Joseph D. Jr., 5642

Martin, Robert A., 3417

Martin, Robert E., 2722

Martin, Robert F., 4529, 6285

Martin, T. R., 8155

Martin, Tony, 5466

Martins, Charles, 6283

Marvel, W. Marcy, 8947

Marx, Rudolf, 0233

Mashberg, Michael, 9134, 9659

Maskin, Melvin R., 5256

Masland, John W., 7553

Mason, Alpheus T., 6927, 6928, 6961, 6987, 7036, 7037, 7038

Mason, Bruce, 6286, 6833

Mason, David T., and Elwood R. Maunder, 2723

Mason, Ernest D., 5467

Mason, Jeffrey D., 3234

Mason, Mark E., 1844

Mason, Philip P., 9660

Mason, Richard, 1762, 1763

Mason, Robert, 9358

Massey, Robert K. Jr., 6611, 6754

Masson, Jack K., and Donald L. Guimary, 2293

Masteller, Richard N., 3675

Masters, Nick, 4530

Mastny, Vojtech, 8623, 8864, 8865

Matheny, David L., 1143

Matheny, Robert L., 2571

Mathes, Michael, 9054

Mathews, Allan, 1546

Mathews, Jane D., 5142, 5081

Mathews, John M., 6167

Matloff, Maurice, 0485, 0486, 4945, 8624, 8866, 9359

Matray, James I., 8951, 9565

Matson, Robert W., 9503

Matson, William L., 7782

Matsumoto, Valeria J., 8379, 8380

Mattern, Carolyn J., 0939

Matteson, Barbara H., and Stanley Gwynn, 3419

Matthews, Geoffrey, 1263

Matthews, Glenna C., 2294, 2295, 2572

Matthews, James W., 3418

Matthews, Thomas G., 6612

Mattison, Robert S., 3676

Matz, Eliahu, 9135

Mauchly, Kathleen R., 4946

Mauney, Connie P., 6979

Maurer, Alfred, 9360

Maurer, D.W., 4249

Maurer, David J., 1632, 1633, 2993

Maurer, Joyce C., 5257

Maw, Herbert B., 5200

Maxwell, James A., and Margaret N. Balcom, 8193

Maxwell, John C., 4221

Maxwell, Margaret F., 1634

May, Dale B., 3174

May, Dean L., 1999, 2041

May, Ernest R., 8867, 9027, 9361

May, George S., 6124

May, Gerry A., 8909

May, Irvin M., Jr., 1081, 1082, 2724, 1487, 1488, 2852, 4032

May, Larry, and Stephen Lassonde, 3795

Mayberry, Virginia, 8224

Mayer, George H., 6077, 6078, 6079

Mayer, Milton, 4033

Mayer, Thomas, and Monojit Chatterji, 2020

Mayers, David, 0852, 0853

Mayle, Paul D., 8625, 8626

Mayo, Selz C., and C. Horace Hamilton, 5468

Maze, John, and Graham White, 0642

Mazon, Mauricio, 5698, 5699

Mazuzan, George T., and Nancy Walker, 8462

Mazuzan, George T., 1243, 1244, 1245, 8301

McAfee, Ward W., 8381

McArthur, Benjamin, 4364

McArthur, Judith N., 9766

McArthur, Priscilla G., 8756

McAvoy, Thomas, 0331

McBane, Richard L., 7978

McBride, David, and Monroe H. Little, 9614

McBride, James D., 6613

McBride, William M., 4947

McCaffrey, Joseph E., and Elwood R. Maunder, 3113

McCain, Johnny M., 9055, 9056

McCain, Linda, 0976

McCain, William D., 1126, 9566

McCandless, Amy M.T., 4365

McCann, Carole R., 5469

McCann, Frank D. Jr., 7659, 9041, 9042, 9143

McCann, Hugh W., 5470

McCann, John B., 1359, 2725

McCarley, J. Britt, 0961

McCarron, Margaret P., 1017

McCarthy, Harold T., 3420

McCarthy, James S., 6614

McCarty, Kenneth G., Jr., 0821

McCaughey, Robert A., 4366

McChesney, Robert W., 3902, 3903, 3904

McClay, Wilfred M., 4166

McClintock, James I., 4948

McCloud, Emma G., 1692

McCloy, John F., 9362

McClung, Hunter, 9848

McClure, Arthur F., and Donna Costigan, 0609

McColloch, Mark, 2296

McCollum, Pat, 2994

McConaghy, Lorraine, 8156

McConnell, Gary R., 6287

McConnell, Grant, 6080

McConnell, Robert L., 3796

McCord, Joan, and William McCord, 4728

McCorkle, James L., Jr., 1360

McCoy, Donald R., 0504, 1764, 2995, 6081, 6082, 6615, 6616, 6617, 6618, 6774, 6775, 6834, 6835, 6836, 7947, 8530, 9661, 9767, 9824

McCoy, Donald R., and Richard T. Ruetten, 5471, 5472

McCoy, Garnett, 3677, 3678, 3679

McCoy, Ron, 5874
McCraw, Thomas K., 3114, 3115, 6988
McCraw, Willam, 6391
McCray, Sandra B., 5143
McCreath, Harrison W., 3235
McCue, Leo F. Jr, 6083
McCusker, John J., 0199
McDaniel, Boyce, 4949
McDaniel, Dennis K., 6881
McDaniel, George W., 1247
McDean, Harry C., 1294, 1361, 1362, 9768
McDermott, Douglas, 5082
McDonald, David J., and Edward Lynch, 2297
McDonald, James L., 3421
McDonald, Judith L., 3422
McDonald, Michael J., 9662
McDonald, Michael J., and John Muldowny, 3116, 3117
McDonald, Susan S. W., 3423
McDonald, William F., 5144
McDonnell, James R., 2298
McDonough, J. E., 2726
McDowell, Winston, 5473
McEdwards, Mary, 6619
McElvaine, Robert S., 1693, 2727
McEnteer, James B., 4034
McEvoy, Richard E., 5145
McFarland, C. K., 2445
McFarland, Keith D., 0666, 0667, 0668, 0669
McFarland, Stephen L., 8978, 9504
McGhee, Flora A. C., 5474
McGhee, Richard D., 3797
McGinn, Robert E., 4950
McGinty, Brian, 1295, 3424, 4729
McGirr, Newman F., 0200
McGoff, Kevin, 2097
McGovern, James R., 5980
McGown, Washington E., 9663
McGreen, John D., 6288
McGrew, Paul C., 1489
McGruder, Larry, 5475
McGuire, Jack B., 6084
McGuire, Phillip, 5618, 5619, 5620, 5621, 5622, 5623, 5624
McGurn, Barrett, 7051
McHale, James M., 0838, 1845
McIlvaine, Bill, 4951
McIlvenna, Don E., 0487, 8157
McIntosh, Clarence F., 6620
McJimsey, George, 0695
McKale, Donald M., 9066
McKay, Marilyn L., 3236
McKay, R. Reynolds, 4167, 7691
McKee, Sister Mary J., 1224
McKelvey, Blake, 1694
McKenna, James F., 3070
McKenna, Marian C., 0985

McKenzie, Kermit E., 7442
McKinzie, Kathleen O., 5146
McKinzie, Richard D., 5147, 5148
McKorkle, James L., Jr., 1394
McLaren, Joseph, 5476
McLaughlin, Doris B., 9849
McLewin, Philip J., 2573
McLoughlin, William G., 4531
McMahaon, Edward J., 2299
McMahon, Robert J., 8955
McMains, Howard F., 6755
McMeekin, Dorothy, 3680
McMilen, Neil R., 5477
McMilian, Elizabeth J., 3175
McMillan, James E., 1020, 1021
McMillen, Neil R., 4035, 6392
McMurtry, Walter L., 8248
McNally, Michael J.T., 4532
McNeal, Patricia, 8034
McNeal, Robert H., 9224
McNeil, William C., 7298
McNeil, William H., 8657
McNutt, James C., 3425
McPherson, Dolly A., 5478
McPherson, Donald S., 2300
McQuaid, Kim, 0553, 2574, 2575, 2576, 2728, 4656, 6168, 6169
McSeveney, Samuel T., 6621
McVicker, Eugene R., 4533
McWilliams, Carey, 3426
McWilliams, John C., 4730, 6874
McWilliams, Wilson C., 7018
Mead, Howard N., 1204
Meador, Prentice A., Jr., 0839
Medeiros, Patricia, 3798
Medhurst, Martin J., 4534
Medicine, Beatrice, 5875
Medley, Keith Weldon, 5479
Meehan, James, 3551, 4222
Meek, Edwin E., 3905
Meeks, Kenneth W., 4036
Meerse, David E., 8531
Megaw, M. Ruth, 7250
Mehlman, Michael H., 2996
Mehren, Peter, 5258, 5259
Meier, August, 5482
Meier, August and Elliott Rudwick, 2301, 5480, 5481
Meier, Kenneth J. and Jeff Worsham, 2577
Meigs, Montgomery C., 4952
Meijer, Hank, 1272
Meikle, Jeffery L., 2578, 4953
Meiland, Jack W., 9769
Meister, Richard J., 6622
Meixner, Mary L., 3681, 5260
Melbourne, Robert E., 1490

Melcher, Daniel P., 6623
Mellon, Knox, 1695
Mellon, Paul, 3682
Melosh, Barbara, 5149, 5150
Melosi, Martin V., 1765, 7554, 7555, 7556, 7557
Melton, George E., 8707
Melton, Gloria B., 5483
Meltzer, Milton, 0746, 3146, 5083
Menard, Wilmon, 3799
Mencken, Henry L., 4037, 6085
Mendelsohn, John, 9664, 9665, 9666
Mendelson, Wallace, 6980, 7019, 7039
Mendoza, Barbara M., 3237
Menig, Harry, 3552
Mercer, L. J., and W. D. Morgan, 2579
Mercier, Laurie K., 2580, 5981
Meredith, Howard L., 1491
Mergen, Bernard M., 2302, 2478
Merola, Vito A., 4774
Merrill, Jeffery, 4223
Merritt, Russell, 3800
Merson, Martin, 7646
Mertz, Paul E., 2853, 3118
Mervis, Leonard J., 4535
Meschutt, David, 3683
Messer, Robert L., 1135, 9505
Messick, Ben, 3667
Mets, David R., 8035
Metting, Fred B., 3427
Meyer, Donald B., 4536, 4799
Meyer, Gerald J., 1229
Meyer, L. Donald, and William C. Moldenhauer, 1492
Meyerowitz, Ruth S., 2303
Meyers, Jeffrey, 3428
Meyers, W. Cameron, 4038
Meyerson, Harold, 5982
Mezzrow, Mezz, and Bernard Wolfe, 3553
"HMS Collections: When Stars 'Fell' on Minnesota", 4807
Michels, Edward H. Jr., 2997
Michelson, Charles, 0166
Michelson, Paul F., 3429
Mickey, David H., 7859
Mickey, Rosie, 4367
Midgette, Nancy S., 4954
Mierzejewski, Alfred C., 9363
Mihelich, Dennis N., 5484, 5485, 6289
Mikesh, Robert C., 9364
Milford, Navey, 3430
Milkis, Sidney M., 0332, 0505, 0406, 6086
Milkman, Ruth, 5983, 5984, 8225
Miller, Aaron D., 8989
Miller, Anthony B., 6624
Miller, Charles A., 3801
Miller, D. C., 0234
Miller, David B., 1363

Miller, Donald L., 6290, 6291
Miller, Duane Ernest, 8463
Miller, George A., 4039
Miller, Hope R., 0379
Miller, James E., 4775, 6806, 8785
Miller, Jean-Donald, 8661
Miller, Jeanne-Marie A., 5261
Miller, Joan, 6887
Miller, John A., 9567
Miller, John E., 3802, 6625, 6626, 6837, 6838
Miller, John R., 0957, 1547
Miller, Jordan Y., 3238
Miller, Kathleen A., 3431, 5885
Miller, M. Lawrence, 5084
Miller, Marc S., 5886, 8082, 8158
Miller, Martin J. Jr., 9365
Miller, Michael H., 6839
Miller, Nathan, 0011, 0121
Miller, Patricia M., 3432
Miller, Patrick, 4611
Miller, Robert A., 4955
Miller, Robert M., 4537, 4538, 4539, 4540
Miller, Robert O., 1098
Miller, Samuel D., 9628
Miller, Vivian I., 6756
Miller, William D., 6627
Millett, John D., 9770
Millett, Stephen M., 6929
Millis, Walter, 0012, 7558
Mills, C. Wright, 2418
Mills, Geofrey, and Hugh Rockoff, 8194
Mills, Geofrey T., 8159
Mills, George, 4657
Mills, Herb, and David Wellman, 2304
Millsap, Mary R., 7346
Milton, David, 2305
Milton, John D., 2998
Milum, Betty, 0506
Minear, Richard H., 5721
Miner, Curtis, 8302
Miner, Curtis, and Paul Roberts, 8160
Miner, Deborah N., 7559
Miner, Stephen M., 8868
Mings, Stephen D., 9366
Minton, Henry L. 4368
Minton, John, 3554
Mintz, Frank Paul, 7560
Miranti, Paul J., Jr., 2581
Mirel, Jeffrey E., 4369, 4370
Miscamble, Wilson D., 2582, 4541
Mishkin, Frederick S., 2042
Mishler, Paul C., 6292
Misse, Frederick B., 6807, 8799
Mitchell, David, 1736
Mitchell, Franklin D., 6170

Mitchell, Greg, 6628
Mitchell, H. L., 1548, 2306
Mitchell, John B., 4956
Mitchell, John G., 2854
Mitchell, Reavis L., Jr., 5486
Mitchell, Virgil L., 2999, 3000
Mitson, Betty E., 8382
Mittelman, Karen S., 5887
Miyamoto, S. Frank, 8383
Mizejewski, Linda, 3239
Modell, John, 1696, 2307, 5722
Modell, John, and Duane Steffey, 4683
Modell, John, Marc Goulden, and Sigurder Magnusson, 5487
Modisett, Lawrence E., 8815
Modras, Ronald, 7131, 7132
Moehring, Eugene P., 5262, 8161
Moellering, Ralph L., 4542, 4543
Mogren, Paul A., 1493
Mohl, Raymond A., 5263
Mohl, Raymond A., and Neil Betten, 4776
Mohler, Stanley R., 1892
Mohn, I.H., 5280
Mohrmann, G. P., and Eugene F. Scot, 3555
Moley, Raymond, 0707, 0708
Moltmann, Gunther, 7299
Mommsen, Wolfgang, and L. Kettenacker, 7300
Monroe, Douglas K., 2446
Monroe, Gerald M., 5085
Monroy, Douglas G., 4777, 5700, 5701, 5702
Montalto, Nicholas V., 4371, 4372
Montejano, David, 5703
Monterio, George, 3597
Montgomery, David, 2309
Montgomery, David, and Ronald Schatz, 2308
Montgomery, Edrene S., 7133
Montgomery, Marion, 3598
Montgomery, Mary I., 3684
Montrose, Charles, 0333
Moody, Eric N., 6629
Moody, Frank K., 0249
Moon, Henry Lee, 5662
Moon, John Ellis van Courtland, 9137, 9367
Mooney, Booth, 1099
Mooney, Rex O., 7134
Moore, Carl, 1050
Moore, Colleen A., 2583
Moore, David G., 2584
Moore, Gerald L, 5488
Moore, Gilbert W., 2310
Moore, Glen, 6630
Moore, Jaime W., 7948
Moore, James R., 2057, 7216
Moore, James T., 3803, 5489
Moore, Jamie W., 7217, 7561, 7562, 7783
Moore, Jesse T. Jr., 5490

Moore, John H., 5491, 8083, 8464, 8465, 8466
Moore, John R., 1109, 6125, 7135
Moore, Libba G., 2658
Moore, Ray Nichols, 5492
Moore, Stanley J., 6631
Moore, Thomas W., 3804
Moore, William V., 6632
Moore, Winfred B., Jr., 1136, 1137, 1138, 1139
Moramarco, Fred S., 3433
Moran, Charles M. Wilson, Lord, 9199
Moran, Robert E. Sr., 6633
Moreau, John A., 1181, 6171
Morehouse, Ward, 3240
Moreno, Tom, 5201
Morey, Loren, 3906
Morgan, Alda C. M., 4373
Morgan, Alfred L., 6634
Morgan, Carl C. Jr., 8162
Morgan, Charlotte T., 5493
Morgan, Chester M., 1127, 1128, 1129
Morgan, Georgia Cook, 5888
Morgan, Hugh J., 4040
Morgan, Iwan, 1635, 1809, 6635, 6636
Morgan, Sir Frederick E., 9368
Morgan, Ted, 0013
Morgan, Thomas S. Jr., 5202
Morgenstein, George, 7563
Morgenthau, Henry, Jr., 0656
Morgher, Fred, 6962
Morimoto, Toyotomi, 5723
Morison, Elting E., 0884, 0978
Morison, Samuel E., 0201, 8627, 9369
Morita, Hideyuki, 9568
Morkowitz, Gerald, and David Rosner, 2080
Morlan, Donald B., 4544
Mormino, Gary R., 4778, 5494
Moroney, Robert M., and Jesse McClure, 4224
Morrill, George, 4731
Morris, Allen, 5889
Morris, Cynthia Hastas, 8036
Morris, Harry W., 6087
Morris, James K., 1697
Morris, James O., 2311, 2312
Morris, Richard B., Paul A. Freund, and Herbert Wechsler, 6971
Morris, Robert L., 7443
Morris, William G., 9506
Morrison A., 5495
Morrison, David E., 4658
Morrison, Joseph L., 0799, 0800, 4041, 8532
Morrison, Rodney J., 6963
Morrissey, Charles T., 9850
Morsberger, Robert E., 3805
Morse, Arthur D., 9138
Morson, Gary S., 3907

Morton, Jacqueline, 3434
Morton, Louis, 4957, 4958, 4959, 7564, 7565, 8628, 8629,
    8869, 9370, 9615, 9667, 9668, 9771, 9772, 9773
Morton, Marian J., 3806
Mosch, Theodore R., 4374
Moscow, Warren, 6637, 6793
Mosely, Philip E., 8630, 8800, 9225, 9569
Moses, Robert, 3001
Moskow, Michael G., 9139
Mosley, Leonard, 7218
Moss, Bobby G., 3435
Moss, Kenneth B., 0868, 7301, 7302
Mosse, George L., 5781
Moszer, Max, 8163
Mott, Frank L., 3436, 4042
Mott, James C., 6739
Motter, David C., 8164
Motter, T. H. Vail, 8870
Motzozky, Eliytho, 9136
Mouledous, Joseph C., 5496
Mount, Barbara L., 3147
Mountcastle, John W., 9371
Mower, A. Glenn, Jt., 0079
Mowry, George E., 9774
Mowry, George E., and Blaine A. Brownell, 2855
Moyers, David M., 2313
Mrozek, Donald J., 2585, 9372
Mruck, Armin, 9570
Muccigrosso, Robert, 6126
Muchmore, Lynn, 2586
Muessig, Raymond H., 0014
Mui, Kan-Chi, 8165
Muir, Malcolm Jr., 7979, 9373, 9374, 9375
Mulcahy, Judith M., 3437
Mulch, Barbara E. G., 0926
Mulder, Robert A., 6088, 6089, 7136, 7137
Mulkin, Barb, 9376
Mullay, M. Camilla, 2422
Muller, Herman J., 2856
Mullholland, Robet J., 3908
Mulligan, Timothy P., 9377
Mullin, John R., 2587
Mullins, William H., 1698, 7138
Muncy, Robyn, 5890
Munley, Kathleen P., 6638
Munnelly, Robert J., 4375
Munro, Dana G., 7682
Muraskin, William, 5497
Murdock, Eugene, 4612
Murdock, Steve, 6293
Muro, Douglas, 5086
Murphy, Bruce A., 6989, 7020
Murphy, Daniel P., 7873
Murphy, Frederick I., 9215
Murphy, Jacqueline L., 3438

Murphy, Paul L., 1364, 6866, 6930, 6931
Murphy, Robert D., 0873
Murphy, William B., 9378
Murphy, William T., 8533
Murray, G. Patrick, 8757, 9379
Murray, Gail S., 1699
Murray, Mary H., 6639, 7139
Murray, Paul T., 8303
Murray, Robert K., 8304
Murray, Stanley N., 1893
Murtha, Donald, 2729
Muse, Clifford L. Jr., 4376
Musgrove, Susan M., 4960
Muste, John M., 7379
Muzzey, D. S., 9669
Myer, Dillon S., 8384
Myers, Carol F., 9616
Myers, Constance A., 5891, 6294, 6295
Myers, Harold P., 8871
Myers, J. Walter, Jr., 1494
Myers, James, 8467
Myhra, David, 0715
Myung, Inn S., 3241

Naber, Gregg R., and Lea Rosson DeLong, 5203
Nachbar, Jack, 3807
Nadeau, Remi A., 9507
Naficy, Azar, 3439
Nagai, Yonosuke, and Akira Iriye, 9508
Nagel, Stuart S., 0407
Nahshon, Edna, 6296
Nairab, Mohammad M., 8990
Naison, Mark D., 1549, 1810, 3440, 5498, 5499, 5500,
    6297, 6298, 6299, 6300
Nall, Gary L., 3119
Namorato, Michael V., 4659
Napoli, Donald S., 4225, 8305
Nardinelli, Clark, 4613
Nash, Al, 2314
Nash, Anedith J. B., 1863
Nash, Gerald D., 0015, 0408, 2588, 9571
Nash, Gerald D., Noel H. Pugach, and Richard Tommasson,
    5151
Nash, Michael, 5992
Nash, Philleo, 4961
Nash, Roderick, 1495
Naske, Claus-M, 5501, 6640, 9380, 8385, 9140
Natanson, Nicholas A., 5087, 5502
Nathanson, Nathaniel L., 6990
National Park Service, 0016
Natoli, Marie D., 0610
Navarro, Vicente, 7380
Nawyn, William E., 9141
Neal, Donn C., 0759
Neal, Nevin E., 1197

Neal, Steve, 0770
Neef, Diana L., 3071
Neff, Robert R., 6641
Neher, Arlen B., 8964
Neidle, Cecyle S., 4168
Nelsen, Claire, 3072, 6757
Nelson, Bruce, 2315, 2316, 2730
Nelson, Daniel M., 2317, 2318, 2319, 2320, 2321, 2322, 2323, 2436, 2857, 2858, 4962
Nelson, H. Viscount, 5503
Nelson, Harland S., 3441
Nelson, John K., 8037
Nelson, Joseph B., 2324
Nelson, Joyce, 3808
Nelson, Lawrence J., 1365, 1366, 1566, 2859, 2860
Nelson, Michael, 6964
Nelson, Richard, 9775
Nelson, Stephen C., 3242
Nelson, Steve, and Donald L. Miller, 7381
Nelson, W. R., 1930
Nelson-Cisneros, Victor B., 2325, 2326
Nemecek, Maureen J., 9381
Nenninger, Timothy K., 8306
Nerad, Maresi, 4377
Nesbitt, Eddie, 4043
Nesbitt, Victoria H. K., 0377
Neth, Mary, 1550
Neuberger, Richard L., and S. B. Kahn, 1034
Neugebauer, Janet M., 1296
Neumann, Robert G., 0409
Neumann, William L., 0488, 7566, 7784, 7784, 7785, 9572
Neuse, Steven M., 3120
Neustadt, Richard E., 0334, 0410
Neustadt-Noy, Isaac, 5782
Neve, Brian, 3809
Neville, Howard R., 2589
Nevins, Allan, 0445, 0752, 1963
Newbill, James G., 2327, 2328, 7003
Newby, Idus A., 3442
Newland, Samuel J., 5876
Newman, Ernest R. Jr., 4378
Newquist, Gloria W., 0630
Newsome, A.R., 4379
Newton, Craig A., 7140
Nicholls, William H., 2590
Nichols, Carole, and Joyce Pendery, 5993
Nichols, Jeannette P., 2058, 7786, 7949
Nichols, Roy F., 6642
Nichols, Sheridan, 9382, 9383
Nickel, Steve, 4732
Nickerson, Edward A., 3599
Nicoll, Christine, and Robert G. Weisbord, 4684
Niedziela, Theresa A., 6965
Nielsen, Michael C., 2329
Nielsen, Stephen F., 0986

Niemi, Albert W. Jr., 5994
Niksch, Larry A., 8965
Ninkovich, Frank A., 3685, 8910, 9459, 9776
Ninneman, Thomas R., 1051, 1052
Nipp, Robert E., 2731
Nisbet, Robert, 7787
Nitschke, Marie M., 4044
Nixon, Edgar B., 0411, 7788
Niznik, Monica L., 0673
Noble, Dennis L.,7465
Noble, Richard A., 1700
Nobles, William S., 0643
Nochlin, Linda, 3686
Noggle, Burl F., 5281
Nolan, William F., 8911
Nomura, Gail M., 5724
Noorzoy, Mohammad S., 2000
Norden, Margaret K., 4045
Nore, Ellen, 9777
Norflett, Linda K., 5504
Norman, John, 8534
Norrell, Robert J., II, 5505, 5663
Norris, Frank, 2591
Norris, L. David, 6643
Norris, Parthenia E., 7248
Norris, Richard P., 1551
Norris, Thomas D., 4545
North, Paul H., Jr., 3443
Norton, Hugh S., 2059
Norton, Lucretia et al., 5204
Notarianni, Philip F., 2419
Notaro, Carmen A., 6301
Nourse, Edwin G., 2861
Nouryeh, Andrea J., 3243
Novack, George, 6302
Novak, Estelle, G., 3600
Noverr, Douglas A., 3687, 3688
Novick, Peter, 9778
Nuechterlein, James A., 5506, 6172
Nuemann, William L., 9629
Nuerburg, Norman, 3176
Nye, Russel B., 4250, 6090

O'Brien, Anthony P., 1864, 1921, 2021
O'Brien, Charles F., 9384
O'Brien, David J., 2330, 4546, 4547, 5783
O'Brien, Frances W., 7141
O'Brien, Michael, 3444, 9779
O'Brien, Patrick G., Thomas D. Isern, and R. Daniel Lumley, 8468
O'Coin, Andre R., 2732
O'Connor, Francis V., 5088, 5205, 5206
O'Connor, J. F. T., 1636
O'Connor, John, 5282
O'Connor, Joseph E., 7444

O'Connor, Michael, 3177
O'Connor, Raymond G., 4963, 8631, 9670
O'Farrell, M. Brigid, and Lydia Kleiner, 2470
O'Gara, James, 7950
O'Hara, Maureen, and David Easley, 2001
O'Hara, Michael J., 1737
O'Keane, Josephine, 1063
O'Leary, Paul M., 8195
O'Leary-Archer, Lynne M., 5995
O'Neal, Bill, 9851
O'Neill, Daniel J., 2462
O'Neill, James E., 9671, 9825
O'Neill, James E., and Robert W. Krauskopf, 9385, 9672
O'Neill, Maureen, 4380
O'Neill, Robert K., 5207
O'Reilly, Kenneth, 6875, 6876, 6882
O'Rourke, James S., 4047
O'Rourke, Paul A., 4046, 6644
O'Sullivan, John J., 0335, 8307, 9386
Ober, Michael J., 3121
Obermayr, Lorna, 8226
Ochillo, Yvonne, 5507
Oden, Jack P., 4964
Oehling, Richard A., 3810, 3811
Oermann, Robert K., 3556
Oestreicher, Richard, 6091
Offner, Arnold A., 0811, 7219, 7303, 7304, 7305, 7789
Ogden, Gerald R., 5877
Ogdon, Montell, 0894
Ogle, Stephanie F., 6303
Ogles, Robert M., and Herbert H. Howard, 7142
Oglesby, Richard, 1496
Ohl, John K., 0701, 0702
Ohrn, Karin B., 8386
Okamura, Raymond Y., 8387
Okihiro, Gary Y., 8388, 8389, 8390, 8391
Okihiro, Gary Y., and Julie Sly, 8392
Oko, Dorothy K., 9617
Okumiya, Masatake, 9387
Olien, Diana D., 1766
Olinger, John C., 8308
Oliver, Robert T., 0167
Olmstead, Robert T., 3445
Olmstead, Timothy, 8393
Olney, Martha L., 1865, 2592
Olsen, Darryll, 1738
Olsen, Michael L., 1367
Olsen, Nils A., 1368
Olsgaard, John N., 1025
Olson, James S., 2002, 2593, 2659, 2733, 2734, 2735, 2862, 5508, 6645
Olson, James S., and Sharon Phair, 5509
Olson, James S. and Liz Byford, 1767
Olson, Keith W., 4226
Olson, Lester C., 3689

Olson, Margaret P., 5510
Olson, Thomas L, 4660
Omura, James Matsumoto; Hansen Arthur, interviewer, 5725
Onunwa, Paschal U., 3244
Opie, John, 1497
Oppenheimer, Robert, 5704
Orange, Vincent, 7567
Orbach, William, 5784
Orlansky, H., 0235
Orleck, Annelise, 5996
Orloff, Ann S., 4227
Orr, Kenneth B., 4381
Orsagh, Jacqueline E., 5089
Orser, Edward W., 4548, 4549, 4550, 8309
Ortquist, Richard T., 6646, 6647, 6648
Orzell, Laurence J., 9509
Osborn, George C., 4048
Osborne, John W., 8535
Osgood, Richard, 3909
Osnos, N.F., 5152
Ostrander, Gilman M., 5090
Ostrower, Gary B., 0662, 7220
Osur, Alan M., 5625
Otley, George N., 4685
Ottanelli, Michele F., 6304
Otto, John S., 3557, 9852
Ourada, Patricia K., 8310
Overacker, Louise, 6758, 6808
Overholt, James, 8166
Overmyer, Deborah A., 4049
Overton, Richard C., 1922
Owen, Gordon R., 1260
Owsley, Harriet C., 1283
Oxford, Edward, 3558, 3812, 3910
Oxley, Frances E., 2331
Oye, Kenneth A., 1964
Oyos, Lynwood E., 2332, 7568
Ozanne, Robert, 2081
Ozinga, Thomas J., 2594
Ozment, Robert, 1320

Paananen, Donna M., 1498
Pacelle, Richard L. Jr., 6932
Padvaiskas, Edmund R., 8872
Page, Kirby, 8038
Pahl, Thomas L., 6305, 6306
Paine, Jeffery, 3813
Painter, David S., 1768, 1769
Painter, Linda L., 3911
Painter, Nell, and Hosea Hudson, 6307
Palacio, 3605
Palladino, Grace, 2333
Palmer, Annette C., 9047, 9833
Palmer, David, 2334
Palmer, Pamela L., 3446

Palmer, Thomas, 9389

Palquist, Eben O., 4382

Palumbo, John C., 7569

Pamphile, Leon D., 7683, 7684

Pan, Stephen, 8632

Pang, Alex Soojung-Kim, 4965

Papachristou, Judith R., 7445, 7570, 7790

Papaleo, Ralph J., 6649

Papanikolas, Helen Z., 2335

Papenfuse, Edward C., 9673

Papke, David Ray, 6840

Parascandola, John, 4966

Parfit, Michael, 1297

Parham, Byron A. P., 7951

Parillo, Mark P., 7571

Park, Bert E., 4228

Park, Edwards, 4967

Park, Hong-Kyu, 8952

Park, Marlene, and Gerald E. Markowitz, 5153

Parker, James R., 9780

Parker, John W., 5511

Parker, Mary H., 0336

Parker, Nancy W., 0202

Parker, R. A. C., 8758

Parker, Robert D., 3447

Parker, Russell D., 2595, 5512

Parker, Sally J., 8759

Parkison, Robert W., 4251

Parks, Jimmy D., 8873

Parks, Lillian R., 0122

Parks, Robert J., 5626

Parman, Donald L., 5878, 5879, 5880

Parmenter, William Q., 4050

Parmet, H. S., and M. B. Hecht, 6794

Parnell, Ben, 9390

Parrish, Michael E., 2736, 6933

Parrish, N. F., 0898

Parrish, Robert, 8536

Parry, Sally E., 3448

Parson, K.C., 5154

Parsteck, Bennet J., 6650

Partick, James, 3559

Partin, John W., 0993, 1140, 6809

Parton, James, 0903

Parzen, Herbert, 9003

Paschal, Andrew G., 5513

Pashigan, B. Peter, 1369

Paszek, Lawrence J., 5627

Patenaude, Lionel V., 0564, 1701, 6092, 6651, 6759, 6966

Paterson, James T., 3122, 7791

Patinkin, Don, 2043

Patrick, Sue C., 2596

Patterson, J. T., 6652

Patterson, J. W., 1273, 1274

Patterson, James A., 4551

Patterson, James T., 0412, 1264, 2082, 2737, 3002, 6841, 7143, 7144

Patterson, Michael S., 1150

Patton, James G., 1370

Patton, Lillian, and Thomas Patton, 0080

Patton, Randal L., 2451, 6653

Paul, Carol L., 4051

Paul, Justus F., 0991, 0992, 6654, 6655, 7860, 8394

Paulette, Irene Carson, 8084

Paulsell, William O., 4552

Paulsen, George E., 2863, 2864, 2865

Pauly, Thomas H., 3814, 3815

Pauw, Alan D., 9510

Pavlak, Raymond T., 4383

Pavli, Robert C., 1499

Pavlowitch, K. St., 8816

Payne, Burnice D., 6173

Payne, Elizabeth A., 2467

Payne, Howard C., Raymond Callahan, and Edward M. Bennett, 7221, 7222

Payne, Ladell, 3449

Payne, Stanley G., 7382

Payne-Carter, David, 3245

Peace, Otis, 2597

Pear, Richard H., 7328

Pearlman, Michael D., 7980, 9391

Pebbles, Robert W., 4385

Peck, David R., 3148, 3450, 4052

Peck, Jeffrey W., 3816

Peck, Jim, 8912

Pecora, Ferdinand, 2598

Pecorella, Robert F., 6656

Pedersen, Sharon, 4384

Pederson, James H., 8772

Peebles, Robert H., 2599

Peel, Roy V., and Thomas C. Donnelly, 6760

Peeler, David P., 3149, 4252

Peeps, J. M. Stephen, 8433

Peffer, E. Louise, 9028

Peffer, Nathaniel, 8913

Peltzman, Sam, 2003

Pelz, Stephen E., 7572

Pena, Luis, 7709

Penick, James L., 0737

Penkower, Monty N., 5155, 9004, 9005, 9142, 9143, 9144, 9145, 9146

Penlower, Monty N., 0081

Penrod, John A., 3451

Penrod, Paul L., 8311

Peoples, Morgan D., 6657

Perdue, Charles L. Jr., 5264

Perett, Geoffery, 8085

Peretti, Burton W., 3560

Perez-Reilly, A. Mario, 7952

Perkins, Bradford, 8086

Perkins, Dexter, 0413, 7052, 7792, 9781

Perkins, Frances, 0414

Perkins, John H., 4968

Perkins, Van L., 2866, 2867

Perkinson, Henry J., 4386

Perling, Joseph J., 0096

Perlman, Daniel, 4553

Perlmutter, Oscar, 0776, 0777

Perloff, Harvey S., 7707

Perna, Francis M., 2868

Perry, Hamilton E., 7573

Perry, Thelma D., 4053

Persky, Marvin, 2463

Person, H. S., 2869

Pescatello, Paul R., 6658

Peselj, Branko M., 7408

Pessen, Edward, 0415, 1702, 3561

Peters, C. Brooks, 4054, 7874

Peters, Ronald J., and Jeanne M. McCarrick, 2336

Peterson, Anne E., 3690

Peterson, Barbara B., 4969

Peterson, Bernard L., Jr., 3817

Peterson, Edward N., 7306

Peterson, Gale E., 4970

Peterson, Hans J., 8714, 9573

Peterson, John M., 2600

Peterson, Joyce S., 2337

Peterson, Leland D., 3601

Peterson, Merrill D., 9782

Peterson, Patti M., 6308, 8039

Peterson, Sally, 5265

Peterson, Susan, 4253

Peterson, Tarla Rai, 1298

Peterson, Theodore, 4055

Peterson, Trudy H., 5208

Peterson, Wilbur, 4056

Petersons, Stow, 4800

Petillo, Carol M., 0940, 0941, 0942

Petrov, Vladimir, 0864

Pettit, William, 7040

Petty, Anne W., 4387

Pew, Thomas W., Jr., 1866

Peyser, Joan, 3246

Peyton, Rupert, 1182

Pfaff, Daniel W., 4057, 4058

Pfau, Richard A., 8874, 8979

Pfiffner, James P., 0529

Pfitzer, Gregory M., 9783

Pfleger, James R., 1770

Pflug, Warner W., 2464

Phelan, Craig L., 2429

Phelps, Bernard F., 0169

Phelps, Marianne R., 4388

Philp, Kenneth R., 5881, 5882, 5883, 5884, 5885

Philipose, Thomas, 6093

Phillips, Bill, 3562

Phillips, Cabell, 1572

Phillips, Cable, 4254

Phillips, Hugh D., 7446, 8875

Phillips, Norma K., 4661

Phillips, Waite, and Clifford E. Trafzer, 7145

Phillips, William H., 2601, 2602, 3452, 3423

Pickens, Donald K., 4229

Pickens, William H., 6659, 6660

Picket, William B., 6661

Pickler, Gordon K., 8914

Picklesmier, Dorman, Jr., 1044

Piehl, Mel 4554

Pierce, Robert C., 6174

Pietrusza, David A., 7146

Pifer, Richard L., 8312

Pika, Joseph A., 0337, 0378

Pike, Frederick B., 7647

Pilat, Oliver, 4059

Pilcher, George W., 0446

Pill, Michael, 2870

Pilot, Drew, 4060

Pilschke, Elmer, 0447

Pinckney, Orde S., 0987

Pinkerton, Jan, 3454

Pinkett, Harold T., 1500, 9674, 9675, 9676

Pinnington, Paul J., 0168

Pinsker, Sanford, 3455

Pinsky, Edward D., 5785, 9147

Pinto, Alfonso, 3818

Pious, Richard M., 0416

Pirjevec, Joze, 8817

Pirsein, Robert W., 9392

Pisana, Dominick A., 8434

Pitt, Carl A., 0771

Pitterman, Marvin, 5786

Pittman, Dan W., 3003

Pittman, Von V., Jr., 1018

Pittman, Walter E., 6175

Pitts, Ethel L., 5514

Pitz, Arthur H., 8708

Pivar, David J., 6662

Plambeck, Herb, 6776

Platt, Rorin M., 6663

Pleasants, Julian M., 1196, 6664

Plesur, Milton, 6783, 9006

Plotke, David C., 2871, 6094

Plotkins, Marilyn J., 3247

Plumb, Milton M., 9677

Plummer, Brenda G., 5515, 7685

Pluth, Edward J., 8469, 8470

Pogue, Forrest C., 0489, 0916, 0917, 0949, 0950, 9393, 9394

Pohl, Frederik, 3456

Pohl, James W., 4614

Pois, Anne M., 5597, 6842

Polenberg, Richard, 0417, 0418, 0530, 0554, 0555, 2872, 6665, 6883, 7147, 8087, 8167
Polisky, Jerome, and Frances R. Wolpaw, 9007
Pollack, Norman, 9784
Pollak, Oliver B., 5787
Pollard, Clarice F., 8313
Pollard, Darrell, 1771
Pollard, James E., 0463
Pollock, Bradley H., 5516
Pollock, Fred E., 7794
Pommer, Richard, 1811, 5091
Pomper, Gerald, 6095
Pond, M. Allen, 4230
Ponko, Vincent Jr., 9395
Pope, Robert D., 1192, 1193
Poppendieck, Janet, 1371
Porter, David L., 0531, 0532, 1002, 1059, 1152, 1246, 1855, 7861, 7862, 7953, 8314
Porter, Laura S., 4389
Posner, Russell N., 6666, 6761
Potenziani, David, 1205
Potter, Barrett G., 3004, 3005, 3006, 3007
Potter, E. B., 0977
Potter, Richard H., 4555
Potts, Margaret H., 7034
Pound, Ezra, 3457, 3912
Powaski, Ronald, 4971
Powell, Charles S., 1703
Powell, Daniel A., 2338
Powell, David O., 6843, 6844, 6845
Powell, Lawrence C., 1704
Powers, Jimmy, 4615
Powers, Richard G., 3819, 6888, 6895, 6896
Pozzetta, George E., and Harry A. Kersey Jr., 8395
Prados, John, 9396
Prago, Albert, 6846
Prange, Gordon W., 7574, 7575
Pratt, Carol I., 3913
Pratt, Julius W., 0840, 0841, 9208
Pratt, William C., 1552, 6309, 6310, 6667, 6847
Presley, Delma E., 3458
Presley, James, 3459
Pressman, Jack D., 4231
Preston, C. Thomas, Jr., 0338
Preston, Edmund R., 9511
Preston, William Jr., 8088, 9785
Price, Allen, 3460
Price, Charles M., and Joseph Boskin, 0533
Price, Clement A., 5517, 5518
Price, Don K., 8578
Price, John A., 3820
Price, Joseph L., 4556
Price, Michael E., 4390
Prickett, James R., 2339, 2340, 2465, 6311
Priebe, Paul M., and Michael W. Rubinoff, 4391

Prince, Gregory S. Jr., 7466
Prince, Jack E., 6668
Prindle, David F., 1772, 6669
Pringle, Robert W., 6312
Prior, Leon O., 9397
Pritchard, Robert L., 6670
Pritchett, C. Herman, 3123, 6934, 6935, 6936
Pritchett, Merrill R., and William L. Shea, 8472, 8471, 8473
Privratsky, Kenneth L., 9398
Propas, Frederick L., 7447, 7448
Prothro, James W., 7148
Prude, Jonathan, 6127
Prudy, Roger W., 7576
Pruitt, Mary C., 5998
Puckett, Patty L., 0663
Pulda, Arnold H., 4061
Pulley, Raymond H., 7676
Pundeff, Martin, 8760
Purcell, Edward A. Jr., 4801, 6096
Purdy, Virginia C., 1299, 9678
Pursell, Carroll W. Jr., 0556, 4686, 4972, 4973, 4974, 4975, 4686
Puryear, Elmer L., 6671
Pusateri, C. Joseph, 0339
Pusey, Merlo J., 4062, 6937, 7053, 7060
Putnam, Carl M., 2873
Pyle, Norman R., 8537

Quadagno, Jill S., and Madonna H. Meyer, 4232
Quadagno, Jill S., 5092
Quam, Lois, and Peter J. Rachleff, 2341
Quantic, Diane C., 3461
Quantz, Richard, 4392
Queenan, Thomas J., 6672
Querry, Ronald B., 3821
Quick, Paddy, 8227
Quinn, Larry D., 4755, 6673
Quinn, R. Thomas, 6674
Quinten, B. T., 5886

Rabe, Stephen G., 7710, 9018
Rabel, Robert G., 8801, 9512
Rabinowitz, Paula, 5999, 6000
Rabinowitz, William Scott, 4616, 4617
Rabkin, Gerald E., 3248
Rable, George C., 4618, 5519
Radar, Frank J., 0696, 0697, 5209, 5210
Radford, Gail Eileen, 1812
Radosh, Ronald, 2738
Radrianarivony-Koziol, Liliane C., 3249
Rae, John B., 1867, 1868, 1894, 1895
Raether, Carl N., 8876
Ragg, Albrecht, 4169
Ragland, James F., 0340, 0464, 7383
Rahman, A. F. M., 8915

Railsback, Brian, 3462
Raimer, Edward A., 7981
Rainard, R. Lyn, 1637
Rainbolt, Rosemary, 6001, 8040
Raksin, David, 3822
Ralph, Joyce P., 0623
Ramset, Frederick Jr. and Chalres E. Smith, 3563
Ramsey, B. Caryle, 1211
Randall, Stephen J., 0644, 1896
Randall, Susan L., 6002
Randle, Mallory B., 5211
Randolph, Mary, 0082
Range, Willard, 0490, 7795
Raper, Arthur F., 5520
Rapf, Joanna, 3823
Rapport, Leonard, 5283, 9679
Raskin, Max, 1705
Raskin, Richard, 3824
Rasler, Karen, 8089
Rasmussen, Wayne D., and Gladys Baker, 2874
Rauch, Basil, 2739, 7796
Raucher, Alan R., 1869
Rausch, David A., 9148
Rawick, George P., 6313, 6314
Rawls, Shirley N., 0784
Rawsome, Frank Jr., 4255
Ray, Deborah W., 7797, 7798
Ray, J. M., and F. G. Gosling, 4233
Ray, Joseph M., 3124
Ray, Robert F., 6810
Raylance, Daniel, 1014
Raymond, C. Elizabeth, 6675
Raymond, Raymond J., 8761, 8780
Raymond, Raymond J., and Garry J. Clifford, 8779
Raymond, Richard D., 5521
Reading, Don C., 2022, 2740
Reagon, Bernice, 5522, 5523
Rebhorn, Marlette, 9209
Reccow, Louis, 2342
Recken, Stephen L., 4063
Record, Wilson C., 5524, 5525, 5526
Reddick, David B., 3825
Redmond, Kent C., 4976
Redmond, Kent G., 0885
Redmond, Mary S., 6676
Reed, Christopher R., 5527, 5528, 5664
Reed, John J., 8669
Reed, John S., 5529
Reed, Linda, 0557
Reed, Merl E., 0645, 4234, 5530, 5531, 5532
Reed, Richard W., 1870
Reed, Thomas V., 6176
Reeder, Rudolph R., 7655
Rees, Maureen, 6003
Reese, John R., 9399

Reese, Trevor R., 8670
Reeves, Mary G., 4393
Reeves, William D., 0419
Regensburger, William E., 2343
Regnery, Henry, 3463, 9786
Rehnquist, William H., 6938
Reich, Murray H., 4394
Reichardt, Otto H., 1897, 1898
Reid, Herbert G., 1183
Reid, Jack J., 4064
Reid, Robert L., eds., 5212
Reiff, Robert F., 3691
Reilly, Michael F., 0341
Reiman, Richard A., 2875, 5266
Reimer, Milton K., 1222
Reingold, Nathan, 9574
Reinhardt, Richard, 6677
Reinsch, J. Leonard, 6740
Reisler, Mark, 4170, 5705
Reiten, Sister Paula, 5093
Reiter, Howard L., 6097
Reitzes, Lisa B., 2741
Reitzes, Robert S., 7449
Remak, Joachim, 7307, 7308, 7309
Remele, Larry, 1553
Remley, David A., 8249
Renaghan, Thomas M., 2004, 2023
Renfro, Robert B., 3464
Rennick, Robert M., 4687
Renov, Michael, 3826
Renshaw, Edward F., 4395
Renstrom, Peter G., 6939
Repko, Allen F., 7310, 7311
"Report to F. D. R.", 4433
Resis, Albert, 9513
Ress, George, 0203
Reszin, M., 6884
Reuss, Richard A., 3564, 3565
Reuter, Paul H., Jr., 0877
Reutter, Mark, 2603
Revold, Daryl L., 7982
Reynolds, Charles V. Jr., 4977
Reynolds, Clark G., 0973, 4978, 9400
Reynolds, David, 7329, 7799, 7800, 9514
Reynolds, Douglas, 2344
Reynolds, Morgan O., 2345
Reynolds, Richard C., 3250
Rezler, Julius, 2346
Rhee, Tong-Chin, 8916
Rhoades, William B., 3150, 3151, 3178, 3179
Rhoads, Esther A., 8396
Rhodes, Benjamin D., 6777, 7223, 7224, 7225, 7330, 7801,
    7863, 8709
Rhodes, Dennis H., 1198
Ribuffo, Leo P., 4557, 6128

Riccards, Michael P., 9200
Ricciotti, Dominic, 3180, 3181
Rice, Charles Owne, 6315
Rice, Grantland, 4619
Rice, Howard C., Jr., 3465
Richards, Johnetta G., 5533
Richards, Pamela S., 8538, 8539, 9401
Richards, Paul D., 2347
Richards, Raymond K., 4235
Richardson, Elmo R., 1502, 1503, 2742, 5213, 5214, 6678
Richardson, James, and George C. Dyer, 7577
Richardson, Truman, 1100
Richberg, Donald R., 0754, 2876
Richey, Susan, 8041
Richey, Suzanne, 9402
Richman, John 7450
Richman, Sheldon, 7149
Richmond, Al, 1504
Richstad, Jim A., 8090
Richter, Anton H., 8474
Riddick, F. M., 0534
Riddle, Donald H., 6098
Rider, Mary M., 8540
Rider, Robin E., 9149
Ridge, Patricia L., 3251
Riebsame, William E., 1300
Riefler, Winfield W., 8168
Riesch-Owen, A. L., 1505
Rifkind, Bernard D., 8710
Riggio, Thomas P., 3466
Righter, Robert W., 1506, 1739
Riley, Glenda, and Richard S. Kirkendall, 0584
Riney-Kehrberg, Pamela, 1301
Ring, Daniel F., 3073, 5215, 5267
Ring, Jeremiah J., 9057
Rippa, Alexander S., 4396, 4397, 4398, 7150
Rise, Eric W., 4399
Rison, David E., 1573, 5216
Risse, Guenter B., 4400
Rist, Peter H., 3827
Riste, Olav, 7802
Ritchie, Donald A., 0535, 0745, 2604
Roach, Fred, Jr., 1899
Roach, Leigh Anne, 1813
Roach, S. Fred, 4979
Robb, Dennis M., 4558
Robbins, Peggy, 3467
Robbins, William A., 3125
Robbins, William G., 2605, 2606, 8169
Robert, Garyn G., 4065
Roberts, Nancy L., 4066
Roberts, Sally R., 4401
Robertson, Charles L., 0842
Robertson, Walter R., 8818
Robinson, Arthur H., 9403

Robinson, Donald W., 4402
Robinson, E. E., 0420
Robinson, George L., Jr., 1554
Robinson, George W., 1120, 2607
Robinson, James E., 4067
Robinson, Jo Ann O., 4559, 8042, 2454
Robinson, John L., 1574
Robinson, Paul, 4403
Rocha, Guy L., 2348
Roche, George C., 8917
Rock, Virginia J., 6129
Rockaway, Robert A., 4733
Rockoff, Hugh, 8170, 8315
Rodabaugh, Karl, 1212
Rodnitzski, Jerome L., 3566
Rodriguez, Louis J., 3074, 7384
Roebling, Karl, 7226
Roedding, Robert H., 1501
Rogers, Agnes, and Frederick L. Allen, 4688
Rogers, Ben F., 8171
Rogers, Benjamin F., 1931, 5534
Rogers, David, 3468
Rogers, Jane, 5217, 5218
Rogers, Joe D., 8475
Rogers, Nathan, 0204
Rogers, Raymond S., and Phillip Lujan, 5887
Rohfeld, Rae W., 4404
Rohr, Mary A., 7660
Rohwer, Jurgen, 9404
Roland, Carol, 4068
Rollins, Alfred B., 0250, 0251, 0252, 0743, 7151
Rollins, Peter C., 3714, 3828, 3829, 3831, 4069
Rollins, Peter C., and Harris J. Elder, 3830
Romano, Michael J., 0565
Romanus, Charles, and Riley Sunderland, 8918, 8919, 8920
Romasco, Albert U., 2743, 7152
Romeo, Mary Ellen, 2877
Romero, Patricia W., 5535, 5536
Romine, Ronald H., 6940
Rominger, Donald W. Jr., 4620
Rony, Vera, 5537
Roorda, Eric P., 7677
Roosa, Wayne L., 3692
Roosevelt, Eleanor, 0083, 0084, 0085, 0086
Roosevelt, Elliot and Joseph P. Lash, 9680
Roosevelt, Elliott, 0097, 0124
Roosevelt, Elliott, and J. Brought, 0123
Roosevelt, Franklin D., 0170, 0171, 0465, 0760, 7803, 9834, 9835
Roosevelt, James, 0507
Roosevelt, James, and Bill Libby, 0125
Roosevelt, James, and S. Shallet, 0126
Roosevelt Library, 9826
Roosevelt, Sara Delano, 0253
Root, Waverly L., 7227

Ropp, Theodore, 9405
Rosales, Francisco A., and Daniel T. Simon, 5706, 5707
Rosar, William H., 3832
Rose, Barbara, 3693, 5094
Rose, Ernest D., 7578
Rose, Gerald A., 2349, 2350
Rose, Mark H., 1871
Rose, Nancy E., 2878, 2879, 4236
Roseboom, Eugene H., and Alfred E. Eckes Jr., 6741
Rosembaum, Karen J., 2880
Rosen, Elliot A., 0342, 6763, 9787, 6762, 4980
Rosen, Harvey M., 6316
Rosen, Philip T., 3914
Rosenbaum, Herbert, and Elizabeth Bartlme, 9836
Rosenberg, Joseph L., 7335
Rosenberg, Bernard, 6317
Rosenberg, Edwin A., 6795
Rosenberg, J. Mitchell, 6941
Rosenberg, Roger E., 6318
Rosenberg-Naparsteck, Ruth, 4662
Rosenfield, Alvin H., 9150
Rosengarten, Adolph G. Jr., 9406
Rosengarten, Theodore, 4621
Rosenman, Samuel I., 0343
Rosenman, Samuel I., And Dorothy Rosenman, 0421
Rosenof, Theodore, 0585, 1255, 2005, 2744, 6319, 6889, 9788
Rosenstone, Robert A., 4070, 7385, 7386, 7387
Rosenthal, Jakob, 8877
Rosenthal, Macha L., 6320
Rosentreter, Roger L., 3008
Rosenzweig, Roy, 2479, 2480, 3833
Rosner, David, and Gerald Markowitz, 2745, 2746
Ross, David R., 2083
Ross, Davis, 9575
Ross, Earle D., 1555
Ross, Hugh, 0772, 2447, 6796
Ross, Irwin, 4734
Ross, Red, 7347
Ross, Rodney A., 5538, 5539
Ross, Ronald P., 5095, 5156
Ross, Theophil W. Jr., 5157
Ross, Thomas W., 2881
Rossi, John P., 3834, 6679
Rossiter, Clinton L., 0344, 0345, 0448
Rostagno, Irene, 3469
Rostow, Eugene V., 8397
Roswell, Mary M., 3252
Rotblat, Joseph, 9407
Rotge, Larry R., 8633
Rothberg, Abraham, 6321
Rothchild, Donald S., 0263
Rothfels, Hans, 7312
Rothman, Hal K., 2747
Rothrock, Thomas, 1395
Rothstein, Arthur, 4689

Rothstein, Joan L., 4690
Rothwell, C. L., 0205
Rotunda, R. D., 0346
Rouse, David S., 3009
Rout, Leslie B., Jr., 3567, 9037
Rovin, Fern R., 6811
Rowe, Marjorie Anne, 7263
Rowen, Milton, 4981
Rowland, Benjamin M., 1965, 7331, 8762, 8763
Rowland, Diane B., 6004
Rowley, William D., 1567, 2748, 6322
Rozakis, Laurie E., 4071
Rubenstein, Harry R., 2351
Rubin, Barry M., 4405, 8973
Rubin, Joan S., 4802
Rubinstein, Annette T., 3253
Ruby, Christine N., 5219, 5220
Ruchames, Louis, 6099
Ruck, Robert L., 4622
Rucker, Randal R., and Lee J. Alston, 2882
Ruddy, Thomas M., 0779
Rudgers, David F., 9029
Rudolph, Frederick, 7153
Rudwick, Elliott M., 5540
Ruetten, Richard T., 1066, 4072, 6680, 9789
Rugh, Susan Sessions, 4691
Ruiz, Vicki L., 2352, 5708
Ruland, Richard, 3254
Rumbarger, John J., 8091
Runde, William H., 9576
Rundell, Walter A. Jr., 3470, 4663, 8316, 9408, 9409, 9853
Rupp, Leila J., 8228
Rusco, Elmer R., 5888
Rushing, Conrad L, 4735
Ruskaup, Calvin F., 3915
Rusnak, Andrew J., 4779
Russell, Andrew, 5726
Russell, Mary A., 3471
Russell, Michael B., 7467
Russell, R. R., 8317
Russett, Bruce M., 8172
Rutman, Herbert S., 5788
Ryan, Carl G., 2608, 2609
Ryan, Fortune, and Penelope Dixon, 2883
Ryan, Halford R., 0172, 0173
Ryan, Hartford K., 0347
Ryan, James G., 6323
Ryan, John P., 8980
Ryan, Nancy M., 3472
Ryan, Paul B., 0951
Ryan, Paul B., and Thomas A. Bailey, 7313
Ryant, Carl G., 4073, 4074
Rydell, Robert W., 4982
Rye, Jack, 3916
Rylance, Daniel U., 1045

Rymer, Jeanne S., 3010
Rynder, Constance B., 6005

Saalberg, John J., 0422
Sadeghi, Khosrow, 8634
Sadkin, David, 3255
Sadler, Charles G. , 6848, 7804, 9515, 9577
Sadler, Christine, 0098
Sagan, Scott D., 7579
Sage, Leland L., 1321
Sageser, A. Bower, 1900
Saindon, Bob, and Bunky Sullivan, 1507
Saint-Etienne, Christian, 1575
Salamon, Lester M., 2749
Salapatas, John S., 7228
Salawak, Dale, 4132
Salisburg, Dorothy C., 0348
Sallach, David L., 2353
Salmond, John A., 0722, 0723, 0721, 2354, 2452, 2884, 2885, 5268
Salo, Mauno, 1901, 1902
Saloutos, Theodore, 1372, 1373, 2750, 2886, 2887, 2888, 7154, 7155
Salstrom, Paul, 3011, 3126
Salter, John R., Jr., 2355
Saltmarsh, John A., 6324
Saltvig, Robert, 4736
Salvaneschi, Lenore, 1740
Salyers, James Ernest, 6681
Salzman, Jack, 3473, 4075
Samosky, Jack A., 1232, 1233
Samponaro, Frank N., 9019
Sanchez, Jose M., 4406
Sandeen, Eric J., 1814, 3835
Sanders, Lynn M., 5541
Sandler, Mark, 4407
Sandweiss, Martha A., 3694
Sanford, Dudley Gregory, 6682
Sanford, Fillmore H., 0423
Sannes, Earling N., 2356, 2357, 2358
Sansom, Sir George, 7580
Sanson, Jerry P., 6683, 6684, 6685, 6686, 7875, 7876
Santoro, Carmela E., 9058
Santos, Michael W., 2610
Sapp, Steven P., 8711
Sapper, Neil G., 5542, 5543
Sapphire, William, 1932
Sargent, James E., 0424, 0675, 0709, 1107, 1108, 2006, 9854
Sargent, John A., 3836
Sargent, Raymond M., 3474
Sargent, Shirley, 1706
Sarvetnick, Lois, 4408
Sasso, Claude R., 7581
Sathre, Eugene R., 7582
Sato, Susie, 5727

Saturday Evening Post, 0032
Saunders, Doris E., 6812
Saunders, James R., 3475
Saunderson, Mont H., 0773
Savage, Hugh J., 6100
Savage, Sean J., 0425
Savory, Douglas, 7336, 8781
Sawada, Mitziko, 8398
Sawak, Dale, 9618
Sawrey, Robert D., 8318
Sayen, Jamie, 4983
Sayler, James A., 4076
Sayles, Stephen, 0998
Sayre, J. L., 1046
Sbrega, John J., 7332, 8764, 8765, 8766, 8878, 9578, 9579
Scales, Junius I. And Richard Nickson, 5544
Scalia, Antonin, 6942
Scanlan, Alfred L., 6943
Scarpio, Philip V., 1508
Schacht, John N., 2359, 2360, 6687, 6688, 6689
Schaffel, Kenneth, 9410
Schaffer, Alan, 1230
Schaffer, Daniel, 2889, 3127, 3128, 4664
Schaffer, Ronald, 1240, 7954, 9411
Schaller, Michael R., 0927, 4737, 8921, 8922, 9412, 9413
Schap, David J., 1741
Schapsmeier, Edward L., 0586, 0592, 4078
Schapsmeier, Edward L. and Frederick H. Schapsmeier, 0587, 0588, 0589, 0590, 0591, 1248, 1258, 1374, 1375, 4077
Scharf, Lois, 0087, 6006
Schatz, Arthur W., 0843, 0844, 1846
Schatz, Ronald W., 2361, 2362, 2363
Schauble, Jeanne, 0349
Scheiber, Harry N., and Jane L. Scheiber, 8399
Scheiner, Georganne J., 3837
Schell, Ernest H., 4984
Scherwood, Robert E., 0698
Schick, Sandor E., 1815
Schiesl, Martin, 8173
Schiffman, Joseph, 0174, 8435
Schifter, Jacobo, 9048, 9516
Schimdt, Kimberly, 6007
Schimmel, Barbara B., 7047
Schisgall, Jane, 8436
Schlatter, Richard, 6325
Schlauch, Wolfgang, 9580
Schlebecker, John T., 1509, 1872
Schlenker, Gerald, 8400
Schlesinger, Arthur M., Jr., 0239, 0426, 0427, 1576, 1577, 2751, 6967, 7805
Schlundt, Chritena L., 3152
Schmaltz, Norma J., 1510
Schmelzer, Janet L., 1087
Schmidt, Earl R., 7473
Schmidt, Hans, 0966

Schmidt, Jacqueline S., 7955
Schmidt, Louis B., 6849
Schmidt, Sanford M., 3838
Schmidt, William T., 1707, 8092, 8174
Schmidtlein, Eugene F., 0611, 0612, 0613
Schmitt, Robert C., 2481
Schmitz, David F., 7348, 7349
Schmitz, Mark, and Price V. Fishback, 2024
Schnapper, M. B., 6101
Schneider, Charles F., 7583
Schneider, James C., 7877, 7878, 7956
Schneiderman, Howard G., 0449
Schnell, J. Christopher, 0380, 6764
Schnell, James C., 7156
Schnell, Rodolph L., 6326
Schnorf, Richard A., 7229
Schoenberg, Loren, 3568
Schoenberger, Walter S., 9414
Schoenherr, Steven E., 0733
Schofield, Ann, 6008
Scholnick, Myron I., 5789
Schonback, Morris, 6393
Schott, Charles J., 4409
Schott, Linda K., 8043
Schott, Matthew J., 1184, 8476
Schottenhamel, George C., 1773
Schrader, Robert F., 5096, 5889
Schramm, Leroy H., 2364
Schrems, Suzanne H., 5221, 6327
Schrenders, Piet, 3476
Schriftgiesser, Karl, 0127
Schriver, Joe M., 4665
Schrivner, John H., 4985
Schrode, George, 2365
Schroder, Hans-Jurgen, 7314
Schroeder, Fred H., 3917
Schroeder, Paul W., 7584
Schruben, Francis W., 6690
Schubart, Richard D., 7157
Schuller, Linda A., 8229
Schulman, Bruce J., 1943
Schulman, Judy P., 8319
Schulte, Steven C., 5890
Schultz, Dagmer, 2366
Schuman, Frederick L., 7230
Schumpeter, Joseph A., 1638
Schuster, Ruth, 9151
Schuyler, Michael W., 0593, 2752, 2890, 3012, 3013
Schwantes, Carlos A., 1923, 2367, 8175
Schwar, Jane D., 7983
Schwark, Stephen J., 9581
Schwarts, Harvey, 2368
Schwartz, Andrew J., 8879
Schwartz, Betty, 0508
Schwartz, Bonnie F., 2891, 2892, 3014

Schwartz, Gerald, 4692
Schwartz, Harvey, 2421
Schwartz, Joel, 1816, 1817
Schwartz, Jordan A., 0566, 0725, 0730, 0761
Schwartz, Lawrence H., 6328
Schwartz, Nancy L., 3839
Schweber, S.S., 4986
Schwedes, Jeffrey T., 9201
Schweigert, Harold F., 8401
Schweik, Susan M., 8230, 8231
Schweitzer, Mary M., 8232
Schwieder, Dorothy, 3075, 6010
Schwieder, Dorothy, and Deborah Fink, 6009
Scigliano, Robert G., 6691
Scime, Joy A., 6011
Scobie, Ingrid W., 6130, 6692, 6693
Scott, Andrew M., 6102
Scott, Anne Firor, 8233
Scott, Carole E., 2753
Scott, George W., 6694, 6695
Scott, Hugh A., 4079
Scott, Kesho Y., 5545
Scott, Robert L., 3695
Scott, William R., 5546, 7244, 7245, 7246
Scriabine, Christine B., 2482, 6329
Scrivner, John H., 4987
Scrovonick, Nathan B., 3918
Scruggs, Charles, 5547
Scruggs, Otey M., 4171, 4172, 4173, 4174, 4175
Sculle, Keith A., 3182
Scweikart, Larry, 2611
Seabrook, John H., 5548
Seabury, Paul, 7957
Sealander, Judith A., 6012, 6013
Sear, Mary., 4176
Sears, James M., 5665
Sears, Louis M., 9790
Sears, Paul B., 1302
Sears, Stephen W., 2369
Seastone, Don A., 2612
Seaton, Douglas P., 2370, 4560
Seawright, Sally, 5643
Seeber, Frances M., 0088, 9839
Segal, Elizabeth A., 4237
Segal, Errol, 6330
Segal, Howard P., 2613
Segur, W. H., and Varden Fuller, 3015
Sehlinger, Peter J., and Sabine Jessnet, 0782
Seidler, Murray B., 6331, 6332, 6333
Seidman, Joel, 2427, 6334
Seigel, Fred, 4238
Seiler, John, 0865
Selby, John G., 2371
Selby, Robert H., 9220
Seligman, G. L., and E. E. Cornwell, 0558

Seligmann, G. L., 6696
Selvin, David F., 2372
Senese, Guy B., 5891
Seretan, L. Glen, 4738
Service, John S., 8923, 8924
Sessions, Gene A., 6131
Sessions, William L., 2614
Sethachuay, Vivat, 8966
Severeson, Robert F., Jr., 2893
Severin, Werner J., 5097
Severo, Richard, and Lewis Milford, 9582
Sewall, Arthur F., 1060, 1061
Seward, Adrieene L., 5549
Sewell, J. Richard, 1933
Sexton, Brendan, 2448
Sexton, Robert F., 6697
Seybold, George H., 0350
Sgan-Cohen, Michael S., 3183
Shaber, Sarah R., 7388
"Shadows of an Era: The FSA Collection of Virginia Photographs.", 5165
Shaffer, Robert, 6335
Shafir, Shlomo, 9152, 9153, 9154, 9155, 9156, 9157
Shain, Russell E., 3840
Shale, Richard A., 3841
Shankman, Arnold, 5550, 6014, 6336
Shanks, Alexander C., 1101, 1102
Shanks, Alexander Graham, 6765
Shanley, Kevin M., 7984
Shanley, Robert A., 4239
Shannon, David A., 6337
Shannon, William V., 4780
Shao, Otis H., 7585
Shapiro, Edward S., 3129, 3130, 4080, 4561, 4562, 4623, 5790, 5791, 6132, 7158
Shapiro, William, 2373
Shappee, Nathan D., 4739
Sharon, John H., 0175
Sharp, Ansel M., 2007
Sharp, Edward F., 9791
Sharp, Tony, 9583
Shaw, Chonghal P., 8925
Shaw, Malcolm, 0351
Shea, William L., 8478
Shea, William L., and Pritchett, Merrill R., 8477
Sheehy, Donald G., 3502
Sheffer, Martin S., 0509, 7044
Shelley, Fred, 9681
Shelley, Mack C., 6133
Shenker, Israel, 6780
Shenton, James P., 7159, 7160
Shepard, David H., 9584
Shepardson, D. E., 4081
Shephard, John E. Jr., 8926
Sherer, Michael D., 8541

Sheridan, Richard B., 4410
Sheridan, Richard C., 1284
Sherman, Jacqueline G., 2660
Sherr, Paul C., 3256, 9619
Sherraden, Michael W., 2894
Sherrill, Robert, 3131
Sherry, Michael S., 4988, 9517, 9585
Sherwin, Mark, and Charles L. Markmann, 7315
Sherwin, Martin J. Jr., 0491, 9415, 9518, 9519, 9520
Sherwood, Foster H., 6944
Sherwood, Leland H., 5222
Shewmaker, Kenneth E., 8927, 9416
Shi, David E., 9792
Shiner, John F., 1903, 2374, 4989, 4990
Shinn, Paul L., 1708
Shipman, Fred, 9837
Shirley, Susan, 4693
Shivanna, K.S., 7472
Shively, W. Phillips, 6103
Shloss, Carol, 3696
Shmueli, Efriam, 5792
Shockley, Dennis M., 1022
Shoemaker, Nancy, 5892
Shofner, Jerrell H., 1396, 3016, 5551
Shor, Francis, 4666
Shore, Paul J., 4411
Short, John D., Jr., 3477
Short, K. R. M., 8542, 8543, 9682
Shortal, John F., 9417
Shoup, Laurence H., 9586
Shouse, Sarah N., 4803
Shout, John D., 3842
Shover, John L., 1376, 1556, 1557, 1639, 1709, 2754, 4781, 6338, 6698
Shover, John L., and Michael P. Rogin, 6699
Showan, Daniel P., 7161
Shuff, Stephen M., 6104
Shughart, William F., II, 2755
Shulimson, Jack, 8093
Shull, Paul, 2615
Shulman, Holly C., 8544, 8545
Shulman, Jeffrey, 7389
Shuman, R. Baird, 3257, 8044
Sicius, Francis J., 4563
Sievers, Harry J., 0352
Sigal, Leon V., 9418
Silver, Paul L., 6134
Silverman, Sheldon A., 1275
Silverstein, Mark., 7021
Simmons, Dennis E., 4667
Simon, Carol J., 2616
Simon, James F., 7004
Simon, Paul L., 0719
Simon, Rita J., 6105
Simpson, B. Mitchell III, 0980

Sims, Robert C., 6700
Sinclair, Andrew, 4756
Sinclair, Karen K., 8045
Sindell, Gail A., 6394
Singer, David F., 9158
Singer, Stanford P., 3258
Singleton, Jeffrey C., 2483
Sinks, George W., 9587
Sinnett, Ronald F., 0176
Sipe, Daniel A., 2895
Sirgiovannia, George, 6135
Sirvag, Torbjrn, 0594
Sisay, Hassan B., 7249
Sitkoff, Howard, 5098, 5552, 5553, 5627
Sitton, Thomas J., 6701
Skates, John R., 4082
Skinner, Byron R., 5554
Skocpol, Theda, and Kenneth Finegold, 2896
Skold, Karen B., 8234
Slack, Walter H., 2466
Slate, Daniel M., 1285
Sloan, Alfred P., Jr., 2617, 2618
Sloan, Charles W. Jr., 8094
Small, Melvin, 7231
Smallwood, Johnny B., 1035
Smiley, David L., 2897
Smith, A. Meriman, 0510
Smith, Alonzo N., 5555
Smith, C. Calvin, 8320
Smith, Charles P., 1130
Smith, Charles W., Jr., 0353
Smith, Charlie C., 6702
Smith, Clyde Jr., 9044
Smith, Cynthia Z., 4083
Smith, Daniel B., 1847
Smith, Douglas L, 5269, 5284
Smith, Elaine M., 2756
Smith, Gaddis, 7848, 8579
Smith, Gary L., 2375
Smith, Gene, 7162
Smith, Geoffrey S., 6402
Smith, Gibson B., 0735
Smith, Gilbert E., III, 4413
Smith, Glenn H., 1257, 7958
Smith, Harold P., 3017
Smith, Ivan E. Jr., 9793
Smith, Jesse R. Jr., 9460
Smith, John K., 2619
Smith, Mark C., 4412
Smith, Melden E., 9419
Smith, Merriman, 0354
Smith, Myron J. Jr., 9630
Smith, Perry M., 9588
Smith, Richard H., 7163, 9420
Smith, Richard N., 6813

Smith, Robert F., 7232
Smith, Robert J., 8635
Smith, Robert M., 2620
Smith, Robert R., 3919
Smith, Robert T., 0928
Smith, Rodney D., 4084
Smith, T. V., 2757
Smith, Terence J., 2898
Smith, Thaddeus, M., 4782
Smith, Thomas G., 0676
Smith, Wilda M., 3018
Smulyan, Susan R., 3920
Smyrl, Frank H., 1144
Snell, John L., 8636, 8637, 8638
Sneller, Maurice P., Jr., 2098
Sniegoski, Stephen J., 7985
Snyder, Robert E., 6877
Snyder, Robert L., 5158
Soapes, Thomas F., 6703
Soebel, Robert, 8880
Sofchalk, Donald G., 2376
Soffar, Allan J., 1511
Sokoll, Carl A., 6395
Solomon, Eric, 4133
"Some Thoughts on Prisoners of War in Iowa, 1943–1946.", 8444
Somers, A. Norman, 2758
Sosna, Morton P., 6177
South Dakota History, 2914
South, Lawren, 0595
Southern Cotton Textile Workers, 2061
Sova, Harry W., 3921
Spangler, Earl, 0453
Sparagana, Eleanor A., 9421
Speierl, Charles F. Jr., 4414
Spencer, Thomas T., 6766, 6778
Spero, Herbert, 1924
Spicehandler, Daniel, 3478
Spiller, Robert, 3479
Spinelli, Lawrence, 4757
Spotswood, Roger D., 7586
Spragens, William C., 0450
Spritzer, Donald E., 1024
St. Armand, Barton L., 4085
St. Louis, Terence R., 9422
Staats, Gegory R., 3569
Stack, John F. Jr., 4783, 5793
Stackman, Ralph R., 8795, 0879
Staff, Michael B., 8767
Staff, Michael E., 1944
Stafford, William, 3480
Stahnke, Herbert, 8479
Standley, William H., 8881
Stanfield, John H., 5556
Stanley, Jerry, 4415

Stanley, Judith M., 0845
Starling, Edmond W., 0355
State, U.S. Department of, 0183
Stater, Mark C., 2899
Stathis, Stephen W., 8639
Staub, Michael E., 3481
Stave, Bruce M., 6704, 6705, 6767, 6768
Stedman, Murray S. Jr., and Susan W. Stedman, 6850
Steeholm, Clara, and Hardy Steeholm, 0128
Steel, Ronald, 0466
Steele, Anne L., 1512
Steele, Richard W., 0467, 3843, 4991, 7806, 7807, 8546, 8547, 9423, 9589
Steen, Harold K., 0356, 1513, 1514
Stefon, Frederick J., 5893, 5894
Stegh. Leslie J., 4758
Stegmaier, Harry I., 9059
Stegner, Wallace, 5794
Steigerwald, David, 6178, 7986
Stein, Anne, Mary Sonnenberg, Katherine Archibald, and Augusta Clawson, 8235
Stein, Bruno, 8321
Stein, C. W., 6797
Stein, Herbert, 2008, 2621
Stein, Jacob A., 3153
Stein, Judith, 6706, 6707
Stein, Pauline A., 5223
Stein, Shifra, and Bob Barrett, 3184
Stein, Walter J., 1303, 1397
Steindl, Frank G., 2009
Steiner, Frederick, 3570
Steiner, Michael C., 1710, 9794
Steiner, T. R., 3482
Steinitz, Hans J., 9159
Steinmeyer, George W., 9590
Stellhorn, Paul A., 6708
Stelzner, Herman, 0177
Stenehjem, Michele F., 7959
Stephanson, Anders, 6339
Stephenson, Frank W., 4564
Stephenson, William, 3844
Steppenoff, Bonnie, 3076
Sterling, Keir B., 0567
Stern, Guy, 9067, 9160
Stern, Harold L., 8095
Stern, Robert H., 3922
Stern, Siegfried, 1966
Sternberg, Joel, 3923
Sternsher, Bernard, 0451, 0622, 0716, 1711, 2377, 2759, 6769, 6779, 7808, 9795, ed., 5557
Stetson, Dorothy M., 6015
Stetson, Frederick W., 2900
Stettinius, Edward R. Jr., 0880, 7233, 8640
Stevens, Errol W., 5224
Stevens, John D., 3845, 4086, 8402

Stevens, Joseph E., 4992
Stevens, Kenneth R., 4740
Stevenson, Janet, 8046
Stevenson, Marshall F. Jr., 5558
Stevenson, W., 9424
Steward, Dick H., 1848, 7648
Stewart, Barbara M., 4177, 9161
Stewart, Garrett, 3846
Stewart, William J., 2084, 9620, 9827
Stewart, William J., and Charyl C. Pollard, 0206
Stickle, Warren E., 6340, 6709
Stielow, Frederick J., 0511
Stiles, Lela, 0744
Stiller, Jesse H., 0869
Stillwell, Paul, 7587
Stilwell, Joseph, 0958, 0959
Stimson, Henry L., and McGeorge Bundy, 0886
Stitt, Peter A., 3603
Stock, Catherine M., 1712
Stocker, Glenn M., 1223
Stocker, Joseph, 6710
Stoeckle, John D., and George A. White, 4240
Stoesen, Alexander R., 1194, 1195
Stoff, Michael B., 8176, 8991, 9591
Stokes, Thomas L., 2760
Stokesbury, James L., 9425
Stoler, Mark A., 8580, 8581, 8641, 9426, 9427, 9796
Stone, Albert E. Jr., 6396
Stone, Edward, 3847
Stone, Goldie, 8177
Stone, Kirk, 0089
Stone, Richard, 4624
Storer, Louise K., 8548
Storman, John A., 8047
Story, Kenneth, 3185
Story, Ralph D, 5559
Stott, William M., 3848
Stourzh, Gerald D., 9797
Stout, Joe A., Jr., 1515
Stovall, A. J., 5666
Strange, Joseph L., 8582
Strange, Maren, 5099
Strange, Meren E., 2761
Straub, Eleanor F., 8236, 8237, 8238
Strauss, David, 0357
Streater, John B., 5667
Street, Paul, 5560
Street, Richard S., 4087
Streeter, Jean D., 1904
Streit, Clarence, 7809
Streitmatter, Roger A., 0468
Stricker, Frank, 3849
Strickland, Aravarh E., 6711, 1398
Strickland, Julie Z., 2622
Striner, Richard A., 3697, 3850, 4993

Strom, Sharon H., 2378
Stromberg, Ronald N., 8057, 9592
Strong, Donald S., 5795
Strong Elizabeth, 4994
Strong, Kenneth, 9428
Strout, Cushing, 8058
Strum, Harvey, 5796, 9162
Stryker, Robin, 2901, 2902
Stuart, Graham H., 0870
Stuart, Paul, 5895
Stuhler, Barbara, 6814, 7864
Stuhr, Margaret D., 3483
Stump, Winifred B., 6712
Suber, Howard, 3851
Sudheendran, K., 4741
Suggs, George G., Jr., 2379
Suggs, John C., 3484
Suhl, Yuri, 9163
Sullivan, John A., 7810
Sullivan, John J., 3077
Sullivan, Kip, 1640, 4416
Sullivan, Lawrence, 1641
Sullivan, Martin E., 5270
Sullivan, Patricia A., 4668
Sumner, Scott, 2010
Sun, You-Li, 8928
Sundell, Michael G., 1818
Sunderland, Riley, 9219
Sundquist, Eric J., 8403
Sunness, Sheldon D., 6341
Sussman, Leila A., 0358, 0469, 6106, 9838
Sutro, Edmund, 4417
Sutton, Anthony C., 0428
Svobida, Lawrence, 1304
Swabeck, Arne, 6342
Swadesh, Frances L., 5709
Swadoz, Harvey, 3485
Swain, Bruce, 0596
Swain, Donald C., 0646, 1516, 1517
Swain, Martha H., 0536, 1153, 1154, 1155, 5159, 5160, 5225
Swanberg, W. A., 7468
Swansinger, A. Jacqueline, 8974
Swanson, Evadene B., 4784
Swanson, Harlan J., 7588
Swanson, Louis E., 1518
Swanson, Merwin R., 1642, 3019, 3132, 4241, 4418, 8178, 9855
Sward, Keith, 2623
Swartzlander, Larry R., 2624
Sweeney, Eugene T., 2380
Sweeney, Jerry K., 8786, 8787, 8788, 8789, 8790
Sweet, Dana R., 7656
Sweezy, Alan, 2044
Sweezy, Paul M., and Harry Magdoff, 6343
Sweezy, Paul M., Sungar Savran, and Ahmet E. Tonak, 6344

Swerczek, Ronald E., 0817
Swetnam, Ford, 4088
Swisher, C. B., 0625
Swisher, Perry, 8096, 1713
Sykes, Patricia L., 0429
Sykin, Marie, 9164
Sylvers, Malcolm, 6345
Synott, Marcia G., 1377, 4625
Syrett, David, 9798
Syrett, John, 0454, 6713, 6714, 6715
Syvertsen, Thomas H., 6716
Szajkowski, Zosa, 5797, 9165, 9166, 9167, 9168, 9169
Szasz, Margaret C., 5896, 5897, 5898
Szymczak, Robert, 9429

Tabari, Keyvan, 8981
Taber, Ronald W., 5226, 5227, 5285
Taft, Philip, 2381, 2382, 6346
Takezawa, Yasuko I., 8404
Talbert, Roy, Jr., 0710, 3133, 3134, 3135
Talley, Paul M., 3571
Tampa Bay History, 3607, 8061
Tamplin, John C., 4089
Tamura, Linda, 8405
Tannenbaum, Frank, 7234
Tanner, Doris B., 8239
Tansill, Charles C., 7811
Taplin, Iam M., 2383
Tarr, Curtis W., 9430
Tarr, Daniel L., 9461
Tarter, Brent, 6717
Tascher, John, 4995
Taschner, Mary, 8179
Tate, James P., 4996
Tate, Merze, 4997
Tate, Roger D., Jr., 3020, 3021
Tatum, Elbert L., 5668
Taylor, A. J. P., 7235
Taylor, Arthur R., 2625
Taylor, Eleanor K., 4419
Taylor, F. Jay, 7390
Taylor, Frances, 5561
Taylor, Graham D., 2762, 5899, 5900, 5901, 9020
Taylor, John C., 3078
Taylor, John M., 0178
Taylor, Joseph E. Sr., 5562
Taylor, Joshua C., 3698
Taylor, Leah M., 6107
Taylor, Myron C., 7812
Taylor, Paul F., 2384, 6878
Taylor, Paul S., 0747, 1399, 1400
Taylor, Philip B., 9021
Taylor, Quintard, 5563
Taylor, Sally, 4090
Taylor, Sandra C., 7589, 7590, 8406, 8407

Taylor, Thomas H., Jr., 3186
Tays, Dwight L., 0359
Tebbe, Jennifer, 3715
Tebbel, John, and Sara M. Watts, 0470
Tedesco, Marie, 2626
Tedlow, Richard S., 2627, 2628, 2629
Teichroew, Allan, 1401
Telotte, J. P., 3852
Temfer, Diane, 3699
Temin, Peter, and Barrie A., Wigmore, 2011
Temme, Walter F., 3572
TenBroek, Jacobus, Edward N. Barnhart, and Floyd W. Matson, 5728
Tenenbaum, Joseph, 6397, 9170
Tenenbaum, Shelly, 9171
Tenney, Craig D., 3924
Tentarelli, Ronda C., 3486, 4091
Terkel, Studs, 9856
Terrill, Tom E., and Jerrold Hirsch, 5286, 5287
Teti, Frank M., 0674
Thackrah, J. R., 9521
Thaddeus, Janice, 3487
Tharp, Mel, 4256
Thatcher, Mary A., 4178
Theobald, Robert A., 7591
Theoharis, Athan G., 1141, 6879, 6890, 8642, 8643, 9522, 9523
Theoharis, Athan G., and John S. Cos, 6897
Thies, Clifford F., 2630
Thomas, Donald W., 1905
Thomas, Dorothy S., and Richard Nishimoto, 8408
Thomas, Edmund B., Jr., 1643
Thomas, Edward J. F., 9593
Thomas, H. Glyn, 4420
Thomas, James W., 3488
Thomas, Joseph D., 5228
Thomas, Mary M., 8097, 8240, 8241, 8242
Thomas, Patricia, 8243
Thomas, Richard W., 5564
Thomas, William B., 4421, 4422, 5565
Thomison, Dennis, 0512
Thompsom, Dean K., 4565
Thompson, Dwayne T., 1934
Thompson, Ellen M., 8048
Thompson, Kenneth W., 7350, 7987
Thompson, William F., 4257
Thomson, James C. Jr., 7469
Thorne, Christopher, 8768, 8769, 8884
Thorne, Frederick C., 4423
Thornton, Harrison J., 0179
Thorp, Willard, 3489
Thorpe, James A., 8975, 8982
Thorson, Winston B., 7879, 7880
Thrasher, Sue, and Leah Wise, 1558
Thurber, James, 4092

Tidd, James F., Jr., 3079
Tietje, Louis H., 6347
Tifft, Thomas W., 4566
Tillapaugh, James C., 9022
Tillman, Rick, 2631
Tilman, Lee R., 7164
Tilman, Rick, 6179
Timberlake, Richard H., 2763
Timmons, Bascom N., 0568, 0705
Tindall, George B., 4669, 6867
Tingley, Ralph R., 0360
Tischauser. Leslie V., 4785
Tissing, Robert Warren, 8480
Titus, James E., 6180, 8098
Tobin, James E., 1945, 8549
Tobin, John, 2085
Tobin, Sidney, 4093
Toepfer, Marcia L., 7451, 7452, 9799
Toews, Paul, 4567
Toland, John, 7592, 7593
Toledano, Ralph de, 6898
Tomayko, James E., 4998
Tomita, Saku, 8409
Tomlins, Christopher L., 2086, 2385, 2386, 2764
Tompkins, C. David, 1276
Toner, James H., 0943
Tonilli, Edith A., 5229
Tontz, Robert L., 2765
Torigian, Michael, 2387
Torodash, Martin, 2766
Toulhouse, Mark G., 4568
Tourtellot, Arthur B., 0180
Towell, William P., 0819
Towey, Martin G., 1644
Towle, W. Wilder, 1559
Towne, Ralph L., 0181
Towns, Stuart, 1185
Townsend, Helen A.B., 5230
Toy, Eckard V., Jr., 2087
Tozer, Warren W., 8929
Trafzer, Clifford E., 4804
Trainer, Kathleen M., 3259
Trains, Richard P., 7391
Trani, Eugene P., 0647, 7054
Trask, David F., 9800
Trask, Robert R., 4742
Trask, Roger, 7402, 7403, 7404
Traylor, Jack W., 7165
Traynor, William L., 9431
Treadway, Sandra G., 6718
Trefousse, Hans L., 7316, 7317, 7594
Trennert, Robert A. Jr., 5902
Tresch, John W., 4424
Trescott, Paul B., 2632
Trey, Joan Ellen, 8244

Tribe, Ivan M., 3925

Trigg, Mary K., 6016

Trilling, Lionel, 3490

Trimble, Stanley W., 1519

Trimble, William F., 9432

Tritschler, Thomas C., 3700

Trolander, Judith A., 1645, 1714, 4694

Trombley, Kenneth E., 1742

Trommald, Elliott C., 2633

Trotter, Agnes A., 8059

Trotter, Ann, 7333

Trotter, Joe William, 5566

Trout, Charles H., 2767, 3080, 5271, 9801

Troy, Bill, and Claude Williams, 4569

Troy, Leo, 2388, 2389

Troy, Robert, 5567

Trubey, Lillian P., 6017

Truck, Isaiah, 5798

Tschirgi, Robert D., 9008

Tselos, George D., 2484, 6851, 6348

Tsou, T., 7470

Tsoumas, George J., 4570

Tuchman, Barbara W., 8930, 9228

Tucker, Albert B., 3853

Tucker, Kathryn, and Theodore L. Tucker, 4571

Tucker, Ray T., 0430

Tucker, Robert C., 9226

Tucker, Robert W., 0129

Tucker, S. W., 5568

Tucker, Susan, 9857

Tufte, Virginia J., 3604

Tugwell, Rexford G., 0017, 0018, 0019, 0264, 0270, 0361,
    0362, 0363, 0364, 0365, 0431, 0432, 0433, 0434, 0513,
    0717, 0718, 2099, 2634, 2768, 2903, 2904, 4805, 6770,
    7166

Tugwell, Rexford G., and E.C. Banfield, 4670

Tulchin, Joseph S., 9030

Tulis, Jeffrey, 0182

Tull, Charles J., 7167

Tulledo, Stan, 2088

Tullos, Allen, and Candace Waid, 3926

Tully, Grace, 0020

Turaj, Frank, 4094

Turim, Gayle, 4999

Turnbaugh, Roy C., 6891, 7168

Turner, Arthur C., 8658

Turner, Bobbie G., 5569

Turner, Norma, 8437

Turner, Stanton B., 8410

Tushnet, Mark V., 5570, 5644

Tuska, Jon, 3491, 3854

Tuttle, Dwight W., 0699

Tuttle, William M. Jr., 4425, 7988, 7989, 7990, 8438, 8180,
    8439

Twentieth Century Fund, Inc., 7169

Twight, Charlotte, 1848

Twombly, Robert C., 4671

Tyack, David, Robert Lowe, and Elisabeth Hansot, 4426

Tyler, Bruce M., 5571

Tyler, Pamela, 6018, 6719

Tyler, Robert L., 2089

Tynes, Sheryl R., 5100

Tyson, Carl N., 4095

U.S. Commission on Wartime Relocation and Internment of
    Civilians, 8411

U.S. Congress, 9683

U.S. Congress. Joint Committee on the Investigation of the
    Pearl Harbor Attack, 7595

U.S. Department of Defense, 9684

U.S. Department of State, 9685, 9686, 9687, 9688, 9689,
    9690

U.S. Department of the Army, 9691

U.S. National Archives and Record Service, 9692

U.S. President, 9693

U.S. Senate, 9694, 9695

Uchida, Yoshiko, 8412

Udelson, Joseph H., 3927

Ueno, Harry, Arthur A. Hansen, Betty E. Mitson, and Sue K.
    Embrey, 8413

Ugland, Richard M., 8440, 8441, 8442

Uhlig, Frank and William R. Matthews, 0435

Ulam, Adam B., 9227

Uldricks, Teddy J., 7453

Ullman, Richard, 0805

Ulmer, S. Sidney, 5572

Ulrich, Kenneth G., 3701

Underwood, Jeffery S., 5000

Underwood, Thomas A., 3492

Ungar, Sanford J., 6892

Unofficial Observer, 0514

Unrau, Harlan D., 1520

Urban, Wayne J., 5573

Urbanki, Andrew A., and Joseph O. Baylor, 4786

Urmann, Michael F., 2390

Urofsky, Melvin I., 6991, 7005

Urwin, Cathy K., 2391

Utley, Jonathan, 0846

Utley, Jonathan G., 7596, 7597, 7598

Uyeunten, Sandra O., 8414

Vaca, John E., 5101

Vacha, John E., 5272, 6798

Vaeth, J. Gordon, 5001

Valaik, J. David, 7392, 7393, 7394, 7395, 7396

Valelly, Richard M., 6852

Valentine, Jerry W., 5231

Valentine, John, 0207

Valilew, Eugene, 6349

Valocchi, Steve, 2485

Van Alstyne, Richard W., 7599, 8882

Van Deusen, Marshall, 6350

Van Devanter, Willis, 7049

Van Dyke, Vernon, and Edward Lane, 1265

Van Dyne, Larry, 2769

Van Edgerton, F., 9433

Van Everen, Brooks, 7813, 7814

Van Horn, Susan H., 6019

Van Loon, Hendrik W., 0208

Van Patten, Paul L., Jr., 0436, 0515

Van Raaphorst, Donna L., 2392, 2393

Van Wyk, Russel D., 7318

Vand De Mark, Brian, 9802

Vandenberg, Arthur H., 1277

Vannucci, Albert P., 9031

VanSickle, Frederick M., 1646

Varg, Paul A., 1850, 7319, 8931

Varma, Premdatta, 5670

Vatter, Harold G., 8181

Vaughn, Cortney, 1186

Vaughn, Herbert W., 0366

Vaughn, Stephen, 3855

Vaughn, William P., 1715

Vazzano, Frank P., 7170

Vedder, Richard K., 2012

Venis, Linda, 3493

Venkataramani, M. S., 0367, 3136, 6853, 8943, 8944

Venkataramani, M. S., and B. K, Shrivastava, 8945

Ventresco, Fiorello B., 4787, 4788

Verba, Sidney, and Kay L. Schlozman, 6351

Verge, Arthur C., 8322

Verrier, Anthony, 9434

Vexler, Richard B., 3574

Vexler, Robert I., 0516

Vialt, Birdsail S., 7849

Vickers, Ruth P., 8415

Vidger, Leonard P., 1819

Vidor, King, 3260

Viehe, Fred W., 6720

Viereck, Peter, 2770, 4427

Vieth, Jane K., 0859, 0860, 0861

Vigneras, Marcel, 8712

Villa, Brian L., 7815, 8583

Vinca, Robert H., 4572

Vincent, Charles, 2771

Vincenti, Walter G., 1906, 5002

Vindex, Charles, 1716

Vinikas, Vincent A., 2635

Vinson, J. C., 1011

Viola, Herman J., 9696

Violas, Paul C., 4428

Viorst, Milton, 9210

Virdicchio, Joseph L., 3081

Virginia Cavalcade, 2915, 3265, 8487

Virginia Law Review, 2661

Viseltear, Arthur J., 4242

Vitas, Robart A., 7454

Vittoz, Stanley, 2090

Vitz, Robert C., 2394, 3702, 5102

Vivas, Eliseo, 4429

Vlack, Don, 3187

Vlahos, Michael, 9435

Vlasek, Dale R., 5574

Vlasich, James A., 5903

Vlaton, Elias, 8584

Vloyantes, John P., 8585

Voeltz, Herman C., 1743

Vogel, Hal, 5003

Vogt, Daniel C., 3022, 6721

Voight, David Q., 4626

Volan, Denys, 8099

Volkomer, Walter E., 0680

Volpenhein, Mark, 8250

Volyn, Robert P., 2636

VonHoffman, Nicholas, 0368

Vose, Clement E., 4759

Vovko, Andrej, 8060

Wachs, Theodore R., 8049

Wachtel, Dennis F., 9211

Wacker, Fred, 5575, 5576

Wada, George, and James C. Davis, 8416

Waddell, Karen, 5577

Wade, Michael G., 2772, 4672

Wagner, David, 3856, 6352

Wagner, Jonathan F., 2395, 6398

Wagon, William O., Jr., 0559

Wald, Alan M., 3494, 6353, 6354, 6355

Waldau, Roy S., 3261

Walden, Daniel, 3857

Waldman, Diane, 3858

Waldmeir, Joseph J., 3495, 4134

Walker, Chip, 8481

Walker, Donald E., 1218

Walker, Forrest A., 2905, 2906

Walker, Henry, Jr., 1104

Walker, John S., 0597

Walker, Kenneth P., 2091

Walker, Maridith, 3703

Walker, Randolph M., 4573

Walker, Richard P., 8482

Walker, Samuel E., 4743, 6356

Walker, Thomas C., 6108

Walker, Thomas G., Lee Esptein, and William J. Dixon, 6945

Walker, Thomas J. E., 2396

Walker, Turnley, 0236

Walker, William O. III, 7649, 7692

Wall, Forrest B. Jr., 8483

Wall, Joseph F., 1378

Wallace, H Lew, 9803
Wallace, Henry A., 0598
Wallace, Teresa A., 6020
Waller, G. M., 7600
Waller, Robert A., 1236, 1237
Waller-Zuckerman, Mary E., 4096
Wallich, Mable T., and Hery C. Wallich, 2013
Walling, William, 3576
Walling, William, and Roger Shatzkin, 3575
Wallinger, Michael J., 8417
Wallis, John J., 2014, 2486, 2773, 2774
Wallis, John J., and Daniel K. Benjamin, 2775
Walsh, Andrea S., 6021
Walsh, Elizabeth E., 5161
Walsh, Francis R., 3859
Walsh, James A., 1402, 7022
Walston, Mark, 2637
Walt, Joseph W., 8986
Walter, Austin F., 8671
Walter, John C., 0979, 2424, 2425, 5004, 5005, 7991
Walter, John C., and Jill L. Ansheles, 4179
Walter, Nancy P., 5904
Walters, Betty L., 4430
Walters, Raymond, 2907
Walters, Ronald G., 5578
Waltzer, Kenneth, 6357
Wandersee, Winifred D., 6022
Wann, Andrew. J., 0437, 0560, 1967
Ward, Charles S., 2638
Ward, Cynthia L., 4097
Ward, Geoffrey C., 0029, 0090, 0209, 0237, 0369, 9828
Ward, Richard J., 2397, 2398
Ware, Gilbert, 5579, 5645
Ware, James W., 1305, 3023, 5006
Ware, Susan, 6023
Warken, Philip W., 0561
Warne, Barbara F., 2399
Warner, C. A., 1774
Warner, Emily S., and Daniel Hawthorne, 0762
Warner, Geoffrey, 7816
Warner, Richard S., 8484
Warnock, Herny Y., 4574
Warren, Ann L., 3860
Warren, F. A., and M. Wreszin, 9804
Warren, Frank A., 6181, 6182
Warren, Wilson J., 2400
Warren-Findley, Jannelle, 5288
Warshall, Peter, 1521
Warshow, R., 6358
Warth, Robert D., 9524
Washburn, Patrick S., 0471, 5580, 5581, 6899
Washburn, Wilcomb E., 5905
Wasko, Janet M., 3861
Wassenaar, Michael, 3862
Wasserman, Benno, 7601
Waters, Enoch P., 4098

Waters, Maurice, 0700
Watkins, Charles A., 1717
Watkins, Floyd C., 5729
Watkins, Thomas H., 0648, 5007
Watkinson, James D., 3137
Watson, Craig A., 3496
Watson, Judson D., III, 3497, 3498
Watson, Mark S., 0438, 5008
Watson, Richard A., 0537
Watson, Richard L. Jr., 9805
Watson, Thomas, 3024
Watson, William B., 7397, 7398
Watt, Donald C., 7236, 7661, 7817, 9806
Wattenberg, Albert, 5009, 5010
Watts, Jill M., 4575
Wax, Rosalie H., 8418
Weales, Gerald, 5103
Weart, Spencer R., 5011
Weathers, Bynum E. Jr., 9023
Weatherspoon, Michael A., 1012
Weaver, Bill, 7602
Weaver, Bobby D., 1775
Weaver, Carolyn C., 2908
Weaver, John C., 6722
Webb, David D., 2015
Webb, Pamela, 1718, 2639
Webb, Robert G., 1217
Weber, Vevra A., 1403, 3025
Webster, Grove, 5012
Weckesser, Ernest P., Jr., 2449
Wecter, Dixon, 1647, 2092
Wedemeyer, Albert C., 0962, 8932, 9436
Weed, Clyde P., 6109, 6110
Weeks, Charles J. Jr., 5906, 8967
Wehle, Louis B., 0765
Weigle, Marta, 1719
Weigley, Russell F., 5013, 9437, 9438
Weiler, Richard M., 0599
Weinberg, Arthur, and Lila Weinberg, 6723
Weinberg, Gerhard L., 9216
Weinberg, Sydney S., 8550, 9439
Weinberg, William, 6724
Weinberger, James M., 0988
Weiner, Charles, 5014, 5015, 5016
Weiner, Lynn, 6024
Weingast, David E., 4099
Weinrich, William A., 0439
Weinrott, Lester A., 3928
Weir, Jean B., 3082
Weir, Kathy C., 8713
Weir, Stan, 2093
Weisblat, Abraham M., 4695
Weisbord, Robert G., 5582
Weisbord, Robert G., and Arthur Stein, 5799
Weisenberger, Carol A., 3026, 3027
Weiss, Leonard W., 8196

Weiss, Nancy J., 5583
Weiss, Richard 4789
Weiss, Stuart L, 0731, 1213, 6183, 6725, 7818
Welburn, Ronald G., 3577
Welch, Richard E. Jr., 7455
Welge, William D., 5907
Weller, Cecil E., Jr., 1199, 1200
Welles, Sumner, 7237, 7850
Wells, Henry C., 6726
Wells, Lloyd M., 2640
Wells, Robert E., 1907
Welsch, Roger L., 5104
Welsh, Carol H., 8551
Welsh, Michael E., 1522, 5017, 5908
Wendt, Bruce H., 5909
Wendt, Lloyd, 4100
Wengert, Norman, 2909, 2910
Wenn, Stephen R., 7851
Wennersten, John R., 5584
Wentz, Frederick K., 4576, 9068
Werly, John M., 6399
Werner, Alfred, 5162, 5800
Wernick, Robert, 3704
Werrell, Kenneth P., 5585, 9440, 9441, 9631
Wershoven, Carol, 3499
Wert, Hal E., 9172
Wertheim, Arthur F., 3929
Werthman, Joan B., 5289
Wesbrook, Stephen D., 8323
Wessel, Thomas R., 1523
Wesser, Robert F., 1036
West, Elliott, 9525
West, James W. III, 3500
West, John F., 3501
West, Kenneth B., 2401, 2402
West, Michael A., 7992
West, Truett, 5586
Westbrook, Brett, 8552
Westbrook, Max, 3502
Westbrook, Robert B., 1946, 4101
Westling, Louise, 3705
Wetzel, Charles J., 9173
Whalen, Richard, 4744
Wharton, Don, 0112
Whatley, Larry, 5232
Whatley, Warren C., 1379, 1524, 2776
Whealey, Robert H., 7399, 7400
Wheat, Ellen H., 3706, 3707
Wheeler, Gerald E., 5018, 5019, 7238, 7603, 7618
Wheeler, Lonnie, and John Baskin, 4627
Wheelock, David C., 2016
Whelan, Paul A., 9442
Whisenhunt, Donald W., 1187, 1648, 1649, 1720, 1721, 1722, 1723, 1724, 2060, 2094, 3138, 6359, 6854
Whitaker, Rosemary, 3503
Whitaker, W. Richard, 5801

Whitcomb, Philip W., 9697
White, David H. Jr., 7993, 8948
White, Donald W., 9594
White, Dorothy S., 9212
White, G. Edward, 8419
White, George A., 3504
White, Gerald T., 5020, 9698
White, Gilbert F., 1525
White, Graham J., 0472
White, Graham J., and John Maze, 0649
White, Larry, 4760
White, Leslie, 3262
White, Ralph K., 8553
White, Ray L., 3505
White, Robert G., Jr., 3930
White, Suzanne, 3863
White, Theodore H., 8933
White, Vibert L., 5587
White, William G. Jr., 6727
White, William T., 2403
Whited, Fred E., Jr., 1019
Whitehead, Albert, 0989
Whitehead, D. F., 7239
Whitehead, James L., 0210, 1725
Whitehurst, Clinton H., Jr., 2641
Whiteman, Marjorie M., 0091
Whiteside, Barbara J.T., 4577
Whiting, Cecile M., 3708, 3709
Whitnah, Donald R., 5021, 9595
Whitney, Simon N., 3864
Whittemore, Bert R., 0895
Whyatt, Nelson T., 6184
Wickens, James F., 3028, 5233
Wicker, Elmus, 2017
Widenor, William C., 9462
Wiecek, William M., 6946
Wiesse, Ruth R., 5803
Wiggins, David K., 4628
Wiggins, William H Sr., 4629
Wigmore, Barrie A., 1650, 2642
Wilbur, J. R. H., 1851
Wilbur, Susan K., 3931
Wilburn, James R., 1908
Wilburn, Mark S., 0614, 7994
Wilcox, Jerome, 9621
Wilcox, Leonard I., 6360
Wilcox, Walter W., 1404
Wilder, Judith C., 1526
Wilder, Robin G., 6185
Wilentz, Gay, 3506
Wiles, Timothy J., 3263
Wilhelm, Gene, Jr., 1527
Wilkins, Mira, 7604
Wilkins, Robert P., 7960
Wilkinson, J. R., 1852
Willard, Timothy A., 8182

Willen, Paul, 7881
Willett, Donald E., 2426
Williams, Alma R., 0720
Williams, Bernard O., 5022
Williams, Bobby J., 3083
Williams, C. Arthur, Jr., 2487
Williams, Christopher Y., 8664
Williams, Colleen I., 3029
Williams, David, 6893
Williams, Elizabeth E., 1560, 4102
Williams, Griffith H., 1856
Williams, Harry M. Jr., 5588
Williams, Jeanne P., 6025
Williams, John, 6361
Williams, Michael R., 5589
Williams, Oscar R. Jr., 5802
Williams, Robert C., 3710, 5023
Williams, Roger, 3507
Williams, T. Harry, 1189, 1190, 6362
Williams, T. Harry, and John M. Price, 1188
Williams, William A., 0370, 0990, 7456, 9526
Willis, Wayne C., 3154
Willoughby, William R., 8676
Willson, John P., 0820
Willson, Paul T., 3932
Wilmont, Chester, 7819
Wilmoth, Carol, 3578
Wilson, Craig A., 9463
Wilson, Deborah S., 3508
Wilson, Donald, 9443
Wilson, E. Raymond, 8324
Wilson, Edmond, 3509
Wilson, Hugh R. Jr., 7320
Wilson, J. H., 7457
Wilson, James Q., 5669
Wilson, Jerry, 3510
Wilson, Joan H., 1241
Wilson, John F., 0184
Wilson, John P., 9174
Wilson, Richard G., 5024
Wilson, Richard L., 5025
Wilson, Robert R., 5026
Wilson, Terry P., 8485
Wilson, Theodore A., 0615, 8644, 8645, 9807
Wilson, Theodore A., and Richard D. McKinzie, 7820
Wilson, William H., 1925, 1926, 1927, 2911, 9808
Wiltz, John E., 0538, 1047, 6111, 7961
Winant, John G., 8770
Wind, Herbert W., 4630
Winfield, Betty H., 0092, 0093, 0094, 0113, 0473, 0474, 0475, 0476
Wingard, Joel D., 3511, 6855
Winger, Sarah E., 3139
Wingfield, Marie G., 6728
Wingfield, Marshall, 4578
Winid, Boguslaw W., 2643

Winkler, Allan M., 2404, 8554
Winkler, Fred H., 7240, 7241, 7821
Winnacker, Rudolph A., 8646
Winograd, Leonard, 9175
Winpenny, Thomas R., 2644
Winslow, Susan, 1726
Winstead, Billy W., 0682
Winter, Frank H., 5027
Winter, William, 6729
Winter, Willis L., 4103
Wiseman, John B., 3865
Witt, Alan F., 8715
Witt, Shirley H., 5910
Witte, Edwin E., 5163
Witte, William D., 8050
Wittner, Lawrence S., 5590, 8051, 8773
Wix, William M., 9596
Wladaver-Morgan, Susan, 5105, 5164
Wohlstetter, Roberta, 7605, 7606, 7607
Woirol, Gregory, R., 2488
Woito, Robert, 7995
Wojciechowski, Marian, 7242
Wojtowicz, Robert, 3188
Wolf, Gerald W., and Joseph H. Cash, 9858
Wolf, T. Phillip, 0997, 6730
Wolf, William, 1909
Wolfe, Donald H., 3264
Wolfe, G. Joseph, 3933
Wolfe, Jonathan J., 8555
Wolfe, Thomas K., 6363
Wolfskill, George, 6112
Wolfskill, George, and J. A. Hudson, 7171
Wolfson, Adam, 5804
Wolfstein, Judith, 3579
Wolk, Herman S., 9444
Woll, Allen L., 3866, 3867
Wollenberg, Charles, 2405, 5591, 5629, 5710, 8420
Wolozin, Harold, 2018
Wolters, Raymond R., 1727, 2406, 5592
Wolthuis, Robert K., 8956
Wolvin, Andrew D., 2912
Wood, Bryce, 7650, 7651, 7652, 7653
Wood, Herbert J., 0849
Wood, William S., 9060
Woodbury, Robert L., 6731
Woodman, Lyman L., 1928
Woodress, James, 3512
Woodruff, Nan E., 8325
Woods, James R., 2913
Woods, Randall B., 7822, 8647, 9032, 9033, 9034
Woodward, C. Vann, 3513
Woodward, Katherine, S., 3868
Woodward, Robert H., 3514
Woodyatt, Lyle J., 2777
Word, James P., 3716
Worrall, Janet E., 8486

Worster, Donald, 1306, 1307, 1308
Worth, Steve, 4806
Worthy, Barbara A., 5593
Wortman, Roy T., 2407, 2408
Woytak, Richard A., 7823
Wray, J. D. Buck, 9445
Wreszin, Michael, 0539, 6113
Wright, Almon R., 9446
Wright, C. Ben, 0854
Wright, Christopher C., 5028
Wright, Esmond, 2778
Wright, Gavin, 2779, 3140
Wright, George C., 4431
Wright, Gordon, 0787
Wright, Howard T., 5029
Wright, Louis E., 4790
Wright, Monte D., and Lawrence J. Paszek, 9699
Wright, Peter M., 5911
Wright, Richard, 5594
Wright, Theodore P. Jr., 7243
Wrigley, Linda, 0681
Wroth, William, 3155
Wu, Chien-Shiung, 4791
Wutke, Eugene R., 4673
Wyche, Billy H., 2409, 2780, 4104
Wye, Christopher G., 5595, 5596, 5597
Wymann, David S., 4180, 9447
Wyne, Lewis N., and Guy P. Harrison, 1528
Wynes, Charles E., 5598
Wynn, Neil A., 5630, 5631, 5632
Wynne, Lewis N., and Carolyn J. Barnes, 5030
Wyszomirski, Margaret J., 0562

Xydis, Stephen G., 8774, 8775

Yale, Andres, 9859
Yankelovich, Daniel, 7882
Yarbrough, Tinsley E., 5599
Yard, Alexander, 1405
Yarmus, Marsha D., 3515
Yasko, Karel, 3711
Yates, Lawrence W., 0813
Yaung, Emily, 8648
Yavis, Constantine G., and Dan Georgakas, 8556
Yeck, Joanne L., 3869
Yedweb, Stanley, 5805
Yee, Robert, 6364
Yeh, Susan F., 3712
Yeilding, Thomas D., 9024
Yellowitz, Irwin, 2489
Yerxa, Donald A., 5031, 7700
Yetman, Norman R., 9860
York, Hildreth, 5234
Yoshikawa, Takeo, and Norman Stanford, 7608
Yoshino, Ronald W., 5032
Yoshpe, Harry B., 5033, 5034

Yost, Harry, 1857
Yound, William H., Jr., 4136
Young, Arthur N., 8934
Young, James E., 9176
Young, James O., 5600
Young, Kenneth R., 0960
Young, Lowell T., 7824, 7825, 7826
Young, Michael, 8052
Young, William H., Jr., 4105, 4135
Youngs, J. William T., 0095
Yovat, Shlomo, 9009
Yu, Renqiu, 4792
Yumiba, Carol K., 8421

Zahavi, Gerald, 2095, 2410
Zahn, Gordon C., 8053
Zalampas, Mehale A., 9217
Zangrando, Robert L., 5601, 5602, 5603
Zaring, Russell A., 1529
Zaslowsky, Dyan, 1530
Zavin, Howard S., 0440
Zebroski, Shirley, 0540
Zedenfelt, Alex, 9448
Zeidel, Robert F., 4761
Zeiger, Robert H., 2450
Zeigler, Luther H. Jr., 6732
Zeigler, Stephen M., 5604
Zeitzer, Glen, 8055, 8056
Zeitzer, Glen, and Charles F. Howlett, 8054
Zelinsky, Wilbur A., 2645
Zeller, William D., 8422
Zelman, Donald L., 1406, 1820
Zhao, Yifan, 6026
Ziaukas, Tim, 3516
Zieger, Robert H., 2411, 2412, 2413, 2414, 9809
Ziegler, Janet, 9632
Zielinski, Martin A., 4579
Ziemke, Earl F., 9449
Zigelmueller, George W., 7172
Zimmerman, Robert W., 9450
Zimmerman, Tom, 2490
Zimmerman, William Jr., 5912
Zinn, Howard, 9810
Zlotnick, Joan, 4137
Zobrist, Benedict K., 9829, 9830
Zook, Mervin D., 4106
Zotos, Constance E., 4107
Zubatsky, David S., 4432
Zuccarello, Louis C., 0763
Zucker, Bat-Ami, 5605
Zucker, Norman L., 1037, 1038, 1039
Zuercher, Roger L., 7883
Zuroff, Efraim, 9177, 9178
Zweig, Ronald, 9179
Zwerin, Kenneth C., 5806
Zwicky, John F., 8100

Subject Index

Note: Numbers refer to entries.

A. M. Byers Wrought Iron Company, Unionization, 2610

Abbott, Edith, Evaluated as Teacher and Person, 4419

Abbott, Grace, and Edith, Their Career as Social Activists, 5931; Early Life and Career, 4199

Abraham Lincoln Brigade: (1936–1939), 7355; Analysis of Participants, 7386, 7387; Jewish Participants, 7367

Absalom, Absalom! (1936), Analysis, 3288

Academic Freedom: at St. Louis University, (1937–1939), 4406; in Higher Education, Five Case Studies, 4373

Academicians in Government from Roosevelt to Roosevelt, 4288

Acheson, Dean G.: Assistant Secretary of State, 0775; Memoir of Relationship with Roosevelt and the New Deal, 2662; Political Philosophy, 0777; Personal Letters, (1918–1971), 0774; World War II Diplomat, 0776

Acreage Limitation Controversy, Origins, (1933), 1474

Action Comics, Entertainment and Ideology, (1938), 3977

Actors as Laborers (1930s), 3736

Adamic, Louis: Americanization, 3310; Autobiography, 4243; Political Views, 6142

Adler, Mortimer, Relationship with Robert M Hutchins, (1929–1941), 4259

Administrative Office Act (1939), 6914

Adorno, Theodor W.: and the Meaning of Culture and Cultural Improvement (1930s), 4658; His Experience in America during the 1930s and 1940s, 4138

Adult Education in America, (1930–1939), 4326; in Harlem during the Great Depression, 5493

Adventure Comics during the Great Depression, (1929–1938), 4136

Advertising Campaigns: and American Mores, (1920–1940), 2635; Campaigns for Vitamins, (1925–1940), 4184; during the Great Depression and World War II, 3716; Federal Regulation, 2627; Influence, (1920–1940), 2597; Techniques, (1920–1940), 2570

Advisory Commission to the Council of National Defense, Establishment (1940), 4825

Aerial Spraying of Pesticides, Origins, 1498

Agar, Hubert S., And the agrarian De-centralist Movement (1930–1936), 6832

Agee, James; Analysis of His Book *Let Us Now Praise Famous Men*, 3472; Compares the Photography of Walker Evans with that of Margaret Bourke-White, 3696; His Description of the Southern Tenant Farmer in *Let Us Now Praise Famous Men*, (1941), 3381; Plans to Create a Magazine for the Criticism of Popular culture (1930s), 4015

Agrarians: Analysis of Idealism, 1326; and Marxists Compared, 6855; as High Priests of Traditional Southern Values, 4654; Attitudes toward the City between the Wars, 1325; Movement, 1283; Role and Techniques of Pressure Groups, 6849

Agricultural Adjustment Act (1933): Background, 2839; Farmer Opinion, 2812; Passage, 2813; Pro and Con Debates, 2754

Agricultural Adjustment Act (1937), Impact on the Dairy Industry, 2842

Agricultural Adjustment Act (1938): Origins, 2890; Political Impact in Kansas, 2995

Agricultural Adjustment Administration: Activities in South Dakota, (1933–1935), 2992; Analysis, 1373; and Southern Tenant Farmers, 2687; and Texas Cattlemen, (1933–1935), 2986; Appraisal, (1937), 2861; Corn-Hog Production Control Measures, 2846; Corn-Hog Program in Iowa, 2953; Development of Production Control Policy, 2866; Impact on Cotton Industry, 2817; Impact on Louisiana, 2956; Impact on New York Milk Producers, 2916; Origins, 2867; Purge of Liberals, (1935), 2860; Reorganization, (1935), 2668

Agricultural: Adjustment Program, Archival Records, 9655; Depression, (1921–1934), 1350; Evaluation of Labor Legislation, 2818; Experiment Stations in the South, 1394; Exports and Imports (1930s), 1336; Mexican and American Reform Efforts Compared, 2776; Origins of Referendum System, 2722; Planning during World War II, 1351; Policies, (1929–1933), 1332; Policy and the

Farm Bureau Federation, 1341; Policy Making in Congress, (1919–1980), 1353; Records, National Archives, 9674; Reform, 1356; Towns in Pennsylvania, 1430; Unions in the Imperial Valley of California, 1403

Agriculture: and the Battle for Managed Money, (1920–1941), 2015; Department Economics Bureau, Study of Correlation between Community Quality and Agricultural Plot Size in California, 2984; Department and Scientific Research (1933–1940), 4974; in Utah, Decline, 1310

Aiken, George D., And the 1936 Gubernatorial Campaign in Vermont, 6532; Considers a Run for the Presidency (1937–1939), 6682

Aimes, Jessie D., As Founder of the Association of Southern Women for the Prevention of Lynching, (1930), 4713, 5943

Air Bombardment, Evolution of the Idea, 1900 to World War II, 4988

Air Intelligence Prior to Pearl Harbor, 4930

Air National Guard, Birth (1943–1946), 9297

Air Passenger Service in Alaska, (1934–1940), 1883

Air Pollution in St Louis, (1930s), 1496

Air Power, Influence on the Roosevelt Administration (1933–1941), 5000

Air Ships, Development and Use, (1930s), 1889

Air Strategy, Origins (1933–1934), 9443

Aircraft Carriers, Development by the United States, Great Britain and Japan Compared, 4978

Aircraft Industry, Development during World War II, 1897; during World War II, 1898; Social and Economic Impact on Los Angeles, 1908

Airline Pilots Association, (1931–1938), 2238; Origins, 2243

Airmail: Delivery, Failed Army Air Corps Attempts, 1903; Invention of System, 1886; Service Suspended, (1934), 1873

Airplanes, Debate over Stability versus Control, (1930s), 1906

Airport Policy Development, (1926–1952), 1874

Alabama: Governors, Reflect on State Politics (1930–1955), 6478; Gubernatorial Election (1942), 6419; Progressive Education, (1935–1951), 4353; Repeal of Prohibition, 4754

Alaska: (Alcan) Highway, 1854; (Alcan) Highway, Origins, 1856; (Alcan) Highway, Photographic History of Construction, 1857; Decline of Gold Mining after 1942, 8115; Highway, History, 8249; Railroad, (1923–1941), 1925; Railroad and Coal, (1914–1939), 1927; Railroad and Tourism,(1924–1941), 1926; Tourist Trade, (1878–1941), 2591

Alaskan Flight of the Ten B-10's (1934), 4882

Albok, John, Depression Era Photographs, 1725

Alcoa, Tennessee, Impact of Union Movement on the Black Community (1930s–1940s), 5512

Alcohol Motor Fuel Movement (1930s), 1753

Alder, Cyrus, And the Rescue of Jewish Scholars, 9085

All American Girls Baseball League, (1943–1954), 4582

Allen, Edison B., Discussion of His Cartoons, 4108

Allen, Fred: His Career in Hollywood, 4124; His views on the Radio Broadcasting Industry, 4123

Allen, Frederick Louis, His Liberal Views, 6173

Allen, William Harvey, Popularity of His Novel *Anthony Adverse* (1933), 3516

Allred, James V., Political Biography, 6415

Almanac Singers, Contributions to American Folk Music, (1930s–1940s), 3526

Alperovitz, Gar, Critical Analysis of his book *Atomic Diplomacy,* 9765

Alsop, Joseph, and American Foreign Policy, 3990

Alssell, Harold D., Noted Political Scientist (1930s), 4639

Alternative Broadcasting Groups (1920s to the 1970s), 3915

Aluminum Company of America, Changing Labor Policies after 1940s, 2595

Alwler, Vanett, Her Career in Music Education, 4334

Amana Society of Iowa, and Automobile Service Stations (1930s), 3182

Amature Politicians in the United States Congress (1930–1984), 6042

America: and Germany during the First Week of March, 1933, 7315; and Poland, Economic Connections (1918–1939), 7212; and the Neutrality of Ireland, (1933–1935), 7335; and the Oil Cartel (1934–1945), 7486; as Seen by Swedish Writers, (1920s–1940s), 3335; Contributions to State Capitalism during the New Deal, 1951; Documented in Photographs, (1935–1943), 3643; Fails to Cooperate with Great Britain in the Far East (1914–1941), 7495; Foreign Policy and the South African Grape Controversy (1930s), 7186; from the Wall Street Crash to Pearl Harbor, 1726; on the Verge of War (1941), 8075; Rise of Mass Culture, (1929–1939), 4248; and the Sexual Revolution between World War I and World War II, 4249; Transforms Itself, (1900–1950), 2062

America First Committee: 7898; and Repeal of the Neutrality Act (1939), 7955; Fails in the South (1940–1941), 7967; Opposes Intervention (1940–1941), 7899; Rhetoric, 7931

American: Abstract Artists, (1937–1941), 3700, 3670; Actors, Socio-Political Activities, (1920–1940), 3200; Agriculture, Development, 1281; Agriculture, Regulation and Innovation, 1344; Aircraft Industry Financial Problems, (1906–1940), 1894; and British Appeasement of Germany (1933–1939), 7314; and Canadian Economies Compared, (1929–1956), 1961; and German Anti-Depression Policies Compared, (1933–1936), 1958; and Italian Architecture during the 1930s, Compared, 3168; Anti-Nazi Boycott Movement (1939–1941), 5761; Appeasement of Germany, 7209; Archivists and the Search for Professional Identity (1909–1936), 9636; Art of the Twentieth Century, 3654; Art Since 1900, 3693; Art Theory and Criticism during the 1930s, 3692; Artist's

Congress, Rise and Fall, 3679; Artists and the Great Depression, 3702; Artists School, Founding, (1936), 3674; Association of Scientific Workers, Efforts to Involve Scientists in Social Issues, (1938–1948), 4898; Authors of the New Deal and World War II Eras, 3402; Blacks, and Selective Service during World War II, 5611; Broadcast Radio, Commercialization, (1920–1934), 3920; Business and Banking Thought, Development, (1913–1936), 2506; Business and Germany (1930–1941), 7294; Business and Recognition of the Soviet Union, 7457; Business Attitudes toward the Soviet Union, (1933–1947), 2498; Business Periodicals, Political Attitudes, (1930–1935), 3986; Business Practices, Critique, 2507; Businessmen and Japanese Trade (1931–1941), 7524; Businessmen, Their Image in the Popular Press, (1928–1941), 4036; Canadian Relations (1937–1941), 7258; Catholic Church on the Spanish Civil War, 4486; Catholics and Anti-Semitism (1930s), 5783; Catholics and the Second Spanish Republic, 7393; Character in the Twentieth Century, 4245; Cinema and World War I, (1914–1941), 3774; Changes Since 1940, 4271; Colonial Revival Architecture (1930s), 3167; Comic Strips during the Great Depression, (1929–1938), 4135; Committee for Non-Participation in Japanese Aggression (1938–1941), 7923; Cultural Metaphors found in Popeye the Sailor Cartoons (1930s), 3862; Defense Policy, Transformation (1932–1941), 4862; Devaluation of the Dollar, (1933), 2011; Diplomacy (1919–1939), 7187; Diplomacy and Nazi Germany (1933–1938), 7303; Diplomacy (1930s), 7195; Diplomatic Relations With Neutral Nations (1933–1940), 7182; Diplomatic Reporting from the Soviet Union (1940–1941), 7427; Diplomatic Reports from the 1936 Berlin Olympiad, 0810; Direct Investment in Japan, (1899–1952), 1844; Discussion of World War II Leaders, 4827; Dollar Diplomacy in Canada (1921–1947), 7256; Drama and World War II, 3218; Drama, Dissident Character (1930s), 3259; Economic Foreign Policy toward Germany (1933–1939), 7266; Economic Performance (1930s), 1949; Economic Thought, Institutional School, 1944; Economy, (1917–1945), 1940; Economy, Analysis, (1925–1962), 1941; Editorial Response to the Rise of Adolph Hitler, 4045; Educational Theater Association, Formative Years, (1936–1950), 3212; Entry into World War II, 7191; Exceptionalism Examined, 2079; Extremism (1933–1941), 6402; Failure in China, (1940–1941), 7470; Far Eastern Policy (1937–1938), 7474; Fashion Work, Transformation, (1930–1955), 2495; Federation of Musicians Strike, (1942), 2111; Federation of Teachers, Social and Educational Position, (1929–1941), 4300; Film, History, (1929–1939), 3777; Film Industry, Analysis, (1929–1945), 3795; Film Industry, Its Financing (1930s), 3763; Film Noir, (1941–1949), Analysis, 3780; Folk Music, Origins of Communist Interest (1930s), 3564;

Foreign Relations (1940–1942), 7232; Foreign Service in China (1905–1941), 7466; German Commercial Rivalry in Brazil (1933–1940), 7311; Government Sports and Physical Training Policies During World War II, 4620; Governors, Content Analysis of their Inaugural Addresses (1943–1971), 6551; Humor and Depression, Bibliography, 9618; Humor Relating to Economic Depression, A Checklist, (1936–1974), 4132; Hungarian Relations (1918–1944), 7407; Immigration Policy, (1924–1952), 4149; Imprints Inventory (1937–1942), 5136; Independent Marxists, Their Disillusionment with Stalinist Russia, 6274; Ineffective Nature of Communist influence on Social Theater Movement, 3219; Indian Image in Films (1919–1976), 5811; Indian Policy, An Evaluation of Assimilation, 5818; Indians and the Environment, 5822; Indians and the Self Government Controversy, 5833; Indians and World War II, 5814; Intellectual History, Critical Appraisal (1961), 9746; Intellectuals and Stalin's Russia (1930–1940), 6273; Intellectuals, Racial Attitudes (1909–1954), 5510; Interest Groups and the Formation of Chinese Policy (1925–1927), 7463; Interventions in Cuba (1901–1934), 7243; Japanists and their Images of Japan (1940s), 5721; Jazz in France, (1917–1940), 3545; Journalism, History, (1690–1960), 4042; Journalistic Perceptions of the Death of the Weimar Republic, (1932–1933), 3998; Journalists in Berlin, Perceptions, (1939–1941), 3957; Jurisprudence between the Wars, 6096; Labor Movement, History, (1935–1941), 2211; Labor on the Defensive, A Personal Narrative, 2093; Labor Unions, (1836–1985), 2227; Liberal Press and German Writers in Exile, Their Relationship, (1933–1945), 4051; Liberal Response to the Recession (1937), 1999; Manipulation of the German Economy before the Great Depression, 7298; Medical Association, History, (1847–1947), 4203; Membership in International Labor Organization (ILO), 0662; Military in China (1901–1937), 7465; Motion Picture Industry and the Banking Industry, 3861; Movie Views of Organized Labor, (1934–1954), 3859; Musical Productions, Libretti (1930s), 9619; Musical Theater during World War II, 3542; National Power as Reflected in Film, (1919–1965), 3787; Negro Theater, History (1940–1949), 5514; News Media and Soviet Diplomacy, (1934–1941), 4028; Newsreels, History, (1927–1950), 3885; Physicians and the Battle of Britain, (1940), 4187; Political Cartoons, History, 4126; Political Culture, History and Rhetoric, 6176; Political Fiction, Change of Focus (1930s), 3283; Political Tradition (1930s), 6055; Politics as Portrayed in *Mr. Smith Goes to Washington* (1939), 3808; Popular Music during World War II, 3555; Presbyterian Perceptions of the Oxford Conference, (1937), 4506; Presidency in Political Cartoons, (1776–1976), 4112; Press Coverage of Mexico, (1934–1940), 4040; Proletarian Novel, Theory and Practice, 3511; Protest Songs, Evolution, 3566; Protestant Reports from China

(1914–1950), 7462; Psychiatry and the Troublesome Child, (1890–1940), 4210; Public Culture in the 1930s as Reflected in Popular Magazines, 4061; Public Opinion on China and Japan (1914–1950), 7461; Public, Reading Tastes (1930s and 1940s), 3436; Radio Broadcasting, Debate over Control and Structure, (1930–1935), 3903; Railroads and the Bracero Program, (1943–1946), 1919; Reaction to the November Pogrom, (1938), 7299; Recognition and Soviet Far Eastern Policy (1932–1934), 7416; Religious Press, Attitudes toward the Soviet Union, (1939–1941), 4029; Reshaping of the Economy, 1935; Review of the Economy (1940), 1939; Russian Chamber of Commerce, 7436; Russian Relations (1781–1947), 7456; Seamen, Unionism, 2219; Silver Policy and China (1933–1936), 7467; Small Business Organizations, 2501; Social Drama, Development (1930s), 3250; Society and Culture, (1890–1940), 5090; Society of Newspaper Editors Attempts to Shape World War II Peace Treaties, 3949; Soldier Poets of World War II, 3584,3585; South, An Intellectual Perception, (1920–1944), 3444; Spanish Relations during World War II, 7384; Steel Makers and the Coming of World War II, 2562; Student Movement (1931–1941), 6839; Technotax Society, Whittier, California, (1934–1935), 2488; Television, Early Development, (1937–1946), 3921 American Thought Between the Wars, (1919–1941), 4801; History, 4796; Topical Reviews, Theatrical Satires (1920s and 1930s), 3229; Tractors, Use in the USSR, (1930s), 2513; Trade Policy and Nazi Germany (1933–1938), 7302; Trotskyists, (1920–1941), 6295; Undeclared Naval War with Germany (1939), 7274; War Novels, 3478; War Veterans, History of Treatment, 2092; World War II Novels, Historical and Ideological Aspects, 3225; Writers and Radical Politics, (1900–1939), 3371; Writers on the Left (1930s), 3489; Youth Commission, History (1935–1942), 5058; Zionist Emergency Council, 9079

American Civil Liberties Union: and Agricultural Labor Disturbances in the Imperial Valley of California (1930, 1934), 2221; Kentucky Miners (1930s), 6878; Organization and Growth, 6868

American Committee for the Defense of Leon Trotsky, 7432

American Council for Judaism, (1942–1948), 5774

American Council on Education, Activities (1930s), 4375

American Farm Bureau Federation and Farm Policy (1933–1945), 7155; and Agricultural Politics from the 1930s to the 1940s, 6980

American Federation of Labor: and the Congress of Industrial Organizations, Conflicting Ideologies, 2245; and the Philippine Independence Question, (1920–1935), 2275; and the Third Party Question (1930–1938), 6830; Changing Attitudes toward Business and Government, (1929–1933), 2186; Definition of a Good Citizen, Changes, (1920–1940), 2380; Internal Conflict during the New Deal, 2312; Opposes Military Conscription, (1920–1940), 2135; Unions in the 1930s, Evaluation of

Performance, 2385; versus the Congress of Industrial Organizations in the Pacific Northwest, (1937–1941), 2287

American Foreign Policy: and National Security, (1914–1945), 4832, (1900–1949), 7193; (1929–1941), 7197; and Disarmament (1926–1935), 7240; and Fascist Italy (1932–1940), 7348, 7349; and Nazi Germany (1933–1939), 7276; and Nazi Germany (1933–1938), 7305; and Nazi Germany (1933–1940), 7304; and Spain (1931–1936), 7376; and Spain (1934–1944), 7377; and the Serbo-Croatian Agreement (1939), 7408; and the Soviet Union (1919–1939), 7437; and the Soviet Union (1929–1969), 7413; Between the Wars, 7176; Compared to Japan and Germany (1932–1942), 7203; Cyclical Trends, 7208; European Perceptions, 7221, 7222; Evaluated (1939), 7178; Evaluated (1956), 7190; From Wilson to Reagan, 7199; Military Conceptions (1904–1940), 4881

American Friends Service Committee, Activities (1917–1937), 4511

American Historical Association Commission on the Social Studies (1926–1934), 4382

American Japanese Relations (1919–1941), 7487; (1940–1941), 7478

American Jewish Committee, Response to Anti-Jewish Policies of Nazi Germany (1933–1939), 5778

American Jewish Community, and Anti-Nazi Boycott (1933–1941), 5763; Efforts to Unify (1916–1943), 5782

American Jewish Labor Movement, Cultural Dimensions, 5798

American Jewry, Development, (1919–1964), 5792

American Jews: and the Presidential Elections (1940 and 1944), 5758; and Their Struggle against Nazism in the 1930s, 5797; Reaction to the Liquidation of B'Nai B'rith in Nazi Germany (1937), 5762; Response to Nazi Programs, 5753; Their Efforts to Rescue European Jews (1939–1945), 5785

American Labor Party in New York City, 6456

American Left: Impact on Literature, 3267; Theater Movement Magazines (1930s), 3980

American Legations at Ottawa, (1937–1941), 7257

American Liberalism: and Communism (1930s), 6180, 6182; Its Changing Political Trends (1930s to the 1960s), 6172

American Liberals: and American Business, 6164; and the Moscow Trials (1936–1938), 6163

American Liberty League (1934–1936), 7146; (1934–1940), 7153, 6821; Founding, 7149

American Library Association and Inter-Library Cooperation, (1922–1945), 4432

American Life: as Portrayed in Hollywood Films (1930s), 3813; Between the Two World Wars, 4244; (1940')s, 4254

American Literature; Bibliography (1930s), 9616; (1930s), 3348; Analysis, 3473; (1940s), 3349; of War (Civil War,

World War I, World War II), 3410; Trends and Themes Influencing (1930s and Early 1940s), 3479

American Newspaper Guild: and the Newark, New Jersey Strike, (1934–1935), 2278; Formation, (1933–1936), 2276; History, 4016

American Novel in World War II: As Social Criticism, 3445; Ideological Aspects, 3495; Radicalism (1930s), 3308

American Olympic Committee, (1896–1940), 4607

American Painting: during the Great Depression, 3642; (1930s), 3644, 3660; Responds to Fascism, (1933–1945), 3708

American Peace Mobilization (1940–1941), 6356

American Peace Movement: (1941–1960), 8051; during World War II, 8055

American Poetry: about the Second Word War, Dramatic Guide, 3580; during World War II, 3592; of World War II, 3589

American Police-Community Relations Movement, Origins (1940s), 4743

American Policy: Alternatives in the Far East (1938), 7500; and Nationalist China (1928–1937), 7469; and the Italo-Ethiopian Crisis (1935–1936), 7337; in the Far East (1931–1941), 7480; toward the Soviet Union (1938), 7451; toward the Soviet Union (1938), 7452

American Presidential Social Theater (1930s), 3192

American Relations: with Asia (1931–1937), 7458; with Indo-China (1900–1940), 7473; with the Far East, Evaluated (1962), 7185; with the Soviet Union (1933–1941), 7439, with Soviet Union (1933–1939), 7179

American Review, Pro-Fascist Periodical (1933–1937), 6396

American Theater: during the 1930s, Leftist Influence on, 3210; (1930s), 3240; Radical Aspects (1930s), 3253; Advertising during the Great Depression, 2516

American Veteran's Committee, History, 2089

American Women: Depression Experience, 1593; Novelists, (1930–1955), 3423; Drama, (1900–1937), 3232

American-Polish Chamber of Commerce, (1920–1939), 2643

Americanism in Late Afternoon Adventure Radio Serials, (1940–1945), 3892

Americans Reaffirm Community Values, 4063

"American Wave," Origins in the Great Depression, 3612

Amerind Foundation Museum, Dragoon, Arizona, (1936), 3637

Amish Attitudes Toward the New Deal, 4526

Amlie, Thomas R: And the Farmer Labor Party, 6831; Political Biography, 6277, Political Career, 1213, Political Evolution, 6319

Ammons, Governor Teller, Discovers the Colorado Governor's Office is Bugged (1937), 6547

Amos 'N' Andy, Protested by Black Groups, 5550

Anaconda Company of Montana as Newspaper Owner, 4072

Analog and Digital Computing Methods Compared, 5022

Ancient Thought, Influence on Indian Art, 3652

Anderson, Herbert L., Recalls his Work on Nuclear Fission at Columbia University, 4815

Anderson, Jane, Nazi Propagandist, 8498

Anderson, Maxwell: Dramatic Theory, 3234; Views on American Government as Seen in *Both Your Houses*, 3279

Anderson, Orville A., Biography, 4987

Anderson, Sherwood, Political Thought, 6213

Angell, Sir Norman, Promotes Anglo-American Friendship in World War II, 8746

Angelou, Maya, Autobiographical Works, 5478

Anglo-American: Diplomacy and the Pacific War, 7538; Diplomatic Cooperation (1927–1936), 7603; Diplomatic Relations with Spain during World War II, 7370; Naval Collaboration (1937–1941), 7327; Naval Relations (1927–1937), 7323; Naval Relations (1938–1946), 4932; Perceptions of German Economic Preparations for War (1937–1939), 7295; Reaction to the Ethiopian War (1935–1936), 7343; Relations (1932–1938), 7331; Relations and Colonialism in East Asia (1932–1940), 7332; Relations and East Asia (1933–1937), 7333; Relations and Lord Lothlan (1929–1940), 7329; Relations and the Far East (1937–1941), 7510; Relations and the Far East (1941), 7511

Animated Film Industry Labor Problems, (1937), 2173

Anschulss, (1938), 7281

Anslinger, Harry J.: As Commissioner of the Federal Bureau of Narcotics (1930–1962), 4730, 6874

Anti-Trust Measures, Evolution, 2503

Anti-Union Agencies, (1865–1985), 2620

Anti-American Sentiment in Latin America, Origins, 7635

Anti-Communist Opinion in World War II America, 6135

Anti-Insurrection Law in Georgia, Use (1932), 5373

Anti-Lynching Bill: of 1935, Legislative History, 6063; Bills (1937–1938), 5365

Anti-Nazi Boycott: (1933–1941), 5784; Movement in America, 6397

Anti-Semitism: and American Jewish Leaders (1928–1933), 9152; and Isolationism (1939–1941), 5791; in America (1930–1940), 5795; in America, Decline After World War II, 5735; in Minnesota during the Great Depression, 5736; in Nazi Germany Pictured by the New York *Times*, (1933), 5801; in St. Louis (1933–1945), 5737, 5738; in the American South (1942–1945), 5796

Anti-Tank Strategy, Evolution, 1928 to World War II, 4878

Anti-War Movements and Students in America (1900–1960), 8039

Anti-War Strategies (1930s), 7965

Antitrust actions Against Major Motion Picture Producers, (1938), 3864

Antonini, Luigi, And the Italian Anti-Fascist Movement in the United States (1920–1943), 6210

Antonius, George, Promotes the Palestinian Cause in American Universities (1930–1936), 9001

Apex, Arizona, Lumber Company Town, (1928–1936), 1504

Appalachia, Historiography (1930–1970), 9729

Appalachian Culture and Migration to Baltimore (1880–1945), 4782

Appalachian Economic Development, The Case of Rayon
    Plants in Elizabethton, Tennessee, 2626
Apple Growing in Northwestern Arkansas, (1890s–1930s),
    1395
Appleby, Paul H., Career in Department of Agriculture,
    0670
Apricot Industry in California, Impact of Great Depression,
    2572
Aptheker, Herbert, Memoirs (1930s), 6189
Arab Stereotypes in the United States, 7620
Architecture: and Public Housing (1930s), 1811; of Urban
    Housing in the United States (Early 1930s), 5091
Archival Movement, History, 9635
Ardennes Offensive, 0914
Argenta Conference, 8610, 8644, 8645
Argentina and the Export-Import Bank (1934–1945), 7654
Arizona in the Great Depression, 1568
Arkansas and Conscientious Objectors, 8036
Arkansas, Economic and Social Tensions (1940–1945), 6702
Arkansas, Louisiana, and Mississippi, Rural Resettlement,
    1461
Arkansas Valley Authority, Proposed (1941), 1442
Armenia and International Rights, 7405
"Armed Services Editions," Condensed Editions of Works of
    Major Authors Prepared for Servicemen in World War II,
    3443
Arms Control (1931–1937), 9301
Armstrong Cork Company, Transformation to a War Time
    Industry (1940–1945), 8120
Army Air Corps, Evolution (1919–1941), 4996
Army Corps of Engineers: and Flood Control in the Red
    River Valley (1936–1946), 5006; Archaeological Work
    (1930s), 4821; As Developer and Administrator of Oak
    Ridge Tennessee, 4911; History of Construction Projects,
    4871; in the Middle Rio Grande Valley (1935–1955),
    5017; Albuquerque District, History, 1522
Arnall, Elise G., As Governor of Georgia (1933–1947), 6653
Arnold, Henry H.: Memoirs, 0897; Relationship with
    Historians, 0898
Arnold, Thurman: Anti Trust Activities, (1938–1943), 2582;
    New Deal Antitrust Efforts, (1933–1941), 2536
Arrington, Leonard J., His Childhood in Idaho, 4674
Art: and Literature (1930s), 3148, 3149; and the State
    Department, (1938–1947), 3685; for the Constitutional
    Sesquicentennial, 3673; for the Public, (1920–1943), 3669
Art Deco: Architecture in New York, (1920–1940), Pictorial
    Essay, 3187; Buildings in Kansas City, (1920s–1930s),
    3184; District of South Miami, Florida, (1930s–1940s),
    3177; Movement of the Inter-War Years, 3697
Arthurdale, West Virginia: as an Experiment in Social
    Planing, 4641; Experiment in Community Planning,
    (1933–1947), 1801; Experiment in West Virginia, 3010;
    Project in West Virginia, 3052
Artists: Their Relationship with the National Government
    from the Great Depression until 1973, 5079; Circles,

Their Variations as Discerned in the 1930s, 5042;
    Confront the 1930s, 2394; in Germany, Letters from
    (1933–1938), 3649; Interviewed, (1936–1945), 3678; of
    the Great Depression Era, 3698; of the Roosevelt Era,
    3668
Asian Indians, Their Struggle for Equality in the United
    States (1900–1946), 5670
Associated Charities of Washington, DC, (1882–1935), 4207
Associated Press Antitrust Suit, (1942–1945), 3948
Association of Archivists, 9641
Association of Catholic Trade Unionists: Activities, 2382;
    Role in the Labor Movement, 2397, 2398
Association of Southern Woman for the Prevention of
    Lynching: History (1930–1942), 5366, 5529;
    (1930–1942), 5985; (1933–1942), 5942; (1930–1942),
    5915
Astoria Studio of Queens, New York, History, (1920–1942),
    3745
Astral, Sinking of by U-43, (December 2, 1941), 7282
Aswell, James B. Jr., Political Career, 6686
At Liberty, Tennessee Williams "Lost" Play (1941), 5103
Atlanta Georgian, Letters Received from the Public,
    (1920s–1930s), 3945
Atlanta Municipal Graft Investigation, (1929–1935), 4741
Atlantic Wall (1941–1944), 8715
Atomic Bomb: as a Critical Issue in American History,
    9245; Development and Decision to use (1939–1950),
    4822; Development (1940–1945), 4952; Discussion of
    Historiographic Controversy, 9708; Evolution of
    Theoretical Framework to Construct (1932–1945); in
    American Science-Fiction, (1930–1960), 3284
Atomic Energy Commission, History (1939–1946), 4897
Atomic Energy, Debate over International Control, 4816
Atomic Weapons and the Question of International Control
    (1943–1946), 9293
Auburn-Lewiston, Maine Shoe Workers Strike, (1937), 2164
Auraud, Lt. General Henry S., Life, 9399
Austin, Warren R.: Foreign Policy Views, 1245; Senate
    Election (1934), 1244; Views on Neutrality, 1243,1246
Australian Representation in the United States (1915–1939),
    7250
Auto Union Factionalism, (1935–1936), 2140
Auto Worker Militancy and Factory Life, (1937–1955), 2283
Automobile: History in America, 1867; Impact on American
    Life, 1868; Industry, Capacity Utilization, (1921–1940),
    2579; Industry, Documentary Holding on Unionization,
    9660; Industry, Union-Management Conflict,
    (1937–1950), 2282; Workers before Unionization,
    (1900–1933), 2337; Workers Unions and the Formation
    of Labor Parties, (1930s), 2286; Wrecks and American
    Culture, (1920–1940), 1863
Avant Garde Novelists (1930s), 3508
Avant Garde Music, Stylistic diversity (1929–1945), 3529
Aviation Industry in Louisiana, Development,
    (1920s–1930s), 1884

B'Nai B'Rith, Response to Hitler's Anti-Jewish Policies, 5777

Bailey Amendment of 1944, Origins, 1514

Bailey, Carl E., As Governor of Arkansas (1936–1939), 6545

Bailey, Mildred, Discussion of Her Music, 3568

Bailey, Senator Josiah W.: As Opponent of the New Deal, 7135; Leader of the Southern Senate Conservatives, (1931–1946), 1109

Baker, Karle Wilson, Major Writer of the Regionalist Movement, (1920s–1030s), 3446

Baker, Newton D.: and the Adult Education Movement, 4404; And the Democratic Convention (1932), 6762

Balding, Sarah G., Career, 4266

Baldwin, Roger: and the Communists (1920–1940), 6191; Career, 5450

Balfour, John, Evaluation of American Culture (1939), 7202

Balkan Question and the Foundation of the Grand Alliance (1940–1942), 7424

Baltic States and U.S.-Soviet Relations (1939–1942), 7229

Baltimore: Politics (1920–1950), 6411; Transient Relief (1933–1937), 5235

Bank: Closures, Impact of New Deal Reforms, 1612; Collapse in Detroit, (1929–1933), 2543, 2589; Crisis (1933), 1582, 1584, 2522; Crisis in Iowa, (1933), 2586; Crisis in Michigan, (1933), 2557; Crisis in Nevada, (1932–1933), 2593: Crisis, National, (1933), 2558; Failures in Chicago, (1930–1932), 2521; Holiday in Arizona, (1933), 2550; Holiday in Arkansas, (1933), 2639; Holiday in Nevada, (1932), 2556; Holiday of (1933), International Causes, 2642; Holiday, Pro Hoover Analysis, 1641; of Douglas, Arizona, Fight for Control, (1933), 2611; Panic (1930), Causes, 1611

Bankhead, Senator John H.: Introduces Bill to Require the Federal Government to Purchase War Bond Advertising in Smaller Newspapers, (1943), 3952; Senate Career, 1110

Bankhead, William B., Supports New Deal Programs, 1068

Bankhead-Jones Farm Tenant Act (1937), 1333

Banking and the Securities Act (1933), 2661; Origins, 2755; Act (1935), Impact, 2003; Act (1935), Influence of Marriner Eccles, 2519; History, (1932–1951), 2517

Banking Industry Regulation, (1935–1980), 2577

Banking Reform, (1933–1935), 2504

Barkley, Alben W.: and the 1938 Gubernatorial Primary Campaign in Kentucky, 6534; and Kentucky Senate Election, (1938), 1118; Dispute with Roosevelt over Tax Bill (1944), 1112, 1120; Early Political Career, 1117; Elected Democratic Floor Leader, 1937, 111; Memoir, 1111; Senate Majority Leader, 1113, 1114; Speaking Ability, 1119

Barnard, Chester I., Writings, 2553

Barnes, Harry Elmer: And the "Historical Blackout", 9789; As Critic of the New Deal, 7168; Revisionist Historian, 9726; World War II Revisionist, 9700

Barnett, Claude, Career, (1919–1945), 4002

Barnstorming, History, (1920–1935), 1890

Barr, Frank, Bush Pilot, 1878

Barrage Balloons, History, 4828

Barton, Bruce: As Opponent of the New Deal, 7133; As Republican Speech Writer, 6034; Career, 1214

Baruch, Bernard M.: Efforts to Promote Orderly Economic Mobilization Planning (1920–1939), 5033; Influence on President Roosevelt, 0725; Memoir, 0724

Baseball: and Pennsylvania's Sunday Blue Laws, (1926–1943), 4609; and the American Presidency, 4618; Cincinnati Red Stockings Win the World Series (1940), 4589; in America (1930s and 1940s), 4626; Personalities (1930s), 4615; Urban and Rural Images (1920s and 1930s), 4587; in American Film (1940s), 3800

Bates, Sanford, and Prison Problems (1930s), 4697

Battleships, Rise and Fall (1898–1941), 4947

Bauhaus Faculty, Influence on American Architectural Development, 3172

Bayen, Walkue, Ethiopian Ambassador to the United States (1936–1941), 7246

Beach, Sylvia: And the Shakespeare and Company Bookstore in Paris (1920s and 1930s), 3344; Description of Her Collection of Papers and Books in the Princeton University Library, 3465

Beal, Fred E., Autobiography, 6193

Beard, Charles A.: Analysis of his Interpretation of Foreign Policy, 9797; And Foreign Policy, 9759; And Historical Relativism, 9769; And the New Deal, 9714; And the Writing of History, 9713; Biography, 9777; Comment on Roosevelt's Place in History, 9705; Criticizes Walter Lippmann (1937), 9802; His Changing Views on War, 7939; His Concept of National Interest Compared to that of Reinhold Neibuhr, 9728; His Views Compared with those of Archibald MacLeish, 6145; Opposes Naval Rearmament (1930s), 7937; Opposes Roosevelt's Foreign Policy, 7936, 7938; Opposes U.S. Foreign Policy (1941), 7854; Political and Social Thought, 9711; The Evolution of his Views on American Foreign Policy, 9750

Beaumont, Texas Race Riot (1943), 5509, 5329

Beck, Dave and Pacific Northwest Transportation Workers, (1917–1941), 2168

Beck, James M., And the Politics of Conservatism, 7122

Becker, Carl, Influence as an Historian, 9775

Bell, Daniel, And the Rise of Modernist Sociology, 6204

Bellgeddes, Norman, Popularizer of Streamlining (1930s), 4953

Bell Telephone and Company Unions, (1919–1937), 2360

Ben-Gurion, David, Visits the U.S. (1940–1941), 9004

Bendiner, Robert, Coming of Age as a Journalist (1930s), 3940

Bendix Trophy Cross Country Air Race, (1936), 1907

Benet, Stephen Vincent, Letters to George Abbey, (1935–1943), 3270

Benjamin Franklin High School in New York City, History (1930s and 1940s), 4385

Bennett, Gwendolyn, Diaries, 5419

Bennett, John C., Christian Social Activist, 4462

Benson, Elmer A., Reflects on Minnesota Politics (1920s and 1930s), 6427

Benton, Thomas Hart: Analysis of His Art, 3665; Career and Political Attitudes, 3610; Political and Social Implications of His Art, 3624

Berkeley, Busby, Use of Mechanized Dances in His Films during the 1920 and 1930s to Depict Man's Relationship to the Advance of Technology, 3850

Berle, Adolph A., Jr.: and Corporate Power, 2631; As a Student of the Corporation, 0728; Biography, 0730; Political theory, 0729; Public Career, 0726; Views on Corporate Economic Power, 0727; Writings, 5052

Berlin, Irving, Biographical Sketch, 3558

Berlin Journalists in New York, (1933–1945), 4152

Berlin, New Hampshire, Local Politics (1932–1936), 6472

Berlin Riot (1935), 9108

Bernard, Congressman John T., Opposes American Foreign Policy (1937–1939), 7864

Berry Pickers Strike, El Monte, California, (1933), 2236

Berryman, John, Memoir (1930s), 3591

Berwanger, Jay, First Winner of the Hiesman Trophy, (1935), 4584

Bethune, Marry McCloud: and the National Youth Administration, 2756; Biographical Sketch, 5454; Career, 5314

Better Homes Movement, (1922–1935), 1803

Better Housing League of Cincinnati, (1916–1939), 1794

Bible, Dana X., As Football Coach at the University of Texas (1937–1946), 4614

Biddle, Anthony J., D., Diplomatic Papers, 0778

Big Bend National Park, Origins, 1467

Big Bombers, Development, 4865

Big Business: and Radio (1930s), 3870; and the Federal Government, Relationship, (1933–1981), 2576; Ideological Defense, (1933–1953), 2640; Public Image, (1880–1940), 2531

Big Steel, Rise and Decline, 2603

Bilbo, Theodore G.: Elected to Senate, (1934), 1122; Election Campaigns in the Mississippi Delta, 1126; Notorious Racist, 1130; Opposes Fair Employment Practices, 1121; Political Career, 1124, 1125; Racial Rhetoric, 1123 Supports New Deal Programs, 1127, 1128, 1129

Bill of Rights, Ratified by Connecticut, Georgia, Massachusetts (1939), 6475

Billboard Advertising, Origin, Design, and Development, 3623

Bingham, Alfred M.: And Non-Marxian Radicalism, 6291; Liberal Views, 6181; Non-Marxian Radical of the New Deal Era, 6290

Biology, Transformation into a Modern Discipline (1930s), 4921

Birmingham, Alabama: and Racial Violence (1930s), 4721 Labor Unions and Jim Crow (1930s and 1940s), 5505

Birth Control Politics (1920–1945), 5469

Bishop, Elizabeth, Correspondence with Marianne Moore, (1930s–1940s), 3662

Bishop, John P., Analysis of His Works as a Novelist, 3340

Bishop, W. Howard, As President of the National Catholic Rural Life Conference, (1928–1944), 4514

Bituminous Coal Acts (1935 and 1937), 2954

Bituminous Coal Industry, Impact of New Deal, 2159, 2566, 4942

Black Agrarian Radicalism in the Great Depression, 1549

Black Agricultural Labor, Efforts of Socialists to Reform (1930s), 5537

Black America and the Ethiopian Crisis, 5582

Black American: Art in the 1920s and 1930s, 5072; Authors (1896–1981), 5559; Communities in Seattle and Portland during the 1930s, 5563; Elite, Statistical Profile (1930–1940), 9614; Experience in Sports (1900–1950), 4611; Leaders and American Civil Religion (1880–1968), 5426; Males, Changes in Economic Status (1940s), 5521; Migration (1915–1940), 5350; Novelists during the Great Depression, 3297; Opposition to America's Wars in the Twentieth Century, 5390; Seen in William Faulkner's Novels, (1926–1936), 3326; Women as Represented in Hollywood Feature Films, (1915–1949), 3744; Writers: Studies James Weldon Johnson, Langston Hughes, Zora Neale Hurston, and Richard Wright, 3475

Black Americans: and Communism, 5442; and Ethiopian Relief (1935–1936), 5539, 7347; between the Two World Wars, 5556; Child Ballads, Analysis (1927–1942), 3554; in Two World Wars, 5632; Reaction to the Persecution of European Jews (1933–1945), 5605; Their Political Status during the Age of Roosevelt, 5652; Their Role in the Armed Services (1948), 5609; Their Views on Haiti, Liberia, The Virgin Islands, and Ethiopia, (1929–1936), 5538

Black and Jewish Ethnic Identity (1930s and 1940s), 4767

Black and White Intellectuals, Their Views on Social and Racial Issues Compared, 5524

Black Anti-Semitism in America, Origins, 5747

Black Attitudes and the American War Effort (1941–1945), 5630

Black Cabinet Members, 0624

Black Chicagoans: And Direct Action to Implement Public School Integration (1936), 5636; And the Politics of Public Education (1910–1941), 5637

Black Clergy in Memphis During the Crump Era, (1920s to the 1940s), 4573

Black Communists in Alabama, (1930–1935), 5439

Black Community: in Columbia, South Carolina (1930s), 5458; Influence on American Foreign Policy since the 1930s, 5515

Black County Agent System, (1906–1940), 5352

Black Culture in Urban Texas, (1930–1954), 5543

Black Employment: in Los Angeles (1938–1948), 5555; in New York (1920–1963), 5317, 5318

Black Female Tobacco Workers in Durham, North Carolina (1920–1940), 5973

Black Film and Folk Tradition, 5549

Black Fliers in Western Pennsylvania, (1906–1945), 5300

Black Harlem Poetry, (1919–1981), 3587

Black Hebrew Communities in America, Origins, 5436

Black History Records, National Archives, 9675

Black, Hugo L., 6972–6980

Black Industrial Working Class in Detroit, Formation and Development of (1915–1945), 5564

Black Jazz Community in Detroit (1917–1940), 5313

Black Jive, The Zoot Suit and White Repression, 5571

Black, John D., Farm Policy Advisor, 1319

Black Journalism in Mississippi, (1867–1945), 4035

Black Leaders and the 1932 Election, 5661

Black Leadership: (1930s), 5353; in the 1936 Election Year, 5657

Black Legion: 6401; American Fascist Organization, 6366; in Detroit (1930s), 6385

Black Literary Magazines (1930s), 4009

Black Migrant Youth in Buffalo, New York, (1917–1940), 4422

Black Migration to the Central Appalachian Coal Fields, (1880–1940), 5457

Black Nationalism and the Italo-Ethiopian Conflict (1934–1936), 7244

Black Newspaper Correspondents and World War II, 4086

Black Newspapers in Mississippi, (1867–1984), 5474

Black Nuns in Louisiana, Efforts to Accredit them as Teachers (1920s to the 1930s), 5376

Black People of Texas, History (1930–1954), 5542

Black Perceptions of the Jews between the Wars, 5799

Black Physicians, And Segregation in Pre-World War II South, 5306

Black Political Thought, Changes (1915–1940), 5668

Black Politics and Protest in Chicago (1930–1939), 5664

Black Population Shifts in the American South (1940–1960), 5468

Black Press: and the Image of Success, (1920–1939), 5578; History in America, 4098; Investigated by the Federal Government during World War II, 5580

Black Protest: at the Chicago's World's Fair (1933–1934), 5481; during World War II, 5628

Black Radicals in Chicago (1930s), 5594

Black Reaction to *Gone with the Wind*, 3845

Black School Teachers in Maryland (1930s), 5584

Black Shipyard Workers and the Union Movement in California during World War II, 5591

Black Social Movement (1900–1960), 5322

Black Teachers and Salary Discrimination (1930s and 1940s), 5307

Black Urban Boycott Movements, (1929–1941), 5431

Black Voters: and the New Deal, 5646; Increase Participation in the South after 1944, 5662

Black Voting Patterns: in Chicago during the New Deal, 5656; in Knoxville, Tennessee (1929–1936), 5655; in Providence, Rhode Island (1930s), 5654

Black/White Relations and the Capitalist System in the United States, (1930–1950), 5321

Black Women in America, Their Survival Strategies, 5545

Black Workers: and Organized Labor, 5381; in the Chicago Meat Packing Industry (1915–1940), 5560

Black Writers: and the Harlem Renaissance, 5547; Their Impressions of the South (1929–1953), 5382

Black-Jewish Relations in Detroit (1937–1962), 5558

Blacks: and the Air Force (1939–1949), 5627; and Education as Portrayed in the 1940 Census, 5641; and Education in the South during the Depression, 5613; and Politics in San Francisco (1920–1940), 5651; and the Communist Party (1930s and 1940s), 5465; and the Destruction of the Democratic White Primary (1935–1944), 5658; and the Struggle against the Texas Democratic White Primary (1932–1945), 5659; and Presidential Politics in Cincinnati, 5653; and their Efforts to Gain the Right to Vote in Macon County, Alabama, (1941–1972), 5663; in American History Text Books, 5486; Memphis, Tennessee, (1920–1955), 5483; in the Army Air Force During World War II, 5625; in Norfolk, Virginia, (1919–1945), 5456

Blaine, Peter Sr., As Representative of the Papagao Indians in Washington (1930s), 5816

Blankenhorn, Hebert, Role in the LaFollette Committee, 2212

Blitzstein, Marc: Analysis of His Play "The Cradle will Rock" (1937), 3544; Social Criticism in His Librettos', 3571

Bloch, Julius, Analysis of His Work (1930s), 3640

Blood, Henry H., As Governor of Utah, 6674

Bloomington, Indiana, Social Networks (1939), 4764

Bloor, L. R., Autobiography, 6202

Blue Ridge Parkway, Early History, 1480

Blues, Cultural History, 3518

Blues Music, Sexual Imagery (1920s and 1930s), 3569

Blumenson, Martin, Discussion of Official Histories, 9709

Boeing B-29, Development, 4913

Boetticher, Freidrich Von, German Military Attache in Washington (1933–1941), 7267

Boettiger, John and Anna, 0114

Bogle, Cathryn: Recounts her Experience as a Member of the Black Minority in Oregon, 5320; Reprint of her Essay "An American Negro Speaks of Color", *Portland Sunday Oregonian* (February 14, 1937), 5319

Bohlen, Charles, E., Diplomatic Career, 0779

Boileau, Gerald J., Supports Dairy Farmers, 1215

Boland, John P., Catholic Labor Organizer in Buffalo, New York, 2128

Bonacci, Frank, Career, 2419

Bond, Horace M.: And Black Education in Alabama, 5573; His Views on Black Education and Society, 5387

Bonus Army, History, 2096, 2097, 2098

Borah, William E.: Biographical Sketch, 0981; Biography, 0985; British View, 0988; Foreign Policy Views, 0984; Letter to Henry Stimpson, 1932, 0990; Opposition to New Deal Programs, 0986; Political Campaigns, 0983; Reelection (1936), 0987; Speaking Ability, 0989

Borden, Neil H., His Books on Advertising, (1932–1942), 3713

Borsodi, Myrtle M., Spokesperson for the Homemaker, 5934

Borsodi, Ralph: As Opponent of the New Deal, 7157; Spokesman for American Agrarian Movement, (1918–1941), 1551; Subsistence Farming Ideas, 1544

Boston: Ethnic Conflict (1935–1944), 4783, 5793

Boston's Elders During the New Deal Years, 4680

Botkin, B.A., As National Folklore Editor of the New Deal Federal Writers Project, 5069

Boulder Canyon Project, Origins, 1930

Boulder Dam, Origins, 1475

Bourke-White, Margaret, As target of the House Un-American Activities Committee (1944), 6877

Bowers, Claude G.: As American Ambassador to Spain (1933–1939), 7356; Biography, 0782; Career, 0780; Mission to Spain, (1939), 0781

Bowles, Chester, His Secret Plan to End World War II, 8006

Bowles, Edward, Career at MIT (1920–1940), 4965

Bracero Movement in the Pacific North West (1940–1950), 5678

Bracero Policy Experiment (1942–1945), 5679

Bracero Program: 4175; (1942–1947), 9055; (1942–1951), 9053; and Railroad Labor during World War II, 1913; and Texas, (1942–1947), 4172; under the Farm Security Administration, (1942–1943), 4174

Braden, Spruille: Memoirs, 0783; Political Career, 0784

Bradley, Omar N., Memoir, 0899

Braithwaite, W.S., His Experience on the Faculty of Atlanta University (1935–1945), 5331

Branch Banking, Origins in California, (1905), 2515

Brandies, Louis D.: 6981–6991

Brandt, Irving, as an Advisor to Roosevelt, 1422

Brawley, Benjamin, Biography, 5511

Brazos River Authority, History, (1929–1979), 2965

Brecht, Bertholt, American Play, (1921–1941), 3254; Analysis of His Relationship with America, 3252

Bretton woods Conference, 2518

Brewster Aeronautical Corporation, History, (1932–1942), 1891

Brickell, Herschel, His Interest in Spanish Literature, 5674

Bridenstine, Ellenore M., Political Career in Montana, 6437

Bridges, Harry: Career, 2421; Role in Maritime Strike (1934), 2420

Brighton Seminole Reservation Florida, (1935–1938), 5829

Bristol, Horace, Photographs of Life in the San Joaquin Valley, (1937), 3295

British Embassy Views of Prominent Americans (1939), 8739

British Foreign Policy: American Evaluation (1930s), 7215 and Germany (1935–1938), 7273

British Propaganda in America (1939–1941), 8535

British Royalty Visit the United States (1939), 7325

Broadcast News, Debate over Editorializing, (1943), 3924

Broadcasting, History in the United States, (1933–1953), 3871; in Kentucky, (1922–1942), 3874

Broadway Plays, Social Significance, 3208

Brodie, J. C., Demands Deportation of all Aliens (1930s), 4157

Brookhart, Smith W., Political Career, 1247

Brookings Institute, Early History (1916–1952), 7092

Brooklyn Public Libraries Baby Naming Service, (1937–1938), 4687

Brookwood Labor College, History, (1921–1937), 4331

Brophy, John, Career, 2422

"Brother Rat" as Theater and Symbol, 3198

Brotherhood of Sleeping Car Porters, Early History, (1925–1937), 2229

Broun, Haywood: Career and Thought, 6171; Leading Columnist (1920s and 1930s), 6185

Browder, Earl R., And American Communism at High Tide (1934–1935), 6323; American Spokesmen for Communism (1930–1945), 6216; Biography, 6318; Rise and Fall, 6259

Brown, Harold, His Experiences with Racial Discrimination in Buffalo, New York, 5312

Brown, Homer S., Civil Rights Activist in Pittsburgh, 5355

Brown, John, As Portrayed in *The Santa Fe Trail* (1940), 3805

Brown, John M., His Dramatic and Theatrical Criticism, 3241

Browning, Gordon: and Tennessee Politics (1937–1953), 6600; and Tennessee Politics (1930s), 6601; and the 1936 Gubernatorial Election in Tennessee, 6405; Political Feud with Boss Ed Crump of Memphis, 6627

Brownlow, Louis, Career, 0671

Brussel's Conference, and Conflict with Japan, 7482

Bryan, Julian, His Documentary Films on Latin America, (1941–1945), 3791

Bryn Mawr, Summer School for Women Workers, (1921–1938), 4323

Bubley, Esther, Photographs of Inner City Bus Travelers, (1942–1943), 3635

Buck, Pearl, Popular Expert on China, (1931–1949), 3385

Buckman, Frank, As Founder of the Moral Rearmament Movement (1938), 4492

Budget Westerns (1930s and 1940s), 3853

Buell, Raymond L., And the Decline of Wilsonism, 7986

Building America, Educational Publishing Experiment, (1935, 1948), 4378

Biltmore Hotel Water Shows, Miami, (1928–1942), 4253

Bullitt, William C.: and the Soviet Union, 7421; Ambassador to France, 0786; Diplomatic Career, (1936–1943), 0785; Witness to the Fall of France, 0787

Bunche, Ralph J.: And Black Radical Thought (1930s), 5445; Intellectual Development and Political Career, 0788

Bunnell, Helen E., Her Experiences as Wife and Mother in Utah During the Great Depression, 4676

Bureau of Indian Affairs: Evaluation of Activities (1933–1950), 5912; Under Charles Burke (1921–1928) and John Collier (1933–1945), 5897

Bureau of Intelligence, Criticism of Hollywood, (1942–1943), 3727

Bureau of Reclamation under the New Deal, 1516

Burma-Shave Advertisements along American Highways, 4255

Burnham, James, Biography, 6254

Burns, Evelyn M., Views on Social Security, 4645

Busbice, E. Hollace, Memoir, 1656

Bush, Oliva Ward, Career, 3367

Bush, Vannever, Press Reaction to his Post War Report on Scientific Research, 4915

Business Advisory Council, 0550

Business: and Government, Historical Analysis of Relationship, 2544; and Public Relations, (1900–1950), 2628; Community Demands Retrenchment in Public Education, (1932–1934), 4396; Liquidity during and after the Great Depression, 2548; Policies in San Francisco and Los Angeles, (1890s–1930s), 2549; Response to Keynesian Economics, (1929–1964), 2029; Responses to New Deal, 1598

Butler, Hugh: and Aid to Latin America (1943–1944), 7860; Biographical Sketch, 0991; Political Career, 0992

Butler, Marion, And North Carolina Politics, 6550

Butler, Smedley D.: Biography, 0966; Court Martial, 0965

Buy-American Act of 1933, Impact, 2000

Byrd, Admiral Richard E., And the Peace Crusade (1930s), 8019

Byrd, Harry F.: As Virginia's Favorite Son Candidate for President (1932), 6717; Life and Political Career, 1132; Opposed by Roosevelt, 1131; Presidential Candidate, (1932), 1133

Byrnes, James F.: 0291, 7040; Attitude toward USSR, 1135; Early Life, 1137; Involvement in Yalta Myth, 1141; Memoir, 1134; Political Career, 1136, 1138; Racial Attitudes, 1139; Wartime Services, 1140

Byrns, Joseph W., Supports New Deal Programs, 1069

Bywaters, Jerry, Biography, 3626

Cabell, James B., Evaluated as Romantic Escapist, 3304

Caffery, Jefferson: Ambassador to France, 0789; Career, 0790

Cain, James M., Analysis of His Contributions to the Tough Guy Novels (1920s and 1930s), 3413; And the Los Angeles Novel (1930s and 1940s), 3342

Cairo and Tehran Conferences, Documents, 9687

Cairo Conference, 8597, 8619

Caldwell, Erskine: Analysis of Works Produced (1930s), 3375; Early Novels, (1930–1935), 3382; Use of Country-Folk Comedy (1930s and 1940s), 3361

Caldwell, Hemingway, and Steinbeck as World War II Journalists, 3464

Caldwell, Sam, and Louisiana Politics (1940s), 6684

California: Agricultural Land Policy, (1900–1966), 1429; Life Payments Plan, Rise and Fall, 2490; Lynching of Two Accused Murders Condoned by the Governor, (1933), 4729; Novelists (1930s), 3391; Peace Movement (1915–1935), 8028; Politics (1920–1932), 6623; Response to the "New Education" (1930s), 4324; Water Politics, (1933–1944), 1476

California Institute of Technology (1930s), 4312

California National Labor Relations Act, (1935), 3015

California Medical Association, Proposes Compulsory Health Insurance (1935), 4242

Caliver, Ambrose, Contribution to Black Education (1930s), 5404

Callahan, Patrick H.: And Kentucky Politics, 6491; Attempts to Reconcile Catholicism with the Southern Ethos, 4480; His Correspondence with H. L. Mencken, (1925–1940), 4120

Callicott, Burton, His Hernando DeSoto Murals in the Pink Palace Museum, Memphis, 3684

Calverton, V. F.: Biography, 6360; His Influence Among Black Intellectuals (1920–1940), 5389; His Views on Black American Writers, 5357; Radical Publisher (1920s and 1930s), 4004

Cambridge-Somerville Youth Study in Massachusetts, (1935–1958), 4728

Camen, Martin D., Recalls his Work at the Lawrence Radiation Laboratory, University of California (1936–1939), 4917

Camp Shelby, Impact on Hattiesbergh, Mississippi, 8092, 8174

Campaign Finance Regulation (1925–1939), 6074

Campbell, Thomas D., Early Large Scale Farmer, 1437

Canadian Foreign Policy (1935–1957), 7251

Canadian-American Trade Agreement (1935), 1841

Canadian-American Trade during the Great Depression, 1851

Canadian-American Rivalry over Greenland, 7254

Cannon, Clarence A., Speaking Skills, 1070

Cannon, Walter B. and L. J. Henderson, Their Differing Views on the Nature of Social Systems, 4854

Capehart, Homer E., Entry into Republican Party Politics in Indiana (1938), 6661

Capitalism and Social Change, Nineteenth and Early Twentieth Centuries, 1957

Capper, Arthur, Foreign Policy Views, 0993

Capra, Frank: American Values as Reflected in His Films, (1930–1950), 3828; And the *Why We Fight* Series, 8507; His Film, *Prelude to War* (1942), Analyzed, 3843; Individualism versus the Masses in His Films, 3849

Carbon County, Utah Coal Strike, (1933), 2335

Cardozo, Benjamin, 6992–6994

Caribbean Immigrants in the Harlem Renaissance, 4179

Carl Mackley Houses in Philadelphia, First New Deal Public housing Project, 1814

Carlson, Evans F.: As U.S. Intelligence Officer in China (1937–1947), 9416; His Mission to China (1937–1938), 6233

Carlson, Chester F., Discover of Xerography (1938), 4879

Carnegie Corporation of New York, Arts Project of during the Inter War Period, 3636

Carnegie Endowment for International Peace (1931–1941), 7973

Caron, Will and the Virginia Conservation Commission, (1926–1934), 1462

Carpenter, Farrington R., Profile, 1457

Carr, Wilbur J., As Minister to Czechoslovakia (1937–1939), 7834

Carroll County, Maryland Children's Aid Society in the Great Depression, 4218

Carstensen, Vernon, Teaching Experiences at Central Washington College of Education (1930s), 4282

Carter, Boake: Radio Commentator, (1931–1938), 3891; (1935–1938), 3881

Carter, Hodding, Southern Liberal, (1907–1972), 4067

Carter, William Hodding, Jr., Crusading Journalist in Mississippi, (1930s to 1950s), 3983

Cartoons, Use and Analysis of during World War II, 3935

Casablanca (1942) and American Foreign Policy in Regard to Vichy France, 3824

Casablanca Conference, 8587, 8604

Cascade Springs, Georgia, History, 1529

Case, Francis H.: Conservative South Dakota Congressman, 1216; Foreign Policy Views, 1217

Casey, A. G., As Australian Minster to U.S. (1940–1942), 8668

Cash, Rosaland, Her Experience as a Black Actress (1930s to the 1980s), 5338

Cash, W. J.: Analysis of His Life and Work, 3435; Editorialist of the South, 4041

Cason, Clarence, Southern Liberal (1930s), 6167

Casteel, John L., Diary of a University of Oregon Speech Professor, (1931–1942), 4430

Castellow, Bryant T., Biographical Sketch, 1071

Castle, William R., Opposes U.S. Involvement in an Asian War (1939–1941), 7895

Catholic Church and Organized Labor (1930s), 2330; and Social Reform (1930s), 4546; and the Congress of Industrial Organizations, (1937–1950), 2370, 4560; and the Spanish Civil War, 7353; Attitudes toward Great Britain (1940), 7206

Catholic Committee for the Ratification for the Child Labor Amendment (1935–1937), 4681

Catholic Committee of the South, (1939–1956), 4528

Catholic: Conscientious Objectors during World War II, 8034; Inter-Racial Council of New York, (1935–1964), 4579; Lay Evangelization (1930s), 4464; Lay Movements in New York City, (1930s–1940s), 4476; Missionaries in China, (1918–1941), 4458; Periodicals, Their Views on Domestic Problems (1920s and 1930s), 3941; Program for Social Action During the Great Depression, 4435; Radicalism in America, 4444; Reaction to the Persecutions of the Church in Mexico, (1926–1936),

4572; Social Thought (1930s), 4547; Thought and World War II Labor Legislation, 4495; Welfare Conference (1935–1945), 4455

Catholicworker Movement, Role in American Pacificism, (1933–1972), 2279; Content Analysis, (1933–1982), 4066; History, (1933–1965), 4554; Origins, 2129

Catholics: Achieve Greater Political Power During the New Deal Era, 4490; in an Era of Disillusionment, (1920–1940), 4496; in the Labor Movement, (1937–1949), 2228

Catholicism: and Industrial Reform, (1937–1940), 4445; in South Florida, (1868–1968), 4532

Caughey, John W., Survey of his Work as an Historian, 9706

Census of 1940, Analysis, 1802

Central Valley Project in California, (1933–1967), 1730

Centrist Liberals, Views (1914–1940), 6178

Cermak, Anton J., And the Public Schools of Chicago (1931–1933), 4416

Chaco Peace Conference, 9037

Chaffee, Zechariah Jr., Conservative Supporter of Free Speech, 6127

Chain Reaction Pile, Building the first, 5010

Chain Stores: Regulation in Kentucky, (1925–1945), 2608; Opposition in Portland, Oregon, (1928–1935), 2545; Opposition in the South, 2609

Chamberlain, Neville, 9180

Champion, Gower, and the American Musical Theater, 3245

Champion of Youth, Organ of the Young Communist League, (1936–1938), 3987

Chandler, Raymond, Analysis of His Works (1939–1940), 3380

Chandler, Walter, Congressional Career, 1072

Chaplain, Charles Autobiography, 3734; His film *Modern Times* (1936) compared to Charles Dickens' story *Hard Times* (1854), 3846

Chaplin, Ralph: Autobiography, 6215; Career in the Industrial Workers of the World, 2355

Chapman, Oscar L., New Deal Career, 2709

Chase, Stuart: Biography of a Liberal Economist, 4650; Economic Thought, 1946

Chavez, Dennis, Supports New Deal, 0994

Chemical Fertilizers, 1284

Chemical Weed Killer, 2,4–D, Development, 4970

Chennault, Claire Lee.: And China (1937–1958), 8886; Leader of Flying Tigers, 0900; Memoir, 8891

Chiang, Kai-Shek, 9218–9219

Chicago: and Ethnic Politics (1890–1936), 4762; and German Question (1914–1941), 4785; and Political Bossism, 6403; Area Project, (1933–1958), 4726; Black Voting Patterns (1918–1936), 5292; Burlington & Quincy Railroad, Abandonment of Rail Lines, (1943), 1922; Catholic Movement, 4563; Changes in Child Birth Patterns (1920s and 1930s), 4691; Changes in Mass Culture (1920s to the 1930s), 4765; Economists, Views on Deficit Budgets (Early 1930s), 2045; (1930s), 4209;

Newspaper Guild #71, Origins, 2272; Newspaper Hoax in the 1936 Election Campaign, 4038; O'Hare International Airport, Development, 1879; Public School Crisis, (1933), 4349; Public Schools and the Great Depression (1929–1937), 4278; Radio, Glory Days, (1930–1940), 3928; School Economists Reaction to Keynesianism, 2043; School of Television, Role in the history of Television, 3923; Social and Cultural Environment (Late 1930s), 4142; *Tribune*, Reveals Advanced Knowledge of Japanese Plan for Attack on Midway Island (June 7, 1942), 9284; Worlds Fair, (1933–1934), Its Impact on Black Demands for Justice and Equal Rights, 5527

Chicanos: in Chicago, 5680; in Ontario, California and Civil Rights (1937–1947), 5695; Labor Movement (1930s), 5677

Child Protective Care, Origins between the Wars, 4182

Childcare, Politics (1940s), 4677

Children: and Federal Legislation (1949–1971), 4690; as Portrayed in American Film, (1935–1975), 3775

Chilocco Indian Agricultural Boarding School, (1920–1940), 5870, 5871

China: and the Quest for an Anti-Japanese Alliance (1931–1941), 8928; Communists and their American Supporters (1926–1929), 7869; Market (1943–1950), 8885

China Clipper, 1881

Chinese-American Community in Nanking (1928–1945), 8904

Chinese Communists, Visited by Foreign Journalist (1944), 8929

Chinese Hand Laundry Alliance of New York City, Campaigns to Repeal Chinese Exclusion Act of 1882, 4792

Chinese Digest, History, (1935–1940), 4018

Chisum, Melvin J., Supports Roosevelt in His Newspaper *The Tribune*, 4053

Christian Century: Civil Liberties Stance between the Wars, 3997; Opposes Diplomatic Relations with the Vatican, (1940–1952), 4544

Christian, Marcus, Career, 5417

Christian Pacifists and Political Strategy, 8041

Christian Science Monitor, Reaction to the First Phase of Nazi Persecution of Jews, 4022

Christopher, Paul R., Career, 2423

Church Peace Union, (1914–1941), 8045

Church, Robert R. Jr., Black Republican Leader in Memphis, (1928–1940), 5648

Church, Verne V., Recollections of a Civilian Conservation Corps Camp Superintendent, 2799

Churchill, Winston: 9181–9201; and the Second Front Question, 8720

Ciechanowski, Jan, As Polish Ambassador to the U.S. (1941–1945), 8808

Cincinnati: Use of Charter Committee System (1933–1936), 6504; Her Black Baseball Players (1920s to the 1940s), 4627

Circle Stock Repertoire Theater in America, (1907–1955), 3233

Cities and Federal Policy, (1933–1960), 2699

City Bosses, Discussion, 6482

City of Flint, American Merchant Ship Captured by Germans (1939), 7271

City of Portland, Riding on, (1935), 1923

City University of New York, Struggles for Freedom of Speech (1930s), 4340

Civil Liberties Crisis in Pacific Northwest (1917–1940), 5402

Civil Rights: Consciousness (1940s), 5440; in New York City (1941–1943), 6449: Evolution of Policy in America, (1937–1982), 5340; Lawyers from the New Deal to the New Frontier, 5587; Movement (1940–1954), 5471; Movement, and Public Argumentation, 5348; Movement (1930s), 5552, 5553; Movement, Origins (1930s), 5298; Movement, Origins (1940s), 5449

Civil Works Administration: Conflict with American Federation of Labor, 2892; Corruption, 2892; Health Project in Louisiana, 2999; History, (1933–1934), 2891, 2906; in California, 3014; in Idaho, 3019; in Louisiana, 3000; in Pennsylvania, (1933–1934), 2966

Civilian Conservation Corps: Accomplishments in the Area of Farming, 2828; and Black Youth in California, 5345; and Politics, 2742; and Politics in Maine, (1933–1936), 2952; and Racial Issues, 5434; and Roosevelt's Impact, 2913; and the Farm Island Causeway, 2914; and the Indians, 5880; and the Negro, 2885; and the Negro Question in New York, 3007; and Wisconsin State Park Development, 2919; Army Participation in, 2873; Brief History, 2856; Camp William James Project, Vermont, (1940–1941), 3060; Conservatism, Censorship, and Controversy in, 2821; Education Program, 2822; Efforts to Make Permanent, 2820; Evaluation, 2893; Fosters Emergence of State Forestry Departments in the South, 3113; History, 2884; in Alaska, 2959; in Buck Meadows, California, 3072; in California, 2931; in Elko County, Nevada, 3071; in Florida, 3016; in Glacier National Park, 3121; in Idaho, 2921; in Louisiana, 2975, 2976; in Michigan, 3008; in Minnesota, 2978; in New Hampshire, 2854, 2947; in New York, 3004, 3005, 3006; in New Jersey, 5213; in New Mexico, 2963, 5214; in Oklahoma, 2971; in Pennsylvania, 5192; in South Dakota, 5193; in the Northern Rocky Mountains, 3099; in Tulsa and Oklahoma City, 3063; in Utah, 2925; in Vermont, 2900; in Wisconsin, 3009; in Yellowstone Park, 3065; Indian Division, 2951; Military Participation, 2894; Military Role, 2898; Myakka River State Park Project, Florida, 3077; Opposition, 7100; Origins, 2714; Reclamation Work in Utah, 2926; Relationship with the Army, 2837; Sherwood Forest Project, Missouri, 3076; Struggle of Blacks to Gain Leadership Positions, 5399

Civilian Pilot Training Program, Origins (1939), 5012

Civilian Public Service during World War II, 8007, 8053

Clark, James E., As Critic of the New Deal, 7086

Clark, Jay Ruben, As Opponent of the New Deal, 6131

Clark, Walter Van Tilburg, Analysis of His Novel *The Ox-Bow Incident* (1942), 3502

Class Confrontation in Hollywood's Romantic Comedies, (1934–1942), 3838

Clawson, Augusta, Remembers Working as a Welder in World War II, 8264

Clayton, Will, Papers, 1828

Clements, Earle C., And Kentucky Politics, 6716

Clerical Opinion on Peace, Prohibition and Poverty in the 1930s, 4457

Cleveland Chamber of Commerce and the Great Depression, 1583

Cleveland, Patterns of Black Life and Thought (1929–1945), 5596

Cleveland Rocket Society: (1933–1938), 4995; History, 5027

Close Up, A Film Journal Operated between 1927 and 1933, 3982

Cloud, Henry R., Winnebago Indian Reformer, 5831

Coal: and Clean Air Acts as Amendments to New Deal Legislation, 1407; Industry, Impact of Union Growth, 2383; Strike (1943), 2202, 2391

Coastal Defense, Development (1919–1941), 4989

Coeur D'Alene Indians and the Dawes Act, 5828

Cohen, Benjamin V., Biography, 0672

Cohen, Wilbur J., Remembers Roosevelt's Efforts to Establish a Welfare System, 5047

Cohn, George W. Jr., Selected as Director of the WPA in North Carolina (1935), 6609

Cold War: and U.S. Policy toward German Scientists, 9288; Historiography, 9703; Origins, 8834, 8840, 8853, 8868, 9464–9526; Revisionists and their Critics (1979), 9791

Coldest Winter, Hottest Summer Ever in Iowa, (1936), 1689

Coldwell, Oliver J., Experience in China (1944–1945), 8890

Collective Bargaining: in Industry, Development under National Government Regulation, (1933–1935), 2638; Origins and Development, 2176

Collective Security: American Response (1929–1936), 7228; and the Italo-Ethiopian Crisis, 7350; Failure, 7987

College Athletics, Aborted Efforts to De-emphasize (1935), 4624

Collier, John: and the Florida Cattle Tick Controversy, 5884; and the Creation of the Inter-American Institute (1940), 5882; and the Hopi Constitution (1936), 5850; and the Oklahoma Indian Welfare Act (1936), 5911; and the Pueblo Lands Act, 5860; As Commissioner of Indian Affairs (1933–1945), 5844, 5868 5881, Encounter with the Florida Seminoles (1935), 5862; Evaluation of the Philosophical Origins of his Policies, 5893; Social Philosophy, 5867

Colorado River Dispute, Arizona vs. California, 1521

Colorado River Land Company and Mexican Agrarian Reform in Baja California, (1902–1944), 1470

Columbia Scholastic Press Association, (1924–1981), 4327

Columbia University Department of Psychology, Golden Age, (1920–1940), 4423

Comedic Heroes of Leo McCarey Compared to those of Frank Capra, 3759

Comfort, Nicholas, Social Activist in Oklahoma, 4473

Comintern: Activities (1933–1935), 7417; Patterns (1928–1943), 7442

Commercial Air Transportation in North Dakota, (1928–1945), 1893

Commercial Aviation and the Colonization of the Equatorial Islands, (1934–1936), 4899

Commercial Trade Policy of the United States: (1922–1952), Analysis, 1829, 1830; Origins, 1831

Commission on Inter-Racial Cooperation: Activities (1919–1944), 5371; and the New Deal in Georgia, 5372

Committee for Political Defense and Hemispheric Security, 9019

Committee on Industrial Organization, and Black Leaders (1936–1945), 5508

Committee on Militarism in Education, (1925–1940), 4265

Committee on the Status of Black Americans of the National Research Council, History and Work, 5433

Committee to Defend America by Aiding the Allies: (1940–1941), 7966; in Minneapolis, 7972

Common Ground: An American Literary Magazine, Its Views on Education and Politics (1940s), 3942; Comments on America's Minorities, (1940–1949), 4049

Commonwealth College: (1925–1935), 4286; Fund Supports Children's Health Care Projects, (1920s–1930s), 4196; History, 4290; Library, (1925–1940), 4407; VS. Arkansas' General Assembly, (1935–1937), 4287

Commonweal, The Williams-Schuster Years, (1924–1938), 3964

Communication Workers of America, Organization, (1935–1937), 2359

Communism: and Black Nationalism during the Depression, 6297; and the American Labor Movement (1920–1950), 6311; and Unionism in the United States and Mexico (1935–1939), 6276; in the Motion Picture Industry Investigated, (1933–1953), 3851, Appeal (1930s), 3266

Communist Party: Activities in Harlem, 5498; and Blacks during the New Deal and World War II, 5526; and Harlem Intellectuals during the Great Depression, 5500; in America (1930s), 6211; Activities (1930s), 6268; Adaptability (1933–1945), 6304; and American Farmers (1940s and 1950s), 6309, 6232; and Black Protest in Harlem (1930s), 6298; and Black Radicals in Alabama, (1929–1941), 6266; America and Children (1922–1950), 6292; and College Students (1930s and 1940s), 6242; and Congressional Investigations (1919–1935), 6212; and Labor Policy during World War II, 6334; and Literary and Cultural Issues, 6328; and Sports during the Great Depression, 6299; and State Politics (1930s and 1940s), 6250; and the Alabama Negro (1930s), 6361; and the

American Labor Party (1930s), 6357; and the Angelo Herndon Case (1932–1937), 6283, 6284; and the Congress of Industrial Organizations, 6263; and the Labor Movement in Minnesota (1936–1949), 6249; and the Midwest Farm Crisis (1933), 6338; and the Popular Front Period, 6345; and the Spanish Civil War (1936–1939), 6280; and the Worker's Theatrical Alliance (1935–1940), 6296; and the Writings of Meridel Le Sueur and Tillie Olsen, 6218; and Women (1929–1941), 6228, (1930–1940), 6335; and World War II, 6201; Belief System, 6270; as Critic of Roosevelt, 6339; Criticized by the New Left. 6243; De-Radicalization, 6269; Development of the Party Line (1928–1939), 6314; during World War II, 6258; History (1919–1957), 6256; Ideological Shifts (1930s), 6221; Infiltration into American Public Life, (1953), 6194; Influence on the Origins of the Congress of Industrial Organizations, 2390; in the Automobile Industry in Detroit before 1935, 2340; in Harlem (1928–1936), 6300; in Philadelphia, (1936–1956), 6282; Opposition to Stalin in America (1930s), 6188; Political Influence in California (1930–1970), 6293; Propaganda, 6209, Response to the New Deal (1933–1945), 6198, and the Effort to Organize the Steel Industry, (1936), 6244, and the Unemployed (1928–1935), 6846, Shifting Ideology on Race (1941–1964), 5496; Unions and Racism, 2070; with West Coast Waterfront Workers, (1930s), 2315

Communist Politics and the International Longshoremen's and Warehousemen's Union during World War II, 7283

Community Organizing Movement, Origins, (1920–1939), 4633

Company Unionism at Thompson Products, (1934–1964), 2253

Comparative Responses to Three International Economic Crises, 1960

Composer Collective, Activities, (1931–1936), 3535

Compton, Arthur, Discussion of his Scientific Career, 4824

Compulsory Education Enforcement in Providence Rhode Island, (1883–1935), 4283

Conant, James B.: And National Defense (1933–1945), 7990: His Career during the Roosevelt Years, 4846; Ideas on Educational Reform, (1933–1948), 4269; Speaks out on Social and Educational Issues, (1933–1953), 4261

Confessions of a Nazi Spy (1938), Anti Nazi Sentiment on Film, 3835

Congress and China (1941–1950), 8896

Congress of Industrial Organizations (CIO): Investigated by Smith Committee, (1939–1940), 2416; and American Foreign Policy, (1935–1955), 2280; and the Tobacco Workers of Winston-Salem, NC, (1943–1950), 2270; Bibliographical Report, 9809; Commitment to Education, 2373; Foreign Policy, (1935–1955), 2353; in Los Angeles, (1938–1950), 2105; Origins, 2215, 2311; Politics during World War II, 2284; Rise of in Buffalo, NY, (1936–1942), 2298; Survey of Early Activities, 2299

Congress of Racial Equality, Origins, 5482

Congress, Opinions on Japan (1937–1941), 7547

Congressional Mavericks, (1935–1939), 6289

Connally, Tom: Foreign Policy Speeches, 1143; Memoir, 1142; Senate Career, 1144

Connecticut Peace Movement (1919–1939), 8027

Conner, Fox, Most Influential Officer in the U.S. Army between the Two World Wars, 0901

Conner, Governor Mike, And the Sales Tax Question in Mississippi (1932), 6729

Connolly, Vera, Life and Career, 4096

Connor, R. D. W., Archivist of the United States, 0504

Conroy, Jack: Evaluation of His Work, 3271; Six Articles in *American Mercury*, (1930–1933), 4075

Conscientious Objectors: and Pacifist Thought (1940–1945), 8049; and the Northern Baptist Convention (1940), 4437; as Viewed by National Consumer Magazines, (1939–1947), 4106; at Camp Downey, Idaho, 8308; at Patapasco State Park, Maryland, 8309; in Idaho, 8310; in World War II, 8031; Perils, 8029

Conservation: Controversies between Agriculture and Interior, (1898–1938), 1511; Government Role, 1424; in the Trans Mississippi West, Bibliography, 9601; Movement in the New Deal, 1505; Planning in the Early New Deal, 1427

Conservatism in American: Culture (1900–1949), 6115; Thought (1930–1955), 6122

Conservative Coalition in Congress (1933–1939), 7143, 7144

Consolidated Tenant's League of Harlem, 1817

Consumer Education During the Great Depression, 4333

Consumer Society in America, Attitudes toward, 1677

Consumers League of Ohio, Political Activities (1909–1937), 5947

Consumers Union, The Movement and the Magazine, (1936–1957), 4012

Continental Congress of Workers and Farmers (1933), 6359

Control of Consumer Credit, (1941–1949), 2018

Conway, Michael P., Political Career in Iowa, 6476

Cooke, Morris L.: Biography, 2798; Career, 1742; Land and Water Conservation Ideas, 2797; Recollections of the Rural Electrification Administration, 2689

Coolidge, Calvin, and the 1932 Presidential Campaign, 6742, 6755

Cooper, Hugh Lincoln, And Recognition of the Soviet Union, 7420

Cooperative Housing Movement, Growth, (1917–1955), 1777

Cooperative League of the United States (1916–1961), 5742

Cooperative Living at the Rutgers University College of Agriculture (1930s), 4408

Corcoran, Thomas G.: Biography, 0672; Career, 0673

Corey, Lewis: Bibliography, 6220; Political and Social Thought, 6205

Corporate: Capitalism as Represented in Western Films (1930s and 1940s), 3748; Elites in the American Economy, 2502

Corporate Liberalism (1920–1940), 6168

Cosmic Rays, Debate over their Source (1930s), 4858

Costigan, Edward P., Support for New Deal, 0995, 0996

Cotton: Culture in Eastern Oklahoma, Decline, 1314; Farming in Bell County, Texas, 1320; Farming, Mechanization, 1524; Programs in the South, 1384; Subsidy Payment Controversy, (1936–1937), 1366; Textile Industry, Emergence of National Trade Organization, 2533; Textile Industry, Trade Association Movement, (1900–1935), 2532

Cotton, Tobacco, and Rice Culture, Decline, 1345

Couch, Harvey C., And the Reconstruction Finance Corporation, 2735

Coughlin, Father Charles E., Analysis and Criticism of his Rhetoric, 7099; and Anti-Semitism, 7131, 7132; and Anti-Semitism in the United States, (1938–1954), 4439; and Fascism, 7159; and the Election of 1936, 6773, 7167; and the Periodical Press (1931–1942), 7142; and Mussolini, 7081; and the National Union for Social Justice, 7140; Career, 7105; Criticized for his Anti-Semitic Statements, 5759; Depression Era Activities, 7076; Evaluation, 4438; Portrait of an Anti-Semite, 5794; Public Career, 7095; Rise and Fall, 4530; Selected Radio Speeches, 7087

Counter-Cyclical Aspects of Government Fiscal Policy, (1929–1940), 2007

Country and Western Music, Origins (1920s and 1930s), 3517; Radio Stations, How they Were Funded (1930s), 3925; Role of Women between World War I and World War II, 3556

County Poor Farm System in Texas, 2648

Courtenay Mill: Labor Market in a Southern Textile Mill Village, Newry, South Carolina, (1937–1941), 2601; of South Carolina, Conditions on the Eve of World War II, 2602

Cowley, Malcolm, Explains Why American Intellectuals Embraced Marxist Philosophy (1930s), 6223; His Literary, Social and Political Thought to 1940, 6208; Infatuation with Revolutionary Marxism, 3274; Memoir, 3317; Reflects on his Failure to Understand the True Nature of Stalinist Russia, 6222

Cox, James M.; Catholic Social Activist, 4472; His Impact on the Creation of the New Deal Coalition, 6044; Memoir, 6467

Coyotes, Poisoning, 1440

Cozzens, James Gould, analysis of His Works, 3370

Cradle Will Rock, The (1937), Creation and Production, 3246

Craft, Rebecca, And the Women's Civic League of San Diego, 5460

Craig Air Force Base, Impact on Selma, Alabama (1940–1947), 8162

Cram, Ralph A., A Conservative who Supported the New Deal, 6126

Crane, R.S., Career, 4322

Crawford, David L., Attempts to Broker a Peace Pact Between the U.S. and Japan (1940–1941), 7842

Credit Financing of Automobiles, Origins, 1865

Crescent Lake, Oregon during the Great Depression, 1452

Crime in New York City and Chicago, Pictorial History, 4714

Cripps Mission to India (1942), 8945

Crisis of 1937–1938, 1594

Criterion, Objectives and Content, (1922 to 1939), 4010

Critical Episodes in American History, 7173

Cross Compliance Concepts in Agricultural Programs, 2711

Cross, Wilbur L., As Governor of Connecticut (1930–1938), 6639, 6731, 7139

Crossett, Arkansas Lumber worker's Strike, (1940), 2313

Crosswaith, Frank R., and Labor Unionization in Harlem, (1939–1945), 2424; and the Negro Labor Committee in Harlem, 2425; Career, 5548

Crowley, Leo T., Public Career, 0731

Crump, Edward, and the 1932 Gubernatorial Election in Tennessee, 6588

Cuba, Conditions in (1933), 7666

Cudahy, John: Career, 0793; Diplomatic Career, 0791; Interview with Hitler (1940), 7296; Mission to Ireland, 0792; And the Search for Peace in Europe, 7839

Culbertson Mission to the Middle East, (1941–1945), 8971

Cullen, Countee, Rise and Fall of His Popularity, (1920s–1930s), 3595

Cultural Tension as Perceived by the Mass Media (1918–1941), 3715

Cultural Thought as Portrayed in the Films of Chaplain, Ford, Capra, and Wells, (1936–1941), 3793

Cultural Values as Portrayed in *Mr Deeds Goes to Town* (1936), 3794

Cummings, Homer S.: And the Presidential Campaign (1932), 6766; Selected Papers, 0625

Cunningham, Agnes, Oklahoma Radical (1930s), 6327

Curley, James M.: As Governor of Mashuesettes (1930s), 6611; Biography, 6477

Curose, Oki Kato, Experience of a Nisei, 5714

Currency Outflow, (1929–1933), 2632

Currran, Joe, And the National Maritime Union, 2426

Cushman, Helen Caldwell, Remembers Her Marriage to Erskine Caldwell, (1925–1938), 3320

Cutting, Bronson: and the 1934 Senatorial Election in New Mexico, 6659, 6660, 6696, 6730; Opposed by Roosevelt for Reelection (1934), 0997

Dabney, Virginius: Career, 4044; Memoir, 3968

Dade, William E., As Ambassador to Germany (1933–1937), 7835

Dahlberg, Edward, Analysis of His Works, 3433

Dairy Farmer's Strike in New York, (1939), 1535

Dallas Morning News and Communist Russia, 3950

Danaher, Senator John A., Opposes American Intervention in World War II, 7896

Dance: Education in American Schools, (1925–1935), 4356; Marathon Craze, (1920–1930), 3521; Sequences in Fred Astaire-Ginger Rogers Films (1930–1939), Analyzed, 3852

Dania Indian School, Florida (1927–1936), 5865

Daniels, Josephus: 0458; Ambassador to Mexico, 0796, 0799; Attitude toward New Deal of, 0794; Autobiography, 0797; Decision not to Run for Office, 0795; Relationship with Franklin Delano Roosevelt, 0798, 0800

Daniels, Jonathan, His Changing Attitudes on Segregation (1930s to the 1950s), 5368

Darling, J. Norwood: Cartoons from the Roosevelt Years, 4116; Economic Conditions and Political Events Which Inspired His Cartoons, (1920s–1930s), 4125; Political Cartoons, (1917–1945), 3650

Darrow, Clarence, Life and Career, 6723

Davenport, Frederick M., Biography, 0674

David, Goode B., Recalls Painting President Roosevelt (1939), 3634

David, John W., And the Presidential Campaign (1936), 7116

Davidson, Donald, Critic of Liberalism and Progressivism (1920s and 1930s), 7125

Davidson, Jo, Autobiography, 3632

Davies, John P., Jr., 0388

Davies, Joseph E.: Ambassador to USSR, (1937–1941), 0801 0805; Biography, 0804; Contact with Soviet Leaders of, 0803; Mission to Moscow (1941), 8824

Davis, Benjamin J. Jr., Life and Career, 5375

Davis, David B., Recalls his Experience as a World War II MP in Germany, 9272

Davis, David R., His Mysterious Air Foil Shape (1938), 5002

Davis, Elmer and CBS News, (1939–1941), 3896

Davis, John H., Career as Agricultural Economist, 1562

Davis, John W., Biography, 6119

Davis, Jonathan M., Political Career in Kansas (1920s to the 1940s), 6496

Davis, Lorenzo Pipper, Recollections of a Negro Baseball Player (1930s and 1940s), 4621

Davis, Norman H.: And Arms Control (1931–1938), 7207; Career, 0806

Dawson, Congressman William L., Prevents the Nomination of James F. Byrnes as Vice Presidential Candidate (1944), 6812

De Beck, Billy, His Research for His Comic Strip *Barney Google and Snuffy Smith*, (1934–1942), 4127

De Gaulle, Charles, 9202–9212

Dearfield, Black Agricultural Colony in Colorado, (1910–1940), 5577

Debt Peonage in Florida Turpentine Camps, 1396

DeCaaux, Len, Autobiography, 2167

Declaration of Independence and Constitution, Transfer to the National Archives, 0546

Decorative Arts (1930s), 3614

Defense Plant Corporation Leases, Origins, 5020

Dehn, Adolph, Influence of his Minnesota Life on his Art, 3629

Delano Family, 0116

Delmo Home's Project, History, 1559

Deloach, William G., Diary, 1296

Delta and Providence Farm Project, (1936–1956), 1531

Demand for Money: during the Great Depression, (1929–1933), 1987; from the Great Depression to the Present, 1988

Demiashkevich, Micheal J., And the Committee for the Advancement of American Education, 4284

DeMille Dynasty, 3783

Democratic Majority, Creation (1928–1936), 6027

Democratic Party: and Domestic Politics during World War II, 8502; and the Politics of Sectionalism (1941–1948), 6057; and Urban Politics (1928–1932), 6474; and Efforts to Attract Republican Voters (1936), 6081; History (1932–1945), 6059; Ideological Turmoil (1929–1932), 6144; in Lackawanna, Pennsylvania (1920–1950), 6638; in Oregon, History (1900–1956), 6446; Resurgence of in California in the 1930s, 6699; Transformation (1918–1932), 6039

Democratic Political Order, Development and Maintenance (1932–1972), 6094

Denhardt, Henry H., Murder (1936), 4708

Dennis, Lawrence, And World War II, 7910

Dennison, Henry S. and Industrial Reform (1900–1950), 6169

Deposit Insurance Legislation (1933), Antecedents and Purposes, 2820

Depression: and World War II as Seen Through Country Music, 4273; Desperados, 4715; Era America and its Films, 3722; Era Writing, Photography, and Painting, 4252; Letters from Farmers to Milo Reno, 1709; Photographs of Mennonite Farmers, 1401; Plays and Idealism, 3227; Pop Art, As a Reflection of Life in America (1930s), 5045

DePriest, Oscar, Efforts to Integrate the Restaurant in the House of Representatives (1929–1935), 5540

Deregulation of Depository Institutions (1979–1983) versus Regulation (1927–1935), 2497

Desert Laboratory in Arizona, History, 1526

Detroit: and Black Elected Officers (1870–1993), 5666; and the Evolution of Reform Groups (1912–1932), 6500; City Elections (1937) and Organized Labor, 6598; Educational Retrenchment, (1929–1935), 4370; Ethnic Patterns in the Composition of High Elected Offices (1900–1950), 6610; Founding of an Economic Club, (1934), 2594; Public Education, (1929–1940), 4369; Race Riot (1933), British View, 8736; Race Riot (1943), 5451; Zionist Movement (1930s and 1940s), 5766

Detzer, Dorothy: Her Career in the Women's International League for Peace and Freedom, 6001; As Lobbyist for the Women's International League for Peace and Freedom, 8009

Dewey, John: and Pacifism (1917–1945), 8024; and the League for Independent Political Action, 6820; and the Struggle for World Peace, 8025; Educational Policies of applied to Negroes in Detroit (1930–1940), 4304; Political Activities (1928–1936), 6818

Dewey, Thomas E.: and the Politics of Accommodation (1940–1952), 6083; Biography, 6033, 6813; Early Career, 6631; Political Leadership (1937–1947), 6428

DeWitt, John, Proposes Internment of German and Italian Aliens, 0902

Dewson, Mary, And the Minimum Wage Movement, 2082

Dewson, Molly, Biography, 6023

Diamond, Anthony J., Delegate to Congress from Alaska (1933–1945), 6607

Dickenson, Clement C., Political Career in Missouri, 6454

Dieckhoff, Hans Heinrich: German Ambassador in Washington (1937–1941), 7291; His View of German American Relations (1937–1941), 7293

Dies Committee (1938), 6113

Dies, Congressman Martin: and the House Un-American Committee (1938–1945), 6880; Biography, 6881

Diesel Powered Locomotive, Invention, 1912

Digital Computers, Pre-History, (1935–1945), 4840

Diplomatic History, Methodical Analysis, 9776

Diplomats of the Inter-War Period, 7833

Dirt Wall Housing Project in Mount Olive, Alabama, 1813

Disability Programs at the Federal Level, (1935–1954), 4189

Disarmament Movement (1918–1945), 7181

Disney, Walt, Discussion of His Film *Victory through Air Power* (1943), 3742

Doctor–Patient Relations, Pictorial History (1930s), 4240

Document Editing, History, 9634

Documentary Films: Evolution into an Independent Art Form (1930s), 3768; (1930s), 3779 3848; of the New Deal Era, 3829

Documentary Photography, Mode and Style, (1900–1934), 2761

Dodd, William E.: Ambassador to Germany, (1933–1937), 0811; Diary, 0809; Diplomatic Career, 0807; Public Career, 0808

Dog Trot House, Mythic Image of Southern Culture, 3339

Dollinger, Genora, Her Views on Labor Unionism (1930s), 5982

Domei News Agency (1936–1945), 7576

Don't Spend Your Money Where You Can't Work Movement, 5595

Dos Pasos, John: Contributions to the American Theater, (1920s–1930s), 3215; Cultural Historian, 9793

Douglas DC-1, Development, 1902

Douglas, Helen G., Political Career, 6692

Douglas, Lewis A.: Public Career, 0676; Relationship with Franklin Delano Roosevelt, 0675

Douglas, Lloyd C., Interpretation of His Works, 3471

Douglas, Melvyn: and the New Deal, 6412; Donations to Occidental College, (1921–1946), 4263; Political Activities during the Roosevelt Era, 3719

Douglas, Paul H., Supports World War II, 1248

Douglas, William O., 6995–7005

Down Home Blues, Recording, (1929–1940), 3557

Downtown Gallery, Greenwich Village, (1926–1940), 3699

Draft Age, Lowering (1942), 4826

Drake, G. Bryant, Liberal Minister in the Bible Belt, (1925–1937), 4479

Draper, Theodore, Discusses his Involvement in the American Communist Movement, 6229

Dreier, Mary, Opposes the Equal Rights Amendment, 6008

Dreiser-Mencken Correspondence, (1907–1945), 3333

Dreiser, Theodore: Correspondence with Rufus Jones, (1938–1945), 3353; Decline of His Career (1930s), 3355; His Views on American Society, (1939), 3466

Dresden, Bombing (1945), 9262

Drew, Charles Richard, Research in Hematology, (1935–1950), 4191

Drive-in Theater Industry, (1933–1983), 3825

Drought: and Depression in Custer County, Nebraska, 1291; in Utah, (1934), 1414; on the Southern Great Plains, 1463; in West Texas, 1420

Drought-Walsh Mission to Japan, 7485

Dru Deal, a Sample of Anti-New Deal Hate Literature, 3275

Drug Stores in Alabama, Social Function (1930s and 1940s), 4247

Drury, Allen, His Senate Journal (1943–1945), 6051

Dubinsky, David: and the International Ladies Garment Workers Union, 2427; and the Labor Movement, 2381

DuBois, Philip H., As Psychology Instructor in Idaho and New Mexico (1930s), 4297

DuBois Rachel D., As Founder of Group Conversation Theory (1937), 4291

Dubois, W. E. B.: and Marcus Gervey Compared, 5534; And the Cold War (1944–1963), 5424; As a Journalist, 5385; Biography, 5363; Demands Creation of a First Class College in Missouri, 5359; His Concept of the Racial Problem in America, 5339; His Social and Economic Views, 5323 His Theory of Economic Cooperation 1940, 5360; Influence, 5513; Major Facets of his Life, 5567

Dubrovsky, Gertrude W., Remembers Growing up in Farmingdale, New Jersey (1920s and 1930s), 5748

Duerksen, Menno, Memoir, 1661

Duke University, Launching (1925–1935), 4299

Dulles, Eleanor L., Public Career, 0812

Dulles, John Foster: and the Arab Israel Conflict (1948–1954), 8998; and the Federal Council of Churches, (1937–1945), 4568; and the Federal Council of Churches (1937–1949), 4516; and the Protestant World Order Movement on the Eve of World War II, 4517; Attitude toward Bipartisanship and Foreign Policy, 0813

Dumbarton Oaks Conference, 9452

Dunjee, Roscoe, Career of a Black Educator (1930–1955), 4316

Dunn, Dorothy, Her Art collection at the Museum of New Mexico, 3701

DuPont, Research and Development Practices, (1900–1940), 2619

Dupriest, Oscar S., Black Congressman from Illinois (1929–1934), 5461

Durable Goods Expenditures between World War I and World War II, 2592

Durand, Earl, Death of a Fugitive Elk Poacher, 4731

Duranty, Walter, Moscow Correspondent for the *New York Times*, (1931–1941), 4090

Durr, Clifford, Career in the Federal Communications Commission, (1941–1948), 3926

Dust Bowl: 1297, 1300, 1305, 1306; and Agricultural Technology, 1290; Causes, 1307; Diary, 1293; Effects, 1308; Farming, 1304; Hardships, 1295; Historiography (1986), 9768; in Kansas, 1301; Introduction, 1286; Letters from Farmers, 1680; Migration, 1303; Photographs of Conditions, 1287; Photographic Record of Conditions, 1663; Refugees Literature, 3510

Dust Storms on the high Plains, 1302

Dyess Colony in Arkansas, Photographic Record, 3185

Eaker, Ira C., Architect of American Air Power, 0903

Earhart, Amelia: Biography, 1901; Death, 1905; Last Flight, 5960; Research, 1882

Earle, George H.: and the 1934 Gubernatorial Election in Pennsylvania, 6438; As Governor of Pennsylvania, 6565

Early, Stephen T.: As Press Secretary to Franklin Delano Roosevelt, 0733; Role in Roosevelt Campaign (1920), 0732

Easel Painting in New York (1940s), 3646

East European Jews in Atlanta (1920s and 1930s), 5733

East Texas Oil Boom of 1931, Social Problems, 1767

Eastman, Max F.: As Model for Character in Fitzgerald's *Last Tycoon*, 1941, 3393; His Critique of Philosophical Marxism, 6227

Eberstadt, Ferdinand, And Economic Mobilization for War (1939–1943), 8111

Eccles, Marriner S., Life and Career, 0677

Echo Park Dam in Wyoming, 1455

Echuca, Take, As Intelligence Agent in Honolulu, 7608

Economic Development, Tennessee Valley and Piedmont Compared, (1931–1954), 2590

Economic History, Research Committee on, (1940–1959), 1937

Economic Ideas of American Political Leaders, (1933–1938), 2005

Economic Mobilization for World War II, 4912, 4962

Economic Mobilization Planning Between the Wars, 5034

Economic Policies in America, Britain, Germany, France, and Sweden, (1929), 1959

Economic Strategies of Southern Urban Black Families (1900–1936), 5430

Economic Theory in America, Development, 1948

Economy Act (1932), Impact on Working Families, 6011

Economy Act (1933), 2006

Economy of the American South, Conditions in the late 1860s and 1930s Compared, 1623

Eden, Anthony: Autobiography, 8725; As British Foreign Secretary, 8724

Edmondson, Robert E., His Libel Trial for Anti-Semitic Publications (1936–1938), 5756

Edmunds, Sterling E., As Critic of the New Deal, 7101

Education: Historiography (1900–1976), 9721; History in America, (1865–1965), 4386; History in America, (1900–1950), 4348; in Tennessee During the Great Depression, 4268; within Organized Labor, (1900–1945), 2336

Educational Achievement in Segregated School Systems, Analysis, 5463

Educational Issues and Reforms (1930s and 1940s), 4398

Educational Rebels (1930s), 4275

Educational Thought During the Great Depression, 4267

Edwards Family, A Black Success Story in Oklahoma City, 5455

Edwards, India, Biography, 5988

Eichelberger, General Robert L., Unknown War Time Commander, 9417

Eicher, Edward C., And the Sedition Trial (1944), 6382

Einstein, Albert, His Career in America, 4983

Eisenhower, Dwight D.: Decision Making Methods, 0904; Decision to Halt at the Elbe, 0906, 0917; Diary, 0909; Gives Up French Items of historical Value, 0915; Letters to George C. Marshall, 0912; Memoir of Wartime Experiences, 0911; Preparations for the Normandy Invasion, 0905; Presidential Library, 9649; Review of the Literature (1979), 9767; Success as Supreme Commander, 0916; Summary of Military Career, 0908; Tenure of Allied Expeditionary Force, 0910; War Years Biography, 0907; Wartime Papers, 0913

Ekern, Herman L., And Wisconsin Politics (1930s), 6492

Ekirch, Arthur A., As Conscientious Objector during World War II, 8012

El Monte, California Berry Picker's Strike, (1933), 2405

El Paseo County Democratic Convention (1944), 6549

Election (1932): 6744; As Viewed from the British Embassy in Washington, 7224

Election (1936): 6775; and Non-Party Groups, 6778; and the Union Party, 6843; Establishes the Ascendancy of the Democratic Party, 6779

Election (1944): 6802; and Foreign Policy, 6801; and Minnesota Politics, 6814; and Party Politics, 6811; and the Service Vote, 6805

Elections, (1932–1935), 6734

Electric Power Industry, Growth, (1882–1942), 1733

Electrical Manufacturing Industry, Class Struggle, (1933–1950), 2362

Electrical Power Policy in the Pacific Northwest, Development, 1738

Electrical Workers, Efforts to Organize, (1930–1950), 2361

Electronic Numerical Integrator and Computer (ENIAC): Development (1943–1946), 4866; Origins, 4830

Elevator Operators and Automation, (1934–1970), 2333

Eliot, T. S., Views on the American South, (1933), 3296

Ellington, Duke, His Contribution to American Culture, 5476

Ellsworth, Lincoln, First Man to Cross Antarctica in an Airplane (1935), 4868

Embick, General Stanley D., Favors Isolationism, 7954

Emergency Banking Act (1933), 2002

Emergency Cattle Purchase Program, (1934–1935), 2844

Emergency Hog Marketing Program, (1933), 3067

Emigre Photography in America, (1933–1938), 4083

Empire State Building, Symbolism (1930s), 3166

Employment during the Great Depression, Analysis, 2486

End Poverty in California Movement (EPIC), Significance, 6620

Endicott Johnson Corporation and Welfare Capitalism, 2095

Energy and the Federal Government, (1900–1946), 1747

Engle, Clair, Biography, 0998

Environmental History in New Deal Documentaries, *The Plow that Broke the Plains* (1936) and *The River* (1938), 3830

Environmental Relationship of People and Land during the Great Depression, 1421

Episcopal Church: Social Attitudes, (1919–1939), 4539; Pacifist Fellowship, 8048

Epstein, Abraham, and the Movement for Old Age Security, 4217

Epstein, Melech, Autobiographical Sketch, 6235

Equal Employment Opportunity in the United States since the New Deal, 2677

Equal Opportunity Commission, Bibliography, 9603

Equal Protection Clause of the 14th Amendment, As Interpreted by W. E. B. DuBois and Charles H. Houston, 5570

Equal Rights Amendment, Legislative History (1923–1960), 6002

Erosion Expeditions, (1930s), 1466

Esquire Magazine, Evaluation of Its Contents, (1933–1941), 3944

Ethnic Groups, Relationships to American Culture (1930s), 4789

Ethnic Workers and the Rise of the CIO, 2218

Europe on the Eve of War, 7230

European Intellectuals and Anti-Americanism (1920–1950), 8058

Evangelical Protestantism, Rise, (1929–1942), 4466

Evans, Maurice, Presents Shakespeare to Troops in the Pacific Theater, 8093

Evans, Walker, Evaluation of His Photography, 3631

Evian Conference (1938), 9071

Exchange Rates and Economic Recovery (1930s), 1953

Export-Import Bank and American Foreign Policy: (1933–1939), 1947; (1934–1941), 2492; (1939–1944), 2496

Eyster, Warren, Conversations with James Agee, (1937–1941), 3337

Ezekiel, Mordecai; Myers, William I.; Tugwell, Rexford G.; Warren, George F.; Wilson, M. L., New Deal Careers, 1565

Fain, Sarah Lee, Political Career, 6718

Fair Employment Practices Act, Bibliography, 9603

Fair Employment Practices Committee: Activities in New York City (1941–1943), 5336; Activities (1941–1951), 6099; Activities (1941–1946), 5506; and Southern Ship Yards, 5532; Efforts to Eliminate Racial Discrimination in West Coast Ship Yards during World War II, 5412; Efforts to End Discrimination in the Iron, Steel, and Ship Building Industries in Pennsylvania, (1941–1945), 5530; Efforts to End Employment Discrimination in the South During World War II, 5531; Investigation into Discrimination on Southern Railroads during World War II, 5415

Fair Labor Standards Act of 1938: Analysis, 2729; Child Labor Provisions, 4679; Discriminatory Effects on Women, 5948; Enforcement Problems, 2803; Origins, 2865

Fairbanks, Douglas, Jr., Biography, 3738

Falknerian Lawyer Character, Development, 3497, 3498

Family Farms in the Twentieth Century, Survival, 1388

Family Structure, Impact on Wisconsin Farming (1940–1960), 4695

Fang, H. Ber, His Personal Narrative (1930s to 1945), 5672

Farley, James A.: and the Gubernatorial Campaign in New York State (1942), 6714; Autobiography, 0627; Biography, 0626; Democratic Party Leader, 0628; Dispute with Huey Long, 0629; Rebuilding the Democratic Party, 0630

Farm: and Factory Earnings Compared, (1925–1941), 1381; Chemical Council and the Department of Agriculture (1935–1939), 4975; Consolidation, (1935–1974), 1382; Debt Adjustment in the Early 1930s, 1342; Debt Adjustments during the Depression, 1348; Depression, Origins in Iowa, 1321; Failures and Government Intervention (1930s), 2882; Families in the Midwest, (1900–1940), 1550; Foreclosures between the Wars, 1323; Holiday Movement, History, 1534; Holiday Movement in Iowa, 1532; Holiday Movement in Nebraska, 1556; Holiday Movement in North Dakota, 1533; Holiday Movement in South Dakota, 1547; Income on the Great Plains, (1920–1940), 1413; Journals and the Constitutional Issues of the New Deal, 3975; Labor in California, 1399, 1400; Life in Marion County, Mississippi, (1938), 2647; Policies in the U.S., Origins and Development, 1337; Policies on the North American Plains, Canada and the U.S. Compared, 1362; Policy Between the Wars, 1315; Policy from Roosevelt to Eisenhower, 1374; Prices, Industrial Wages, and Capital Earning, Analysis, (1942), 1936; Protest Movements, (1930s), 1552; Farm Strikes of 1932 and 1962 Compared, 1543; Subsidies, History, 1358; Women in New Mexico, (1920–1940), 1390; Workers in California, (1930–1942), 1387

Farm Security Administration: 1330; Activities in Kern County, California, 3045; Decline, 1331; Evaluation of Nine Resettlement Projects, (1943), 2800; in North

Dakota, 2932; Medical Care Program, (1935), 2824; Photo Documentary Project and Black Americans, 5087; Photo-Journalists, 5097; Photographs, 2690; Photographs by Marion Walcott, 5111; Photographs of a Minnesota Logging Camp, 5244; Photographs of Virginia Life, 5165; Photography Project, 5118; Photography Project Coverage of Black Life, 5502; Photography Project Evaluated, 5099; Photography Project in California, 5185; in Indiana, 5212; in Kentucky, 5174; in South Carolina, 1941, 2943

Farmer, Hallie, Biographical Sketch, 6015

Farmer-Labor: Association in Minnesota, 6544; Movement in Idaho, (1933–1938), 6829; Movement in Ohio, 6829; Parties, Failure (1936–1938), 6828; Party in Michigan, (1935–1937), 6597; in Minnesota, (1918–1944), 6851, 6852; in Minnesota and the Coming of World War II, 6511; Rise and Fall, 2309

Farmer Protests in Plymouth County, Iowa, 1318

Farmers' Holiday Association: History, 1376; Strike, (1932), 1557

Farmers' Picketing Movement during the Great Depression, 1545

Farmers: and the Industrial Workers of the World in the Yakima Valley, (1933), 2327; and World War II, 1404, Economic Problems, 1370, Independent Council of America (1935–1938), 7082, Relationship with the Federal Government, (1920–1956), 2750, Role in American Life, 1555

Farming: and Improved Technology, 1412; in Kit Carson County, Colorado, 1289; in the Depression Years, 1444

Farrell, James T.: Analysis of His Rhetoric, (1932–1939), 3338; Analysis of His Works (1930s and the1940s), 3438

Fascism: and Communism Compared, 6389; and the American Writer, 6378; and the Italian-American Immigrants of Utica, New York, 6369; in America (1930s and 1940s), 6393; in America (1930s), 6365; in Detroit (1933–1935), 6374; in Georgia (1930s), 6390; in Spain (1931–1942), 7382

Father Devine and the Peace Mission Movement, (1879–1942), 4575

Faulkner, William: Analysis of His Fiction, (1930–1936), 3447; Analysis of His Racial Views, 3289, 3306; Analysis of His Story *The Afternoon of a Cow,* 3365; Analysis of His Use of the Cow Motif. 3377; Analysis of His Work, (1939–1942), 3330; Analysis of His Works, 3417; and the New Deal, 3383; and William Wright Compared, 3327; Depression Humor in *The Hamlet,* 3331; Race and Gender Themes in his Novels, 3299; Use of the Handshake as a Metaphor for Southern Race Relations in *The Unvanquished* (1938), 3468; Use of wilderness Theme in *The Bear,* 3356

Fausal, Robert W., Describes his Efforts to Sell Airplanes to Cuba (1937), 7671

Faymonville, Colonel Philip R.: As Military Attache in Moscow (1933–1938), 7433; His Views of the Red Army, 8847

Federal Aid to Education: and the Churches, (1933–1939), 4470; History, (1937–1950), 4413

Federal Aid to the Poor, (1935–1971), 4219

Federal Art Project: and the Social Realists, 5162; Art Works, Efforts to Locate and Restore, 3711; Black Representation, 5383; Community Art Centers in Iowa, 5222; Evaluation, 5127; History, 5144, 5289; in California, 5247; in Iowa, 5190; in Massachusetts, 5229; in New Jersey, 5234; in New York, 5205, 5206; in San Francisco, 5246; in Southern California, 5223; in Tennessee, 5230; in Texas, 5194; Influence on Sculptures, 5115; Mural Painting Program in New York City, 5238; Murals Project in California, 5186; Role of the Library of Congress, 5117

Federal Bureau of Investigation: and German Saboteurs, 6887; and Harry Elmer Barnes, (1936–1944), 6891; and Political Surveillance, (1924–1936), 6893; and Popular Culture (1933–1939), 6888; and Presidential Directives (1936–1953), 6890; and the Japanese American Community (1931–1942), 6886; and the New York City Photo League, 6885; and the Pearl Harbor Attack, 6894; History (1908–1980), 6869; History, 6892

Federal Communication Act (1934): 5143; Analysis, 3887

Federal Communications Commission, Activities, (1934–1952), 3932

Federal Cotton Acreage Programs, Effect on Out Migration, 1340

Federal Crop Insurance, History, (1938–1982), 2710

Federal Dance Project: (1936–1939), 5133; History, 5138

Federal Daycare Centers in Oklahoma, (1933–1946), 4685

Federal Deposit Insurance Corporation, History, (1934–1964), 2012

Federal Economic Policy, from Hoover to Truman, 2059

Federal Educational Projects (1933–1944), 5128

Federal Emergency Relief Administration: and Blackfoot Indian Crafts in Montana, 5809; Impact on Key West Florida, 3040

Federal Environmental Protection Policies, Survey, 1765

Federal Farm Board: Activities, 1363; and Agricultural Adjustment Administration Compared, 1357

Federal Farmland Preservation Policy, Origins, 1477

Federal Fiscal Policy during the Great Depression, 1976

Federal Food Programs in Arkansas, (1933–1942), 2967

Federal Home Loan Bank system: Creation, 2524; Origins, 2726

Federal Housing Policy, Presidential Perspectives, 1787

Federal Income Dispersal Policies in the Southeast, 1989

Federal Indian Policy and Anthropologist (before 1940), 5873

Federal Labor Regulations Policy, (1933–1955), 2086

Federal Music Project: and Cultural Nationalism, 5110; and Nationalism, 5169; History, 5107; in New Mexico, 5178; in Oklahoma, 5191, 5221; Opera Unit in San Diego, 5258

Federal National Mortgage Association (Fannie Mae), Early Years, 1819

Federal Park Policy in Utah, 1503

Federal Power Commission and Regulation of Natural Gas, 1746, 1756

Federal Probation System, Struggle to Transfer From Prison Bureau to Administrative Office of the Federal Courts, (1930–1940), 4709

Federal Public Housing in Atlanta, Origins, 1806

Federal Records Centers, Discussions, 9698

Federal Relief: Administration in Louisiana, 2977; Policy, Analysis, 2832; Surplus Corporation and Emergency Work, (1934–1935), 2852

Federal Reserve System: Monetary Policy, (1924–1933), 2016; Role in Money Stock Decline, (1929–1933), 2009; (1914–1938), 1998; (1930s), 2013; New Deal Reforms, 2596

Federal Securities Regulation, Origins, 2792

Federal Surplus Relief Corporation: (1933–1935), History, 2724, 2816; Evaluation, 2847

Federal Tax Policy: (1929–1939), 2023; During the Roosevelt Era, 1991

Federal Theater Project: and Black Drama, 5156; and Black Playwrites, 5261; and Constitutional Issues, 5149; and Medical Themes, 5150: and the Living Newspaper, 5065, 5068, 5082 5101; and the New York City Children's Theater Unit, (1935–1939), 5067; and the War on Syphilis, (1937–1939), 5063; as a Forum for New Plays, 5075; Black Version of Macbeth, 5124; Evaluation, 5157; Evaluation of the Negro Unit, 5050; History, 5113, 5114, 5142, 5161; in Cincinnati, 5257; in Florida, 5197, 5198; in Los Angeles, 5251; in Oklahoma, 5221; in San Francisco, 5254; in the Midwestern States, 5277; in the South, 5134, 5282; Influence of Hallie Flangan Davis, 5135; Influence on Design, 5109; Its Forgotten Productions (1935–1939), 5077; Legacy, 5116; Negro Repertory Company of Seattle (1935–1939), 5253; Performs *The Cradle Will Rock* in New York (1937), 5252, 5272; Protest Plays, (1936–1939), 5084; Research on the History of Black Theater, 5112; Role of Blacks (1935–1939), 5095; Shakespearian Productions, 5125; Supports Performance of *Heaven Bound* by Big Bethal African Methodist Episcopal Church, Atlanta (1937–1938), 5255

Federal Wildlife Conservation Policy, (1933–1940), 1426

Federal Writers' Project: Analysis of the American Guide Series, 5123; and Ex-Slave Narratives, 5130, 5187, 5278, 5311, 5316; and Tennessee Ghost Stories, 5078; and the Preservation of Iroquois Tribal Folklore and History, 5132; Authenticity of Life History Program 5283, 5286; Collects Folklore in Wise County, Virginia, 5264; Discussion of Life History Program, 5287; Evaluation of Activities (1937–1939), 5155; Florida Slave Narratives, 5494; Folklore Collection Program in S E Massachusetts,5204; for Blacks in Louisiana, 5176, 5196; History, 5140, 5146; Horse Trading Stories (1930s to the 1940s), 5104; in Idaho, 5226; in Indiana, 5207, 5224;in

Iowa, 5183; in Louisiana, 2936; in Massachusetts, 5228; in New Bedford, Massachusetts, 5182; in Pennsylvania, 5265; in the Pacific Northwest, 5285; in Washington State, 5227; in Wyoming, 5189; Massachusetts State Guide,5179; New England Life Histories Program (1938–1939), 5121; Southern Life Histories Program, 5276; Studies of Tobacco Farming, 5108

Federal-City Relations during World War II, 2696

Federation of Flat Glass Workers in America, Origins, 2213

Feingold, Henry L., Remembers His Education in Nazi Germany, 5752

Feis, Herbert: and the Search for National Security before World War II, 7837; and the Search for Rubber, 0735; As Economic Advisor to State Department, 0734

Fellowship of Reconciliation: (1915–1960), 7998; and World War II, 8056

Fellowship of Southern Churchmen, History, (1934–1957), 4529

Female Adolescents as Portrayed on Film, (1920–1970), 3837

Female Performer and Female Character, Relationship in the American Musical, (1920–1974), 3236

Female Teachers in Hamilton, Ohio, Oppose Unionization (1930s), 4392

Feminist Movement, Changes (1910–1940), 6016

Fermi, Enrico and the First Self Sustained Nuclear Reaction (1942), 5009

Feuer, Leon, The Birth of the Jewish Lobby (1940s), 5755

Fiction and Non-Fiction Books, Best Sellers, (1933–1945), 3369

Fields, Alonzo, 0372

Fighter Aircraft Development (1933–1945), 4906

Fighter Plane, Evolution of Offensive Doctrine, (1917–1939), 5032

Filene, Edward A.: and the Parameters of Industrial Reform (1890–1947), 4656; Career, 5750

Filipino-Americans in California, Efforts to Organize, (1934–1938), 2150

Filipinos in Stockton, California, (1920s–1930s), 4153

Film: and Radio History, Documents, 9682; Censorship, (1930–1940), 3776; Comedians (1940s), 3847; Music and Hollywood's Promise of Utopia in Film Noir and the Woman's Film, 3753; Musicals as Popular Art Forms (1930s), 3842; of the Great Depression, 3728

Finnish-American Left, Decline (1925–1945), 4771

Finnish-Americans: and Crisis in Finland (1918–1958), 4770

Finnish-Amcrican Communists (1920s–1940s), 6187

First American Artist's Congress, History, 3142

First American Writer's Congress, Memories, 3269

Fiscal Policy in the 1930s, Analysis, 2004

Fisher, Harry B., And Clandestine Surveillance at Yale University (1937–1952), 4296

Fisher, Irving: Economic Theories, 2048; Monetary Economic Theory, 1978

Fisher's Business Cycle Model, 2010

Fitzgerald, Edmond J., And the U. S. Geological Survey (1930s), 3619

Fitzgerald, F. Scott: and Ernest Hemingway, Correspondence, (1924–1937), 3298; His Declining Talent after 1935, 3500; His Health Problems While Writing *The Last Tycoon*, 3374

Fitzgerald, Zelda, Biography, 3430

Flanagan, Barney L., Memoir of Utah State Highway Commission Hiring Inspector, 2948

Flanagan, Hallie: Biography, 3251; Role in American Theater, (1924–1935), 3237

Flaring of Natural Gas, Elimination in Texas, (1930–1949), 1772

Flat Glass Worker's Union, Internal Discord, (1936–1937), 2115

Fleischer, Nat, Comments on the Sport of Boxing (1930s), 4592

Fleischer Studios Animation Workers Strike, (1937), 2174

Fletcher, Frank, Aircraft Carrier Commander, 0967

"Flight," Restoration of a New Deal Mural at the La Guardia Marine Air Terminal in New York, 5237

Florida: and Lynching (1930–1940), 4719; and the Jim Crow Labor System (1940s), 5551; and the Sponge Industry, (1930s–1940), 2511; Photographs during the Depression, 3608; Seminoles and Acculturation Policy, (1927–1954), 5863; Seminoles and the New Deal (1933–1942), 5864; State League of Women Voters, 5927

Florida Barge Canal Project, (1927–1968), 1929, 1931, 1933

Flynn, Edward J., Autobiography, 0736

Flynn, Elizabeth Gurley, Career, 5916

Flynn, John T.: And the New York Chapter of the American First Committee (1940–1941), 7959; As Roosevelt Hater, 7107, 7108

Fokine, Michel, Life and Career, 3145

Folk Idioms of the Cumberland Mountain Region of Kentucky as Preserved in the Writings of Jesse Stuart, 3311

Folk Music: of the South (1930s–1960s), 3538 Style, Use by Leftist Movements during the 1930s, 3527

Folk Remedies in Maury County, Tennessee, (1936), 4204

Folklore: How Recordings were made (1930s), 3546; Growth of Profession since the 1930s, 3376

Folsom, James E., And His Four Electoral Defeats (1933–1942), 6517

Fong, Hiram L., Political Career, 1249

Food and Drug Administration and the Ergot Controversy, (1930), 4208

Food Assistance Programs, History, 1371

Ford and General Motors, Competition, (1920s–1930s). 1864

Ford, Arnold, History of his Back to Ethiopia Movement (1930–1935), 5546

Ford Factory at Cherry Hill, 2085

Ford, Henry: Amazon Rubber Venture, (1920s–1940s), 2534; and His Plastic Car, 4933; Hostile Biography, 2623; Industrial Village Experiments (1918–1944), 2613; Public Image, 2565; Village Industry Experiment, (1914–1941), 2587

Ford Hunger March, (1932), 2117

Ford, John: and the War Time Documentary, 8533, 8536; His Early Films, (1917–1934), 3827

Foreign Correspondents on American Radio, (1930–1940), 3894

Foreign Nationalities Branch, 8077

Foreign Oil Policy, America, (1941–1954), 1769

Foreign Policy and Presidential Elections, (1940–1948; 1952–1960), 6735

Foreign Policy Association and American Foreign Policy, 7174

Foreign Relations, Documents Series (1943–1946), 9657

Foreign Trade and Government Regulation, 1849

Forest Conservation in South Dakota, 1425

Forest Farmers' Association, Activities, 1494

Forest Pathology in the Southern Appalachians, (1900–1940), 1460

Forest Service: Proposed transfer from the Department of Agriculture to the Department of the Interior, 2872; History, 1513

Forests, Their Role in American History, 1431

Forrestal, James V.: Diaries, 0816; Foreign Policy Philosophy, 0815

Fort, Corenlia, Female Pilot during World War II, 8239

Fort Gibson (Oklahoma), Restoration (1935), 5172

Fort Ontario Refugee Shelter (1944–1946), 9162

Fort Peck Dam, Origins, 1507

Fortis, Abe, 0501

Fortune Magazine, Anti-New Deal Philosophy, 4007

Forty Hour Workweek, Origins, 2078

Fourteenth Amendment and Personal Liberties (1920–1941), 6871

Fosdick, Harry Emerson, Writings (1930s), 4555

Fosdick, Raymond B., Biography, 7982

Foulois, Benjamin D., and the Development of the Air Corps, (1931–1945), 4990

Fram, Leon, Remembers his Role as a Leader of the League of Human Rights in Detroit (1930s and 1940s), 5757

France: and the Sino-Japanese War (1937–1939), 7261; Documents Concerning German Occupation, 9697

Franco-Soviet Pact, (1936–1937), 7262

Frank, Glenn, Becomes President of the University of Wisconsin (1930s), 4352

Frank, Jerome N.: Analysis of Liberal Left Position, 0679; Impact on American Law, 0678; Papers, 0681; Political Philosophy, 0680; Spokesmen for Legal Realism, 6941

Frankfurt School of Marxist Social Philosophy, Activities in America (1933–1950), 6260

Frankfurter, Felix, 7006–7022

Franklin, John Hope, His Personal Account of Black Participation in World War II, 5612

Frazier, E. Franklin, Economic Thought, 5574

Frazier, Lynn J., Supports Neutrality, 1250

Free Reserve Adjustments by Commercial Banks, (1933–1942), 2535

Free Trade and New Deal Farm Program, Conflict, 1834

Freedom of Expression Supported by Large City Newspapers, (1920–1940), 3953

Freeman, Joseph: Autobiography, 6195; Political Views, 6287

Friedman, Colonel William F., Master Cartographer, 9260

Frisch, Otto R., And the Atomic Bomb, 9285

Friske, Leo J., Recalls His Family's Participation in Various New Deal Programs in Milwaukee, 5245

Frontier Films, *People of the Cumberland* (1938), Analysis, 3751

Frost, Robert: and Life Crises, (1938–1942), 3602; and Nature Poetry, 3582; and the Politics of Self, 3597

Fruit Workers of the Santa Clara Valley, Unionization, 2295

Fry, Ralph L., Experiences in the Pacific during World War II, 0918

Fuchs, Daniel, Analysis of His Works (1930s), 3429

Fulbright, J. William, Political Disputes with Allen Elender, 6423

Full Employment, Debates, (1930s–1980s), 1984

Fund Raising in the United States, History, 4200

Fundamentalism, Renewal in American, (1930–1945), 4467

Fundamentalist Religious Ideas, Development, (1930–1941), 4503

Futrell, Governor Junis M., And the Effort to Curb Legislative Spending in Arkansas (1932–1934), 6643

Futures Markets, Opposition, 1369

Gallop, New Mexico Coal Strike, (1933), 2351

Gangster Films, Rise and Fall, (1930–1940), 3782; of the 1930s, 3718

Gangster Stereotypes in American Social Drama (1930s), 3199

Gannett, Frank, Views on Presidential Powers (1937), 4313

Gardner, Earl, Last Man Legally Hanged in Arizona (1936), 4727

Garland, Claude M., As Critic of Roosevelt, 7109

Garner, John Nance: 0564–0566; And the Democratic Convention (1932), 6759; Biography, 0568; Relationship with Roosevelt, 0567

Garrett, Garet, As *Saturday Evening* Post Writer, (1940–1942), 4074

Garvey, Marcus, And the Universal Negro Improvement Organization, 5346; His Views on Fascism, (1935–1939), 5443

Gary, Indiana: History (1930–1940), 6622; Immigrants and Social Welfare, 4776

Gates, John, Autobiography, 6238

Gavin, James M., Combat Experiences, 0919

Gay, Peter, Reflections on the Holocaust, 9100

Gellhorn, Martha, As New Deal Relief Investigator, 5089

Gender: Ideology (1930s), 5975; Relations in American Film, (1930–1980), 3792; Stratification at the University of California, (1916–1962), 4377

General Electric Company Leaders, Relationship with New Deal Advisors and Agencies, 2574

General Motors: and Impact of Automation on Unionization, (1930–1940), 2344; and the XP-75 Fiasco, 8138; Copes with the Great Depression, 2618; Sit Down Strike, (1936–1937), 2193, 2401, 2402; Tool and Die Makers Strike, (1939), 2116, 2143

General Records Company, Promotion of Folk Music, (1939–1942), 3540

General Strike: at Pekin, Illinois, (1936), 2148; in Terre Haute, Indiana, (1935), 2114

General Textile Strike (1934), 2250

Genetics Studies Between the Wars, Germany and the United States Compared, 4892

Geneva Disarmament Conference (1932–1933), German Withdrawal, 7264

Geneva Naval Conference (1927), 7196

George, Walter F., Attacked by Roosevelt, 1145

George-Deen Act (1936), Evaluation, 5173

Georgia: And the 1936 Election, 6484; Anti-Insurrection Law (1933), 5370; Congressmen and the Early New Deal, 2688; Sterilization Statute (1937), 6586

German American Bund: (1933–1941), 6367; and Nazi Germany (1936–1941), 6387; History (1924–1946), 6370, 6371, 6395; in New Jersey, 6383

German-American Relations: (1922–1939), 7318; and the Soviet Union (1933–1938), 7210

German-Americans and Isolationism, 6406

German Book Trade, (1933–1945), 4145

German Declarations of War against the United States, 1917 and 1941 Compared, 7288

German Exchange Control (1931–1938), 7183

German Foreign Policy, Documents (1918–1945), 9685

German Intelligence Operations, Failure in the United States (1935–1945), 7316; in the United States (1933–1941), 7277

German Jewish Immigration, (1930–1940), 4164

German Opposition, Difficulties in Contacting, 7290

German Propaganda: Abroad, 9066; in America (1939–1941), 8535; in the Americas, (1933–1941), 9065

German Re-armament and Trade Policies (1930s), 7306

German Refugees: and American Social Thought, (1932–1965), 4166; in Princeton (1930s and 1940s), 8437; in Southern California, (1933–1950), 4160

German Resistance Movement, Analysis, 7312

German Scholars of the Nazi Period in America, 4151

German Socialist Immigration to the United States, (1933–1945), 4169

German Unrestricted Submarine Warfare Policy and German American Relations (1939–1941), 7297

German Views of the United States (after 1937), 7309

German Writers, Reception in California, (1933–1950), 3282

German-American Bund: 6375, 6376, 7307

Germans, Changing Roles in Hollywood Films, 3810

Germany: and American Neutrality (1935–1941), 7317; and the United States (1933–1939), 7308; Economic and Productive Infrastructure (1929–1933), 7269

Germer, Adolph: As Conservative Congress of Industrial Organizations Leader, 2154; Career, 2428

GI Bill of Rights, Origins, 2083, 4374

Giannini, A. P.: and the California Banking Crisis (1933), 2614; And the 1934 Gubernatorial Campaign in California, 6409, 6666

Gibson, Hugh, Diplomatic Career, 0817

Gide, Andre, Translations of His Works by Justin O'Brien, (1937–1949), 3434

Gilders, Joseph, Kidnaped and Flogged in Birmingham, Alabama (1936), 4722

Gillette, Guy, Political Career, 1251

Gilpin, Laura, Biography, 3694

Ginther, R. D., Biographical Sketch, 3606

Girdler, Tom M., Career, 2512

Gitlow, Benjamin, Critic of the Communist Party during the New Deal, 6241

Glasgow, Ellen, and the Southern Agrarians, 3301

Glass, Carter: Clashes with Bishop James Cannon, 1150; Opposes National Recovery Administration, 1147; Role in 1936 Election, 1148; Senate Career, 1146,1149

Glass House Concept, History, 3162

Glavis, Louis R., Biographical Sketch, 0737

Goddard, Robert H., Life and Career, 4831

Gold, Michael: Biography, 6253; Marxist Literary Figure (1930s), 6199; Study of the Background and Development of His Literary Ideas, (1920–1941), 3439

Gold Standard Diplomacy, (1919–1933), 1997

Golden Gate Bridge, Building, 4860

Golden Gate International Exposition (1939), 4251

Goldstein, David, As Catholic Street Lecturer, 4463

Golf in America, (1930–1945), 4630

Gone with the Wind: (1939), Discussion of the Creation and Maintenance of the 5,500 Costumes used in the Movie, 3760; and *The Grapes of Wrath* Compared, 3814 ; Portrayal of Blacks, 3789

Gooch, Arthur, Only Person ever Executed under the Lindbergh Law, 4700

Good Neighbor Policy: and the Nationalization of Mexican Oil, 1760; and Argentina, (1933–1939), 1827; As Interpreted by Various Historians, 9780

Good Soldier Schweik and Beatle Bailey Compared, 3276

Goodbye to Berlin (1939), As Cultural Representation of German Fascism in Relationship to Female Eroticism, 3239

Goodyear Rubber Strike (1936), 2321

Gordon, Caroline: Analysis of Her Early Works, (1930s–1940s), 3414; Analysis of Her Novels, (1924–1937), 3292

Gore, Thomas P.: Opposition to National Industrial Recovery Act, 0999; Opposition to New Deal Programs, 1000, 1001

Gorky, Arshile, Analysis of His art, (1943–1948), 3691

Gosiute Indians and the Skull Valley Reservation, Utah, 5832

Gospel Blues in Black Old Line Churches in Chicago, Introduction, 5410

Gottlieb, Adolph, Discussion of His Art, (1923–1974), 3672

Government: Documentary Film as a Teaching Tool, 3767; Intervention in the Housing Market, Origins, 1804; Involvement in financial Institutions (1930s), 1952

Grable, Betty, Exploration of Her Popularity during World War II, 3755

Grady County, Oklahoma, Attempts to Secede from Stephens County (1935, 1940, 1950), 6676

Graham, Ernest, And Florida Politics (1930s), 6572

Graham, Frank, Possible Vice Presidential Candidate (1936), 0308

Graham, John, Discussion of his Art (1920–1950), 3622

Grain Threshing in Kansas, (1930s), 1389

Grand Alliance and Italy (1943–1944), 8876

Grand Army of the Republic, Influence on Education in New Jersey, (1866–1935), 4414

Grand Coolee Dam, Origins, 1732

Grand Rapids, Michigan, Photos of Life on the Home Front during World War II, 3648

Grand Teton National Park, Origins, 1506

Granville Brothers, Famous Air Racers, 1877

Graves, John T. II, His Views on the New Deal, 6856

Gray, David, U.S. Ambassador to Ireland, Attends Seance to Obtain Information on the Progress of the War, 8779

Great Depression: Activities of Mexican Consulate in Los Angeles during, 1653; Analysis, 1647; and American Literature, 3451; and American Writing, 3485; and Income Distribution, 1620, 2024; and Labor Disputes, Review of the Literature (1972), 9738; and Labor Historiography (1970s), 9795; and Labor, Interpretations (1972), 9716; and New Deal Humor, 4111; and Oral History, 9856; and Radicalism, 6056; and Student Protests, 1658; and Tax Protest Campaigns, 1654; and the Frontier Thesis, 9751; and the Politics of Science, 4918; and War Debts, 7198; and the Chicago and New York World Fairs, 4982; and the Temper of the American People, 7113; and Tenant Activism, 1810; as a Watershed in American History, 9752, 9753; as Dividing Line in American Experience, 1610; Bibliography, 9597; Business Response, (1929–1932), 2633; Causes Black Migration to the Cities, 5401; Causes, 1605, 1607, 1621, 1628, 1638; Compared to the 1980s, 1575; Development of Public Policy, 1604; during the Hoover Administration, 2674; Early Years, (1929–1933), 3146; Econometric Analysis, 1969; Effect on a Milwaukee Family, 1683; Explanation for Length, 2494; Formative Years of U.S. Social Spending Policies, 5038; Generates New Interest in the American Past, 3388; How Four Painters Responded in Their Work, 3688; Humor of Galbraith, Leacock, and Mencken, 4110; Impact on Household Balance Sheets, 2042; Impact on International Banking, 1966; Impact on Memphis, 3038; Impact in Texas, 1649; Impact on Real Estate Delinquencies in Cook County, Illinois, 1586; Impact of Price Level Decline, 1609; Impact on Denton, Texas, 1715; Impact on a Family in Plentywood, Montana, 1716; Impact on Academic and Applied Physicists, 5011; Impact on

Allentown, Pennsylvania, 1606; Impact on American Art, 3615; Impact on American Attitudes toward Success, 1596; Impact on American College and University Faculties, (1929–1939), 4381; Impact on American Comic Film, 3823; Impact on American Fathers, 1655; Impact on American Thought, 4800; Impact on Ann Arbor, Michigan, 1618; Impact on Arkansas, 1699; Impact on Arkansas, 1718; Impact on Banks in Boise, Idaho, 1579; Impact on Black and White Urban Working Class Women, 5955, 5956, 5957; Impact on Black Female Domestics in New York City, 5344; Impact on Black Sharecroppers in Missouri, 1667; Impact on Black Writers, 5600; Impact on Blacks in Mississippi, 5398; Impact on California, 1695; Impact on Catholic Workers, 2126; Impact on Chicago's Black Community, 5528; Impact on City of Progress Project in Chicago, 3044; Impact on Colorado, 6700; Impact on Columbia, South Carolina, 6595; Impact on Congressional Election Results, 1608; Impact on Connecticut, 1630; Impact on Cooperative Extension Service in Michigan, 1595; Impact on Custer County, Nebraska, 1626; Impact on Employment in Illinois, 2993; Impact on Eugene, Oregon, 1708; Impact on Fitchburg, Massachusetts, 1643; Impact on Flint, Michigan, 3047; Impact on Fort Wayne, Indiana, 1635; Impact on Forty-six Large American Public Libraries, 1622; Impact on Harlem, 1665; Impact on Higher Education in Georgia, (1930–1940), 4393; Impact on Illinois, 1633; Impact on Immigrant Mexican Labor, 4167; Impact on Individual Americans, 1696; Impact on Iowa Farmers, 6421; Impact on Kansas, 1617; Impact on Kentucky, 1721; Impact on Key West, Florida, 1631; Impact on Lake Forest, Illinois, 1646; Impact on Lee County, Florida, 1637; Impact on Los Angeles, California, 1627; Impact on Major League Baseball, 4616; Impact on Maryland, 6569; Impact on Memphis, 6430; Impact on Middle Class Blacks in Philadelphia, 1669; Impact on Military Man Power Procurement, 4884; Impact on Mississippi, 6721; Impact on Natchitoches, Louisiana, 1685; Impact on New Castle, Pennsylvania as Depicted in the Film *Valley Town*, 3730; Impact on New Mexico, 1719; Impact on New Orleans, 1613; Impact on Newark, New Jersey (1929–1941), 6708; Impact on North Dakota Agriculture, 1312; Impact on Ohio, 1632; Impact on Oklahoma, 1662; Impact on Omaha, Nebraska, 1625; Impact on Orange County California, 6670; Impact on Paterson, New Jersey, 1700; Impact on Protestant Church Social and Welfare Activities in Erie, New York, 4487; Impact on Protestant Churches, 4497; Impact on Public Education, 4426; Impact on Public Opinion in Baltimore, 1624; Impact on Pulp and Sulphate Union, 2411; Impact on Rochester, New York, 1694; Impact on Rural Oregon, 1629; Impact on Rural West Virginia, 3011; Impact on Sharecroppers in Missouri, 1666; Impact on Shoe Workers and Tanners of Endicott Johnson, 2410; Impact on Social and Radical Political Activities, 6105;

Impact on South Dakota Farms, 6010; Impact on Southern Churches, 4441; Impact on Steel Workers, 2071; Impact on Texas Cities, 2939; Impact on Texas Panhandle Farmers, 3119; Impact on the American Mind, 3397; Impact on the Army, 4920; Impact on the Disciples of Christ, (1929–1936), 4552; Impact on the Employment of Married Women, 6006; Impact on the Indian Tribes of Oklahoma, 5886; Impact on the Old Middle Class, 1712; Impact on the Rochester, New York Public Library, 4662; Impact on the Science of Physics, 5016; Impact on the Southwest, 1724; Impact on the St. Louis Cardinals, 4617; Impact on the Thinking of John C. Dancing, 5516; Impact on the United States Army, 4845; Impact on the Work Roles of Women, 5984; Impact on The Master Plan Idea, 4631; Impact on Tobar, Nevada, 1703; Impact on Trans Atlantic Passenger Service, 1932; Impact on Utah, 2968; Impact on Women, 5918; Impact on Women in Atlanta, 5919; Impact on Women in Atlanta, New Orleans and San Antonio, 5920; Impact on Women in San Antonio, 5921; Impact on Women in the 7th Day Adventist Church, 4436; Impact on Working Women, 5923, 5945; Impact on Yavapai County, Arizona, 1634; Impact on Young Lawyers, 1580; in Arkansas, 1573; in East Texas, Oral History Interviews, 9851; in the South, 1574; in the Southwest, 3138; Influence on the Development of American Musical Theater, 3573; International Dimensions, 1954; International Economic Forces as Cause, 1602; Length, 1591; Mythic Impact, 1690; Oral Histories from South Dakota, 9858; Origins, 1585, 1601; Pictorial History, 0109; Political Impact on American Authors, 6252; Response of Urban Settlements, 1645; Spread to the World, 1956; Teaching About, 1570; Writers Translate Words of the Dispossessed into Print, 3481

Great Plains: Farming, Change and Adjustment, 1445; Future, 1525

Great Plains Region before Settlement, 1292

Great Red Scare (1934), 0543

Great Smokey Mountains National Park, Origins, 1447

Greece and the Great Powers (1939–1941), 7334, 8771

Green, Anne B.: Recalls her Experiences in the Women's Army Corps during World War II, 8214, 8283

Greenbelt, Maryland, Project Evaluation, 5195

Greendale, Wisconsin, History, (1935–1980), 4638

Green Mountain Parkway Proposal in Vermont, Defeated (1935), 6442

Green, William, As American Federation of Labor Leader, (1924–1952), 2429

Greenbelt Program, Critique, 2889

Greenbelt Town Program, (1935–1954), 4632

Greenbelt Town Project in Cincinnati, (1935–1939), 3056

Greene, James (Joe), Memories of a Black Baseball Player (1930s), 4597

Greenland, Military Use During World War II, 4875

Gregg, Alan, Supports Research in the Psychosomatic Field

at the Chicago Institute of Psychoanalysis, (1935–1943), 4195

Grew, Joseph C.: Ambassador to Japan, 0819, 7513, 7514, 7828; Diplomatic Career, 0818

Griffith, D. W., His Life during the 1940s, 3721

Grimm, Charley, Memories of a Baseball Man, 4598

Gringrich, Arnold, Considers Publishing a Story by Langston Hughes in *Esquire* Magazine (1934), 5358

Grocery Shopping (1930s), 2563

Grooper, William, His Use of the Seamstress as a Subject for His Paintings (1930s), 3647

Ground Observer Corps, History, 8099

Ground Water Property Rights in Arizona, 1439

Group theater: Record, (1931–1941), 3264; History, (1931–1941), 3255

Groves, Leslie R.: And the Manhattan Project (1943–1945), 9298; Biography, 4929; His Discussion of the Manhattan Project, 4886

Gruening, Ernest, As Territorial Governor of Alaska (1939–1953), 6640

Guam, American Occupation, 7471

Guaranteed Wages in American Industry, History, 2612

Guffey Coal Act (1935), 3137

Guffey, Joseph F., and the New Deal in Pennsylvania, 6530

Guided Missiles, Origins, 4870

Gulf Coast Shipbuilding Industry, Impact of Technology, (1900–1945), 2599

Guthrie, Woody: and John Steinbeck, Aesthetics and Political Expressions Compared, 3141; Bibliography (1968–1986), 9607; Biographical Sketch, (1937–1967), 3579; Biographical Sketch, 3565; Contributions to the Bonneville Power Administration Documentary, (1939–1949), 3552; Influence, 3531

Haas, Father Francis J.: As New Deal Advisor, 0738; As Chairman of the Fair Labor Practices Committee, (1943), 2823; Social Philosophy, 2066; Social Reformer, 4453

Haber, William, Remembers his Work as Relief Administrator in Michigan, 9849

Hague, Frank, And the New Deal in New Jersey, 6480

Haight, Raymond L., And the Commonwealth Progressive Party in California (1934), 6815

Hall, Fred R. and Mabel P. Hall, Memories of Crescent Lake, Oregon, 1915

Halsey, William F., Memoirs, 0968

Hamett, Bill, Career, 2430

Hamline University, Faculty Runs the School, (1932–1933), 4362

Hammett, Daschiell, Analysis of His Career (1930s), 3415; Analysis of His *The Maltese Falcon*, 3416; Career, 3424

Hammon, Stratton, Experiences (1920s and 1930s), 3169

Handbill Collection, University of California, Archives, 9654

Handicapped Parents Movement, (1930s–1960s), 4202

Hankin, Mary A., Adult Education in the American Red Cross, (1940–1947), 4317

Hansen, Alvin H., As Advocate of Keynesian Economics, (1936–1938), 2025; Career, 2028; Contributions to American Economic Policy, (1930s–1940s), 1945

Hanson, David E., and Portland, Oregan Schools during World War II, 4318

Hanson, Sam, Career as a Journalist in San Francisco during World War II, 3992

Hapgood, William P., Efforts to Reform Columbia Conserve Company of Indianapolis, (1917–1943), 2575

Harap, Louis, *Science & Society*, Founding (1930), 4319

Hard Boiled Detectives as Portrayed in American Film since 1941, 3804

Harding, Edwin F., Biography, 0920

Harding, Forrest, And the *Infantry Journal*, (1934–1938), 3934

Harlem Boycott (1934), 5497

Harlem Jobs Campaign (1932–1935), 5473

Harlem Race Riot (1943), 5333

Harmon, Florence, Memoir, 1670

Harriman, W. Averell: Around the World Flight (1941), 0741; As Philosopher of Containment Policy, 0740; As Special Emissary to Churchill and Stalin, 0742; Diplomatic Activities, 0739

Harrison, Pat: Changing Attitude toward New Deal, 1153; Political Career, 1151; Supports Federal Aid to Education, 1155; Supports Reciprocal Trade Program, 1152; Supports Social Security Act, 1154

Hart, Leo Establishes School in California for the Children of Dust Bowl Migrants, 4415

Hart, Moss, *Winged Victory* as a Reflection of the American Mind during World War II, 3211

Harten, Lucille B., Memoirs of a Housewife in Pocatello, Ohio during World War II, 5949

Harvard: and Nazi Propaganda Efforts (1930s), 4425; History Department Personnel (1930s), 4355; Football Break with Princeton, (1926–1934), 4625; Intellectual Giants of the 1930s, 4274

Haskell, Douglas P., Writings, 3158

Hassett, William D., Diary, 0498

Hastie, William H.: and Army Recruitment (1940–1942), 5621; and Military Homophobia (1940–1942), 5623; As Civilian Aid to the Security of War (1940–1942), 5622; His Influence on the Desegregation of the U.S. Army, 5624; Opposes Racism in the Armed Forces during World War II, 5620

Hatch Act, Historical Background, 6054

Hatch, Carl, Political Career, 1002

"Hatter's Disease" in Danbury, Connecticut, (1920–1941), 4206

Hauptman, Bruno, and the Lindbergh Kidnaping, 1935, 4704; Innocent of the Lindbergh Kidnaping, 4725

Havinghurst, Walter, Analysis of His Works, 3390

Hawaii: and the Admission Question (1935–1959), 6049; Agricultural Workers, Interviews, (1930s–1940s), 2119; Sugar Labor Market, Monopoly, 1285

Hawk's Nest Tunnel Disaster, 2508

Hawkins, Ernest and Richard Pounder, Lynched in Tallahassee, Florida, (1937), 4718

Hawks, Howard, Film Production Style, 3778

Hay, Charles M., Changing Liberal Views, 6170

Hayden, Carl T., Papers, 1003

Hayes, Carlton J. H.: Ambassador to Spain, (1942–1945), 0820, 8793, 9174

Haynes, George E., As Director of the Commission on Race Relations of the National Council of the Churches of Christ in America, (1922–1946), 4553

Hays, Brook, Public Career, 6139

Haywood, Harry, Autobiography, 6251

Health Care: and the Medical Profession in New York City, (1890–1940), 4192; Issues of 1935 Compared to those of 1975, 4223; Presidential Initiatives, from Harding to Roosevelt, 4230

Hearst, James, Memoir, 1673

Hearst, William Randolph: Breaks with Roosevelt over Wealth Tax, (1935), 3959; Charges University of Chicago Professors with Subversion, (1935), 4033; His Role in American Progressivism, 4023; His Use of News Control, (1920–1940), 4050; Opposes National Industrial Recovery Act, (1933), 3958; Political Ideas and Influence, 7084; Progressive as Reactionary, 3960

Heavy Construction Companies during the New Deal, 1417

Hebrew Committee of National Liberation, Proposes Use of Poison Gas Against the Axis (1944), 9137

Hebrew Free Loan Association (1933–1950), 5786

Heckscher, William S., Arrives at Princeton from Germany (1936), 4321

Heilbron, Fred A., San Diego County Water Crusader, 1490

Heldon, Karl, Memoirs of a Civil Servant, 0500

Helicopters, Development, 1909

Hellman, Lillian, And Motion Picture Propaganda, 8552

Hemingway, Ernest: Activities in and around Bimini during the 1930s, 3328; and the West, 3347; Background of His Novel *To Have and Have Not*, (1937), 3379; Correspondence with Owen Wister, 3460; Defends the Accuracy of his Dispatches from Spain (1938), 7371; Evaluated As Not a Two-Fisted War Hero, 3455; His Spanish Civil War Dispatches, 7388, 7397; His Transformation from Loyalist Supporter to Partisan of the Republican Insurgency (1937), 7398; Observations on the Spanish Civil War, 7389; Political Views, 3315; Researching His Life, 3428; Retreat from Pacifism as Expressed in *For Whom the Bell Tolls*, (1940), 3394

Hemispheric Defense Initiatives during World War II, 4847

Henderson, Caroline A., Dust Bowl Diary, 1299

Henderson, Loy W., And Soviet American Relations, 7438

Herbst, Josephine F., Perceptions of German Public Opinion (1935), 7287

Heredity-Environment Controversy (1883–1940), 4853

Herndon, Angelo, (1932–1937), 5491

Heroines of American Midwestern Repertoire Theater Comedy Dramas, (1900–1940), 3194

Herring Industry in Alaska, Rise and Fall, 2560

Hershey, Lewis B., Biography, 4874; Defining Conscientious Objectors, 0921

Hershey, Pennsylvania as Paternalistic Industrial Town, (1933–1937), 2539

Hi-Fidelity Sound Reproduction, Development, 4950

Hickham Field, Building, 9378

Hickok, Lorena A.: Career as Journalist, 0617; Federal Emergency Relief Administration Investigator, 0621, 0622; Relationship with Eleanor Roosevelt, 0616, 0620; Reports on Poverty, 0619; Reports on Conditions in the Middle West, 0618; Report to Harry Hopkins Concerning Conditions in Pennsylvania, 0685

Hicks, Granville: American Marxist Critique, 6200; Radical Thought (1931–1939), 6278

Hicks, Mary and Mildred, Socialist Activities (1931–1943), 6336

Higgins, Andrew J.: and the Development of Landing Craft and Patrol Torpedo Boats, 8135; and the Presidential Campaign (1936), 6084

High Altitude Balloon: Development during the Great Depression, 1900; Development of Flight, (1920s–1930s), 1887; Flights, (1934–1935), 1875

Higher Education: Allocation of Resources (1930s), 4345; Responds to Student Activism (1933–1938), 4388

Highlander Folk School: History, (1932–1962), 4310, 4420; in Tennessee, 4390; Workers Education Programs, (1933–1942), 4387

Hill Air Force Base, Establishment and Development (1934–1945), 4928

Hillman, Sidney: Biography, 2433; Career, 2432, 2434; Role in Shaping Federal Labor Policy during the New Deal, 2431

Hinckley, Robert H., Public Service Career, 0682

Hinckley, Ted C., Memoir, 1675

Hindenburgh, Paul Von, American Press Opinions of (1925–1934), 7279

Hinds, Robert, Charged with Raping a White Woman (1937), 4717

Hindus, Maurice, A Russian Immigrant in Upstate New York, 4168

Hirohito, As Initiator of Diplomatic-Military Decisions, 7479

Hirsch, Helmut, Executed in Germany (1937), 9090

Hirth, William, As Critic of the New Deal, 7094

Hispanic Crafts, Revival in New Mexico (1930s), 3155

Hiss, Algier, And the Yalta Conference, 7841

Historians and the Rating of Presidents, 9785

Historic Preservation, Growth in National Park Service, (1930s), 1520

Historical Literature in the U.S. (1929–1949), Analysis (1952), 9741

Historical Records Survey: 9633, 9673, 9679; in Iowa, 5184, 5208; in Michigan, 5215; in Oklahoma, 5175; in Wisconsin, 5171; in Wyoming, (1936–1952), 9652; Juneau County, Wisconsin, 9663; Microfilming Project (1935–1942), 9645

History: and the Objectivity Question, 9778; Use by Presidents, 9774

Hitchcock, Alfred, His Film *Foreign Correspondent* as Anti-Nazi Propaganda, 3834

Hitchhiking in America, History, 1872

Hitler, Adolph, 9213–9217; and the Origins of World War II, 7272; and the Re-militarization of the Rhineland (1936), 7275; Donates Books to the University of Denver, 1936, 4391

Hoboes, 2652

Hobson, Richmond P., Biography, 6175

Hocutt, Thomas R., Attempts to Enter the All White University of North Carolina School of Pharmacy, 5645

Hofer, Philip, And the Harvard Library Department of Printing and Graphic Arts (1930s), 3616

Hoffman, Clare E., Conservative Political Views, 1218

Hoffman, Paul G. and Car Culture in America, 1869

Hofstadter, Richard, Analysis of Factors which Influenced his Work, 9702

Hog Slaughter, 1338

Holiday, Billie, Biographical Sketch, 3575

Holland, Bill, Negro Baseball Player (1920s–1930s), 4601

Holland, Lou E., Public Career, 0683

Holland, Royce Q., Memoir, 1676

Hollins, Jess: Analysis of his Rape Case (1931–1936), 5464; Tried by an All White Jury in Oklahoma (1931), 5354

Hollywood: and Political Issues (1930s), 3796; and the Great Depression, 3729; Impact on the American Mind, 3831; Movie Premiers between the Wars, 3781; Movies as a Barometer of Popular culture, (1930s–1950s), 3743; Novels of the 1930s and 1940s, Themes, 3291; Role in J. Edgar Hoover's rise to Power, 3819; Stars Perform in Minneapolis, (1942), 4807; Years of Fitzgerald, Faulkner, West, Huxley, and Agee, 3323

Holman, Eugene, Life, 1751

Holocaust: 9072, 9073, 9078, 9083, 9088, 9098, 9124; and American Apathy, 9138; and American Catholics, 9110; and American Fundamentalists, 9105, 9148; and American Jews, 9142, 9147, 9164; and American News Media, 9127; and American Popular Culture, 9150; and American Protestant Churches, 9141; and American Radio Coverage, 9097; and Anglo-American Immigration Policy, 9092; and Anti-Semitism, 9125; and Internal Zionist Conflict, 9143; and Jewish Denial, 9123; and Organized Labor, 9121; and Polish Rabbis, 9178; and the American Jewish Press, 9111; and the American Jews, 9089; and the Bermuda Conference (1943), 9145; and the Failure to Bomb Auschwitz, 9139; and the International Red Cross, 9146; and the Press, 9126; and the Public Response of American Jews, 9128; and the War Refugee Board, 9144; and U.S. Army T-Forces, 9116; and Western Indifference, 9154; Compared to Strategic Bombing, 9133; Evaluation of the Literature, 9176; in American Historical Writing (1972), 9756 Records in the National Archives, 9664, 9665, 9666; Rescue Efforts, 9112, 9114, 9177

Holt, Arthur E., And the Ideal of the Rural Lifestyle, 4637

Holt, Rush Dew: As Critic of the New Deal, 7088, 7112; As Senator from West Virginia (1935–1940), 6466

Holts, Alice, Memoir, 2435

Holy Cross Greek Orthodox Theological School, (1937–1942), 4570

Home Owner's Loan Corporation, Racial Policies, 1805

Hook, Sidney: Analysis of His Thought (1930s and 1940s), 3401; and Stalin's Purge (1935–1936), 6255; Social, Political and Educational Philosophy (1930–1970), 4795

Hoover Dam: Architecture, 5024; Building, 4992; Construction, 5007

Hoover, Herbert C.: Account of his Presidency (1934), 7120; and the Congressional Debate over Food Relief (1930–1931), 7128; and the Interregnum Period, 7104; and the New Deal (1933–1940), 7102; and the United States Supreme Court, 7141 and Foreign Policy (1939–1945), 7947; and Post-War Foreign Policy (1942–1945), 7963; and the Road to War (1939–1941), 7887; Anticipates Need to Correct the Imbalance in the Economy, 7152; As Portrayed in the American Press (1932), 6757; As Titular Leader of the Republican Party (1933–1935), 7072; Biography, 7163; His Bid for Leadership of the Republican Party (1936–1939), 7071; His Memoirs of World War I, 7929; Impact of his Policies on San Francisco and Seattle, (1929–1933), 1698; Opposes American Involvement in World War II (1939), 7912, 7928; Opposes National Planning, 4644; Review of the Literature (1979), 9767; Speeches (1933–1938), 7115; The Post Presidential Years (1933–1964), 7073

Hoover, Irwin H., 0374

Hoover, J. Edgar: and the Black Press during World War II, 6899; As Director of the FBI, 6895; Biography, 6896, 6897, 6898

Hooverville in Saint Louis, Missouri, 1644

Hope, Clifford, Supports New Deal Farm Programs, 1219

Hope, John, Biography, 4294

Hopkins, Harry L.: Appointment as Secretary of Commerce, 0690; As Special Diplomatic Agent, 0700; As Works Progress Administration Administrator, 0697; Biography, 0684; Career as Relief Administrator, 0687, 0688; Contributions to the New Deal, 0693; Head of Works Progress Administration, 0694; Impact on Social Welfare Administration, 0692; Influence on Executive Policy, 0691; Major Influences on, 0696; New Deal Career, 0695; Relationship with Franklin Delano Roosevelt, 0698; Relationship with USSR, 0699; Spokesman for Roosevelt, 0689

Hormel Strike, Austin, Minnesota, (1933), 2185

Horn, Ernest, His Contributions to the Commission on the Social Studies in the Schools, (1929–1933), 4344

Hornbeck, Stanley K.: and American Far Eastern Policy, 7831; and the Diplomacy of the Open Door, 7832; Diplomatic Career, 0821; Prevents Summit Meeting (1941), 7545

Horror Films: Musical Scores (1930s), 3832; Their Power as Related to the Sexual Traumas of Adolescence (1930s and 1940s), 3747

Horses, Debate on the Cost of their Use over Tractors (1930s), 4817

Horton, Myles, Discusses Establishment of Highlander Folk School, 4329

Hose, John D., Attempts to Unionize Goodyear Tire and Rubber Plant in Gadsden, Alabama (1941), 2436

Hot Springs Conference (1943), 9463

Hound and Horn, Importance (1920s and 1930s), 3991

House Naval Affairs Committee and the Treaty Navy (1926–1934), 7992

House Un-American Activities Committee: 0518, 0524, 0539

Household Technology and Social Change in the Twentieth Century, 4852

Houseman, John: and the Voice of America, 8544; Reminisces about Working with Orson Wells, (1933–1938), 3222

Houser, Lowell: Analysis of His Mural, *The Development of Corn*, Ames, Iowa Post Office, 3681; Paints Mural in Ames, Iowa Post Office, 5260

Housing Act (1937), Failure, 1784

Housing and Home finance Agency, Origins, 1800

Housing Movements in Cincinnati, (1910–1954), 1793

Hovey, Graham, Memoir (1933), 1678

Howard, Edgar, Political and Journalistic Career, 3962

Howard, Perry W., Black Show Piece of the Republican Party from Mississippi, 5477

Howard, Richard P., Memoir, 1679

Howard University During the New Deal, (1933–1945), 4376

Howard, Willie, Career, 3153

Howe, Irving and Alfred Kazin, As examples of the New York Intellectuals (1930s and 1940s), 4797

Howe, Louis M.: Career, 0744; Relationship with Franklin Delano Roosevelt, 0743

Hoyt, Ross G., Evaluates the P-26, 4907

Huddleston, George Sr., And Alabama Politics (1915–1937), 6418

Hudson, Hosea, Southern Black Radical (1930s), 6307

Hughes, Charles Evans: 7050–7054; As Chief Justice of the United States Supreme Court, 6971

Hughes, Langston: Development of his Character, *Semple,* 5408; His Contributions to American Culture, 5476; Religion in his Poetry, 3586

Hughes, Richard J., Political Career in New Jersey, 6495

Hull, Cordell: and Latin America, (1933–1939), 7626; and Argentina, 9032; and U.S. Argentine Policy during World War II, 9028; Attitude toward Japan, 0826; Biography, 0841; Career and Personality, 0830; Career as Secretary of State, 0842; Concept of a World Organization, 0832; Democratic Party Unity, 0845; Diplomatic Philosophy, 0840; Diplomatic Theory, 0824; Far East Diplomacy, 0846; Foreign Policy Decisions, (1933–1936), 0835; Foreign Policy Decisions, 0827; Foreign Policy

Philosophy, 0836; Influence on Roosevelt, 0829; International Trade Philosophy, 0822, 0823; Liberal Economic Policies, 0831; Memoir, 7843, 0833; Opposes Recognition of USSR, 0825; Post-War Trade Philosophy, 0837; Proposals for Foreign Economic Development, 0838; Relations with Japan, (1933–1936), 0834; Speeches at Montevideo Conference, (1933), 0828; Trade Agreement Philosophy, 0844; Trade Agreement Proposals, 0843; Wartime Speeches, 0839

Hull, Helen Rose, Analysis of Her Works, 3432

Hull-Nomura Conversations (1941), 7491, 7552

Hull-Roosevelt Reciprocal Trade Agreement Act (1934), 1822

Humphrey, Hubert H.: and the Politics of the Cold War (1943–1954), 6469; and the Minneapolis Mayoralty Election (1943), 6606

Hunter, Jane Edna, As Leader of the Phyllis Wheatley Association of Cleveland, 5435

Hunting Magazines and the Image of Hunting During World War II, 4580

Hurley, Patrick J.: American Policy toward China, (1944–1945), 0924; Attacks on John Service and John P. Davies, 0926; Attacks on the Yalta Protocol, 0922; Biography, 0925; Demands Recall of General Joseph W. Stilwell, 0927; Efforts to Unify Nationalist and Communist Military Forces in China, 0928; Failure as a Diplomat, 0923; Interview of (1986), 9845; Mission to China (1944–1945), 8893

Hurst, Fannie, Her Correspondence with Zora Neal Hurston, 3506

Hurston, Zora N., And the Federal Writers Project in Florida, 5188

Hutcheson, William L., As Leader of Brotherhood of Carpenters and Joiners, 2437

Huxman, Walter, Elected Governor of Kansas (1936), 6510

Hybrid Corn in Illinois, Development, 1282

I'm Alone, Controversy (1929–1935), 7255

Ice Cream Suppers in Kentucky (1930s and 1940s), 4256

Iceman Cometh, The (1939), Analysis, 3263

Ickes, Harold L.: Administration Hatchet Man, 0643; Aggressive Progressive, 0640; and Oil Crisis (1933), 0639; Appointment as Secretary of the Interior, 0636; As Federal Administrator, 0631; Autobiography, 0633; Biographical Sketch, 0648; Career as Secretary of the Interior, 0647; Diary, 0634; Hated by Alaskans, 0638; Hiring Quotas for Blacks in Public Works Administration, 0637; Involved in West Virginia Coal Mine Strike (1943), 0645; Political Career, 0635, 0642; Psycho-biography, 0649; Relation with National Park Service, 0641; Relationship with Horace M. Albright, 0646; Use of Federal Power, 0632; Views on Petroleum Policy Planning, 0644; Writings, 5052

Idaho, and the Repeal of Prohibition, 4755

Ignatow, David, Poetry, (1931–1978), 3594

Iijima, Kazu, Discusses Her Life in Oakland, California (1930s), 5719

Illinois: and the Ratification of the 26th Amendment, 6577; Congressional Elections (1942), 6636

Illinois Central Railroad in an Iowa Winter (1936), 1917

Illness, Impact on World Leaders, 4228

Immigration Policies and India, (1917–1946), 4154

Immigration Service and the Chicano Labor Movement in the 1930s, 4148

Important Labor Leaders, Essays, 2415

Income Loss, Impact on Marital Relations during the Great Depression, 1688

Independent Journalists in Texas, Themes, Attitudes, and Methods, 4034

Independent Liberalism, Failure, (1930–1941), 6162

Independent Textile Workers Union of Woonsocket, Rhode Island, (1931–1946), 2214

Indiana Politics (1936–1940), 6635

Indian Arts and Crafts Board as an Aspect of New Deal Indian Policy, 5096

Indian Boarding School, White Earth, Minnesota (1909–1945), 5812

Indian Children and Federal Boarding Schools (1920–1960), 5896

Indian Claims Commission Act of 1942, Evaluated, 5872

Indian Education in the 20th Century, 5898

Indian Fishing Rights in the Pacific North West, (1933–1953), 5878

Indian New Deal: and Indian Women, 5813; and Rehabilitation Policy Among the Sioux (1936–1942), 5820; and the American Indian Federation, 5846; and the Sioux Indians, 5819; and the Western Shoshone of Nevada, 5051; Evaluation, 5810, 5885, 5899, 5900; Promotion of Arts and Crafts, 5889; Use of Anthropological Techniques, 5858

Indian Policy: (1943–1961), 5843; from the Dawes Act to the 1970s, 5895; in the United States from early 19th Century to World War II, 5834

Indian Relocation in the West, 5853

Indian Reorganization Act (1934): 5905; and Education, 5875; and the Indians of Alaska, 5883; and the Iroquois, 5845; and the loss of Tribal Sovereignty, 5826; Evaluation, 5847, 5861 The Responses: Hopi, Western Shoshone, and Southern Utes, 5823, 5824

Indian Rights Association, Opposes Allotment Policy, 5817

Indian Self Determination Policy, Evaluation (1940–1975), 5891

Indian Studies Program and the University of Oklahoma Press, 5830

Indians: and Selective Service, 5839, and Impact of Urbanization (1920–1950), 5892; and Termination Policy (1943–1958), 5894, and White Politicians in South Dakota (1920–1965), 5890, and World War II, 5840, 5851

Industrial Anthropology, Rise and Decline, 2584

Industrial Design Profession, (1925–1939), 2578

Industrial Policy, (1920s–1930s), 2540

Industrial Recreation Movement and Women's Sports (1930s), 4599

Industrial Union of Marine and Shipbuilding Workers of America, History, 2302

Industrial Unionism: in the Los Angeles Furniture Industry, (1918–1954), 2106; Rise in Woonsocket, Rhode Island, (1931–1941), 2216

Industrial Workers of the World (IWW): and the Boulder Canyon Project, 2348; in Chicago, (1919–1939), 2069; in Cleveland, (1918–1950), 2407;in Ohio, (1913–1950), 2408; in Yakima Valley of Washington, 2166, 2328

Institute for Advanced Study: and Foreign Art Historians (1930s), 4401; and Foreign Scholars (1930s), 4394; Founded of at Princeton (1930–1933), 4389

Institute for Social Research, History in America, (1934–1950), 4363

Institutional Development in the United States, (1917–1935), 2622

Insull, Samuel, Attempts to Extradite Him from Europe (1933), 4742

Insull Utility Complex Collapse, Impact on Investors, 2625

Intellectual trends in America (1930s), 4250

Intelligence Testing of Blacks (1930s), 4421

Inter-American Aviation Rivalry, (1927–1940), 1896

Inter-American Coffee Agreement (1940), 7660

Inter-American Commission on Women (1933), 5991

Inter-War Years, 7180

Inter-Service Cooperation, Efforts to Develop (1900–1938), 4958

Interest Payments on Demand Deposits and Bank Behavior, 1588

Interest Rate: Impact on Demand for Money during the Great Depression, 1972; Term Structure, (1920–1939), 2630

International Brotherhood of Teamsters, Organizing Efforts in the Dakotas, (1930s), 2395

International Events as Portrayed in Comic Strips, (1940–1970), 4084

International Financial Relations as a Factor in Diplomacy, 2058

International Labor Institute of Gary, Indiana, 4144

International Labor Organization, Changes in Structure, Function, and Policy, (1935–1955), 2063

International Ladies Garment Workers Union: and Theatrical Propaganda, (1935), 2375; and Mexicans in Los Angeles (1933–1939), 5701; Selected Bibliography, 9617; Strike, Los Angeles, (1933), 2180

International Longshoremen's and Warehousemen's Union: Origins, 2139; Strike in Portland, Oregon, (1934), 2130

International Monetary Diplomacy, (1929–1937), 1964

International Peace Garden, History, 8047

International Relations, Bibliography (1920–1970), 9623

International Sources of American Trade Policy, (1887–1939), 1843

International Studies in America (1930s), 4366

International Union of Mine, Mill, and Smelter Workers, Efforts to Organize Black Workers, (1933–1952), 2248

International Workers Order; Activities (1930s and 1940s), 2396; Role in the Organization of the Congress of Industrial Organizations, 2266

Internationalism: and the South (1930s), 7975; Triumph during World War II, 7968

Interstate Commerce Commission: and the Debate on Railroad Freight Rate Schedules, 1914; and the Impact of the Great Depression on Freight Rates, 1921

Interstate Commercial Motor Vehicle Operators, Federal Regulation (1900–1986), 2624

Interstate Highway Politics, (1939–1956), 1871

Interstate Oil Cartel, Establishment, (1933–1940), 1761

Interventionism, Debates on (March 1941 to December 1941), 7981

Interventionists: Arguments (1939–1941), 7985; in the Middle West (1935–1941), 7994; of 1940, 7964; Propaganda in the U.S. (1937–1941), 7983

Inter-War Monetary Systems, France and England, 1965

Inter-War Period, Analysis, 1938

Intra-Cultural Educational Movement (1924–1941), 4371, 4372

Investment Failure in the Inter-War American Economy, 1974

Iowa: and the 1932 Presidential Election, 6746; Child Welfare Research Station and the Debate on Intelligence, (1940), 4368; Farm Women in the 1930s, 5935; Farmers in Crisis, (1920–1936), 1378; Planning Programs (1930s, 1940s and 1950s), 4657; Produces Leaders: Herbert C. Hoover; John L. Lewis; Henry A. Wallace; and Harry Hopkins, 6687; Progressives: Gilbert N Haugen; Herbert C. Hoover; and Henry A. Wallace, 6689; State College, Research on the Conversion of Agricultural Waste into Marketable Products, (1920–1940), 4361; Violent Episodes Resulting from Farm Foreclosures, 4706; Why a Disproportionate Share of the Influential People Came from there, 6688

Irey, Elmer L., In Pursuit of Tax Dodgers (1930s and 1940s), 4724

Irish Treaty Ports (1940), 7336

Irish-Americans: And Urban Political Machines, 6824; Political, Cultural, Social Activities during the New Deal Years, 4780

Irrigation: Impact on Great Plains Agriculture, 1410; on the Great Plains, (1940–1980), 1409

Irwin, Virginia, *St. Louis Post-Dispatch* War Correspondent, 5974

Irwin, Will, And the Crusade for the League of Nations, 8026

Isolationism: (1919–1933), 7902; (1919–1941), 7925; (1935–1941), 7906; Analyzed, 7820; and Academe (1938–1941), 7930; and American Foreign Policy (1933–1939), 7948; and the Catholic Church, 7950; and

Congressional Foreign Policy Voting Patterns (1914–1941), 7914; and the Early New Deal (1932–1937), 7886; and Pro-Axis Sentiment, 7933; and Southern Senators, 7952; and the Coming of War (1931–1941), 7961; and the Middle East, 7894; and the South, 7905; and the Swedish American Press, 7892; and the Undeclared War (1939–1941), 7942; and the World Crisis (1937–1940), 7941; as a Cause of Military Weakness, 7995; As a Dominant Force in U.S. Policy (1930s), 7885; As Influenced by the End of World War I, 7897; Compared to European Neutralism, 7889; Decline (1937–1941), 7916, 7927, 7932; Explained (1937), 7926; Failure, 7987; Historiographical Essay (1974), 9727; Ideology (1939–1941), 7908; in America (1935–1941), 7935; in Lancaster, Pennsylvania (1935–1939), 7903; in Macintosh County, North Dakota, (1936–1940), 7904; in Missouri (1935–1941), 7951; in North Dakota, 7960; in the Middle West, 7949; Leading Advocates, 7909; Not Strong in Kenton County, Kentucky, 7970; Why it was Abandoned, 7884

Israel and the B'Nai B'Rith, 7622

Italian American Anti-Fascist Movement, 4788, 6379; and the Question of Loyalty, (1939–1940), 4775; in Greenwich Village New York (1930s), 5711; and the Ethiopian Crisis, 4787

Italian Immigrants and Sports (1925–1941), 4778

Italians: and Conflict with the Jews (1930s), 5734; in Courtland, New York, (1905–1940), 4784; in Los Angeles During the Depression, 4773

Italio-Ethiopia Crisis (1934–1936), Afro-American Response, 5296, 5362

Italo-Allied Relations (1943–1944), 8784

Italo-American Press and Pro-Fascist Propaganda in America (1935–1936), 8534

Italo-American Relations: (1919–1936), 7345; (1932–1941), 7341; (1935–1939), 7339; (1937–1941), 7338

Italo-Ethiopian: Dispute (1934–1938), 7184; War, Efforts to Stop it, 7340

Ives, Charles, Influence on American Music, 3520

Jackson, Gardner, Relationship with H. L. Mitchell, 1541

Jackson, Harry L., Letters of a Special Services Officer, 9239

Jackson, Henry M., As Snohomish County Prosecutor (1939–1940), 6512

Jackson, Robert, 7041–7044

Jackson, William Henry, As Painter of Murals for the National Park Service (1930s), 3671

James, C. L. R., Radical Organizer (1930s and 1940s), 6279

Jamison, Alice, Critic of New Deal Indian Policy, 5849

Jamison, J. Franklin, And the Quest for a National Historical Publications Commission, 9760

Japan: and Pro-Japanese Propaganda in America (1937–1941), 8532; and the Oil Embargo (1941), 7475; and Western Style Imperialism, 7499; and the Greater

East Asia Co-Prosperity Sphere, 7535; Blunders into War, 7580; Excluded from American Fisheries (1937–1939), 7597; Foreign Policy (1868–1941), 7533; Foreign Policy Decisions leading to the Pacific War, 7582; Imperialism and Aggression, 7534; Regional Policy in the Far East (1931–1941), 7515; Sees U.S. and British Peace Plans as an Imperialistic Plot, 7526; The Decision for War, 7564

Japanese-American Relations (1931–1941), 7484

Japanese Americans: and Prejudice on the West Coast, 5728; and Unionization in the Fruit Stand Industry, 2307; in Southern Nevada, (1905–1945), 5726; Why They Prospered during the Depression, 4766

Japanese: and Chinese, American Images of (1930–1960), 5713; Empire, Decline and Fall (1936–1945), 7593; Export Policy, (1930–1936), 1837; Farmers in Arizona, Attacks on (1934–1935), 5712; Foreign Policy Decision Making Process (1930s), 7529; Image in Four American Newspapers, (1905–1972), 4020; Immigrants in California Agriculture, 5720; Immigrants in California before 1941, 4155; in Hawaii (1927–1941), 5724; in Los Angeles (1900–1942), 5722; in San Diego (1880's to 1942), 5716; Internment, 8326–8422; International Negotiating Style, 7481; Language Schools in California (1903–1941), 5723; Leaders as Disciples of Alfred Thayer Mahan, 7494; Mandates in the Pacific (1919–1941), 7488; Nationalist Activities in America (1930s), 5718; Policies (1938), 7497; Settlers in Arizona, 5727; Women in America (1900 to World War II), 5717

Jazz: Criticism, (1914–1940), 3577; Development (1930s), 3543; Historiography and Criticism, (1920–1945), 3576; in Los Angeles (1940s), 3550; in the Midwest and Southwest, (1920–1940), 3523; in Transition, (1935–1945), 3528; Men as Romantic Outsiders, (1920s–1940s), 3547; Music Critics Changing Attitudes toward, (1920s–1940s), 3574; Music, History (1930s and 1940s), 3567; Music, Use in American Animated Cartoons (1930s and 1940s), 3539; Musicians Interviewed (1930s), 3563; Origins, 3560

Jeffers, Robinson, An Atypical Lighthearted Poem, 3599

Jefferson National Expansion Memorial: Discussed, 5248; Proposed by Mayor Bernard A. Dickman of St. Louis (1933), 6441

Jefferson, Short History of the State (1941), 6677

Jehovah's Witnesses: and Constitutional Issues (1930s and 1940s), 4500; and the Supreme Court (1938–1960), 4521

Jennings, Frances, Discusses Her Career at Arlington Hall Junior College, 4337

Jersey City, New Jersey, Efforts to Unionize, 2251

Jessup, Philip C., Ambassador at Large, 0847

Jewish Adult Summer Camp (1920s and 1930s), 5744

Jewish Aeronautical Association, 5780

Jewish-American Artists in New York City, (1905–1945), 5800

Jewish-Black Relations: before World War II, 5802; in Detroit during World War II, 5740

Jewish Catastrophe, Bibliography (1939–1945), 9625

Jewish Community Council of Detroit, Founding (1937), 5771

Jewish Community: in America, Response to Depression, New Deal and Nazism, 5743; in Boston and the Rise of Nazism, 5804

Jewish Coordinating Council in St. Louis, 5739

Jewish Crisis and U.S. German Relations (1933–1939), 9157

Jewish Gangster during Prohibition and the Great Depression, Composite Portrait, 4733

Jewish Immigrants of the Holocaust Era, (1933–1953), 5730

Jewish Intellectuals: and Flight to America (1930–1945), 9118; and Refugees in America, 9113; in New York City (1930s), 5803

Jewish Labor: between World War I and World War II, 2145

Jewish Labor Committee and American Immigration Policy (1930s), 4143

Jewish Labor Movement in the United States, from World War I to the 1950s, 2232

Jewish Non-Zionism in the U.S. (1917–1941), 9002

Jewish Overseas Relief (1919–1939), 9165, 9166, 9167

Jewish Pacifists during World War II, 8052

Jewish Radical Writers during the Great Depression, 5764

Jewish Refugees: (1938), 9170; and Alaskan Economic Development, 9140; and American Churches (1933–1945), 9102, 9103; and American Jews (1933–1939), 9106, 9169; and Anglo-American Relations (1944–1948), 9179; and Jewish Loan Societies in the U.S. (1880–1945), 9171; and Zionism, 9168; in Atlanta, 9151; The Rescue of Scholars and Scientists (1933–1945), 9173

Jewish Unions and the American Federation of Labor, (1903–1935), 2108

Jewish Vocation Service of Newark, New Jersey, (1939–1952), 5790

Jews: and Reform Politics in Omaha (1930s), 5787; and the Anti-Nazi Boycott (1933–1941), 9107; and the Early Days of Nazi Rule in Germany, 9109; and the New Deal, 5746; and Protestant Efforts to Convert (1820–1925), 5751; and Tin Pan Alley (1910–1940), 5770; as Portrayed in Jewish-American Novels (1930s), 5805; at Princeton, 5749; in Hawaii (1930s), 5806; in Minneapolis, (1930–1950), 5788

Jobless Party in New Mexico, 6854

John Doe Associates, And Backdoor Diplomacy for Peace (1941), 7492

John Morrell Company and Welfare Capitalism, (1922–1937), 2400

Johnson, Ben, And Kentucky Politics (1927–1937), 6573

Johnson, Evelyn C., Discusses Her Career at Springfield, Missouri Senior High School in the 1940s, 4339

Johnson, Henry, Views on the Teaching of World History (1930s), 4403

Johnson, Hiram: Attitude toward New Deal, 1009; Author of Johnson Act (1934), 1011; Biography, 1008; Impressions

of William E. Borah, 1004; Influence on Foreign Policy, 1006, 1007; Speaking Skills, 1005, 1012; Supports Roosevelt (1932), 1010

Johnson, Hugh S.: As Head of National Recovery Administration, 0702: Biographical Sketch, 0701

Johnson, Jack and Joe Louis as Caricatured in Newspaper Cartoons (1908–1938), 4629

Johnson, James Weldon, Letters to George A. Towns (1896–1934), 5432

Johnson, Keen, As Governor of Kentucky, (1939–1943), 6499

Johnson, Lyndon B.: Attitude toward Blacks, 1073; Campaign Speeches (1941), 1078; Career as Director of National Youth Administration in Texas, 1075; Commemorative Remarks on the 82nd Anniversary of Roosevelt's Birth, 1079; Foreign Policy Background, 1077; Religious Background, 1074; Remarks on the Roosevelt Legacy, 1080; Views on Civil Rights Legislation, 1076

Johnson, Nelson T.: And U.S. Policy toward China (1935–1941), 8889: Minister to China, 0848, 0849

Johnson, Philip, Supports Father Charles Coughlin, 3159

Johnson, Robert, Lynched of in Tampa, Florida, (1934), 4716

Johnson, William H., Life and Work, 3639

Johnston, Frances B., His Photographic Survey of Old Buildings, 3690

Johnston, Henry S., As Attorney for the Oto and Missouri Indians (1930s), 5852

Johnston, Olin D.: As Governor of South Carolina (1935–1939), 6455: Early Political Career (1896–1945), 6624: Efforts to Reorganize the South Caroline State Highway Commission (1935–1936), 6426; Senate Campaigns, 1156

Johnston, Oscar G.: New Deal Career, 1566; Public and Private Career, 2859

Joint Chiefs of Staff: and National Security Policy Making, (1942–1961), 6870; Development of Committee Structure, 4857; History during World War II, 4856; War Reports, 8577

Jolson, Al, Decline of Career (Mid 1930s), 3536

Jonas, Manfred, Flees to America (1936), 9119

Jones, Jesse H.: As Head of Reconstruction Finance Corporation, 0703; Biography, 0705; Relationship with Franklin Delano Roosevelt, 0704

Jones, Marvin, Political Career, 1081,1082

Jones, Sam Houston, And the 1940 Gubernatorial Campaign in Louisiana, 6556

Jorgensen, Arthur W. Sr., Remembers the Depression Years, 4343

Joseph-Gaudet, Frances, How she Brought Social Change in New Orleans, 5325

Josephson, Matthew: Marxist Historian, 9792; Recollection of the Early Days of the Depression, 2554

Journal of Negro History, Impact on Black Historical Scholarship, 9735

Judd, Walter H., Criticizes Roosevelt's China Policy, 1220

Juergensen, Hans, Flees to America (1934), 9120

Julian, Hubert F., And the Italo-Ethiopian War, 7245

Julius Rosenwald Fund and Race Relations (1928–1948), 5309

Junior Novel, Emergence and Development, (1870–1980), 3386

Juoette, Colonel John H., And the Training of Chinese Pilots (1932–1935), 7464

Kaiser, Henry J., Career, 2527

Kaltenborn, H. V.: Biography, 3877; Calls for American International Involvement, (1939–1941), 3893

Kansas City, And Racial Discrimination in Public Accommodations (1939–1964), 5342

Kansas Congressional Delegation and the Selective Service Act, 7924

Kansas Family, History, 1313

Kansas: History of Prohibition, 4745; History of the National Guard (1954–1975), 4876; Indian Units (1920s and 1930s), 5876; Letters from Farmers, 1335; Press and the New Deal, 3974

Kase, Toshikazu, Memoir, 7536

Katyn Forest Massacre, 8839

Kavanagh, Jack, Memories of the Brooklyn Dodgers (1930–1941), 4604

Keck, George F., Career, 3160

Kee, Elizabeth, Career, 5944

Keller, Kent, New Deal Congressman from Illinois, 6725

Kelly, Edward J.: Political Career in Chicago, 6431, 6432; Chicago Controls the Black Vote (1933–1950), 5647

Kelly, Thomas, His letters from Nazi Germany (1938), 7292

Kemmerer, Irwin W.: Career, 1981; Financial Beliefs and Prophecies, 1982

Kendrick, John B., Fight for Western Water Legislation, (1917–1933), 2933

Kennan, George F., Analysis of Memoirs, 0854; Diplomacy, 0850; Diplomatic Philosophy, 0851; Diplomatic Papers, (1938–1940), 7846; Evaluation, 7838; Views on Events in Europe, (1939–1945), 0852; Views on Russia, (1944–1946), 0853

Kennedy, Joseph P.: And the Origins of World War II, 8735; As Ambassador to the Court of Saint James, 0856, 0859, 0860, 0861; Biography, 0858; As Chairman of the Securities and Exchange Commission, 0857; Relationship with Franklin Delano Roosevelt, 0855

Kent, Frank R., As Critic of the New Deal, 7111

Kent, Tyler, Intercepts Confidential Roosevelt-Churchill Correspondence (1940), 4744

Kentucky: Baptist and World War II, 4556; Democratic Politics (1919–1932), 6697; Press and the Democratic Senatorial Primary (1938), 6521

Kester, Howard A., Political and Religious Views, 6285

Keynes, John Maynard, Biography, 2033; Effect on the US during the New Deal, 2032; Reverses Classical Economic Position, 2037

Keynesian Economics: Analysis, 2026; Impact on American Thinking and Policy, 2039; Impact on Government

Policy, (1933–1939), 2044; Impact on Policy from the New Deal to the Great Society, 2040; Theory and Public Administration Theory, 2027

Keynesian Economists, Growing Influence (1920s), 2038; Role in Wartime Policy and Postwar Planning, (1940–1946), 2036

Keys of the Kingdom (1944), As a Propaganda Film, 3724

Kiesler, Frederick, Career (1930s), 3183

Kildahl, Earling E., Memoir of a Flight from Bismark to Spokane, (1936), 1888; Riding the Rails to Jamestown, North Dakota, (1936), 1918

Kilgore, Harley M.: Senate Career, 1158; Supports Wartime mobilization, 1157

Kimmel, Admiral Husband E., And the Pearl Harbor Controversy, 7602; Self-Exoneration for Pearl Harbor Debacle, 0969

King, Carol W., Labor Organizer, 6240

King, Edith, Her Life in Alabama (1929–1936), 4678

King, Ernest J.: Autobiography, 0971; Biography, 0970; Career as Chief of Naval Operations, 0973; Strategic Philosophy, 0972

King Peter II of Yugoslavia Visits the U.S. (1942), 8816

King, William H., Views on Haiti, 1013

King's Canyon National Park, Origins, 1433

Kinley, David, Career, 4315

Knights of Columbus, Activities during the Great Depression, 4513

Knox, Frank: Biography, 0862; Interventionist views, 0863

Koerner, W. H. D., Discussion of His Illustrations of the West, 3655

Kollmorgen, Walter M., Memoir, 1473

Kone, Fumimaro, Efforts for Peace (1941–1945), 7569

Koreans as Enemy Aliens in World War II, 5807

Korson, George, and the Pennsylvania Folk Festival, 3144

Kotov Affair, 8871

Kristallnacht (November 9–10, 1938), American Reaction, 5745

Krivitsky, Walter, Soviet Defector (1937), 6247

Krock, Arthur, And the New Deal Era, (1929–1941), 4076

Krutch, Joseph W., Conservation and Nature Theories, 4948

Ku Klux Klan: History, 6400; in Pennsylvania (1920–1940), 6386; Supports Roosevelt (1932), 6751

Kump, Herman G.: And the Fiscal Crisis in Virginia (1933), 6513, 6514; As Governor of West Virginia (1933–1937), 6515

Kurr, Philip (Lord Lothian), British Ambassador to the United States (1929–1940), 7321

Kurrie, Lauchlin, Economic Theories, 2035

Kurusu Mission to the United States (1941), 7530

La Follette Committee and the Congress of Industrial Organizations, 2109

La Follette, Philip F.: and Wisconsin Politics in the New Deal Era, 6625; His Political Use of the English Language, 6838; Memoir, 0930; Political and Economic Views, 6837

La Follette, Robert M., Jr.: Biography, 1254; Economic and Political Views, 1255; Foreign Policy Views, 1253; Investigates Big Business Anti Labor Practices, 1252

La Guardia, Fiorello H.: and Employment Discrimination in New York City (1931–1938), 6450; and his First Hundred Days as Mayor of New York City, 6458; and The Harlem Crime Wave (1941), 4701; As Mayor of New York City (1930–1945), 6457, 6710; Criticizes the Nazis (1938), 6493; Labor Views, 6562; Speaking Ability (1932–1945), 6614, 6650; Speaking Ability; Views on Racial Discrimination, 5332

Labor and Civil Liberties in the New Deal, 2110

Labor College Movement in America, (1920s and 1930s), 4260

Labor Conflict in Eastern Kentucky Coal Fields, (1930s), 2153

Labor Disputes in the Disney Studios, (1930s–1940s), 3856

Labor History, Sources, 2084

Labor Journals and the Constitutional Issues of the New Deal, 3976

Labor Militancy in Akron, Ohio, (1936–1938), 2320

Labor Movement: Expansion, 2147; in Indiana during World War II,. 2112; in Memphis, Tennessee, (1930s), 2131; in New York City's China town, (1930–1950), 2273; in Windber, Pennsylvania, (1890s–1930s), 2064

Labor Organization: and the New Deal in Baltimore, 2104; at Du Pont, (1920–1960), 2346; in Detroit, Development (1920s and 1930s), 2291

Labor Radicalism and the Law in California (1936–1941), 6236

Labor Relations: during the Roosevelt Years, 2081; in the Steel Industry, (1920–1950), 2267; on the West Coast, (Mid 1930s), 2368

Labor Unions: Activity in Film *United Action Means Victory* (1940), 3833; Growing Influence in Personnel Management, (1930s–1940s), 2254; Growth in the Twentieth Century, 2125; Maintenance of Membership Formula, (1941–1942), 2151; Records, 9658

Labor Unrest in High Point, North Carolina, (Early 1930s), 2371

Laidler, Henry W., And the League for Industrial Democracy (1921–1957), 6316

Lamont, Corliss, And the Struggle for Civil Liberties (1930s to the 1950s), 6872

Land Exchange Act (1937), 5904

Land Grant School Fund in Montana, (1938–1982), 1456

Land Policy, History, 1497

Land Reclamation in the Dust Bowl, 1464

Land Reform in New Mexico during the New Deal, 1434

Land Reservation, Development on Federal Land, 1493

Land Speculation in Iowa, 1311

Land Use Planning on the Great Plains, (1930s), 1454

Landis, James M., New Deal Career, 0745

Landis, Kenesaw Mountain, As First Commissioner of Baseball, 4613

Landon, Alfred M.: and Republican Party Politics in Kansas (1930s), 6615; and the 1936 Presidential Election, 6774,

6777; As Governor of Kansas (1932–1936), 6616; As Leader of the Republican Opposition, 6077; Comments on the Roosevelt Record (1970), 6780

Lane, Arthur B, Diplomatic Career, 0864

Lane, Russell, And Segregation in the Secondary Schools in Indianapolis, (1927–1949), 4367

Lange, Dorothea: Biography, 0746; Culture of the Great Depression Captured in Her Photographs, 3630; Photographing Migrant Pea Pickers, 0747

Langer, Walter C., His Experiences in Austria, (1936–1938), 7259

Langer, William L.: and Conspiracy Trials in North Dakota, 6585; and Farm Policies in North Dakota, 1327; and the 1936 Gubernatorial Campaign in North Dakota, 6712; As Bureaucrat and Diplomatic Historian, 9758; As an Isolationist (1940–1959), 7958; Autobiography, 7213; Isolationist Views, 1256, 1257; Political Career, 1014

Langlie, Arthur B., As Governor of Washington, 6694

Lansdale, Edward G., Father of Special Operations, 0929

Lansing, Michigan Labor Holiday, (June 7, 1937), 2136

Laski, Harold J., As Believer in a Classless Society, 6364; Career (1910–1946), 5760; Political Influence, 6234

Last, Tony (in Evelyn Waugh's *A Handful of Dust*, 1942) and Ike McCaslin (in Faulkner's *Go Down Moses*, 1942), Compared, 3398

Latin America: and Promotional Literature in the United States during the Roosevelt Administration, 3469; Its Image in American Film, (1929–1939), 3866, 3867

Lauck, W. Jett, Biography, 2051

Law, Laura, Murdered (1940), 4736

Lawrence, D. H., Reputation in America (1930s), 3363

Lawrence, Jacob: Analysis of His Art, 3627, 3704; Career, 3706, 3707

Lawson, John H.: Activist Playwright, 3197; Rhetorical Analysis of Plays, 3235; Selective Plays, 3249

Layman, Irving, As Chief Judge of the New York Court of Appeals. 6946

Layton, Edwin T., Memoir, 7543

Leaf, Arthur, Letters to His Family, 1687

League for Independent Political Action (1928–1933), 6140

League of American Writers (1929–1942), 6214, 6363

League of Nations: America Considers Sending an Ambassador (1933), 7220; and Disarmament (1919–1934), 7996

League of United Latin American Citizens, (1933–1940), 5697

Leahy, William D.: Biography, 0974; Favors Naval Expansion, 0975; Influence on Foreign Policy, 0976; Mission to Vichy France, 8698, 8703

Ledyard, H.C., Biography, 4507

Lee, Algernon, His Correspondence with Karl Kautsky (1930–1935), 6230

Lee, Harper, Use of Truman Capote as a Character in *To Kill a Mockingbird*, 3358

Lee, Molly Houston, As Librarian of the Richard B. Harrison Library for Negroes, Raleigh, North Carolina, 5492

Lee, Raymond E., U.S. Military Attache London (1940–1941), 7326

Lee, Russell, Depression Era Photographs, 3651

Left-Wing Musicians (1930s), 3548

Leftist Fiction and Criticism (1930s), 3357

Leftist Politics as seen in Frontier Films' *Native Land* (1942), 3750

Legislative Veto Systems, Rise and Decline (1930–1980), 6593

LeHand, Marguerite, Private Secretary to Franklin D. Roosevelt, 0623

Lehman, Herbert H.: And Milk Price Controls, 0748; As Governor of New York, 0751, 6553; As Lieutenant Governor of New York, 0749; As Political Saint, 0750; Legislative Leadership, 6424; Political Career, 0752

Lemke, William: As Union Party Presidential Candidate (1936), 6817, 6840; Public Career, 1221; Seeks Presidency (1936), 1222; Speaking Style, 1223

Lend Lease: 8656, 8748; and Anglo-American Relations, 8750; and Saudi Arabia, 8984; in Latin America, 9024; in the Middle East (1940–1944), 8974; Policy, 7204; Program, 7233

Lenoire, Rosetta, Career, 5504

LeTournau, R. G., 9220

Lewis, John L.: and the 1940 Election, 2447; and the Rise of the CIO, 2448; As Leader of Anthracite Coal Miners, (1926–1936), 2446: Biography, 2438, 2439, 2450; Comments on GM Sit Down Strike, (1936–1937), 2440; Evaluation, 2443; Interpretation, 2442; Legacy, 2441; Philosophy, 2449; Reflections of Philip Van Gelder, 2444; Relationship with Roosevelt, (1933–1940), 2445

Lewis, Sinclair: Analysis of His Novels Published from (1920–1949), 3406; His Later (after 1930) Works, 3448

Lewisohn, Ludwig, Acculturation, 9158

Lexington, Virginia, Remembering 1939, 9848

Libby, Frederick and the American Peace Movement (1921–1941), 8033

Liberal Attitudes toward the South (1930–1965), 6160

Liberal Journalism during World War II, 6184

Liberal Thought in the 1930s, Transformation, 2703

Liberal Tradition in America, 6154

Liberalism: and its Challenges, (1932–1982), 6153; Demise, 6141

Liberals and the Cold War, 6174

Liberia, American Efforts to Promote Industrial Education (1930s), 4341

Life in Tokyo, (1941), 0814

Life Magazine, Creation, 4005

Light Division, Development (1935–1944), 4905

Lilienthal, David E., His Journals of the Atomic Energy Years, (1945–1950), 4934; Journals (1939–1945), 3111

Lincoln Battalion of the 15th International Brigade (1938), 7362

Lincoln Institute in Kentucky, How It Was Saved During the Depression, 4431

Lincoln, Nebraska Urban League, Formation, 5484

Lindbergh, Charles A.: and Isolationism (1939–1941), 7921; and Munich, 7922; His Attitudes toward Technology, 4960; His Isolationist Views Evaluated, 7957; Isolationist Speeches, 7917; Journal of his European Trip (September-October 1938), 7944; Opposes American Intervention in World War II, 7900, 7940, Papers, 1904, Wartime Journals, 7945

Lindsay, Sir Ronald C., As British Ambassador to the United States (1930–1939), 7330; Portrays Congress as an Archaic Institution lead by a "Bunch of Blundering Individuals," 7863

Lindsey, Ben, Pioneer in the Passage of Child Labor Laws, 4682

Linsdey, Ambassador Sir Ronald, Tells British Government how to Win American Support, 8740

Lippman, Walter: 0466; Analysis of His Political Philosophy and Journalistic Style, 4077; Analysis of his Writings (1913–1955), 7074; and U.S. Foreign Policy (1914–1945), 7883; As Critic of the New Deal (1932–1941), 7077; Content Analysis of His column, (1932–1948), 4099; His Opposition to the New Deal, 7127; Political Ideas, 7096; Political Philosophy, 4078; Writings, 7070

Literary Chronicle (1920s and 1930s), 3509

Literature and Reading in the South and Southwest, Conference, (1935), 3322

Literature of the Great Depression, 3268, 3450

Litvinov, Maxim, Biography, 7446; Disagrees with Stalin's Foreign Policy (1943–1946), 8865; In the United States (1941–1943), 8875

Littell, Norman M., Memoir, 0503

Little Orphan Annie and Her Right Wing Philosophy, 4105

"Little Steel": Efforts to Organize, (1937–1942), 2210, Strike (1937), 2118, 2300, 2376

Little White House, Pictorial History, 0105

Llano del Rio Colony, Gila, New Mexico, (1932–1935), 1697

Lloyd, Lola M., And the Peace Movement, 8046

Locke, Allain L.: Contribution to Black Education (1930s), 5404; His Views on Race Relations, 5467; Race Consciousness, 5507

Log from *The Sea of Cortez*, Analysis, 3278

Logan-Walter Reorganization Bill, 0532

Lone Ranger, The, Birth, (1933), 3909

Long Beach Earthquake, (1933), 1481

Long, Breckinridge, War Diaries, 0706

Long, Earl: His Career as a Corrupt Politician in Louisiana (1939–1960), 6580; His Political Career in Louisiana, 6590; Political Career in Louisiana, 6417, 6657

Long, Frank, His Involvement with the Treasury Section Fine Arts Program, 5168

Long, Huey: And Southern Radicalism 6362; Attention to forming Public Opinion, 1176; Attitude toward New Deal, 1160; Autobiography, 1180; Biographical Sketch, 1179; Biography, 1166, 1190; Challenges New Deal, 1178; Compared to Father Charles Coughlin, 1162;

Criticizes Chaco War, 1172; Criticizes New Deal, 1164; Death, 1170; Evaluation, 1186; Friendship with Rupert Peyton, 1182; Funeral Oration by Gerald L. K. Smith, 1169; His Rise to Political Power Explained, 6548; Influence on Education, 1175; Journalistic Impressions, 1173; Modernizing Force in Louisiana Political and Economic Life, 1183; Papers, 1188; Political Career, 1189; Political Philosophy, 1167; Progressive Leader, 1184; Senate Career, 1165; Share Our Wealth Movement, 1163; Speaking Ability 1159, 1161, 1177; Supports Cotton Acreage Control, (1931), 1187; Supports Hattie Caraway, 1185; Various Interpretations, 1168; Various Views, 1174, 1181

Longstreet, Stephen, Remembers His Friendship with Sinclair Lewis, (1930–1947), 3409

Loosli, Alden, Remembers Working His Way Through College (1930s), 4357

Lorentz, Pare: A Note on *The River* (1938), 3801; As documentary Film Maker, 3786

Loriks, Emil, Comments on Huey Long, 1560

Los Alamos Little Theater, (1943–1946), 3189

Los Angeles as Depicted in Film Noir (1940s), 3790

Los Angeles Daily News, Supports Roosevelt and the New Deal, 4070

Los Angeles Newspaper Guild Strike, (1938), 2207

Los Angeles, And the Development of the Watts Ghetto (1940–1950), 5347

Lost Horizon (1937), and Southern California Locations used, 3754

Louderback, Judge Harold, Impeachment, 6040

Louis, Joe: and His Fights with Max Schmeling, (1936 and 1938), 4583; and His Rematch with Max Schmeling, (1938), 4585, 4590; and Race Relations (1936–1945), 5337; Myth, Legend, and Folklore, 4595; White Attitudes Towards, 5374

Louisiana: Adult Literacy Efforts, (1900–1940), 4346; and Political Humor, 4122; and Public Relief (1928–1960), 6633; History (1939–1945), 6683; Political Opponents of Huey Long and Earl Long (1941–1964), 6452; Public Reaction to the beginning of World War II, 7875; Reform Alliance (1940–1942), 6685; State University as a Center for the Teaching of Literature, (1934–1942), 4292

Louisiana League for the Preservation of Constitutional Rights, 6632

Louisville, Kentucky Flood, (1937), 1453

Loup City Riot (1934), 6322

Lovecraft, Howard P., His Horror Tales (1920s and 1930s), 4085

Lovett, Robert A., As Assistant Secretary of War for Air (1940–1945), 8499

Lowenfels, Walter, Poetry (1930s), 3590

Lower Colorado River Authority, Development, 1408

Lubin, Isador, Ideas and Career of a New Deal Labor Economist, 4651

Lucas, Scott W., Senate Majority Leader, 1258

Luce, Claire Booth, and Anti Communist Rhetoric, 1224

Luce, Henry R.: As Opponent of the New Deal, 7124; Biographical Sketch, 3937; Biography, 7468

Lucy, Robert E., Life and Career, 4461

Ludlow Amendment, Debate (1937–1938), 7855

Ludlow, Louis, And the War Referendum Crusade (1935–1941), 8018

Lumber Industry: History in Arkansas, 2989; Efforts to Organize in California, (1930s–1940s), 2350; Impact of National Recovery Administration on, 2606; in the White Mountains of Arizona, (1919–1942), 2571

Lumberjack Strike in Michigan, (1937), 2123

Lumber Production and Community Stability in the Pacific Northwest (1930s), 2605

Lurie, Harry L., His Contributions to the Development to the Profession of Social Work (1930–1950), 4665

Lutherans: and Social Problems, (1917–1940), 4542; Reactions to War and Pacifism, (1917–1941), 4543

Lyle, Eugene P., Jr., Predicts a Second War with Germany, (September, 1918), 3971

MacArthur, Douglas: Biography, 0935, 0938; Conflict with Roosevelt, 0931; Essays by Subordinate Officers, 0936; Images, 0933; Memoirs, 0937; Philippine Years, 0942; Policy Decisions, 0932; Presidential Campaigns, 0939; Prewar Career, 0943; Relationship with Manuel Quezon, 0940, 0941; Strategy (1945), 0934

MacDonald, Dwight, Political and Journalistic Activities from 1928 through World War II, 4027

Machado, Gerardo, As Dictator of Cuba (1925–1933), 7670

Machine Tools and the Aircraft Industry, (1930s), 1876

Machines as a Symbol of Changes (1920–1939), 4993

MacLeish, Archibald; 0495; Librarian of Congress, 0508, 0511, 0512

MacMillan, Harold, World War II Memoir, 8755

MacNutt, Paul V., Role in the Coming of Philippine Independence, 0866

MacVeagh, Lincoln, Letters to Roosevelt, 0865

Maestri, Robert S., As Mayor of New Orleans (1936–1946), 6528

Magazine Humor: and Popular Morality, (1929–1934), 3994; and the Depression Years, 3995; (1929 through 1933), 3993

Magnetic Sound Recording, Early Development (1928–1950), 4927

Maher, Amy G., And the Public Works Administration in Toledo, 6005

Malta and Yalta Conferences, Documents, 9688

Malta Conference, 8639

Managed Economy, Development (before 1939), 1970

Manfred, Frederick, Analysis of *The Golden Bowl* (1944), A Story of Midwestern Farmers Who Fought the Dust Bowl and Depression, 3461

Manhattan Project: Administrators and U.S. Nuclear Monopoly, 5025; and Washington University at St. Louis, (1940–1946), 5023; and Radiation Safety Problems (1942–1946), 4888

Mannly, John H., Career in the Field of Nuclear Energy (1930s), 4944

Manufacturing: and Fixed Investment during the Great Depression, 1578; Distribution Activity in the United States, (1939–1947), 2645; Output in the United States, (1899–1937), 2523

Mao, Se Tung, 9228

Marble Cannon Trading Post Arizona, Robbery (1935), 4710

Marcantonio, Vito: Congressional Career, 1230; Foreign Policy Views, 1226; Opposes Xenophobic Immigration Laws, 1227; Political Career, 1225, 1229; Pro Labor Activities, 1228

March of Time, Origins (1930s), 3875, 3899

March on Washington Movement (1941), 5466

Mare Island Mutiny Court Martial (1944), 5629

Mareno, Tom, Interviewed by Federal Writers Project (1937), 5201

Marget, Arthur W., Economic Theories, 2031

Marihuana: as a Problem (1930s), 4185; Tax Act (1937), 4737, 5062

Maritime Workers and Working Class Consciousness (1930s), 2324

Marriage as Viewed by Best Selling Women Writers (1930s), 3303

Married Women Battle for the Right to Teach in St. Louis, (1941–1948), 4384

Marsh, Arthur L., And the Washington Education Association (1921–1940), 4285

Marsh, Reginald: His Etchings in the Reissue of John Dos Pasos' *USA* (1946), 3675; Interpretation of His Art, 3313

Marshall, George C.: Biography, 0950; Military Teacher, 0944; Not Chosen to Command Operation Overlord, 0945; Opposes Military Aid to Great Britain, 0947; Papers, 0948; Relationship with his Commanders, 0949; Relationship with Orlando Ward, 0946; Response to Americas' Unreadiness for War (1930s), 5008; Response to Congressional Pearl Harbor Inquiry, 0951

Marshall, Robert: Activities, 1449; Biography, 1489; Profile, 1495; Wilderness Preservation Activities, 1448

Marshall, Thurgood, Legal Career, 5315

Marshall, Verne, And the No Foreign War Committee (1940), 7911

Marston, George W., And Conservative Reform in San Diego, 4502

Martin, Joseph W., Congressional Career, 1231

Martin, Mrs. Thomas E., Congressional Wife in War Time Washington, 5979

Marx Brothers, Their Films as Satirical Social Criticism, 3214

Marxism in the United States (1900–1940), 6207

Marxist Aesthetics, Influence on American Fiction, (1929–1940), 3484

Marxist Intellectuals of the 1930s Depicted as Neurotic Poseurs, 4427

Marxist Literary Criticism (1930s), 6350

Maryknoll Fathers in Manchuria (1941–1947), 4519

Maryland Politics: between Word War I and World War II, 6439; in the 1930s and 1940s, 6445

Mason, David T., Career, 2723

Mason, Lucy R.: and the New Deal, 2452; Career, 2354, 2451

Mason, Noah M.: Anti New Deal Rhetoric of, 1233; Congressional Career, 1232

Mass Production Unionism, Growth, 2146

Mass Transit in Chicago between the Wars, Growth, 1853

Massachusetts: and the 1936 Presidential Election, 6754; Senatorial Election (1936), 6566

Matanuska Colony, Alaska, Early History (1935–1938), 5241

Matanuska Valley, Settlement, 1471

Matteson, Barbara H. and Stanley Gwinn Compare Recollections of the Chicago Century of Progress World's Fair, (1933), 3419

Matthews, J. B., His Shift from Communism to Anti-Communism, 6224

Matthiessen, F. O.: Analysis of His *American Renaissance*, (1941), 3309; Harvard Professor of American Literature, 4360; Influence on American Literary Criticism (since the 1930s), 3504; Views on Henry James, 3300

Mauchly, John, As Developer of the Electronic Digital Computer, 4946

Maugham, Somerset, His Days in Hollywood (1940s), 3799

Mauldin, Bill, Discussion of His Cartoons, 4129

Maupin, Will M., Nebraska Newspaper Man, 3984

Maurer, James H., Socialist Labor Leader in Pennsylvania, 2453

Maverick, Maury: and the Bexar County War Veterans' Relief Camp, (1932–1933), 2094; As Leader of the Liberal Block in Congress, 6183; Mayor of San Antonio, 1083; Political Career, 1084; Views on Civil Liberties, 1085

May, Kenneth O., Career, 4342

Maybank, Burnett: and South Carolina Politics (1930s), 6447; and the 1938 Gubernatorial Election in South Carolina, 6448

Mayberry, Virginia, Memoir of an Army Wife, 8224

McCarran, Patrick: Biography, 1017; Opposition to Court Packing Plan, 1016; Political Power, 1018; Senate Career, 1015; Speaking Ability, 1019

McCarthy, Joe, Background of his Crusade Against Communism, 6873

McCloud, Emma; Memoir, 1692; Story, 1309

McCluskey, Henry S., Supports the Cause of Workingmen in Arizona (1920s to the 1950s), 6613

McCormack, John, Supports Roosevelt's Policies, 1234

McCormick, Robert R., Opposed by Frank Knox, 7956; Opposes Roosevelt's Foreign Policy (1937–1941), 7918

McCormick, Vincent A., Memories of his Time in Rome, (1942–1945), 4501

McCowen, H. C., Economic Theories, 2060

McCreary Tire and Rubber Company, Survival, (1930–1940), 2530

McCullers, Carson, Biographical Sketch, 3458

McDaniel, Boyce, Recalls His Experiences at Las Alamos, 4949

McDonough, Peter M., Boss of San Francisco's Underworld, 4696

McDuffie, John, Political Career, 1086

McEwen, Dr. Currier, His Role in Saving Jews in Nazi Germany, 5741

McFarland, Ernest W.: Attitude toward Censoring the Film Industry, 1021; Senate Career, 1020

McGill, George S.: Defeated for Reelection to the Senate from Kansas in 1938, 6617; Senate Career, 1022

McGill, Ralph: His Views on Human Rights, 4025; Urges Peaceful Desegregation in the South, 5604

McGraw, Myrtle, Press Coverage of her Study of Johnny and Jimmy Woods (1930s), 4859

McGregor Arctic Expedition (1937–1938), 5003

McIntire, Carl, Early Radio Years, (1932–1955), 3908

McKay, Claude, Life and Career, 3316

McKellar, Kenneth D., And the 1934 Campaign in Tennessee, 6518; Political Career, 1192, 1193; Supports TVA, 1191

McMurray, John Van Antwerp, Urges Open Mind toward Japan (1930s), 7830

McNutt, Paul V.: As Governor of Indiana (1933–1936), 6641; As Presidential Candidate (1940), 6795

McPherson, Aimee Semple, Activities and Accomplishments, 3878; Career, 4527, 4531

McReynolds, James C.: 7045, 7046, 7047

McSwain, John J., Political Career in South Carolina, 6722

McWilliams, Carey, Political Rebellion, 3319

Means, Gardner C.: Critique of Classical Economics, 2055; Economic Ideas, 2054

Mechanization, Impact on Agriculture in Pennsylvania, (1930–1960), 1518

Mefkere Incident (1934), 9130

Memorial Day Massacre, 2277

Memphis Inter-Racial Commission, 6728

Memphis Press-Scimitar, Opposition to Boss Edward H. Crump, (1932–1948), 3956

Memphis, The Industrial Labor Movement and Black Workers, (1929–1945), 5423

Memphis Round Table of the National Conference of Christians and Jews, 4578

Mencken, H. L.: and Civil Rights, 5303; and Hitlerism (1933–1941), 6368; As Critic of the New Deal, 7090, 7091,7119; Attacks the Southern Methodist Church, 4008; Biography, 7123; Career, 4019; Comments on Roosevelt and the New Deal, 4037; Diary Analyzed, 3345; Did Not Sympathized with Nazis, 4094 His Coverage of the Democratic and Republican Conventions (1932), 6085; His Role with *American Mercury*, (1920s–1930s), 3936; Life and Works, 4081; Friendship with Bishop James Cannon, 4750

Mend, Elwood, and the Origins of the Resettlement
    Administration, 4636

Mendelsohn, Erich, Influence on American Architecture
    (1930s), 3175

Mennonite Central Committee and Mennonite Refugees,
    9104

Mennonite Peace Theology, (1925–1946), 4567

Mennonite Response to Conscription in World War II, 4518

Menominee Indians Versus the Federal Government
    (1943–1961), 5857

Menorah Group, Leftward Leaning, 6354

Merchant Marine Act (1936), Analysis, 2641

Merchants of Death Theory and American Intervention in
    World War I, 8059

Mercury Theater, History, (1937–1942), 3243

Merman, Ethel, Evaluation of Her Significance in Musical
    Theater, (1930–1960), 3530

Merola, Vito A., Remembers His Youth in the Bronx, New
    York during the Great Depression, 4774

Merriam, Charles E.: 0548; Political Ideas, 4655

Merriman, Robert, As Model for "Robert Jordan" in *For
    Whom the Bell Tolls*, 3334

Messersmith, George S.: Ambassador to Austria, 0867;
    American Diplomat in Nazi Germany (1933–1940),
    7301; And the Jewish Question (1928–1939), 9153;
    Biography, 0869; Diplomatic Career, 0868; Efforts to
    Reform the Consular Service, 0870

Messick, Ben, Assessment of His Work as an Artist in the
    1930s and 1940s, 3667

Metals Manufacturing in Montana, 2580

Methodist Commission on World Peace, and the Anti-
    Conscription Campaign (1940–1948), 8269

Methodist Episcopal Church, South, General Conference,
    (1936), 4564

Methodist Women and Inter Racial Fairness (1930s), 5976

Metropolitan Military Complex in San Francisco, Los
    Angeles, and San Diego, Compared (1919–1941), 4939

Metropolitan Opera Guild, History (1935–1975), 3541

Mexican Aliens: Repatriation, (1920s–1930s), 4156;
    Repatriation, (1929–1939), 4158

Mexican-Americans: and the Race Question in El Paso
    (1936), 5682; Children and Segregation in the California
    Schools (1930s–1940s), 5710; Efforts to end Segregation
    in Texas (World War II to the 1970s), 5703; Festivals in
    New Mexico, 5709; in Politics in Los Angeles
    (1941–1945), 5681; Population in the United States
    (1940), 5687; Relations, From the Mexican Revolution to
    the Good Neighbor Policy, 7234

Mexican: Anti-Clericalism and American Catholics
    1933–1936, 4475; Berry Pickers Strike (1933), 5696;
    Cannery Workers in California, 2352; Community in Los
    Angeles and Educational Reform (1920s and 1940s), 5685;
    in San Antonio (1930–1940), 5683, 5684; Farm Labor
    Agreement (1942), 4171; Farm Workers in California
    (1900–1940), 5688; Immigrants in Kansas (1900 to World
    War II), 5704; Immigrants in the Urban Mid-West
    (1919–1945), 5707; in the United States (1900–1940),
    5705; in the United States, (1926–1934), 5691; Life in
    Gary, Indiana during the Great Depression, 5675; Migrant
    Laborers and American Immigration Policy, (1930–1960),
    4146; Migrants and Relief in Depression Era California,
    1406; Muralists and the New York School (1930s), 3611;
    Radicalism and the Communist Party in Los Angeles
    (1930s), 5700; Repatriation during the Great Depression,
    5694; Repatriation from Texas during the Great
    Depression, 7691; Unionization in Agriculture,
    (1927–1936), 4170; Women and the California Food
    Processing Industry (1937–1950), 5708; Workers and
    Unionism in the Mid-West (1919–1945), 5706; Workers in
    Colorado (1930s), 5690; Workers in the United States
    Before World War II, 5693; Workers in the United States
    from Roosevelt to Nixon, 5692

Mexicanos in Los Angeles (1930–1941), 4777

Mexicans and Radical Politics in Los Angeles between the
    Wars, 5702

Meyer, Eugene, Purchases *Washington Post* (1933), 4062

Mezzrow, Mezz, Career, (1930s–1940s), 3553

Micheaux, Oscar, Black Film Producer, (1918–1948), 3817

Michelson, Charles, 0166

Michigan: and the Legislative Recount (1934), 6691;
    Depression Politics (1929–1933), 6647; Election (1932),
    6646; Gubernatorial Campaign (1938), 6621; Politics in
    the Early Depression Years, 6648; Presidential Election
    (1932), 6747

Mid-Gulf South (Panama City-Mobile Area), Growth
    (1930–1950), 6594

Middletown, Reappraisal, 6501

Midgley, Thomas, Career, 2564

Midwest American Authors, Analysis of their Works,
    (1890–1940), 3496

Midwest and the American Imagination, (1890–1940), 3483

Midwestern Editorial Responses to the New Deal,
    (1932–1940), 3938

Midwestern Industrial Landscapes by Charles Sheeler and
    Philip Evergood, (1930s), 3687

Midwestern Newspapers, and Isolationist Sentiment, 4017

Migration and Economic Opportunities in Tennessee
    Counties, (1940–1950), 4141

Migration, Internal, 1339

Miles, Josephine, Poetry and Criticism, 3593

Military: Between the Wars, 5018; Conscription, Debates,
    4834; Conscription, Origins (1940–1941), 4842;
    Planning, Political Aspects (1920–1942), 4991; Plans and
    Preparations, (1939–1941), 4945; Proceedings of History
    Symposium (1970), 9699; Service and Family Formation
    (1940–1950), 4683; Strategy, Impact on Insect Control
    Practices, 4968; Unification Debate (1943–1947), 4837

Military-Industrial Complex, Origins, 4923

Milkwagon Drivers in Fargo, ND and Morehead, Minnesota,
    Efforts to Organize, (1934), 2357

Miller, Frieda S., Career, 6020

Miller, Henry: His Years in France, (1930–1938), 3405; Impressions of the Writings of D. H. Lawrence, 3302; Parisian Exile (1930s), 3420

Miller, Kelly, Biography, 5475

Miller, Perry, Harvard Professor of History, 4359

Millspaugh, Arthur C., Mission to Iran (1943–1945), 8982

Milton, George F.: and the New Deal, 4001; His role in the Development and Growth of the Tennessee Valley authority, 4039

Milwaukee: and Municipal Socialism (1910–1940), 6203; Art Community in the Depression Era, 3663; Black Community (1915–1945), 5566; Its German American Community and the Nazi Challenge (1930s), 6373; Its Baby Bonds, 1705; Socialist Movement, 6272

Miniature Golf, History, 4581

Minimum Wage: Background of Movement in the United States, (1910–1938), 2841; Employment Effects, (1938–1950), 2600

Minneapolis: Citizen's Alliance (1930s), 2341; Labor Movement (1930s), 6348; Truckers' Strike, (1934), 2133

Minnesota Farmers, Problems of 1930s and 1980s Compared, 2958

Minton, Sherman: Senate Career, 1259; Speaking Style, 1260

Mission San Diego de Alcala, Model, 1941, 3176

Mississippi: Congressional Delegation and the Formation of the Conservative Coalition (1937–1940), 6061; Congressmen (1931–1937), 6520; Efforts to Balance Agriculture with Industry (1936–1958), 6668; Farm Bureau, (1919–1945), 1554; The 1936 Senatorial Primary, 6497

Missouri: and the Presidential Election (1940), 6791; Democratic Party, (1928–1944), 6681; Labor Movement, (1930s), 2199; Presidential Election (1932), 6748; Republican Party Politics (1937–1952), 6703; Shoemakers Avoid New Deal Labor Laws, 2525

Missouri Ex Rel Gaines Verus Canada (1938), 5639

Mitchell, Billy, His Theories on Air Power, 4880

Mitchell, Charles E., Symbol of Shaky Banking and Financial Practices, 2547

Mitchell, Ewing Y., As Opponent of the New Deal, 7156

Mitchell, Margaret: Biographical Sketch, 3366; Her *Gone With the Wind*, (1936), Compared to Faulkner's *Absalom! Absalom!*, (1936), 3418; Impact of Her novel *Gone With the Wind* on Atlanta, 3507; Reception of Her Novel *Gone With the Wind* in Nazi German, 3505

Mitsubishi Trading Company, Activities in San Francisco and Seattle,(1918–1941), 1839

Model Farm Communities Movement, 1377

Modern Agriculture, Development, 1343

Modern American Reform, History, 2700

Modern Architecture Symposium: The Depression Decade (May, 1964), 3164

Modern Art: (1900–1956), 3617; Movement on the Eve of World War II, 3666

Modern Gothic Romance Films (1940s), 3858

Modern Political Economy, Development, 6150

Modern Quarterly, An Independent Radical Magazine, (1923–1940), 3985

Modern Socialism, Evaluated, 6313

Moffat, Jay P., Papers, 0871

Mohammand, Elijah, Political Thought, 4790

Moley, Raymond: Political Views, 0709; Writings, 5052

Molton, Flora, Street Singer in the District of Columbia (1930s), 5522

Molyneaux, Peter, Commentaries on the New Deal, 4032

Mom and Dad (1944), Purportedly Educational Movie about Sex, Birth Control, and Venereal Disease, 3863

Monetary Policy under the Gold Standard, (1928–1936), 1955

Money Demand, (1920–1939), 1990

Monnet, Jean, And Plans to Strengthen the French Air Force, 7974

Montana: Politics (1932–1933), 6605; State Liquor Control System (1933–1968), 6673

Monthly Review, Its Writers and Editors Interviewed about Marxism in America, 6343

Moore, Beatrice H., Political Career, 5971

Moorehouse, Kathleen, Use of North Carolina Folklore in Her Novel *Rain on the Just* (1936), 3501

Morgan, Arthur E.: As Head of Tennessee Authority, 0710, 3084; As President of Antioch College, 3134; Biography, 3135; Personal and Social Philosophy, 3133

Morgan, J. C., As Chairman of the Navajo Tribal Council (1938–1942), 5879

Morgenthau Diary, Selected Entries, 9695

Morgenthau, Henry, Jr.: and U.S. Treasury Policy, 0654; Diaries, (1928–1938), 0651; Diaries, (1938–1941), 0652; Diaries, (1941–1945), 0653; Influence on Foreign Policy, 0650; Plan to Convert Germany into an Agrarian Nation, 0655, 0656

Morison, Samuel Eliot, Analysis of his Works, 9783

Morman Church: Attitudes towards Physical Recreation and Relaxation, 4474; Responses to the Great Depression, 4505

Morrell Packing House Strike (1935–1937, Sioux Falls, South Dakota, 2332

Morris, Wright, Discussion of His Photographs of Life in Nebraska (1940s), 3656

Moscow Conference (1943), 8623, 8862

Mosse, George L., Discusses his German Jewish Legacy in America, 5781

Mothers' Pensions, History, 2658

Motherwell, Robert, His Art (1940s), 3676

Motion Picture: Advertising, Evolution, (1933–1940), 3766; Craft Workers and Unionization, (1912–1948), 2329; Production Code, (1938–1961), 3836; Relief Fund's Screen Guild Radio Program, (1939–1952), 3913

Mountain Broadcast and Prairie Recorder, History (1939–1947), 4043

Mountbatten, Lord Louis, Selected as Allied Supreme Commander in Asia (1943), 8764

Movement for Shorter Workweek, Social History, 2076

Movies: and Politics (1930s), 3735; Censorship, (1934–1968), 3756; During Hollywood's Golden Age, (1930–1950), 3762

Muller, Herman J., Dismissed from Faculty of University of Texas for Marxist Opinions (1936), 4298

Multinational Oil Companies, and American Foreign Policy, (1941–1954), 1768

Mumford, Lewis: Activities, (1922–1962), 3188; and American Sociology, 4647; And the Question of War, 7890; Architectural Criticism, 3161

Muncie, Indiana: Political Power (1930s), 6503; Reconsideration of Municipal Government and Community Power (1925–1935), 6502

Mundelein, Cardinal, Criticizes Hilter's Treatment of Catholics, 4515

Muncie Star, Content Analysis of Editorial Opinion, (1935–1944), 3943

Munich: (1937–1938), 7406; Agreement, 7194; Conference, 8600; Crisis Broadcasts, (1938), 3890; Crisis and the American Press (1938), 7879

Municipal Ownership of Electrical Power in America, 1741

Munitions Manufacturers Promote War, 1042

Murphy, Frank, 7023–7034; Political Career, 0872

Murphy, Robert D.: and Operation Torch, 8682; Memoirs, 0873

Murray, "Alfalfa" Bill: And Oklahoma Politics, 6690; as Governor of Oklahoma (1930s), 6443; Spokesman for Agrarian America, 6479

Murray Case (Maryland) and the 14th Amendment (1935), 5642

Murray, James E.: Senate Career, 1024; Views on Foreign Policy, 1023

Murray, Matthew S., Rise and Fall of his Political Career in Missouri, 6494

Murray, Rex, Remembering the General Tire Sit Down Strike (1934), 2317

Murrow, Edward R., Influence, 3882

Muscle Shoals Controversy, (1920–1932), 3104

Museum of Modern Art, Building, (1939), 3181

Music: and Musicians in the White House, 3522; from the Left, (1930s–1940s), 3525

Musical Films (1930s), 3769

Musser, Elise F., Career, 5925

Mussolini, Benito: 9221; and America, 7342; and the United States (1935–1941), 7346; His Popularity in America (1920s), 6377

Muste, A. J.: And Christian Pacifism, 7999; And Pacifism, 8042; And the Labor Temple in New York City, (1937–1940), 4559; Career, 2454; His Theological and Ethical Thought Compared to that of Reinhold Neibuhr, 6275

Myrdal, Gunnar: Analysis of his book, *American Dilimena* (1944), 5575; Racial Theories, 5576

Nancy Drew Books, Analysis, 3389

Nash, Al, Memoir, 2314

Nash, Philleo, Memoir, 4961

Nashville Agrarians: and Southern Tenant Farmer's Union, Diverse Views on Reform, 1539; Reactionary Views, 6129

Nation of Islam, Basic Ideologies (1932–1975), 4577

Nation, Reflects Split in Liberal Community, (1930–1950), 4071

National Archives: Building, History, 9678; for Black Women's History, Origins, 5958; History, 9681, 9696; Records for the Roosevelt Period, 9648; Struggle to Establish, 9661; Twentieth Anniversary, 0541

National Association for the Advancement of Colored People: Activities in Philadelphia (1930s), 5503; and Anti-Lynching Legislation, (1920–1940), 5519; and Civil Rights, 5601; and The Crusade against Lynching (1909–1950), 5603; and Social Welfare, 5405; and the Communist Party, 5525; and *University of Maryland Vs. Donald G. Murray (1935)*, 5643; and The fight for a Federal Anti-Lynching Bill (1934–1940), 5602 And the Destruction of the Democratic White Primary (1934–1944), 5660; And the Legal Struggle against Segregated Education, (1925–1950), 5644; As an Agent of Equality, 5579; Challenges Segregation at the University of Texas, 5634; Challenges Segregation at the University of Missouri, 5635; Control Shifts From White Progressive to Blacks (1909–1935), 5480; Efforts to Establish an Equalitarian Legal Order (1930–1950), 5414; Efforts to end Discrimination, 5453; in Alabama, (1913–1952), 5299; in Texas, (1937–1957), 5392, 5393

National Association of Manufacturers: and Public Relations during the New Deal, 2629; Attacks Harold Rugg's Textbook, *Man and His Changing Nation*, 4402; Free Enterprise Campaign, (1929–1949), 2583; Seeks to Censor Textbooks, (1940–1941), 4397

National Bureau of Standards, Activities (1935–1941), 4972

National Citizens Political Action Committee, (1944), 2134

National Committee for the Extension of Labor Education, 0542

National Committee to Uphold Constitutional Government (1937–1941), 7147

National Conferences on the Problems of the Negro and the Negro Youth, (1937–1939), 5562

National Cooperative Council and Farm Relief, (1929–1942), 1542

National Council of Catholic Women (1919–1946), 8032

National Council of Women Psychologists, 8202

National Defense: Philosophy, Changes Between (1937–1947), 4848; Policy and Trans-Pacific Air Routes, (1933–1941), 1885; Transformation (1932–1941), 4863

National Economic Planning, History, (1935–1940), 1995

National Emergency Council: 0557; Report on Economic Conditions in the South, (1938), 1983

National Farm Organizations and the Reshaping of Agricultural Policy, (1932), 1468

National Farmer's Process Tax Recovery Association, 2935

National Fine Arts Inventory, 5152

National Gallery of Art, Origins, (1936–1941), 3682

National Geographic Society, Stratospheric Balloon Project (1934), 4985

National Government Growth, Origins, (1933–1940), 2773

National Grasslands Project: Failure, 1478; Origins, 1465

National Income, Composition, (1919–1938), 2019

National Industrial Recovery Act (NIRA): Sect 7A, Impact on Black Workers, 2406; Analysis, 1985, 2717

National Industrial Recovery Administration and the Automobile Industry, (1933–1935), 2194

National Institutes of Health Extramural Research Program (1937–1950), 4877

National Labor Relations Act: Impact on Labor Law and Economics, 2870; Impact on Organized Labor, 2871; Passage, (1935), 2895

National Labor Relations Board: Compared to Federal Trade Commission, 2901; Elimination of Division of Economic Research, 2902; Growth, (1933–1937), 2225; Growth (1937–1947), 2226; History, (1935–1947), 2758; Politicization, 2840

National Lawyers Guild, (1936–1938), 6138

National Negro Business League, History (1900–1945), 5330

National Negro Congress: (1936–1947), 5667; Evaluation, 5590; Movement, 5428

National Nominating Conventions (1940), 6043

National Park Service: and the New Deal, 1517; and U.S. Forest Service Dispute, (1916–1937), 2747

National Party Platforms, (1932, 1936, 1940, and 1944), 6737

National Pay Your Taxes Campaign, 1587

National Planning: and Reciprocal Trade, 1845; Failure (1930s), 6060

National Policy and Military Strategy, Lack of Coordination, 4959

National Progressives of America (1938), 6835

National Recovery Administration: and the Southern Pine Association, 3094; and Georgia's Black Workers, 5421; Automobile Code, (1933–1935), Roosevelt's Attitude Toward, 2809; Blue Eagle Campaign (1933), 2912; Chamber of Commerce Attitude, 2911; Code of Fair Competition for Bituminous Coal Industry, 2838; Conflict with Federal Trade Commission, 2864; Defense, 2708; Evaluation, 2868; Failure, 2876; Henry Ford's Defiance, 2810; Impact on the Oil Industry, 2788; in Oklahoma, 3023; in Virginia, 2962; Influence on Black Wages in the South (1933–1934), 5520; Influence on Newspaper Publishing, 5137; Newspaper code, Evaluation, (1933), 3946; of 1933, Modeled on War industries Board of 1917, 2588; Origins, 2830; Rise and Fall, (1933–1935), 2793; Self Analysis, (1934–1935), 2766

National Relief Programs, Discussion of Need, (1933), 2831

National Research Council, History (1922–1942), 4833

National Resource Planning (1932–1939), 4646

National Resources Planning Board: 0561; Report on Social Security, (1943), 4226

National Science Foundation: Legislative Origins, 4943; Origin and Development (1942–1954), 4981; Origins, 4869

National Security, and American Entry into World War II, 7231

National Urban League: and Social Welfare, 5405; and the New Deal, 5406

National War Labor Board (1942–1945), 8182

National Wildlife Federation, Conservation Policies, 1411

National Women's Party: (1920–1941), 5917; Internal Strife (1920–1947), 5995

National Women's Trade Union League of America, Records, 9677

National Youth Administration: in Cincinnati, 5266; in South Dakota, 2964; in Southern California, 5268; in Texas, 3026, 3027; Origins, 2875; Origins of Resident Training Program, 2772

Nationalism and Democracy in American Arts (1930s), 3154

Native American Art from New Mexico, (1932–1937), 3605

Navajo Code Talkers of World War II, 5874

Navajo Day School Experiment (1935–1945), 5856

Navajo Indians and Opposition to New Deal Policies, 5855

Navajo Nation, Impact of Stock Reduction Programs (1930s), 5910

Navajo Women (1940), 5869

Navajos: and World War II, 5838; The Reservation Years, 5808

Naval and Marine Corp Reserve Center in Los Angeles, History, 9350

Naval Arms Limitations: and the Cruiser Controversy (1932–1936), 9236; Efforts to Regulate Submarines (1921–1941), 9256

Naval Conferences between the Wars, 7324, 7238

Naval Policy, History, 4811

Naval Research Laboratory, Origins, 4812

Naval War College and War Gaming (1919–1942), 9435

Navy Department and the Campaign for Expanded Apportions (1933–1938), 5005

Navy V-5 Aviation Cadet Pilot Training Program, 4935

Nazis: and Book Burning, 9067; and the American Catholic Periodicals, 9068; Propaganda and North Dakota's Germans (1934–1941), 6398; Racism, Impact on American Inter-Group Relations (1933–1940), 5732

Nazism in America, Failure, 6372

NBC Advisory Council, (1927–1941), 3918

Nearing, Scott, Intellectual Biography, 6324

Nebraska Post Office Art, 5167

Nebraska Power Review Board, Development, 1737

Nebraska Republican Party and the Ku Klux Klan (1936), 6655

Nebraska, Voting Patterns in the 1940 Election, 6460

Negative Nominal Interest Rates, Discussion, 1979

Negro Actors Guild of America, (1937–1982), 3204

Negro Colleges and Universities and Philanthropic Support (1930–1973), 4281

Negro Labor Victory Committee of New York City (1941–1945), 5427

Negro Organizations Reaction to Depression, New Deal and World War II, 5452

Negro People in America, A Documentary History, 5295

Negro Soldier (1944), Army Orientation Film, 3739

Negro Theater Project in New York City, History (1935–1939), 5166

Neibuhr, Reinhold: and the Emergence of Liberal Realist Faith (1930–1945), 6147; and U.S. German Relations (1916–1956), 7984; His Liberal Views Compared to those of George Kennan, 6143; Political Conversion, 6196; Was he Ever a Marxist?, 6347

Neighborhood: Change in the Bronx, (1905–1960), 1815; Planning, Evolution, 1798

Nelson, Donald, As Chairman of the War Production Board, 8110

Nelson, Steve, On his Participation in the Abraham Lincoln Brigade, 7381

Nesbitt, Victoria H. K., 0377

Ness, Eliot, Life and Career, 4732

Netherlands Military Intelligence (1939–1940), 9238

Neutrality: and Public Opinion (1935–1939), 7919; In History, Economics, and Law, 7872; Patrol, 7175

Neve, Frederick W., and Mission Education in Virginia, (1888–1948), 4295

New Deal: A Political Disaster for Blacks, 5396; Activity and the States, (1933–1939), 2022; Administrative Apparatus, 2707; Administrative History, 2727; Administrative History of Relief Programs, 2774; Adult Public Library Services, 2785; Agencies in Kentucky, 5170; Agricultural Legislation, 2874; Agricultural Policies and the Constitution, 1364; Agricultural Programs in Kansas, 3012; Analysis, Agricultural Programs, 1372; Aid to Education in Arkansas (1933–1936), 5216; Aid to Education in Louisiana, 5231; Aid to Louisiana Sugar Producers, 3074; Analogue of War, 1571; Analysis and Interpretation, 5064; Analysis, 0708, 1651, 1652, 2691, 2693, 2706, 2738, 2770, 2778; Analysis of Economic Policies, 1986; Analysis of Federal Art Project, 5094; Analysis of Labor Policy, 2896; Analysis of Opposition Rhetoric, 7172; Analysis of Programs, 2855; Analysis of the Two New Deals Concept, 9808; Analytical History, 2721; and Agriculture, Historiography (1971–1976), 9754; and Agricultural Relief Activities, (1933–1936), 2752; and Big Business, 6031; and Black Education, 5256; and Catholic Rural Life Movement, 4562; Agricultural Policies, Critiqued, 1334, 2814; and De-Centralist Intellectuals, 7158; and Democratic Party Politics in Washington State (1932–1940), 6579; and East Asia, 7562; and Economic Changes, 2713; and Economic Planning, 4652, 4653; and Economic, Political, and Social Changes, 2704; and Electoral Realignments, 6037; and Farmer Labor Parties, 6850; and Federal Aid to Archeology in the Southeast (1934–1942), 5279; and Federal Aid to Education (1930–1945), 4409; and Florida Politics, 2692; and Georgia Congressmen during the first One Hundred Days, 6516; and Government use of Propaganda Films, 6863; and Growth of Industrial Democracy, 2493; and Illinois Politics, 6711; and Indian Tribalism, 5901; and Kentucky Youth, 2927; and Labor, 2223; and Labor in Harlan County, Kentucky, (1931–1939), 2234; and Labor Radicalism, 6281; and Liberal Journals, 4046; and Liberal Senators from the Great Plains States, 6146; and Midwestern Progressives, 6090; and Montana Politics, 6604; and National Health, 4220; and North Carolina Blacks, 5290; and Ohio Politics, 7170; and Party Realignment, 6097; and Political Realignment, 6103, 6104; and Politics in Boston, 3080; and Puerto Rican Politics, 6612; and Pragmatic Reform, 6159; and Progressivism in Wisconsin, 6626; and Public Education in Connecticut, (1933–1939), 4383; and Public Opinion Polls, (1935–1946), 5044; and Reciprocal Trade in Latin America, 7648; and South Dakota Politics, 6644; and Taxation, (1933–1939), 1996, 2849; and Texas Politics, 6092; and the American Business Community, (1932–1934), 2676; and the American Farm Bureau Federation, 7154; and the American People, 5060; and the Appalachian Congressmen, 6519; and the Artists, 5147, 5148; and the Blacks of St. Louis, (1932–1940), 5413; and the Business Community, 7150; and the Byrd Machine in Virginia, 6576; and Catholic Agrarian Thought, 4561; and the Chicago Machine, 6560; and the Conservation of Natural Resources, National Archive Holdings, 9676; and the Coughlin Movement, 7160; and the Eastern Cherokee, 5906; and the Electric Utility Industry, (1933–1941), 1735; and the Federal System, 6652; and the Greendale, Wisconsin Community, 3031; and the Historical Debate (1973), 9755; and the House Un-American Activities Committee, 6884; and the Old Progressives, 6152; and the Papagao Indians, 5815; and the Philadelphia Municipal Election (1933), 6525; and the Planning in (1930s), 4643; and the Presidential Campaign (1932), 6756; and the Problem of Monopoly, (1933–1939), 1942, 2541; and the West, 3112; and Voter Mobilization, 5043; and Voter Realignment, 6669, 6769; And Anti-Semitism in America, 5789; And Black Housing in Philadelphia, 5304; And Georgia Congressmen (1933–1938), 6464; And Georgia's Black Youth, 5422; And Investment Bankers, (1933–1940), 2795; And Poverty Programs for Rural Blacks, 5305; And South Dakota Congressmen, 6453; and Southern Rural Poverty, 2853; And Tennessee Congressmen (1933–1938), 6465; And the Black Community, 5597; And the Black Community of Savannah, Georgia, 5437; And the Growth of the Federal Bureaucracy, 6819; And the Inversion of Liberalism (1930s to the 1960s), 6161; And the National Park Service, 2796; And the Rise of the Professional Social Worker, 4634; And the States, 2737; Architecture

and Public Works Administration Projects, 2741; Art Programs and the Influence of the Communist Party on the Art Community, 5102; Art Projects in Wyoming, 5181; Art Projects, Participants Publish their Memoirs, 5088; Artists, Writers, and Photographers Record the History of America, 5281; as a Cause of Voter Realignment, 5057; as Creator of a New Social Philosophy, 5061; as Cultural Phenomenon, 2757; as Reviewed in the Baton Rouge Daily Newspapers, 4093; As a Case Study of the Transformation of Upper Class Ideology, 4798; As Progressive Tradition, 4805; As Seen by Alfred M. Landon, 6618; As Viewed by Thorstein Vebelen, 6179; Assistance to Black Writers, 3290; Attempts to Regulate Household Moving Industry, 2829; Background, 2634; Banking Legislation, 1636; Bonneville Power Administration Project, 3096; Camps and Residence Centers for Women (1933–1944), 5105, 5164; Can it Survive the War? (1942), 7066; Capitalist Planning as seen in the Ideas of Donald Richbergh and Rexford Tugwell, 4659; Cattle Purchase Project, (1934–1935), 3108; Civil works Administration, (1933–1934), 2789; Coalition and the Congressional Election (1946), 6035; Coalition, Break Down, 6064; College Student Aid Programs, 5139; Colorado-Big Thompson Reclamation Project, 3107; Commercial Policy and Germany (1933–1939), 7310; Communitarian Programs, 2669; Communities in the South, (1934–1944), 2970; Community Program, 2802, 2685; Compared to the Progressive Era, 6102; Conflicting Interpretations, 9764; Conservative and Liberal Perspectives, 2701; Conservative Constitutional Critique, 6117; Continuing Effects on America (1950s), 5055; Cost of Public Assistance Programs, 2850; Contributions of Progressive Planners, 2056; Cotton Policy, 1365; County Records Survey in Texas, 5217; Critique, 4806; Critique of Domestic and Foreign Policy, 2666 Cultural Projects in Wyoming, 5180; Cultural Projects of the 1930s, 5081; Decline, (1939–1945), 2679; Demise, 7164; Development of Agricultural Program, 1419; Diplomacy, 7217; Disarmament Attempts (1934), 4997; Discussion of Labor Legislation, 2144; Drought Relief Activities in Kansas, 3013; Early Experiments, 2675; Early History, 2719; Early Period, (1933–1934), 1576; Economic Analysis of Labor Legislation, 2345; Economic Aspects of Diplomacy, 7200; Economic Impact on the South, 2753; Education Efforts, Compared to War on Poverty Education Efforts, 2880; Education Policy, 4303; Education Programs in Civilian Conservation Corps, Works Progress Administration, and National Youth Administration, 5120; Effect of Agricultural Program on Great Plains Farmers, 1361; Efforts to Eliminate Southern Poverty, 3118; Elections and Public Policy, 6038; Electric Policy and the Coming of World War II, 1734; Emergency hog slaughter (1933), 2985; Essays Concerning the National, State, and Local Levels, 2670; Evaluated after Fifty Years (1985), 2682, 5098; Evaluation, 5071; Evaluation of Farm Policy, 2888;

Evaluation of Foreign Policy, 721;4 Evaluation of Policy, 2886; Expenditures in the Western States, (1933–1939), 2665; Farm Policies, 1359; Farm Policy on the Great Plains, 2887; Farm Policy and the Resettlement Idea, 2903; Farm Production Controls, (1933–1936), 2725; Farm Programs in Virginia and North Carolina, 3105; Federal Aid to Archeology in the Southeast (1933–1942), 5275; Federal Records Centers Holdings, 9644; Federal Transient Service, 5066; Financing, (1932–1940), 2014; Food and Drug Law Reform, 2836; Foreign Trade Policy, (1933–1939), 1847; Granger Homestead Project, Iowa, 3075; Grass Roots Programs, 2762; Greenbelt Town Program, (1935–1952), 3034, 5154; Hispanic Programs in New Mexico, 2944; Historical American Building Survey, (1933–1942), 3165; Historical Dictionary, 2733; Historical Writings (1960s), 9736; Historical Writings (1944–1960), 9737; Historiographical Assessment (1961), 9731; Historiography (1975), 9757; Historiography (1966), 9810; History, (1933–1938), 2739; History, 2716, 5048; Homesteading Project in Alaska, (1934), 2994; Housing Projects in Atlanta, 1789; Housing Reform in Miami, 5263 Ideas Concerning the Place of Women in the Economy, 2787; Ideological Analysis, 2744; Impact in Maryland, 6568; Impact of Agricultural Programs on Rice Culture, 3109; Impact of Bank Reform Legislation, 1616; Impact in Oklahoma, 1614; Impact of Farm Policy on Southern Agriculture, 1379; Impact of Farm Programs on Western New York, 3042; Impact of Labor Policy on Radicalism, 2249; Impact of Resettlement Program on Southern Blacks, 5420; Impact on Agricultural Unionism in California, 2940; Impact on American Conservative Ideology, 6132; Impact on American Labor, 2065; Impact on American Thought, 5056; Impact on Atlanta, 3057, 3058; Impact on Black Americans, 1727, 2705, 2907, 5379, 5384, 5441, 5446, 5447, 5557, 5665; Impact on Black Farmers, 5592; Impact on Black Politics in Pennsylvania, 1672; Impact on Black Voting Patterns, 5583; Impact on Boston, 5271; Impact on British Economic and Political Ideals, 7328; Impact on Business Investment, 2020; Impact on Chicago, 6559; Impact on City Politics, 6552; Impact on Class Relations in the California Cotton Industry, 3025; Impact on Colorado, 5233; Impact on Corporate Liberalism, 2728; Impact on Cotton Farmers, 2697; Impact on Farmers in Appalachia, 3126; Impact on Fort Barrancas, Pensacola, Florida, (1933–1941), 3041; Impact on Georgia Politics, (1933–1941), 2949; Impact on Harlan County, Kentucky Coal Miners, 3062; Impact on Labor in the South, (1933–1941), 2780; Impact on Labor Organizations, 2073; Impact on Michigan Oil Business, 1771; Impact on Minden, Louisiana, 3030; Impact on Missouri Farmers, 2945; Impact on New York State Politics, 6707; Impact on North Carolina, 2924; Impact on Organized Labor, 2124; Impact on Pine Mountain Valley, Georgia, 3051; Impact on Pocatello, Idaho, 1642; Impact on Politics in Illinois, 6422;

Impact of Resettlement Programs on Blacks, 2731; Impact on Rural Kentucky, (1933–1941), 2928; Impact on South Carolina, 2957; Impact on Southern Plantation Economy, 3140; Impact on Southern Agriculture, 3106; Impact on Southern Cities, 3037; Impact on Texas Society, 1701; Impact on the American System, 6032; Impact on the Economy and Society of New York City, 6151; Impact on the Elderly in Boston, 3061; Impact on the Professionalization of American Archeology, 5122; Impact of Labor on Southern Cotton Textile Industry, (1933–1941), 3102; Impact on the Urban South, 5269, 5284; Impact on the Views of Wilsonians, 6134; Impact on the Western States, 2664; Impact on Washington, D.C., 2769; Impact on Western Agriculture, 1328; in Baltimore, 3032, 3033, 6410; in Georgia, 2973; in Historical Perspective, (1983), 2698; in Idaho, 2920, 2990;in Milwaukee, 2240; in New Jersey, 2997; in North Carolina, 2923; in Pocatello, Idaho, 3132; in South Carolina, (1931–1941), 2930; in Tennessee, 2998; in the South, 3089; in the Virgin Islands, 3098; in the West, 3122; in Vermont, 2980; in Virginia, 2960; in World Affairs, (1933–1945), 1963; in Wyoming, 2987; Indian Policy (1933–1936), 5841, (1933–1953), 5866; Influence, 6029; Insiders View, 0707; Intellectual Sources, 2751; Interpretive History, 6112; Irrigation Projects in Colorado, (1933–1938), 2983;l Labor Policy, 2819; Labor Policy and the Industrial Economy, 2090; Labor Policy and the Southern Cotton Textile Industry, (1933–1941), 2235; Land Reform Experiments, 2749; Landscape Projects, 2805; Livestock Production Control Program, (1933–1935), 2845; Local Government Archival Program in Albany, New York, 3035; Major Writings (1966), 9804; Middle Period, (1934–1936), 1577; Monetary Legislation, 2763; Montana Contributions to Farm Policy, 2974; Murals in Iowa, 5203; Occupational Safety and Health Policies, 2745, 2746; Operation of Public Relief Programs in Minnesota, 6575; Opinion of the Alabama Clergy, 4452; Opinion of the American Clergy, 4447, 4451; Opinion of the Clergy in the State of Washington, 4446; Opinion of the Episcopalian Clergy, 4449; Opinion of the Massachusetts Clergy,4450; Opinion of the Presbyterian Clergy, 4448; Opposition in North Carolina, 2917; Organized Opposition, (1933–1937), 2607; Origin and Development (1932), 6763; Origins of Land Retirement Program, 1472; Origins of Public Housing Programs, 2777; Party Politics and Administrative Reform (1930s), 6086; Pictorial History, 1572; Planning, 4635; Political Analysis, 2743; Political Analysis of Spending, 2779; Political Impact on Pittsburgh, 6704, 6705; Political Impact on the South, 6522; Political Opposition in the South (1937), 6841; Political Origins of Agricultural Policy, 2811; Political Style, Economic Conditions, and Popular Culture Compared (1920s), 4417; Political Reaction in Minneapolis, 3066; Political Reinterpretation in Light of Populist Achievements, 6341; Politics and Civil

Rights Reform (1933–1948), 4668; Politics in Louisiana, 1171; Post Office Art Program, 5199; Post Office Mural Project, 5153; Proceedings of 50th Anniversary Commemorative Conference, 9733; Programs for Women in Mississippi, 5225; Programs in Colorado, 3028; Programs in Mississippi, 3020; Programs in Providence, Rhode Island, 3053; Projects in Pendleton County, West Virginia, 3078; Promotes Change in Cotton Farming Communities, 1347; Promotes Federal Participation in the Arts (1933–1943), 5059; Public Works Program in Albuquerque, 3036; Public Works Projects in Las Vegas (1933–1940), 5262; Public Works Projects in New York State, 3001; Radio and Newspaper Coverage, (April, 1933 to July, 1934), 3898; Reaction of Farmers to Farm Programs, 3018; Radical Influence on Federal Theater Project, 5046; Recollections of Insiders, 2720; Relief Programs, Impact on Federal Budget, 2775; Relief Programs in Detroit, 5270; Relief Programs in Mississippi, Impact on Race Relations, 3088; Relief Programs in Nevada, (1933–1935), 3017; Relief Programs in Rhode Island, 3002; Relief Projects in New York City, (1933–1938), 3081; Resettlement Program, 2904; Resettlement Projects in Louisiana, 2972; Response to Mexican-American Housing Conditions in San Antonio, 1820; Revenue Acts, 1994; Review of the Literature on Ideology (1987), 9788; Revolutionary or Evolutionary?. 2759; Rural Rehabilitation, the Ropesville Project, 2979; Securities Regulation, 2736; Selected Bibliography, 9605; Social and Economic Impact on the South, 6867; Social Security and Work Relief Programs, 2718; Social Workers in Atlanta, 2656; Soil conservation Programs, 2826; Sources of Economic Policy, 2057; Sources of Realignment, 6041; Source of Reformist Ideas, 2768; South Dakotans' Attitudes toward, 2922; Southern Opposition to Farm Policies, 1380; Southern Support, 7097; Statistical Analysis, (1933–1939), 2740; Successes and Failures in Virginia, 2961; Sympathetic Review, (1936), 2667; The Arthurdale Experiment in West Virginia, 5236; The First One Hundred Days Evaluated, 6068; The Post Office Mural Project (1934–1943), 5054; Theory and Belief, 6889; Thought and Progressive Thought Compared, 2702; Thought Patterns of White Liberals on Racial Issues, 5448; Trade Policies, 1840; Treasury Art Program, 5053; Treasury Department Art Programs (1933–1943), 5049; Unraveling of Party System (1930s to 1970s), 6071; Urban Resettlement Programs, 2825; Use of the Term before Roosevelt, 2680; Vocational Education Programs, (1933–1945), 2732; Water Resource Development Projects in Arkansas, 3093; Welfare Programs, 2767; and the Western Progressive Republican Bloc in the Senate, 0982; Work Relief in North Carolina, 2991; Work Relief in Maine, 2988; Work Relief Programs, (1933–1935), 2878; Work Relief Programs and Public Recreation in New York City, 4588; Work Relief Programs in Mississippi, (1933–1934), 3021; Work Relief Projects in New Bedford,

Massachusetts, 3070; Work Relief Projects in the Cleveland Public Library, 5267; Worker Education Programs in Indiana, (1933–1943), 2955; Worker's Service Program, (1933–1942), 2843, 4350

New Jersey: Gubernatorial Campaign (1940), 6709; Parochial School Bus Bill, (1941), 4302

New Jersey State Board of Mediation, Administrative History, 6724

New Jersey Suffragist (1910–1940), 5940

New Left: Analysis of Political Philosophy, 6137; Revisionism, 6166

New Masses, Development of American Marxist Literary Criticism, 4052

New Mexico, Education and the Spanish Speaking Child, (1920s and 1930s), 4309

New Orleans: Black Education System (1862–1960), 5361; Politics and the Influence of Women (1930–1955), 6719

New Republic, Supports Stalinism (1930s), 3979

New York and German Jewish Immigrants (1930s and 1940s), 9159

New York City: Activities of Housing Authority, 1808; and Economic Retrenchment (1930s), 6656; and Organized Crime in (1930–1944), 4699; and Splinter Parties (1930s and 1940s), 6435; Democrats Lose Local Elections (1933), 6473; Financial Crises (1930s and 1970s) Compared, 1615; Housing Authority, Site Selection Policies, (1934–1939), 1797

New York Intellectuals: and the Function of Criticism, 6262; Community (1930s–1940s), 4794; (1930s to the 1970s), 6165; History, 4163; (1930s and 1940s), 6155; Rise and Decline of the Anti-Stalinist Left (1930s to the 1980s), 6355

New York Jews and Crime, (1900–1940), 5768, 5769

New York Politics (1928–1948), 6637

New York State and Democratic Party Politics (1933–1938), 6649

New York State Liquor Control Act (1933), 6425

New York State Minimum Wage Act (1933), 6554

New York Times: Coverage of Higher Education Finance, (1937–1986), 4107; Editorial Response to International Relations, (1939–1941), 4064; on Nazism, (1930–1939), 3955; Reporters Walter Duranty and Harold Denny Conceal News of Millions of Ukrainian Deaths by Starvation, 3961; Views of U.S.-Soviet Relations, (1939–1941), 3970

New York University, Division of General Education, (1934–1959), 4307

New York Urban League, Activities (1919–1959), 5490

New York World's Fair: (1939–1940), 4891, 4951, 4984, 4999; Visited by the U.S. Fleet (1939), 5028

New Yorker, The Great Depression as Reflected in its Cartoons, 4133

Newark, New Jersey: Growth of its Black Community (1917–1947), 5517; Struggle to Integrate, (1932–1947), 5518

Newman, Alfred, Analysis of His Musical Scores (1930s), 3570

Newspaper Circulation in Relation to Population, (1929–1957), 4056

Nicholas, Johnny, Black Intelligence Agent during World War II, 5470

Niels Bohr Institute, Changes Focus from Atomic to Nuclear Physics (1930s), 4808

Night Life, Resurgence after the Repeal of Prohibition, 4748

Nimitz, Chester W., Biography, 0977

Nineteen Thirties, Pictorial History, 0108

Nineteen Thirty-Two, Analysis, 1674

Nixon, Herman C., Biography, 4803

Nomura, Kichisaburo Diplomacy, 7496

Non-Automotive Sit Down Strikes in Detroit, (1937), 2367

Non-Governmental Organizations and Arms Reduction (1920–1935), 8040

Non-Monetary Effects of Financial Crisis of the Great Depression, 1590

Non-Southern Senators, Voting Patterns on Southern Issues (1938–1963), 6536

Norbeck, Peter, Senate Career, 1025

Norris, George W.: Biography, 1033, 1034; Father of Tennessee Valley Authority, 1029; Favors Public Hydroelectric Power, 1030; Foreign Policy Views, 1027; Losses his Senate Seat (1942), 6471; Moralistic Views, 1038; Political Career, 1037; Political Contributions, 1026; Political Philosophy, 1039; Promoted New Deal Programs in Nebraska, 1031; Promotes Regional Planning, 1035; Promotes Unicameral Legislature in Nebraska, 1036; Reflective View, 1028; Supports Franklin Delano Roosevelt, 1032

Norris, J. Frank, Changing Attitudes on the New Deal and Roosevelt, 4499

North Africa Landing (1942), 8659

North American Aviation Strike, (1941), 2339

North American Indians as Stereotyped in Motion Pictures, 3820

North Carolina: and Democratic Party Factionalism (1925–1936), 6671; and Graduate Education for Blacks (1930–1951), 5633; Movement to Enact Unemployment Insurance Legislation (1935–1936), 5202; Patterns of Segregation (1930–1950), 5327; Senatorial Election (1932), 6664; Tobacco Marketing Crises, (1933), 2941

North Dakota: and the 1938 Election, 6508; Farm Strike, (1932), 1553

Northeast Louisiana State University, Origins (1931), 4336

North Louisiana and Public Opinion at the Beginning of World War II, 7876

Northern Liberal Attitudes toward Black America (1936–1952), 6158

Northern Neo-Orthodox Theologians Aid Southern Share Croppers (1930s), 4509

Norton Company in Germany (1933–1945), 7270

Norton, Mary T., Political Career, 6003

Norwegian Community in Brooklyn, New York (1940s), 4161

Nuclear Arms Race, (1939–1986), 4971

Nuclear Fission: Discovery (1939), 4819; Early Experiments of Columbia University (1939), 4814

Nuclear Physics, Becomes Major Field of Research in Japan, Denmark, and the United States, (1935–1945), 5015

Nuclear Technology, Development, 4896

Nuclear Weapons, Impact on Foreign Policy and Strategy, (1941–1978), 4823

Nye Committee: 1043; (1934), 6111; Evaluation, 1047

Nye, Gerald P.: And the Isolationist Argument, 7943; Influence on Foreign Policy, 1041; Opposition to Roosevelt's Foreign Policy, 1040; Political Career, 1045, 1046; Speaking Ability, 1044

Nylon: Invention (1937), 4893; Origins, 4904

O'Connor, Herbert R., Biography, 6570

O'Connor, Raymond G., Recalls his Service in the Navy (1930s), 4963

O'Grady, John, As Head of Catholic Charities, (1920–1961), 4566

O'Hare, Edward Henry, Life, 2178

O'Keefe, Georgia: and Willa Cather Compared, 3638; Biographical Sketch, 3609

O'Mahoney, Joseph C.: Breaks with Roosevelt over Court Reorganization Bill, 1049, 1051; Election to the U.S. Senate, 1052; Senate Career, 1048, 1050

O'Neill, Eugene: Efforts to Write Plays Dealing with American History, (1935–1946), 3221; His Role in the Federal Theater Project, 3262; Racism and Discrimination Addressed in Plays, 3244

Oak Ridge: Community, Development (1944), 4910; History (1942–1970), 8166

Obermyer, Lorena, Recalls her Experience as a Welder in Milwaukee during World War II, 8226

Odets, Clifford: Early Plays, 3206; Themes of Loneliness and Homelessness in his Plays, 3257

Odom, Howard W.: Analysis of his Folklore Studies (1925–1930), 5541; His Agenda for Social Reform in Southern Race Relations (1930–1936), 5565; His Significance to Southern History, 4669

Office Management in America, (1870–1940), 2568

Office of Indian Affairs and Civilization Policy, (1890–1938), 5835

Office of Price Administration: Activities, (1940–1946), 1971; History (1941–1946), 8105, 8159

Office of War Information, Analyzes Hollywood Films, (1942–1943), 3726

Ogden River Project, (1934–1965), 1415

Ohio, Attempts to Secure State Aid for Private Schools (1930s), 4354

Ohio National Guard and the Steel Strike (1937), 2374

Ohio, Repeal of Prohibition, 4758

Oil Boom in Richardson County, Nebraska, (1938–1942), 1773

Oil Business: Regulation in Texas, (1930–1935), 1750; Regulatory Changes in Texas, (1930–1975), 1749

Oil Industry: Development in Texas, (1941–1957), 1774; Flush Production in the Southwest, 1752

Oil Producers in Kansas, Problems (1930s), 1764

Oil Workers in Texas, Efforts to Organize, (1942–1943), 2257

Okies: as Farm Laborers in California, 1397; Emergence of Subculture in California, 1288; Impact on California, 1668; Migration 1294, 1671; Migration to California, (1930–1950), 4165

Oklahoma: Crime and Law Enforcement (1930s), 4698; Dry Conditions, (1930s–1950s), 1435; Kansas, and Missouri Metalworkers Strike, (1935), 2379; Prohibition, (1907–1959), 4749

Oklahoma! (1943), Plot Analysis, 3533

Oklahoma City WPA Symphony Orchestra (1937–1942), 3578

Oklahomans in California, (1931–1941), 2660

Old Age Assistance in Ohio, (1916–1940), 4232

Oldham, George A., Episcopal Bishop of Albany, (1922–1947), 4477

Olesen, Anna D., Biography, 5970

Olsen, Nils A., Diary, 1368

Olympic Games (1936): 4600 ; American Participation, 7285; American Policy (1933–1936), 7283, and the Issue of Racism, 4603

Olympic Gold Medalists of the 1930s in Hollywood, 3746

Olympic National Park, 1502

Omaha Tram Strike, (1935), 2224

Omer, Lewis, Letters to Allen Nevins, 1317

Omura, James M., Interviewed, 5725

Onion Worker's Strike, Hardin County, Ohio, (1934), 2377

Operation Cross Word, 8821

Operation Overlord, Bibliography, 9626

Opportunity School at the University of Toledo, (1932–1941), 4306

Oral History: and Hard Times in Idaho (1920–1941), 9855; and Slavery, 9846; and the Federal Writers Project (1938–1939), 9842; and the Great Depression, 9840; and the New York Milk Industry, 9843; As a Valuable Tool for Modern Historians, 9854; Collection, Colombia University (1973), 9847; Memories of Beale Street (1930s and 1940s), 9859; Methodological Problems, 9844; Servants and Employers in the South (1900–1965), 9857; Workers at the Studebaker Automobile Plant (1939–1963), 9841

Orange County, California Citrus Strike, (1935–1936), 2342

Organized Labor: and Foreign Policy in Latin American, (1932–1955), 2122 and the Coming of World War II, (1937–1941), 2074; as Viewed by Southern Newspapers in the New Deal Years, 4104

Orientals as Portrayed in Hollywood Films (1910–1950), 3811

Orlemanski, Stanislas, Meets Stalin (1944), 8829

Orphan Annie and the Conservative Tradition, 4128

Osborne, Frances D., British Diplomat in Washington (1933–1945), 7223

Oxford Group and the Seattle Longshoreman's Strike (1934), 2087

Ozark Tales, (1929–1935), Compared to Chaucer, 3312

Pabst, G. W., His Brief Career in Hollywood (1930s), 3771

Pacific Northwest Lumber Industry during Great Depression, 1599

Pacific Northwest Power Agency, Development, 1743

Pacificism: (1919–1941), 8022; and American Military Policy (1930s), 8013; and the Historic Peace Churches, 8030; in America (1914–1941), 8004, 8005, 8037; Viewed as Subversion (1939–1945), 8010

Packing House Workers of America Crusade Against Racism, (1936–1968), 2100

Pafford, Robert J., Post Master of Salina, Kansas, Opposes Post Office Murals, 5242

Page, Kirby, Autobiography of a Pacifist, 8038

Pageantry and Theater in the Service of Jewish Nationalism in the United States, (1933–1946), 3201

Paiute Tribal Council Formation (1934–1936), 5888

Palmer, Charles F., Career, 1799

Palmer, Margaret, Her Letters from Spain, (1936–1939), 3677

Panay Incident: 7539, 7573, 7588; and Public Opinion in Kansas (1937), 7542

Panhandle Oil and Gas Field, Development, 1775

Paperback Books, Growth of the Industry, (1939–1959), 3476

Paper Workers, Efforts to Organize during the New Deal, 2412

Parity, Implementation, (1929–1954), 2765

Parker, Charlie, and Harmonic Sources of Bee Bop Composition, 3559

Parkin, Louise, As a Member of the Women's Army Corps during World War II, 8290

Parking Meter, Invention, 4873

Parrish, Brigadier General Noel F., His Relationship with the Black Flying Program during World War II, 5616

Partisan Review: and World War II, 4026; as a Tool to Evaluate and Appreciate the Literary Output (1930s), 3427; Editorial Shifts (1930s), 6219; Evolution from a Communist Literary Magazine (1934) to an Anti-Stalinist Journal (1937), 3966; Ideological Shift, 6267; Origins, 3452

Patent Struggles, Boeing Versus Douglas over Pressurization Process (1930s and 1940s), 4841

Patman, Wright, Political Career, 1087

Patton, George S.: Ancestry, 0954; Papers, Volume I, (1885–1940), 0952; Papers, Volume II, (1940–1945), 0953

Patton, James G., Career, 2455

Peabody, Endicott, 0021

Peace Movements: and Asia (1941–1961), 8008; and Politics (1930s), 8003; in the 1930s, 8002; during World War II, 8054

Pearl Harbor: Analysis of Japanese Attack, 7560; Analysis of the Week Before, 7523; and American Defense Policy, 7503; and Germany, 7594; and Japanese Intelligence Reports, 7489; and Operation Magic, 7505; and Strategic Miscalculations, 7498; and the Cuban Missile Crisis Compared, 7605; and the 1944 Election, 7555; and the Failure of Intelligence, 7601; and the Limits of Intelligence Operations, 7607; and the Navy Department Investigation, 7517; and the Question of an Ultimatum, 7522; Attack Investigation Documents, 9683; Bibliography, 9615; Causes of Japanese Attack, 7551; Congressional Inquiries, 7531; Congressional Investigation, 7595; Controversy (1941–1946), 7556, 7557; Critique of Congressional Investigation (1947), 7563; Destruction of U.S. Battleships, 7525; Discussion of Revisionist Literature, 9724; Japanese Attack, 7546, 7550, 7567, 7574, 7575, 7587; Kimmel and Short as Scapegoats, 7581; Origins, 7541; Radio Reports, 7578; Washington's Contribution to the Japanese Attack, 7591; Why we were Surprised?, 7606

Pearson, Drew, Biography, 4060

Pecan Shelling in San Antonio during the Great Depression, 2091

Pecora Committee, 0535

Pecora Wall Street Expose, (1934), 2604

Peek, George N.: Biography, 0711; Career, 1561

Peery, George C., As Governor of Virginia (1934–1938), 6507

Pegler, Westbrook, As Critic of Roosevelt and the New Deal, 4059

Pell, Herbert C.: as War Crimes Commissioner, 0875; Diplomatic Career, 0874; Relationship with Roosevelt, 0876

Pelley, William D.: And the Silver Legion, 6388, 6399

Pendergast, Thomas J., and Kansas City Politics (1930s), 6481

Penicillin: allocation during World War II, 4809; Revolution in Modern Medicine (1940s), 4214

Pennsylvania: and the Little New Deal: 2981, 2982; and the Presidential Election (1932), 6753; Gubernatorial Election (1938), 6634; History of the Turnpike, 1862; Politics and Unemployment Relief (1931–1939), 6540; Workers interviewed, (1900–1940), 2137

Penny Auctions during the Great Depression, 1639

Pensions and Old Age Insurance, Canada, Great Britain, and the United States Compared, (1880s–1930s), 4227

People of the Cumberland (1937), Analysis, 3772

People's Institute of Applied Religion, (1940–1975), 4569

Pepper, Claude D., And the Democratic Senatorial Primary Campaign in Florida (1934), 6463; Senatorial Career, 1194; Supports Florida Barge Canal Project, 1195

Perelmen, S. J., Life and Career, 4121

Perkins, Frances: As Secretary of Labor, 0657. 0658, 0663; Career, 0661; Influence on Bureau of Labor Statistics, 0659; Interest in a New Deal for Blacks, 0660; Writings, 5052

Persian Corridor: 8870, 8968

Pessen, Edward, Memoir, 1702

Peterkin, Julia, Analysis of Her Works, 3403

Peters, C. Brooks: American Correspondent in Berlin, (1937–1941), 4054, 7874

Petersen, Hjalmar, As Governor of Minnesota (1936), 6564

Petroleum,:Availability during World War II, 1754; Companies on Trial in Wisconsin, 1937, 1755; Geologists, Activities in Northern Texas, 1763; Industry in the Texas Panhandle, World War II Role, 1770; Policy in Venezuela, (1920–1941), 1759; Resources in Louisiana, Regulation and Conservation, (1901–1940), 1745

Pharmaceutical Industry: Development (1920–1940), 4966; Financial Analysis, (1930–1959), 2500

Philadelphia: Emergence of a Two Party System (1924–1936), 6698; Hosiery Workers and Politics (1929–1935), 6662; Politics, Ethnicity and Religion (1924–1940), 4781; Transit Strike, (1944), 2404

Philadelphia Tribune, Voice of the Black Community, (1912–1941), 3981

Philanthropic Foundations, Impact on Public Education of Blacks in Florida, (1920–1947), 4325

Philippines: Education during the Commonwealth Period (1935–1941), 7610; Independence and Japan, 7613; Independence Question (1933), 7612; Movement to Reverse Independence, (1934–1941), 7618; National Development, 7616; Not Ready for Independence (1936), 7617; Records on the Loss, 9668; Sugar Industry and Independence, 8958

Phillips, Leon C., As Governor of Oklahoma (1939–1943), 6436

Phillips, Waite: A Liberal Republican's Philosophy, (1940), 4804; As Opponent of the New Deal, 7145

Phillips, William, Diplomatic Career, 0877

Phoenix, Arizona, Growth (1915–1920), 6578

Phoenix Indian School (19891–1935), 5902

Phrenology, Rise of Interest (1930s), 4400

Phyllis Wheatley House, A Black Settlement House in Minneapolis, (1924–1940), 5438

Physician Accountability in New York City, (1915–1940), 4183

Physicians and Birth Control, (1936–1947), 4233

Physicists: as Refugees from Europe (1930s), 5014; Flee from Europe to America (1930s), 4159

Pia Machita, The Last Indian Warrior in Arizona (1940–1941), 5837

Picasso's Exploration of Androgyny, (1901–1940), 3645

Piedmont Country Blues, Origins (1930s), 3562

Pierce, Florida, A Black Company Town, 5462

Pierce, Walter M., And the Birth Control Movement, 4692,

Pinchot, Amos, As Opponent of the New Deal, 7134

Pinchot, Cornelia B., As Social Activist, 5937

Pinchot, Gifford: And Emergency Relief in Pennsylvania (1932–1933), 6645; His View of the New Deal, 6563; As Governor of Pennsylvania (1931–1935), 6509

Pittman, Key: Anti-Japanese Views, 1058; Biography, 1054, 1057; Foreign Policy Views, 1060; Leader of the Silverites, 1056; Political Career, 1055; Promotes Silver Legislation, 1059; Quest for the China Market, 1061; Views on Neutrality, 1053

Pittman, Vail, And the Nevada Democratic Senatorial Primary (1944), 6629

Pittsburgh: and the Presidential Election (1932), 6768; Newspapers Comment on the Spanish Civil War, 4031; Public Education of Blacks, (1920–1950), 4332; Sports in the Black Community (1920s to the 1950s), 4622; Treatment of Chinese Immigrants during the Depression and World War II, 4791

Pittsburgh *Courier:* and Black Workers, 5581; Begins Drive to Open all Branches of the Armed Services to Blacks (1938), 5610; Increases Circulation in Mississippi (1935), 5380

Plainfield, New Jersey School System in the Depression, (1930–1937), 4314

Plains Indians, and Dealing with Life After the Passing of the Frontier, 5854

Plan Orange, History (1933–1940), 4864

Planning, History, From Roosevelt to Nixon, 4642

Platt, J. P., Interviewed about Cattle Ranching in Southern Florida, 9852

Playwrights Producing Co, History, (1938–1960), 3226

PM, The Short and Lively History of a New York Tabloid, (1940–1948), 3972

Poetry of Agrarianism, 3603

Pogue, Forrest C., Biographical Sketch of Pioneer Oral Historian, 9803

Poindexter, Joseph B., 0502

Poland, Invasion Coverage by U.S. Newspapers, 8541

Polio in Kentucky, (1920s–1950s), 4193

Polish-American Congress, Formation, 4763

Polish-American Vote in Chicago, 6561

Polish-American Cultural-Educational Policy Towards American Poles, (1918–1935), 4786

Polish, Italian, and Eastern European Immigrants in Connecticut, (1890–1940), 4140

Polish Refugees and U.S. Policy (1939), 9172

Political Campaign Strategies and Modern Technology, 6028

Political Convention Broadcasts, History and Influence, 3880

Political Drama in America (Since 1930), 3190

Political Left, Impact on the Labor Movement (1930s), 6265

Political Parties, and Foreign Policy, 6050

Political Party Platforms (1944–1964), 6095

Political Realignment (1980s Compared to the 1930s), 6072

Political Satire in American Musical Theater (1930s), 3256

Political Spot Advertisement, Evolution, (1936–1956), 3873

Politics, American Anti War Journal Founded (1944), 4101

Politics: and Labor during the Great Depression, 2305; Impact on American Drama (1930s), 3248

Pollack, Norman, Critique of Hofstadter's *The Age of Reform,* 9784

Pollard, Clarice F., Recalls her Experience in the Women's Auxiliary Corps, 8313

Popular Art, Impact on Los Angeles Literature (1940s), 3493

Popular Culture: and the Intellectuals (1930s), 6358; during the Great Depression, 3147

Popular Front: in Minnesota (1936–1950), 6537; in the American South (1930s), 2242

Popular Poetry in Texas during the Great Depression, 1720

Porcupine Mountains State Park, Origins, 1469

Port Alexander, Alaska, History, 2559

Porter, Katherine Anne: Analysis of Her Works, 3346; Letter to Mitzi Berger Hamovitch, 3372

Porter, Quincy, Symphonic Works, 3572

Posetta, Rose, Career, 2456

Positive Thinking in America From Mary Baker Eddy to Norman Vincent Peale, 4799

Post Office Architecture in Colorado, 3156

Post-War Planning, 9527–9596

Post, Wiley, Aerospace Achievements, 1892

Post-Modernism in the Los Angeles Art Community (1940s), 3661

Postal Savings System in the Depression, 2001

Potsdam Conference, 8588, 8598

Pound, Ezra: Analysis of His Work (1930s), 3373; and American Fascism, 6381; And his World War II Propaganda Broadcasts, 8495; and Anti-Semitism, 3583; As Critic of the New Deal, 7080; As Patron of Independent Presses, 4088; His Angry Love Affair with America, 3598; His Effort to Arrive at a Philosophy of History in His Poetry, 3601; His Fascist Views, 6391; Praises Hitler's Economic Policies, 1962; Selected Letters, (Mid 1920s to the Mid 1930s), 3457; Seventeen Articles Published in *Santa Fe New Mexican*, (1935), 3963, Trial (1945), 4735; World War II Radio Speeches, 3912

Pound-Dollar Exchange Rates, (1931–1938), 1992

Poverty: as Reflected in Plays by Six Depression Playwrights, 3203; Attitudes Toward in the United States, 2646; Roles of Church and State in Fighting in the United States, 2654

Powdersmoke Range (1935), Representing the Pioneer Ethic and Image of the Frontiersman, 3854

Powell, Adam Clayton Jr.: Biographical Sketch, 5444; Origins of his Political Career, 5403; Political Success, 5669

Powell, Adam Clayton Sr., Biographical Sketch, 5444

Powell, Jake, The Racist Views of a New York Yankees Ballplayer (1930s), 4586

Powers, Elmer G.: Diary, 1664; Memoirs, 1451

Pransky, Myer, Jewish Leader in Los Angeles, 5775

Pre-Keynesian Economic Policy Proposals during the Great Depression, 2030

Predator Control and the Environment, (1920–1939), 1441

Predicting and Controlling Wind Erosion, 1485

Prentis, Henning Webb, Conservative Economic and Political Views, 2644

Preparedness Movements in the U.S. (1898 to 1941), 7980

Presbyterian Board of Foreign Missions, Internal Conflict, 4551

Presidency, Bibliography, 9600

Presidents and their Transportation, 1860

Presidential Anecdotes as a Form of Humor, 4118

Presidential Automobiles, Picture History, 1861

Presidential Campaign Funds (1944), 6808

Presidential Character, 0275

Presidential Elections: and Campaign Funding (1932), 6758; Described and Analyzed, 6760; of 1940: and Democratic Party Publicity, 6785; and Foreign Affairs, 6788; as Reflected in the Tennessee Metropolitan Press, 6786; Propaganda Features, 6789; (1932, 1936, 1940, 1944, and 1948), 6738; and City Politics (1920–1948), 6489; and the Urban Vote, (1932–1936 and 1940), 6736; Dynamics (1928–1936), 6733

Presidential Ideology (1932–1982), 6067

Presidential Libraries, Guide to Manuscripts (1985), 9832

Presidential Politics (1916–1940), 6073

Presidential Primaries (1928–1960), 6048

Press Reform, Progressive and New Deal Eras Compared, 3947

Press-Radio Competition, (1920–1940), 3888

Price Controls, Effects on Southern Agriculture, 1360

Price, James H.: And his Political Battle with Harry Byrd Sr., 6715; As Governor of Virginia (1938–1942), 6529, 6713

Prisoners of War in America, 8443–8486

Prisons as Portrayed in Motion Pictures (1930s), 3821

Private Foundations and Public Policy, Secondary Education During the Great Depression, 4270

Private Higher Education, Effects of Great Depression, 4328, 4330

Pro-Nazi Sentiment in the United States (1933–1934), 6392

Production Code Administration and the Hollywood Film Industry, (1930–1940), 3725

Profit Rates Falling Prior to the Great Depression, 1600

Progress, American Belief, 1569

Progressive Educators: Promote Unification of School and Society, (1934–1943), 4380; Views on Race and Ethnicity During the Depression, 4311

Progressive Insurgents: and the New Deal (1933–1939), 7137; in the Senate during the Hoover Era, 6100; in the United States Senate (1933–1939), 6088, 6089, 7136

Progressive Republican Senators and the Presidential Election (1932), 6743

Progressives, Their Influence (1930s), 6148

Prohibition: Forum on Fiftieth Anniversary of its Repeal in
    Willimington, Delaware, (1953), 4753; History
    (1920–1932), 4747, 4756; Impact on Anglo-American
    Relations (1919–1935), 4757; Repeal as a Political
    Achievement, 4759; Response of Seventh Day Adventist
    to Repeal, (1932–1934), 4760; Response to Repeal in
    Milwaukee, 4761

Proletarian Literature: Analysis (1930s), 3341; Novels
    (1930–1939), 3329, 3325, 3343; Poetry in America,
    (1926–1939), 3600; Writers (1930s), 3411

Proportional Representation of Workers in the Automobile
    Industry, 2192

Protestant Churches: Attitudes toward the Negro,
    (1919–1939), 4537; and Lynchings, (1919–1939), 4538;
    and Pacifism During World War II, 4549; and the Race
    Issue During World War II, 4548; Decline and Revival of
    Social and Political Liberalism, (1920–1940),
    4469;Diplomacy and Arab Nationalism, (1914–1948),
    4493; Establishment, Ascendency of (1930–1955), 4523;
    Far Right from the Great Depression to the Cold War,
    4557; Influence on American Culture Declines during the
    Great Depression, 4498; Journals and the Nazi Assault on
    Religion, 4576; Reactions to New Deal Issues, 4533;
    Responses to Political and Social Issues, (1917–1941),
    4482; Search for Political Realism, (1919–1941), 4536;
    Social Attitudes during World War II, 4550; Thought and
    the Idea of Progress, (1930–1960), 4468

Protestantism and Social Issues, (1919–1939), 4540

Psychologists: and Unemployment, (1920s–1930s), 2473,
    2474

Psychology, Practice in America, (1920–1945), 4225

Public Accounting, Response to Federal Trade Commission
    (1914) and Securities and Exchange Commission (1934),
    2581

Public Assistance: in the State of Washington during the
    Great Depression, 1592, 2471; Roosevelt and Nixon's
    Policies Compared, 2715

Public Domain, History, 1530

Public Education: and Social Values, Their Relationship
    Debated (1930s), 4428; in the United States,
    (1918–1945), 4264

Public Health Policies in Britain and the United States
    during the Depression and World War II, 4181

Public Health Programs in Washtenaw County, Michigan,
    (1932–1940), 4205

Public Housing: and Eminent Domain, 1795; British Roots
    of American Policy, 1790; Development in Philadelphia,
    1782; in Baltimore, (1937–1954), 1792; in Dayton, Ohio,
    (1933–1935), 1791; in Duluth, (1936), 1796; in Fort
    Wayne, Indiana (1930s), 1809; in the Depression, 1781;
    in Washington, DC, (1943–1946), 1778, 1779; Policy
    Changes, (1920s–1930s), 1812

Public Opinion: and Freedom of Speech, 6866; and
    Immigration Policy, 6861; and New Deal Speakers

(1934–1936), 6862; and the Concentration of Wealth in
    America, 6860; and the Legislative Process, 6859; and
    World War II, 6858

Public Power Crusade in the Pacific Northwest during the
    New Deal, 1731

Public Utility Holding Company Act (1935), Political and
    Legislative History, 5126

Public Utility Holding Company Lobby, Investigated,
    (1935), 2851

Public Welfare in Washington County, Missouri,
    (1939–1941), 1619

Public Works Administration: in Tampa, Florida, 2567;
    Projects in Texas, (1933–1934), 3024; Saves Private
    Enterprise, 2505

Public Works of Art Project in Texas, 5211

Pueblo Agriculture (1938–1948), 5903

Puerto Rican Migrant Women in New York, (1920–1940s),
    5978

Puerto Rico: and National Self Determination (1809–1948),
    7702; and the Nationalist Movement (1930s), 7705; and
    the Sugar Crisis (1930–1935), 7703; and the Tydings Bill
    (1936), 7706; and the Self Government Question (1940s),
    6429

Pulitzer, Joseph, II: And Advertising Censorship,
    (1929–1939), 4057; And the European War, (1938–1945),
    4058

Pullman Sleeping Cars, Humorus Stories, 1916

Pulp and Paper Workers Union, (1933–1934), 2414

Purdue University's Pharmacy Extension Department
    (1930s), 4277

Quakers and Pacificism in the United States (1919–1941),
    8050

Quebec Conference: (1943), 8589; (1944), 8595

Quezon, President Manuel, And Economic Protectionism
    (1935–1941), 7614

Quillen, Robert, Discussion of His Cartoon Character Willie
    Willis, (1920s–1930s), 3653

Rabbis in America and the Social Justice Movement, 4535

Race Mutiny at Army Air Force Station 569 Banber Bridge,
    England (1943), 5585

Race Relations in the Rural South, (1915–1954), 1391

Racial Attitude Confrontation in New Mexico (1933), 5686

Racism: From Roosevelt to Reagan, 5297; in Gary Indiana
    (1906–1940), 5310; in Literary Anthologies, 5386

Radical Artists' Movement, (1926–1945), 3143

Radical Criticism (1940s), 8017

Radical Farm Organizations, Checklist of Journals, 9602

Radical Film Making in the United States, (1930–1942),
    3732

Radical Intellectuals (1930s), 6302

Radical Journals of the 1940s, Analysis, 3988

Radical Literature of the 1930s, Analysis, 3453

Radical Movements in the Southwest (1895–1943), 6246

Radical Politicians of the Great Plains (1930–1936), 6541

Radical Social Service Workers, Their Activities Evaluated, 6352

Radical Student Organizations in Higher Education (1905–1944), 6326

Radical Thought and Education Theory (1930s), 4405

Radical Writers (1930s), 6320

Radicalism, Lack of during the Great Depression, 1711

Radio: and Foreign Affairs (1930s), 3883; and Television, Development during the Roosevelt Era, 3900; Broadcasters and the Federal Government, 3914

Radio Broadcasting: and Comedy in the Great Depression, 3929; Commercial Takeover (1920s and 1930s), 3904; Development, (1925–1940), 3876; Early Years in El Paso, 3916; in Tennessee (1920s and 1930s), 3886; Journalism, Development, (1930–1941), 3879; Libel Laws, (1937), 3895; Programming and American Life, (1920–1960), 3901

Radio City Music Hall Productions, Cultural Significance, (1932–1985), 3534

Rag Town Life in the West Texas Oil Fields, 1766

Railroad: Changes in Financial Structures, (1929–1958), 1911; Coordination, Politics, (1933–1936), 1920; Workers in the Pacific Northwest, (1860s–1930s), 2403

Railway Industry, Growth of Unions, 2388

Rainbow 5, Discussion, 4849

Rainey, Henry T.: Elected Speaker of the House, 1237; Rise to the Speakership, 1236; Supports New Deal Legislation, 1235

Raksin, David, Recalls Working with Charlie Chaplin on *Modern Times* (1936), 3822

Ralston, Jackson, Proposes Tax Reform in California (1930s), 6487

Rancho de los Quiotes, 3174

Rand, Ayn, Analysis of Her Works, 3359

Randolph, A. Philip: As Charismatic Leader (1925–1941), 5411; Biography, 5294; Political Activities, 5416

Rankin, Jeanette: as Peace Activist, 5946; Biographical Sketch, 1238; Career, 1241; Congressional Career, 1240; Life, 1239

Rapport, Joe, Career as a Jewish Radical, 6264

Raskob, John J.: Advocates Repeal of Prohibition, 6070; His Conversion to the New Deal Opposition, 7129

Rayburn, Sam: And the Democratic Convention (1932), 6765; Attitudes toward New Deal Legislation, 1101; Biography, 1092, 1095; Career as Speaker of the House, 1090; Congressional Career, 1091, 1093; Congressional Leadership, 1094; Description of Official and Personal Papers, 1089; Favors Repeal of Arms Embargo, (1939), 1100; Leader of Congressional Democrats, 1096; Majority Leader, (1937–1940), 1097; Persuasive Powers, 1098; Primary Concern with Agriculture, 1102; Promotes Development of Public Power in the Southwest, 1088; Relationship with Roosevelt, 1099

Rayonier's Timber Acquisition Program, (1937–1952), 2526

Re-Thinking Chicago Movement (1930s), 4478

Rea, George B., Supports Japanese Expansionism (1930s), 4006

Reading, Pennsylvania: and the Success of the Socialist Party (1928–1940), 6667; Socialists in Power and in Decline (1932–1939), 6538

Reagan, Ronald, His Secret Service Movies, (1938–1939), 3855

Recession of 1937: Causes, 1980, 2034; Response of Henry Morgenthau and Marriner Eccles Compared, 2041

Reciprocal Trade Agreement Act (1934), Origins, 1832

Reciprocal Trade Agreement Program: in Action, (1937–1940), 1825; Origins, 1823, 1826

Reciprocal Trade: (1930s–1950s), 1852; and the Farm Vote, (1934–1940), 1846; and the Good Neighbor Policy, 1848; and South America, 1850; Use in Combating German Policies, 1835

Reciprocity and North Atlantic Trade Patterns, (1932–1938), 1842

Reconstruction Finance Corporation: (1932–1940), 2734; Activities in Mississippi, (1932–1933), 3022; and the New Deal, (1933–1940), 2862; and the Railroads, (1932–1937), 1924

Recorded Music Format on Radio, Rise, (1934–1954), 3930

Red Caps, Origin, 5536

Red River Bridge Conflict, Dispute between Texas and Oklahoma during the Great Depression, 6498

Red River Oil field and Conservation Measures, (1930s), 1762

Redding, Robert H., Dump Truck Driving in Alaska, (1937), 1501

Redistribution and Political Economy, (1929–1961), 2655

Reed, Daniel B., As Critic of the New Deal, 7079

Reed, William T., And Virginia Politics (1925–1935), 6506

Refugee Crisis, (1938–1941), 4180

Refugee Scholars in America, (1933–1945), 4147

Refugees, 9080

Regional Tennessee Valley Authority Project, Failure, 3110

Regionalism in the Great Depression, 1710

Regionalist Artists Respond to Fascism, 3709

Reinsch, J. Lennard, Discusses use of Radio and Television in Presidential Elections, 6740

Relief Crisis in Illinois, (1930–1940), 1597

Rental Libraries (1920s and 1930s), 2520

Repertoire Theater in America, (1926–1962), 3230

Republican: Decline of Machines in Philadelphia, (1936–1952), 6527; Attitudes towards New Deal Ideals (1956), 7148; Foreign Policy (1939–1942), 6058; Leaders and Foreign Policy (1943–1946), 6093

Republican Party: (1854–1964), 6079; (1932–1952), 6078; and Foreign Policy (1941–1945), 7189, 7856; and Presidential Campaign Speeches (1932), 6750; and the Congressional Elections (1938), 6783; and the Mackinac Island Conference (1943), 6108; as a Minority in Congress (1943–1944), 8518; As Wartime Minority (1933–1944), 6069; Decline in Pennsylvania

(1929–1934), 6413; Dynamics (1932–1938), 6109, 6110; Evolution in Vermont, 6531; First Hundred Years, 6101; in Arkansas (1920–1982), 6535; in Nebraska, (1865–1946), 6654; in New York State, (1932–1938), 6706; in the New Deal Period (1936–1940), 7075; in a Minority Role (1933–1938), 6087

Research Project (Number 7424), 7205

Reserve Officer Training Corps, Opposed (1920–1940), 8020

Resettlement Administration: Greenhills Project, Cincinnati, Ohio, 3068; Impact on Tenant Farmers in Arkansas, (1935–1936), 2996; Music Program in Appalachia, 5288

Retail Activity in Rural Wisconsin, Changes, (1934–1970), 2551

Reusser, Marguerite L.S., And the Utah State Historical Society (1937–1949), 5200

Reuter Organ Company, Survives the Great Depression, 2615

Reuther, Victor, Experiences in the Soviet Union, (1933–1935), 2457

Reuther, Walter: And the Kelsey-Hayes Wheel Company Strike, (1936), 2458; Anti-Communist Views, (1939–1947), 2465; As Leader of the United Automobile Workers of America, 2461; Career, 2460; Ideas, 2466; Political Ideas, 2463; Radical Ideas, 1936, 2459; Speeches, 2462; Two Letters, 2464

Review of Politics: Analysis of Contents, (1939–1989), 4014; Review of Contents, (1939–1963), 3978

Revolutionary Theater in America, Artistic and Social Vision, (1930–1970), 3209

Reynolds, Robert R., Senate Career, 1196

Rhineland Crisis and the American Press (1936), 7880

Rhode Island Birth Control League, Early Years, 4684

Rhode Island Jewish Press in the Twentieth Century, 4021

Rhode Island Self Help Organization (1944–1945), 8069

Rhode Island Textile Strike, (1934), 2191

Rice, Charles O.: Memoir of an Anti-Communist Priest, 6315; Catholic Labor Organizer in Pittsburgh, Pennsylvania, 2127

Rice, Elmer, As a Regional Director in the Federal Theater Project, 5070

Rice, Grantland, Comments on the Sports Champions (1930s), 4619

Richards, James P., Early Political Career, 1103

Richardson, Admiral James O., Memoir, 7577

Richberg, Donald R.: Attitude Toward New Deal, 0753; Memoir, 0754

Ridgway, Matthew B., Leadership Style, 0955

Right to Work Controversy, (1942–1967), 2209

Right Wing Protestants, Examination of their World View And Personalities, 6128

Rio Conference, 8647

Rio Grande Interstate Water Conflicts, (1880–1938), 1482

Rio Grande Treaty (1933), 7689

Ritchie, Albert C.: And the 1934 Gubernatorial Election in Maryland, 6440; And the Democratic Convention (1932), 6752

Rivera, Diego: Destruction of His Controversial Mural at Rockefeller Center, (1934), 3695; Murals Depicting Scientific Research Issues, (1933), 3680

Rivers, Eurith D., As Governor of Georgia (1930s), 6542

Robbins, Margaret D., Opposes New Deal, 2467

Roberts, Elizabeth M., Main Characters in Her Short Stories, 3286

Roberts, Owen J.: 7055–7060

Robertson County, Texas Electric Cooperative, Origins, 1736

Robeson, Paul, And Black Identity in American Movies, 3740

Robinson, Bill "Bojangles," Career (1930–1949), 3551

Robinson, Joseph T.: Biography, 1197; Speeches, 1198; Supports Court Packing Plan, 1199; Supports Robinson-Patman Act, 1200

Robinson-Patman Act (1936), Analysis, 2514, 2881

Roche, Josephine, Career, 5963

Rockefeller Foundation Program in Molecular Biology, (1929–1939), 4922

Rockwell, Norman, His Representation of Roosevelt's Four Freedoms, 3689

Rodeo and the Professional Rodeo Cowboy, Development, 4593

Rogers, Agnes, Memories of the Roosevelt Years, (1933–1941), 4688

Rogers, Will: and Horace Lorimer, Their Ideological Views Compared, 4069; and Wiley Post, Their Careers, 4130; And Presidential Nominations, (1924, 1928, and 1932), 4095; As Cracker-Barrel Humorist, 4114; Biographical Sketch, 3467; Career, 3714; His Support for Military Aviation, 4979; His Use of Rhetorical Irony, 4113; Humor, 4109; Humorist of the Great Depression, 4131; Supports Commercial Aviation, 1899

Rolph, James Jr., As Governor of California (1931–1934), 6459

Romantic Film Comedy in America, (1938–1950), 3868

Ronald, W. R., Life and Journalistic Career, 4102

Roosevelt: Administration, Impact on Organized Labor, 2142; and the Bonus Marchers (1932), 2099; Coalition, History (1932–1952), 6739; Corollary, Efforts to Repudiate, 7634

Roosevelt, Eleanor: A Tribute, 0056; and the National Youth Administration, (1935–1943), 2781; And Education, 0080; And Food, 0068; And Human Rights, 0019; and Racial Justice, 0046, 0047; And Rural Resettlement, 0071; And the Media, 0043, 0044; And the Plight of World Jewry, 0081; And The Press, 0093; And Val-Kill, 0090; And Women in the New Deal, 0088; As First Lady, 0049, 0050, 0059, 0061, 0064, 0065, 0069, 0077, 0082, 0087, 0092, 0094; As Radio Commentator, 0041; As UN Ambassador, 0079; Attitudes Toward American Life and Culture, 0067; Autobiography, 0083, 0086; Biography, 0048, 0052, 0072, 0073, 0074, 0089, 0095; Compared to Jane Addams, 0055; Foreign Policy Views, 0045; Her

Influence, 0076; Her Press Conferences, 0084; Letters to Louis Fischer, 0057; Memoir, 0085; Mission to the Pacific (1943), 0078; Papers, 9839; Personal Relationships, 0075; Personality, 0060, 0066; Photographs, 0063; Political Career, 0051; Press Conferences, 0042; Relations with Sara Delano Roosevelt, 0040; Resigns from DAR, 0058; Role in Women's History, 0070; Social Views, 0039, 0062; Tour of Europe (1929), 0054; Youth, 0053

Roosevelt, Elliott: As Aide to His Father, 0097

Roosevelt Family: (1640s to 1960s), 0115; As Remembered by Marion Dickerman, 0101; History, 0121

Roosevelt, Franklin D.: 0272, 0273; Accedes to Russian Demands at Yalta, 8833; Acceptance Speech (July 2, 1932), 0147, 0167; Accomplishments, 0017; Accused of Incompetence during the Munich Crisis, 7840; Accused of Tricking the United States into World War II, 7747; Address and Opinions, 9834; Advocate of Naval Preparedness, 0488; Affect of Crises on His Presidency, 0345; After Death Communications With, 0217; America during His Presidency, 0402; Analysis of his Foreign Policies, 7789; Analysis of his Foreign Policy (1941–1945), 7734, 7785; Analysis of his Policies toward Germany and Japan, 7792; Analysis of His Importance, 0314; Analysis of State of the Union Messages, 0156; Ancestry, 0120; and American Recognition of the Soviet Union, 7411; and Argentina, 9034; and City Bosses, 6483; and Crime Control, 6875; and Dutch Colonial Architecture, 3178, and Eleanor, 0114, and Endicott Peabody, 0022, and His Critics (1933–1939), 7171; and James L. Fly, Chairman of the Federal Communications Commission, (1941–1944), 3897; and Jerome Davis, 0005; and Libraries, 0026; and Madame Rosat-Sandoz, 0023; and Neutrality Policy (1933–1937), 7188; and Numerology, 0333; and Pearl Harbor, 7592; and Political Mail, 6106; and the American Communists (1933–1941), 6301; and the Architecture of Warm Springs, 3179; and the Coming War with Germany, 7268; and the Congressional Elections (1938), 6782; and the Election (1936), 6591, 6771; and the Good Neighbor Policy, 7201; and the Isolationists (1932–1945), 7901; and the New Deal, 2663; and the Origins of the Welfare State, 2686; and the Politics of Naval Expansion during the New Deal, 5004; and the Presidential Campaign (1936) in Indiana, 6772; and the 1940 Presidential Campaign, 6793, 6794; and the Primary Campaigns (1938), 6781; and the Promotion of State Legislative Action on State Programs (1933–1941), 6589; and the Purge of Congressman John O'Connor of New York, 6665; and the Reconstruction of Italy (1943–1944), 6806; and the South, 5274; and the Spanish Civil War, 7373, 7391; and the Spanish Embargo (1937–1939), 7395; and the Third Term Question (1940), 6797; and the Triumph of Rural Agrarians, 6107; and the Urban Coalition (1940), 6792; and U.S. Soviet Relations, 8838; and the Vatican, 4484;

and Water Pollution Control Policy, 4239; And "Secret Map" of South America (1941), 7723; And Aerial Reconnaissance of Japanese Islands before World War II, 9360; And Aid to the Aviation Industry, 9372; And America's Tiny Islands, 7824; And American Entry into World War II, 7286, 7760; And American Foreign Policy (1932–1945), 7738, 7748; And American Liberalism (1937–1945), 6157; And American Religious Leaders, 4522; And American-Soviet Relations in the Pacific (1933–1941), 7445; And Anglo-American Cooperation, (1934–1937), 7757; And Anti-Colonialism, 7810; And Anti-Imperialism (1930s), 7790; And Anti-Nazi Propaganda, 8492; And Appeasement (1935–1938), 7759; And Asian Colonialism (1941–1945), 7730; And Axis Influence in Latin America, 9016; and California's Role in His Nomination (1932), 6761; And Canadian American Relations (1933–1939), 7782; And Central European Foreign Policy before World War II, 7242; And China Policy (1941–1945), 8894, 8907, 8926; And Christian Pacifism, 8021; And Churchill (1939–1941), 7775; And Civil Liberties, 6879; And Civil Rights, 6883; And Collective Security (1933), 7741; And Congressional Isolationist, 7857; And Correspondence with William C. Bullitt on the Soviet Union (1933–1936), 7418; And Cuba (1933–1945), 7673; And Eastern Europe, 8614; And Efforts to Intimidate Japan (1937–1938), 7752; And Efforts to Prevent Aid to the Spanish Republic, 7352; And Failure of the Plan to Provide the Soviet Union with Battleships (1936–1938), 7979; And Family, 0124, 0125, And Famine in India (1943), 8944; And Foreign Affairs, 7788; And Foreign Policy (1933–1937), 7239; And Foreign Policy (1938–1939), 7803; And Foreign Policy, 7768; And Foreign Policy Issues, 7711; And France (1938–1939), 7754; And France during World War II, 8690; And Franco (1933–1941), 7364; And Franco-American Relations, 7755; And French Reaction to the Quarantine Speech, 8692; And German Naval Policy toward the United States (1939–1941), 7289; And Hate Mongers, 7069; And Herbert Hoover's Opposition to his Foreign Policy (1941), 7733; And His Personal Envoys (1941–1945), 7776; And His Theory of International Relations, 7795; And His Foreign Policy Critics, 7805, 7806; And Hyde Park, 0118; And Imperialism, 7825; And Indian Policy during World War II, 8935; And Indo China (1942–1945), 8946; And Internationalism (1939), 7969; And Internationalism, 7744; And Japan (1913–1933), 7784; And Japanese Policy (1933–1941), 7713; And Jewish Refugees, 9074, 9129; And Lend Lease, 7724; and Lucy Mercer, 0379; And Manchukuo (1933–1941), 7731; And Mid-East Diplomacy, 8970; And Military Planning Before Pearl Harbor, 7745; And Missed Opportunities to Avert World War II, 7781; And Monetary Diplomacy (1933), 7786; And Multinational Corporations in Spain (1930s), 7363; And Mussolini (1933–1941), 7740; And Naval Preparedness

(1932–1940), 7991; And Neutrality Revision (1939), 7791; And New Left Criticism (1972), 9715; And New Left Historiography, 9701; And Opponents of the New Deal, 7063, 7064, 7065; And Palestine, 9000, 9003 And Pearl Harbor, 7476, 7477, 7506, 7507, 7558; And Personal Diplomacy, 7793; And Personal Diplomacy with Great Britain (1936–1937), 7758; And Poland (1943–1945), 8807; And Recognition of the Soviet Union (1933), 7414, 7428, 7450, 7455; And Senate Opposition to Internationalist Foreign Policy, 7726; And Stalin, 7778, 7787; And the 1938 Senatorial Campaign in Georgia, 6732; And the Abrogation of the Platt Amendment, 7749; And the Aftermath of Pearl Harbor, 7554; And the Anglo-Soviet Balkan Agreement (1944), 8635; And the Atlantic Charter, 8607, 8621; And the Atomic Bomb, 9234, 9244; And the Attitude of Hyphenate Americans towards his Foreign Policy, 7868; And the Back Door to War Theory, 7811; And the Baltic State Question (1940–1941), 7736; And the Battle of the Atlantic (1941), 7871; And the Brain Trust, Historiographical Overview (1972), 9787; And the British Empire, 8753; And the British Royal Visit to the United States (1939), 7800, 7801; And the Carlson Mission to China, 9433; And the Coming of War (1941), 7718; And the Coming War with Japan, 7599, 7600; And the Conduct of his Diplomacy, 7820; And the Congressional Elections (1942), 6799; And the Cuban Crisis (1933), 7669; And the Czech Crisis (1933–1939), 7714; And the Decision to Aid Great Britain, 8751; And the Decision to Aid the Soviet Union (1941), 8825, 8831 And the Decision to Aid Tito, 8818; And the Decision to Provide War Planes to Greece, 8757; And the Demand for Unconditional Surrender, 8570; And the Destroyers for Bases Deal (1940),7732, 7774, 8732, 8733; And the Dismemberment of Germany, 8616, 8630; And the Doctrine of Unconditional Surrender, 8596, 8631; And the Dominican Republic (1933–1940), 7676; And the Early Military and Diplomatic History of World War II, 7819; And the End of Isolation (1936–1941), 7751; And the Erosion of State Department Influence, 7735; And the Establishment of the Poughkeepsie, New York Post Office, 3151; And the Expansion of the Monroe Doctrine, 7826; And the Failure of the Post-War Trusteeship Plan, 8792; And the Failure of the Yalta Conference, 8611; And the Failure to Rescue European Jews, 9091; And the Far East (1913–1941), 7727; And the Foreign Policy of his First Administration, 7764; And the Four Freedoms, 8617; And the Geneva Disarmament Conference (1932–1934), 7739; And the German Jews, 9117; And the German Problem (1919–1945), 7813; And the Good Neighbor Policy, 7637, 7750; And the Holocaust, 9093–9096, 9136, 9155, 9163; And the House Un-American Activities Committee, 6882; And the Implementation of Regional Theory, 9794; And the Invasion of North Africa, 9423; And the Invasion of Southern France, 9359; And the Italo-Ethiopian Crisis

(1935–1936), 7344; And the Japanese Invasion of China, 7483; And the Making of the Good Neighbor Policy, 7652; And the Mexican Approbation, 7687; And the Myth of the Hundred Days, 7779; And the Necessity of War, 7772; And the Neutrality Act (1935), 7818; And Neutrality Legislation (1930s), 7756; And the New Deal, 0018; And the New Panama Treaty (1936), 7695; And the Ogdensbergh Agreement (1940), 7794; And the Origin of His Popular Coalition in Pittsburgh (1932), 6767; And the Origins of Lend Lease, 7728, 7769; And the Origins of World War II, 7773; And the Palestine Problem (1933–1945), 8994, 8996; And the Polish-American Congress (1944), 6848; And the Polish-German Frontier Question, 7804; And the Polish Question, (1941–1945), 7763; And the Polish Question at Yalta, 8615; And the Polish Question in the Election (1944), 6803; And the Polish Vote in the Election (1944), 6807; And the Politics of Isolationism (1932–1936), 7777; And the Post-War Plans for China, 8899; And the Presidential Nomination (1940), 6787; And the Problem of Nazi Germany, 7814; And the Progressive National Committee (1936), 6836; And the Promise to Support Britain in the Far East, 7780; And the Proposed Atlantic Union, 7809; And the Quarantine Speech, 7721; And the Rearming of France, 8712; And the Russians (1933), 7725, 8640; And the Science Advisory Board, (1933–1935), 4994; And the Search for Peace and Freedom at Yalta, 8603; And the Second Front Decisions, 9345; And the Spanish Civil War, 7383; And the *St. Louis* Tragedy, 9101; And the Stimpson Doctrine, 7808; And the Surveillance of Black Americans by the FBI, 6876; And the Takoradi Air Route to Africa (1941), 7798; And the Tyler Kent Affair (1940), 7770; And the Third Term Nomination (1940), 6796; And the Trans-African Airbase Program of World War II, 7797; And the Undeclared Naval War with Germany (1939–1941), 7266, 7313, 7746, 9230; And the United Nations, 9458; And the United States Supreme Court, 6967; And the Vice Presidential Question (1944), 6804, 6809; And the Vicente Asper Espionage Ring, 7836; And the War Refugee Board, 9135; And the Welles Memorandum on Inter-American Relations (1933), 7638; And the Welles Mission to Europe (1940), 7762; And the Winter War (1939–1940), 7765; And the World Court Defeat (1935), 7852, 7767; And the World Crisis (1937–1945), 7771; And the World Disarmament Question, 7821; And the Yalta Conference, 8622; And the Yalta Miscalculations, 8608; And The Triumph of American Nationalism, 7822; And those who Hated him, 7085; And U.S. Cuban Policy, 7643; And U.S. Entry into World War II,7729, 7766; And U.S. Occupation Policy in Europe, 7712; And U.S. Oil Exports to Japan, 7598; And U.S. Strategy in World War II, 8620; And Vichy France, 8702; And Vietnam, 7743; And Wartime Correspondence With Pope Pius XII, 7812; And Wartime Policy toward the USSR, 7802; And Wartime Propaganda, 8547, 8550;

And Western Hemisphere Neutrality Zone, 7715; And William Bullitt's Secret Mission to Europe (1933), 7722; And World War II, 7737, 7742; Anti-Roosevelt Documents, 9646; Appraisal of His Presidency, 0413; Approach to National Security, 0483; Artistic Patronage, 3150; As a Conservative, 6120; As Ad-Libber, 0148; As Assistant Secretary of the Navy, 0255–0258; As Latin America's Good Neighbor, 7629; As Mystery Story Writer, 0198; As Newspaper Columnist, 0140; As seen from France (1930s), 7260; As seen in Post War Germany, 8714; Atomic Energy Policy, 0491; Attacked by Republican Conservatives (1944), 6800; Attempt to Assassinate (February, 1933), 4705; Attempts to Enforce Party Discipline, 0533 Attempts to Modify the Party System, 0505; Attitude toward Negro Rights, 0721; Attitude toward Nye Committee, 0522; Attitude Toward the Courts, 0353; Inaugural Speeches, 9693; Bibliography, 9609, 9610, 9611;Bibliography of his Speeches, 9598; Biography, 0002, 0003, 0004, 0007, 0008, 0009, 0010, 0011, 0013, 0016, 0019, 0103, 0282, 0288, 0367, 2694; Biography (1940–1945), 0286; Biography to 1940, 0285; Bird Watcher, 0209, 0210, 0240; Blamed for World War II, 0299; Brains Trust Advisors, 0365; Brief Mention, 0301; British Images (1932–1938), 7322; Campaign Biography (1940), 0262; Campaign for New York State Senate (1910), 0245; Campaign for the Presidency, 0267; Campaign Speeches (1920), 0153; Catalyst for Social Change, 0381; Champion of Naval Preparedness, 0481; Chautauqua Speeches, 0179; Checklist of Anti-Roosevelt Literature, 9621; Christian Convictions, 0348; Chronology of Activities, 0138; Columbia University Connection, 2050; Commander-in-Chief, 0480, 0492; Commemorative Medals, 0297; Comment, 0323; Comment on British Policy (1938–1939), 7799; Compared to Adlai Stevenson as Campaigner, 0307; Compared to Eisenhower, 0393; Compared to Hitler, 0302, 0303, 0477; Compared to Hoover as Speaker, 0144; Compared to Herbert C. Hoover, 7162; Compared to Jefferson, 0331; Compared to Kennedy, 0334; Compared to Lincoln, 0319, 0398; Compared to Lyndon B. Johnson in Recruiting Advisors, 0562; Compared to Mussolini, 6380; Compared to Other Progressive Presidents, 0279; Compared to Theodore Roosevelt, 0362, 0460; Compared with Truman, 0417; Conception of Liberty, 0304; Concern for the City, 0440; Condemned for Repeal of Prohibition, 4746; Conflict with A. Philip Randolph (1941), 5343; Connections with Warm Springs foundation, 0236; Conservation Correspondence, 0411; Conservation Policies, 0294, 0356; Conservative Critique, 0420; Contribution to the American Competitive Ideal, 2782; Contributions to American Political Thought and Practice, 2695; Contributions to the Return of Prosperity, 0399; Conversion to Anti-Prohibitionism, 4752; Court Reform Speeches, 0169; Creates Image of Hoover as Incompetent and Insensitive, 7151; Creation of Federal Field Coordinating Organizations, 0551; Creation of Planning Boards, 0547; Critical Analysis of his Foreign Policy (1933–1940), 7716, 7717; Critical Assessment of the Early New Deal, 0424; Criticism, 0293; Criticism of Selected Speeches, 0184; Critique, 0478; Critique of his Second Inaugural Address, 7093; Critique of Presidential Actions, 0280; Critique of the Revisionist Thesis, 9781; Death, 0223, 0226, 0228, 0231, 0232, 0234; Decision to begin Manhattan Project, 0407; Decision to send War Planes to France (1933–1941), 7263; Democratic National Committee Speeches, 0176; Descendants, 0129; Described as Poor Administrator, 0321; Development of Petroleum Reserves While Assistant Secretary of the Navy, 0254; Disability, 0218; Disciple of Alfred Thayer Mahan, 0435; Discussion of the Arrangement of His Papers at Hyde Park (1948), 9837; Discussion with Joint Chiefs of Staff about Japan, 0499; Dismantling New Deal Programs, 0289; Dutch Heritage, 0117; Early Days as President, 0513; Early Foreign Policy (1932–1933), 7823; Early Life, 0242, 0247; Early Speeches, 0134; Early Years, 0028; Economic Efficacy of New Deal, 0325; Economic Philosophy, 0243; Economic Policy, 0306,1968; Education, 0024, 0027; Effectiveness as Administrator, 0383; Effects of Presidency on Personality, 0497; Efforts to Conceal His Disability, 0224; Efforts to Mediate Peace (1939–1940), 7849; Efforts to Prepare the United States for War, (1933–1939), 4969; Election (1940), 0139; Elitist, 0428; Emphasizes need for National Unity (1938–1940), 6053; Entering World War II, 0482; Establishing the Modern Presidency, 0409; Evaluated as a War-Time Statesmen (1951), 7850; Evaluated as War Leader, 0484–0490; Evaluated by Richard Hofstadter; 6149; Evaluated by Jawaharlal Nehru, 7472; Executive Reorganization, 0418, 0437, 0530, 0549, 0555, 0560; Exercise of Presidential Power, 0410; Extends Christmas Shopping Season, (1939), 2509; Family, 0032, 0033, 0034; Family Life, 0122, 0128; Family Notes, 0373; Family Tree, 0119; Favors a Naval Quarantine of Japan, 7753; Fireside Chats, 0133, 0151, 0175; First Inaugural Address, 0152, 0172; First President to Have a Personal Airplane, 0366; First Year as President, 0364; First Year of New Deal as Told by Speeches and Executive Orders, 0171; Fiscal Policies, 2008; Fondness for Seagoing Experiences, 0194; Four Freedoms Speech, 0146; Fourth Inaugural Address, 0173; Frances Perkins Remembers him, 0414; French View of the New Deal, 0357; From Teheran To Yalta, 7816; General Assessment of His Presidency, 0283; General Survey of his Foreign Policy (1945), 7720; Gold Policies, 1322; Good Neighbor Policy and Paraguay, 7701; Governor of New York, 0265. 0266, 0269; Gradual Loss of Executive Power, 0434; Gubernatorial Speeches, 0168; Guide to Public Papers and Addresses in Early Career, 0160; Health During

World War II, 0211; Heritage, 0127; Hiding His
Disabilities, 0237; His 1944 Campaign Speeches
Compared to those of Thomas E. Dewey, 6810; His
Children, 0098; His Correspondence with Norman
Thomas, 6231; His Foreign Policy from Munich to Pearl
Harbor, 7796; His Foreign Policy Opposed by
International Law Specialists Edwin M. Borchanrd and
John Bassett Moore, 7907; His German Policy
(1933–1941), 7280; His Leadership Style Compared to
Mussolini, 7761; His New Deal Political Philosophy,
6052; His Philosophy of Government as Compared to
Hoover, 7166; His Plan to Establish and Edit a
Newspaper after Retirement, 3939; His Relationship with
Hoover in the Interregumun Period (1932–1933), 7161;
His Religious Views, 4454; His Sons, 0096; His Speech
Writers, 0137; His War Time Speeches Compared to
those of Hitler, 8553; Historians' Ratings, 0405;
Historiographical Essay, 9717; Historiographical Survey
(1970), 9710; Hobbies, 0185, 0186, 0187, 0188, 0190,
0192, 0193, 0196, 0197, 0200, 0204, 0206, 0207; How he
got His Tape Recorder (1940), 4836; Hunting Trip to
Louisiana (1920), 0259; Ideas about Deficit Spending,
0523; Illnesses (1943–1945), 0216, 0233; Images of
Presidential Leadership, 0274; Impact of Democratic
Party Philosophy, 0412; Impact of Ethnic Groups on his
Foreign Policy, 4768; Impact on Public Opinion, 0384,
0401; Impact on the Presidents of the 60s and 70s, 0332;
Inaugural Medals, 0330; Inaugural Addresses, 0141,
0165; Influence of Advisors on, 0544; Influence of Ethnic
Groups on his Foreign Policy, 4769; Influence on Growth
of Presidential Power, 0436; Influence on Passage on
Reciprocal Trade Agreements Act (1934), 0517; Influence
on Succeeding Presidents, 0404; Intention to Revive New
Deal after World War II, 0395; Interest in Farm Matters
While State Senator, 0252; Interest in Harnessing Power
of Nature, 0248; Interest in Labor and Social Reform
Issues, 0251; Interpreted as Conservative, 9707;
Intervenes in the Georgia Senate Race (1938), 6630;
Issues and Personalities Affecting, 0123; Journalistic
Impression, 0510; Labor Record (1910–1913), 0250; Last
Illness, 0219; Last Illness and Death, 0213; Last Speech,
0131; Last Trip to Warm Springs, 0214; Last Year as
President, 0278; Leadership and Personal Qualities, 0403;
Leadership Skills, 0385, 0391, 0397, 0406; Leadership
Style, 0292, 0423; Leading the Nation into World War II,
0426; Legacy, 2684; Legendry Figure, 0313; Legends
Concerning Death, 0230; Letters, 0178; Letters from
Missippians to Roosevelt, (1932–1933), 1707 ; Letters
from Working Class American to Roosevelt, 1691;
Letters received while President, 9838; Liberal Heritage,
0312; Liberalism as a Favorable Symbol, 0346; Lifelong
Afflictions, 0220; Lifestyle and Political Technique,
0354; Literary Style, 0174; Local Historian, 0189, 0191;
Major Appointments, 0516; Man of Faith and
Compassion, 0315; Masonic Activities, 0203, 0205;

Meets Alfred M. Landon in Des Moines (1936), 6776;
Meets King Ibn Saud (1945), 8985; Memoirs of His
Bodyguard, 0341; Militancy, 0494; Monetary Experiment
(1933), 2017; Mother's View, 0253; Nature of His
Presidency, 0351; Naval Art, 0201; New Deal-A Policy
with No Coherent Philosophy, 0300; New Deal and the
Democratic Process, 0317; New Deal as Extension of
Earlier Policies, 0318; New Deal Associates, 0514; New
Deal Years, 0284, 0296; Newspaper Support, 0464;
Opposed by Al Smith, 7114; Opposed by the Socialist
Party, 6248; Orders Army to Seize Montgomery Ward
Plant in Chicago (1941), 8145; Party Leadership, 0425;
Passion for Human Rights, 0298; Personal Letters, 9680;
Personality, 0001, 0006, 0014, 0025, 0126, 0310;
Photographs, Cartoons, and Caricatures, 0112;
Photographs, 0104, 0106, 0107, 0110, 0113; Pictorial
History, 0102; Polio Attack, 0221, 0222; Polio Treatment
Center at Warm Springs, 0349; Political Achievements,
0415; Political Activities (1920s), 0263, 0264; Political
Career, 0276; Political Ideology, 0432; Political
Leadership, 0305; Political Legacy, 0327; Political
Maneuvering, 0431; Political Philosophy, 0344, 0386;
Political Skills, 0012; Portrait, 0099. 0100, 0111, 3683;
Pre-1933 Articles and Speeches, 0170; Presidential
Automobiles, 0202; Presidential Campaigns, 6741;
Presidential Candidate, 0270; Presidential Conferences,
9836; Presidential Integrity, 0382; Presidential Legacy,
0370; Presidential Papers, 0163; Presidential Ranking,
0441–0451; Presidential Skills, 0277; Presidential Style,
0389, 0421; Press Conferences, 0461, 0463; Press
Releases (1929–1939), 0183; Primary Election
Campaigns, 0295; Profile of those who Hated him, 7121;
Progressive Orthodoxy, 6770; Promises to Intervene in
Pacific War, 8728; Promoter of Human Rights, 0396;
Promoting the Saint Lawrence Seaway, 0387; Public and
Private Papers, Arrangement, 0149; Public Papers and
Addresses, 9650; Public Papers, 9835; Public Papers of
His Second Administration, 9669; Public Response to
Quarantine Speech, 0159; Published Writings on
(1950–1957), 9805; Puritanical Themes in Rhetoric of,
0390; Quarantine Speech (1937), 0155; Reaction to
Security, 0359; Reaction to the Neutrality Acts, 7783;
Reactions to Death, 0235; Reading Interests, 0208;
Rearmament, 0438; Receives Letter from Gandhi, 8942;
Receives Letters from Ordinary People in North Carolina,
(1936), 5076; Recollections of His Secretary, 0020;
Recorded Speeches, 0150; Rejects Proposal against and
All Out offensive Against Japan (1942), 8580; Rejects
Summit Meeting (1941), 7490, 7527; Relations with
Congress, 0392; Relations with Congress during World
War II, 8501; Relationship to Business community, 0339;
Relationship to Civilian Conservation Corps, 0422;
Relationship with 78th congress, 0534; Relationship with
American Catholics, (1937–1945), 4485; Relationship
with Arthur Krock, 0322; Relationship with Attorney-

General Robert H. Jackson, 0509; Relationship with Bureau of the Budget, 0515; Relationship with Business Advisory Council, 0553; Relationship with Business before World War II, 0439; Relationship with Churchill and the Atomic Bomb Question (1945), 7719; Relationship with Congress, 0519, 0521, 0526, 0527, 0528, 0529; Relationship with Corporate Elite, 0368; Relationship with George M. Elsey, 0371; Relationship with His Advisors, 0342; Relationship with Interest Groups, 0337; Relationship with National Emergency Council, 0558; Relationship with Neighbors, 0249; Relationship with Samuel Rosenman, 0343; Relationship with Senator Pat Harrison of Mississippi, 0536; Relationship with the 76th Congress, 0531; Relationship with the 77th Congress, 0540; Relationship with the Bureau of the Budget, 0496; Relationship with the Federal Communications Commission, 0552; Relationship with the Forest Service Lobby, 0554; Relationship with the Media, 0455, 0456, 0457, 0462, 0467–0476; Relationship with Various Organizations in the Bureaucracy, 0336; Reliance on Public Opinion, 0340; Religious Activities, 0281; Religious Influences, 0241; Religious Views, 0244; Remembered in Verse Form, 3581; Reorganization of Executive Branch, 0493; Response to Crises, 0394; Review of First Term, 0329; Review of the Literature (1979), 9767; Rhetoric in Prewar Speeches, 0164; Rhetoric of Collective Security, 0161; Rhetorical Style, 0182; Rise to Power, 0239; Role in History, 0015; Role in Rearmament, 0479; Role in the Formulation in the Public Utility Act (1935), 0400; Satirical Assessment, 0430; Scandals, 0380; Scathing Indictment (1940), 7106; Search for Support of Democratic Party Leaders After 1928, 0268; Secret Communications with Neville Chamberlain, (1938–1939), 7817; Secret Service Protection, 0355; Selected Bibliography (1945–1971), 9620; Selecting Staff, 0507 Sense of Humor, 0030, 0031, Social Activities in the White House, 0375; Social and Political Ideas, 9833; Speaking Style, 0132, 0135, 0136, 0142, 0145, 0347; Speaking Style Compared to that of Ronald Reagan, 0338; Speech Preparation (1932), 0154; Speech Training at Harvard, 0143; Speeches in the Northwest from 1914 to World War II, 0238; State of the Union Messages, 0157; State Senator, 0246; Statistical Information on His Elections, 0320; Success as a Campaigner, 0260, 0261; Supported by Missouri Progressives (1932), 6764; Survey of Political Attitudes and Policies, 0328; Takes U.S. off the Gold Standard, (1934), 1977; The Atomic Bomb and the Normandy Invasion, 7815; The Media and the Coming of War (1940–1941), 7807; Third Term Decision, 0352, 0452, 0453, 0454, 6784; Through Foreign Eyes, 0311; Transcripts of Press Conferences, 0459, 0465; Transition from Hoover Administration, 0363; Tree Planting Project, 2730; Trip to Europe during World War I, 0369; Trips to

Warm Springs, 0229; Triumph over Disability, 0225; Triumph over Polio, 0212, 0227; *U.S.S. Sequoia*, 0195; Use of Competitive Theory of Administration, 0419; Use of Executive Power, 0429; Use of Intellectuals, 2053; Use of Presidential Power, 0416; Use of Presidential Power in Conflict with the Constitution, 0427; Use of the Mail as a Political Tool, 0358; Use of the Party System, 0287; Use of the Radio, 0130; Use of Veto Power, 0537; Uses a Positive Image of Jefferson to Unify the Democratic Party, 9782; Various Events of the New Deal Era, 0326; Various Ways of Addressing Him, 0335; Vetoes, 0316; Vicious Attacks, 7098; Views on the Bureau of the Budget, 1967; Viewed as Improviser, Compromiser, and Opportunist, 0433; Views on Racial Matters, 5495; Visit to Liberia (1943), 0350; Visit to National Archives, (June 16, 1937), 0290; Visit to Sidney, Nebraska, 0324; Visit to South Dakota (1936), 0360; Visit with Georgia Farmers (1934), 0361; Vocabulary in War Messages, 0158; War Message (December 8, 1941), 0177; War Messages, 0181; Wash Drawing of the *Alfred*, 0199; What the 1930s Would Have Been Like Without Him, 0309; Will, 0215; World War I Origins of New Deal Labor Policy, 0408; Writings on Presidential Functions, 0180; Youth, 0029, 0036

Roosevelt, James (Father), 0037
Roosevelt Library: 9811–9830; and Oral History (1963), 9850
Roosevelt, Sara Delano, 0035, 0038
Roosevelt-Litvinov Agreement, 7412
Roosevelt Memorial, plans, 0545
Rosary College Catholic Evidence Guild, 4465
Rose, Billy, Theatrical Activities, (1925–1963), 3242
Rosenman, Samuel I.: Biography, 0756; Public Career, 0755
Rosenwald Schools and Black Education in North Carolina, 5407
Ross, Arthur M., Theories of, 2331
Ross, C. Ben: and the New Deal in Idaho, 6603; As Governor of Idaho, 6571; Political Career in Idaho (1923–1930), 6602
Ross, Nellie T., Political Career in Wyoming (1925–1950), 6486
Rotbalt, Joseph, Explains Why he Left the Bomb Project, 9407
ROTC Training, Efforts to Terminate, (1926 and 1936), 4940
Rothstein, Arthur, Photographs of the American People the Depression Years, (1936–1942), 4689
Rourke, Constance, And the Search for a Usable Past, 4802
Route 66, History, 1866
Rubber Workers: and Organized Labor, (1900–1941), 2323; Southern Strategy during the New Deal, 2322
Rubinow, Max, As an Advocate of Social Security, 4648
Rugg, Harold, Analysis of His Writings on Education, 4280
Runyon, Damon, Biography, 3223
Rural Electrification Administration: Activities and Achievements, (1936–1950), 2869; Bibliography, 9639;

Evaluation, (1935–1945), 2899; Impact on Louisiana, (1937–1983), 2946; Impact on Oregon, 2942; Impact on Rural America, 2877; in Arkansas, (1935–1940), 2929, 2934; in Montana, 1729; in North Carolina, 1728; in Sheridan County, Montana, 3069; in the South, (1920–1955), 3086; Origins, (1935), 2790, 2806, 2834

Rural Rehabilitation Corporation Projects in Arkansas, 3003

Rural Social Work Profession in America, 4241

Russell, Bertrand, Advocates Citizenship Education, 4338

Russell, Richard B.: Defends White Supremacy, 1205; Opposes Eugene Talmadge, 1204; Photographic Essay, 1201; Political Career, 1203; Senate Election, 1202

Russian Art and American Money, (1930–1938), 3710

Russian Refugees from Nazi Persecution in Princeton, New Jersey, The Story of Three Women, 4139

Russian Security and American Recognition, 7410

Russo-American Relations (1917–1939), 7409

Ruth, Babe, Myths and Images, 4608

Rutledge, Wiley, 7035

Ryan, John A.: Advocates Shorter Workweek, 2077; As an Opponent of Fascism, 4541; As Director of the Social Action Department of the National Catholic Welfare Conference, (1920–1945), 4443; Biographical Sketch, 4434; Catholic New Dealer, 4460; Critique of Henry George's Single Tax Doctrine, 2049; His Interpretation of Papal Encyclicals, 4459; Social Reform Advocate, (1892–1945), 4534

Rylander Theater of Americus, Georgia, History, 3749

Sabath, Adolph J., Supports New Deal Programs, 1242

Saint Lawrence Project, Origins, 1934

Salinas, California Lettuce Strike, (1934), 2175

San Diego: in Photographs, (1943), 3621; 1935 Fair in Photograph, 3620

San Diego Pacific International Exposition, (1935–1936), 4813

San Francisco: and Human Rights, 5731; and Red Scare, (1934), 2372; and the Bay Bridges, 4889; and the Rise of the Metropolitan-Military Complex, (1919–1941), 4938; and Waterfront Strikes (1934), 2290; Bay Area Press Photographers and the Salinas Valley Lettuce Strike of (1936), 4087; Longshoremen and Contract Sanctioned Worker's Control, (1930s–1960s), 2304; Longshoremen, History, 2157; Machinists from Depression to Cold War, (1930–1950), 2067;Political Development between World War I and World War II, 6596

San Francisco Chronicle: and the Air Mail Emergency (1934), 4047; Metamorphosis, (1935–1965), 4103

San Francisco General Strike, (1934): 2156, 2161, 2260; Newspaper Coverage, 2088; Role of California National Guard, 2247

San Joaquin Cotton Strike, (1933), 2155

San Jose, California, Social History during the Great Depression, 2294

Sanderson, Ross W., As Director of the Council of Churches in Erie County New York (1937–1942), 4488

Sandoz, Mari: Biography, 3422; Literary Apprenticeship, 3364; *Old Jules* (1935) and *Slogum House* (1937) Compared, 3503

Sandstone Creek Project: History, 1512; Western Oklahoma, 1491

Sanger, Margaret, Her Birth Control Views during the New Deal Years, 4212

Santa Clara Pueblo v. Martinez, (1977) 5887

Santayana, George: Analysis of American Culture as seen in the *Last Puritan* (1935), 3281; Letters to Sidney Hook (1929–1938), 6384

Sargent, Fred W. and the Great Depression in Chicago, 1640

Sargent, Shirley, Childhood Experiences during the Great Depression, 1706

Saturday Evening Post: Decline in Popularity (1930s), 4055; From Isolation to Intervention, (1939–1942), 4073

Saudi American Relations, Origins (1931–1943), 7623

Saville, General Gordon P., Career, 9410

Savoy Ballroom Controversy (1943), 5335

Saxon, Lyle, Analysis of His Novel *Children of Strangers* (1937), 3488

Saylesville, Rhode Island Cotton Worker's Strike, (1934), 2179

Sayre, Frances B., As High Commissioner to the Philippines (1939–1942), 7611

Scales, Junius I., Autobiography, 5544

Scalia, Antonin, His Views on Administrative Law, 6942

Scandinavian Politicians in Minnesota, 1393

Scattergood Refugee Hostile, (1939–1943), 9084

Schlatter, Richard, On Being a Communist at Harvard (1930s), 6325

Schlesinger, Arthur M. Jr., His Interpretation of Roosevelt, 9720

Schlesinger Thesis, Evaluation, 9763

Schneiderman, Rose, Labor Philosophy, 2468

Schuyler, George S., Biography, 5588

Science Advisory Board, Failure, 0556

Science Agencies in World War II, 4973

Science and Society, Contributions to Marxist Scholarship, 3989

Science Fiction, Origins (1930s), 3456

Scientific Activism, Birth (1930s), 4925

Scientific Psychiatry, Development in America, (1935–1955), 4231

Scientists as Political Activists (1930s), 4924, 4926

Scott, Anne F., Recalls her War Time Experiences, 8233

Scott, Hugh A., Recalls the Construction of the Bonneville Dam, 4079

Scottsboro Case: (1931–1950), 4702; Discussion, 5395

Screen Biography, (1929–1949), Discussion, 3764

Screen Writer's Guild, Attempts to Organize, (1930s–1940s), 3839

Screen Writers and Social Problems as Portrayed in American Film, (1936–1938), 3809

Screwball Comedies, Analysis, (1934–1941), 3731

Screws V. United States (1945), Analysis, 5425

Sears, Mary, As Public Health Nurse in California, (1938–1944), 4176

Seattle: Amusement Trades Workers Problems, (1921–1935), 2169; Municipal Politics (1930s), 6695; *Post-Intelligence* Strike (1936), 2103

Secondary Schools for Negroes, Evaluation, (1940–1946), 4320

Securities Act (1933): Impact on Stock Market, 2616; Legislative History, 2712

Securities Business and Regulation, (1930–1960), 2499

Securities Exchange Act (1934), Evaluation, 2783

Securities Exchange Commission, Origins, 2807

Securities Industry, Federal Regulation of during the New Deal, 2537

Securities, Marketing, (1930s–1940s), 1993

Segregation: in American Cities, (1940–1950), 5308; in the Military, and the Presidential Election (1940), 5607; in U.S. Army Hospitals, (1940–1942), 5626

Selective Service Act (1940), 4843

Self-Help Associations during the Great Depression, 1686

Seminoles in Oklahoma (1839–1936), 5908

Semple, Jesse B., Origins of this Langston Hughes Character, 3459

Senate: Elections in Kentucky, (1926–1948), 1115; Leadership and International Policy, 0525; Munitions Inquiry (1934–1936), 0538; Silver Bloc and the New Deal, 2672

Senate Survey of Conditions Among Indians of the United States (1928–1945), 5842

Seneca Arts Project (1935–1941), 5848

Seniority Issue in the United Auto Workers, (1934–1946), 2217

Sergeant York (1941), Production, 3788

Service, John S.: Dispatches from China (1941–1945), 8924; Explains the Loss of China, 8923

Serviceman's Readjustment Act (1944): 2075, 8256

Settlement Houses, Impact on Professionalism and Leadership, (1886–1986), 4694

Sewell, Joe and Luke, Their Careers in Major League Baseball, 4612

Sex Research Publications (1930s), 4936

Sexauer, Fred, Role in Shaping New Deal Agricultural Policies, 2938

Shahn, Ben: His Efforts to save Post Office Murals (1938), 3613; How Changes in His Social and Political Thinking Influenced His Art, (1930–1946), 3625

Shapley, Harlow, and the Asylum Fellowship Plan at Harvard, (1938–1940), 4162

Sharecroppers: Decline, 1432; Demonstration in Missouri, (1939), 2152; Plight in Southeast Missouri, 1398

Shaw, Frank L.: Recalled as Mayor of Los Angeles (1938), 6539, 6701; Reevaluation of his Recall as Mayor of Los Angeles (1937), 6720

Shawn, Ted, Performances, (1933–1940), 3152

Sheeler, Charles: Analysis of His Art, 3612; His Paintings and Photographs Representing the Machine Age, (1920s–1940s), 3712

Sheen, Fulton J., As a Reflection of the Changes in American Catholicism in the Twentieth Century, 4483

Shelter Belt Project: 1523; (1935–1942), 1438; in Nebraska, 1483

Shenandoah National Park, Creation (1924–1936), 4667

Shenandoah Resettlements, (1935), 1527

Sheppard, Morris, Political Career, 1206

Sheppard, Muriel Earley, Life, 1717

Sheppard-Towner Maternity and Infancy Act, (1918–1932), 2681

Sherwood, Robert E.: 0162; Pacifist Views, 8044

Ship Building in Tampa during World War II, 5030

Shipstead, Hendrick, Supports New Deal Farm and Labor Legislation, 1261

Shoemaker, Frances H., and Minnesota Politics, 6558

Short Term Capital Movement between the US and Great Britain, (1936–1939), 1950

Shotwell, James T., And the Rise of Internationalism in America, 7976

Shultz, David, As Governor of Florida (1930s), 6468

Silex, Humberto, Career, 2469

Silk Industry in Patterson, New Jersey: Decline, (1920–1935), 2636; Labor Conflict and Technological Improvement, (1920s–1930s), 2573

Silver, Hillel, As Head of American Zionist Emergency Council, 5754

Silver Spring, Maryland, Development (1930s), 2637

Silver Subsidy Proclamation (1933), Origins, 1975

Simmons, Rosco C., And Illinois State Politics (1920s and 1930s), 5649

Simons, Henry C.: Economic Theories, 2046, 2047

Simpson, James A.: And Politics in Birmingham, Alabama (1930s), 6414; Career, 1537; Correspondence with Roosevelt, 1538

Sims, Harold, Consul to Brazil, (1941–1945), 0878

Sims, Harry S., Supports New Deal Programs, 1207

Sims, William B., Promotes Carriers and Submarines, 0978

Sinclair, Harold, Early Writings, 3293

Sinclair, Upton: and California Politics (1924), 6628; and the 1934 Gubernatorial Campaign in California, 6434, 6584, 6619; And the EPIC Movement, 6286, Biographical Sketch, 3400, 6526; Crusade to Make California a Cooperative State, 3193; His Switch from the Socialist Party to the Democratic Party (1934), 6587; Literary and Political Career, 6505; Political Philosophy, 6329; Social and Political Thought, 6237

Sioux City, Unionization of Iowa Packing Houses, (1937–1942), 2244

Sioux Indians: and Federal Policy (1934–1965), 5827; and the Black Hills Claim, 5825; and the Civilian Indian Conservation Corps, 5821

Sit Down Strike: in Flint, Michigan, 2262, 2369; in Detroit, 2113; in Milwaukee, (1937–1938), 2239; (1930s), 2132; in the rubber Industry, (1934–1938), 2319; in the Steel Industry, Origins, 2289

Skidmore, Hubert, Analysis of Novels (1936 and 1938), 3336

Sklar, George, Career, 6330

Skyline Farms Project in Alabama, 3046

Skyscraper Construction, Nature, (1920s–1930s), 3173

Slave Narrative Collection: 9860; Discussion, 5397

Slavic-American Editorial Opinion on the Molotov-Ribbentrop Pact (1939), 4779

"Sleepy Lagoon" Case, Los Angeles (1942), 5676

Sloan, Alfred P., Jr., Memoir of Career as General Motors Chief Executive Officer, 2617

Slum Conditions in America, (1938), 1818

Small Business, Organization in Kansas City Area in World War II, 2585

Smaller War Plants Division, 8134

Smedley, Agnes, Her Activities in China (1927–1949), 6026

Smith Act (1940): Evaluation, 6197; First Use in Minnesota, (1941), 6305, 6306

Smith, Alfred E.: Attitudes and Policies (1930s), 0761; Biography, 0758, 0762, Laudatory Assessment, 0760, Leaves the Democratic Party (1932), 6490; Political Thought, 0757, 0763; Rise to National Prominence, 0759

Smith and Griggs Button and Buckle Company, Failure (1936), 2569

Smith, Gerald L. K.: And the Share Our Wealth Movement, 7117; Biography, 4510, 7118; Depression Era Activities, 7076; Notorious Anti-Semite (1940s), 5767

Smith, Lillian E., An Early White Southern Opponent of Segregation, 5459; Biographical Sketch, 4508; Biography, 3431; Views on Southern Society (1930s), 3294

Smith Mine Disaster at Bear Creek, Montana (1943), 8253

Smith, Wendell, Campaigns to Include Blacks in Organized Baseball (1933–1945), 4628

Smog, Development in Los Angeles, 1423

Smoot-Hawley Tariff: Critical Analysis, 1838; Impact, 1603

Snell, Bertrand H.: and the New Deal (1933–1939), 6114, 7068; Efforts to Salvage the Republican Party (1933–1939), 6030

Snow, Edgar, Views of China, 8900

Snow White and the Seven Dwarfs (1937), and Advanced Animation Techniques, 3812

Soboba Indians, California, A Case Study in the Loss of Kinship Structure, 5836

Social Banditry in Depression America, 4738

Social Consciousness and Moral Outrage as Themes in American Literature during the Great Depression, 3314

Social Drama, Emergence in American Theater (1920s–1930s), 3196

Social Economics, Development at the University of California, Berkley, 4289

Social Education, Changes World View, (1937–1979), 3969

Social Frontier Journal (Founded 1934), Historical Sketch, 3951

Social Gospel Theology (1918–1946), 4442

Social Justice, History, (1936–1942), 4030

Social Justice Movement, Politics, 4471

Social Re-Constructionism, Views from the Left and Right, (1932–1942), 4272

Social Science and the Debate Over its Role in America (1930s), 4412

Social Security Act (1935): Analysis, 2801, 5074, 5119; and Politics (1935–1965), 6036; and Public Opinion, 6857; and Welfare Capitalism, 5092; Background, 2835, 2908; Board, Establishment, 5131; Conservative Critique, (1980), 2808; Conservative Critique, 2827; Critique of Payroll Tax Policy, 2848; Development, 2673; Employment Assurance Provision in Original Version, 2879 Origins, 5037; Evaluation, (1977), 2794, 5151; First Crises, (1935–1939), 2784; Impact of Titles I and II on Elderly Black Americans, 5589; Impact on Black Needy Children (1935–1985), 5569; Impact on the Elderly, 5106; Legislative History, 5163; of the United States and New Zealand Compared, 4235; Policy Changes with Respect to Economic Conditions, 4237; Retirement Program, Origins, 2791; Retirement Program, How it Functions, 5086; Sociological Analysis of Factor Leading to its Political Success, (1935–1985), 5100; State-Federal Cooperation (1935–1946), 5145; Why Work Relief Was Dropped from the Original Measure, 4236

Social Settlement Response to the Great Depression, 1714

Social Welfare: Attitudes in California (1930s), 4221; Guide to Manuscripts, 9831; System, Evolution of, (1900–1940), 4190

Social Work: and Policy in the United States, History, 2653; Development as a Profession, (1930–1960), 4216; in America, Efforts to Reform, (1939–1950), 4660; in St. Louis, (1920–1940), 4213; Social Welfare, and the Social Security Act, 4661

Social Workers, Unionization during the New Deal, 2231

Socialism, Failure in America, 6351

Socialist Movement: in America, History, 6257; Strength (1930s), 6245

Socialist Party: and the Election (1932), 6853; and the Trotskyists, 6294; and Women in Reading, Pennsylvania, (1927–1936), 6310 History, 6337; Impact on the Trade Union Movement, 6333

Socialist Protest Writers, 6206

Socialist Review, Appraisal, 3999

Society for American Archeology, Formation (1934), 4883

Society for the Psychological Study of Social Issues:(1936–1945), 4305; Early History, 2198; Origins, 4931

Society of American Archivists, Founding (1936), 4379

Sociological Journals, Publishing Patterns, (1929–1945), 4301

Sociological Theory in the United States, (1930–1945), 4351

Soft Coal Industry, Failure of New Deal Programs to Revitalize, 2552

Soil Conservation, 1298

Soil Conservation Movement, Evolution, 1416

Soil Conservation Practices, Impact of New Deal, 1519

Soil Conservation Programs, Development, 1418

Soil Conservation Service: Analysis, (1933–1954), 2804; and Anthropologists on the Navajo Reservation (1930s), 5859; and Farm Woodland Management, (1938–1945), 1500; History, 1484; Impact on Great Plains Farmers, 3100

Soil Erosion Research (1930s), 1492

Solid South, Evaluation, 6420

Sommerville, Nelly N. and Lucy S., Political Careers in Mississippi, 5953

Song Writing, Development (1920s and 1930s), 3247

Sorensen, Virginia, Career as a Writer, 5938

Sorghum, Development in South Dakota during the Depression, 1509

Soroyan, William, Theatrical Philosophy, 3228

South Brooklyn, Operation of Political System (1920–1935), 6726

South Carolina Council for the Common Good, (1935–1977) 6014

South Carolina Equal Rights Movement (1930–1939), 5418

South Carolina, and Higher Education for Women, (1920–1940), 4365

South Dakota: Agriculture, Effects of Mechanization, 1446; and Presidential Election (1932), 6745; Women Writers and the Pioneer Heroine, (1922–1939), 3272

South Dakotans', Reaction to *The Plow that Broke the Plains* (1936), 3802

South, Marshal, Life Atop Ghost Mountain, (1932–1946), 4068

South, Politics and Society (1920s to the 1980s), 6433

Southern Agrarian Movement (1930s), 3421

Southern Agrarians: A Thirty Year Perspective, 3442; Their Resentment towards H. L. Mencken, 4080

Southern Agricultural Press and Rural Problems, (1900–1940), 4048

Southern Agriculture, Impact of Out Migration, (1930–1940), 4150

Southern Attitudes toward Industrial Unions, (1933–1941), 2409

Southern Baptists: and the "Okie" Migration, 4545; Response to Threats to Peace (1931–1941), 4481

Southern Black Writers, Bibliography, 9604

Southern Conference for Human Welfare: (1938–1948), 4649; Nashville convention of, (1942), 4234

Southern Congressmen and Foreign Policy (1938–1948), 6555

Southern Cotton Textile Workers Letters to Roosevelt, 2061

Southern Demagogues: Theodore Bilbo, Eugene Talmadge, Huey Long; and Gerald L. K. Smith, 7130

Southern Economic Development and Federal Policy, (1933–1980), 1943

Southern Family Ideology, (1920–1940), 4693; Labor in Politics, (1943–1975), 2338

Southern Liberal Journalists: (1920–1940), 6865; Hodding Carter; Gerald Johnson; and Ralph McGill, (1938–1954), 6864

Southern Literary Renaissance (1930s), 3513

Southern Methodists and Unification, First Phase, (1939), 4574

Southern Negro Youth Congress: (1937–1949), 5429; History, 5533

Southern Newsprint Paper Industry, Birth (1927–1940), 4964

Southern Plantations, Transformation, (1920–1960), 1392

Southern Political Thought (1930–1948), 6047

Southern Poor Whites in the 1930s, Literary Treatment, 1659

Southern Renaissance Writers, 3395

Southern Review: and the Baton Rouge Literary Community, (1935–1942), 3321; History, (1935–1942), 3486, 4091; Origins, (1935), 3954

Southern Scientists (1883–1940), 4954

Southern Sectionalism, Resurgence (1933–1955), 6523

Southern Senators and Role Call Votes (1941–1944), 6046

Southern States Art League, (1922–1950), 3664

Southern Summer School for Women Workers, (1927–1941), 5936

Southern Tenant Farmers' Union: 1329, 1352, 1405; and Commonwealth College, 6217; and Socialist Critics of the New Deal, 6190, 7067; Founding and Early History, 1548; History, 1536, 1558; Origins, 1386, 2138; Pictorial History, 2306

Southern Transient System, Desegregation (1937–1965), 5302

Southern Women as seen by *Progressive Farmer* (1930s), 6018

Southwestern Agricultural Experiment Stations during the New Deal, 1488

Southwestern Pennsylvania, Poverty and Isolation, 0686

Soviet American Relations: (1917–1933), 7425; (1929–1941), 7440; (1933–1938), 7426; and the Far East (1933–1941), 7570

Soviet and American Negotiation Behavior Compared, 7431

Soviet Diplomacy (1918–1930), 7435

Soviet Foreign Policy: (1917–1941), 7423, 7430; and the Great Purges, 7453; as Perceived in the United States, 7441

Soviet Occupation of Lithuania, U.S. Non-Recognition, 7454

Soviet Participation in the War Against Japan, Documents, 9684

Soviet Policies toward the United States (1919–1939), 7449

Soviet Russia: the Munich Crisis and Historiographical Debate, 9799; as Portrayed in Hollywood Films (1940s), 3816

Soviet Union: and American Travelers (1917–1932), 7422; and Diplomatic Recognition, 7443; and Latin America (1918–1936), 7419; and Public Opinion in the United States (1939–1945), 7881; and the Munich Agreement, 8877; and the War in the East, 8867; and the War in the West, 8866; and the War with Japan, 8869; as Viewed by American Diplomats in the Balkans (1944–1946), 8827; under Lenin and Stalin, 7429

Soy Bean Cultivation, Rise, 1349

Spaatz, Carl A., And the U.S. Army Air Force, 9273

Space Race, Origins (1933), 5001

Spanish Civil War: American Response, 7357; and America, 7368; and American and British Literature, 7379; and American Catholic Dissenters, 7392; and American Catholics, 7394, 7396; and American Commissars, 7385; and American Foreign Policy, 7361, 7390; and American Neutrality, 7378; and American Pilots, 7372 and American Volunteers, 7360; and Boston's Catholics (1936–1939), 7359; and Ernest Hemingway, 7375; and the Abraham Lincoln Brigade, 7380; and the Coming of World War II, 7365; and the Economic Influence of the Great Powers, 7399; as Depicted in Art and Literature, 3368; Impact on Liberal Novelists, 7354; Origins, 7366; Reaction in North Dakota, (1936–1939), 7374; Sources of Financial Support for the Nationalists, 7400

Spanish Foreign Policy and World War II, 7351

Spanish Language Films Made in Hollywood (1930s), 3818

Sparkman, John, Promotes Veterans' Benefits, 1104

"Specialized Catholic Action," (1936–1949), 4558

Spellman, Cardinal, Involvement in Politics and Church Activities during the Roosevelt Years, 4489

Squalus, Sinking and Recovery (1939), 4967

St. Louis: Fighting for Civil Rights during World War II, 5291; The Black Community (1920–1940), 5349

St. Louis Tragedy, 9122

Stafford, Jean and Evelyn Scott, Correspondence (1930s), 3324

Stafford, William, Recollections of a Conscientious Objector, 3480

Stalin, Joseph: 9222–9227, and the Politics of the Second Front (1941–1943), 8845; and the Prospects for a Separate Peace, 8864; Refuses to Allow U.S. to Build Air Bases in Soviet Territory, 8849

Standard Oil Company: Operations in Bolivia, (1922–1937), 1758; Operations in Hungary, (1938–1948), 1757

Standard Radio Transcription Company, Rise and Decline, (1934–1954), 3911

Standard-Vacuum Oil Company, And Origins of World War II, (1933–1941), 1744

Standley, Admiral William H.: And the Second London Naval Treaty (1934–1936), 7829; As Ambassador to the Soviet Union (1942–1943), 8881; Promotes Naval Expansion, 0979

Stark, Admiral Harold R.: Memorandum to Roosevelt Concerning Strategy in the Atlantic and Pacific Areas (1940), 8576; Promotes Naval Expansion, 0980

State Aid to Education Improves Quality, (1930–1949), 4395

State Department: and Soviet American Relations (1918–1938), 7448; Efforts to Convince Americans that Big is Better during World War II, 2491; Reports on Red Chinese Strength (1927–1934), 7459; Training of Soviet Experts, (1927–1937), 7447

Stateless European Jews, State Department Documents (1942–1944), 9659

Steagall, Henry B., Political Career, 1105

Steel and Auto Workers in Los Angeles, Problems, (1935–1986), 2177

Steel Industry: Attempts to Organize, (1936–1942), 2274, 2281; Workers Organizing Committee Activities in Granite city, Illinois, (1937), 2072

Steelman, John R., 0559

Steichen, Edward, and Advertising Photography (1920s and 1930s), 3659

Stein, Gertrude: Analysis of Her Works, 3404; Contributions to American Opera, 3524; Her Poem: "Love Like Anything," 3604

Steinbeck, John: 1930s Photo-Recollection, 3477; Analysis of His Works, 3351; and the Federal Migrant Camps, 4024; Background of the Creation of *The Grapes of Wrath,* 3407; Critical Analysis of His Short Stories, 3384; Dating His Short Story "How Mrs. McGillicuddy Met Robert Lewis Stevenson" (1934), 3514; Degree of Realism in *Dubious Battle,* 3287; Efforts to Suppress His Novel *The Grapes of Wrath* in Kern County, California, 3396; First theatrical Production of *Of Mice and Men,* (1937), 3213; His Ideas in *The Grapes of Wrath* (1939) Compared to Those of Charles Darwin Regarding the Role of Man in the Natural World, 3462; His Image of the West, 3470; His Place in American Literature, 3350; His Political Views, 3441; His Preoccupation with the Relationship between Man and the Environment, 3426; and the Influence of the Hispanic World, 3515; Literary Career, 3512; Modern America's Problems as seen in His Novels, 3378; Non-Fiction Writings, 3437; Relationship with Lincoln Steffens, 3408; Social Criticism in his Fiction, 3474; Use of Non-Teleological Thinking in his Mexican-American Characters, 3354

Steinhardt, Laurence A.: And American Policy toward the Soviet Union (1939–1941), 7444; As Ambassador to Turkey, 7827; Diplomatic Career, 0879

Stella, Joseph, His Activities as an Artist (1935–1946), 3657

Stephenson, Riggs, Memories of a Baseball Player (1920s–1930s), 4605

Sterilization Movement in the United States, History, 4229

Stern, Guy, Reflects on German Culture, 9160

Stettheimer, Florine, Analysis of Her Work, (1929–1944), 3686

Stettinius, Edward R. Jr., And the London Mission (1944), 8756; Diaries, 0880

Stevens, Ernest E., New Deal Artist, 5041

Stevens, Lewis M., And Political Reform in Philadelphia (1930s), 6642

Stevens, Wallace: His Poetry (1930s), 3596; Right Wing Political Bias in His Prose, 3454

Stieglitz Circle, Paintings and Photographs (1924–1934), 3628

Stilwell, General Joseph W.: Biography, 8930; Career in Asia, 0960; Conflict with Chiang Kai-Shek, 0957; Failure to Support Chiang Kai-Shek, 0956; In China (1942–1944), 8905; Papers, 0959; Personal File, 0958

Stimpson Doctrine (1929–1940), 8892

Stimpson, Henry L.: Biography, 0884; Combination Memoir and Biography, 0886; Diary Entry, (25 November 1941), 0881; Dispute with Sir John Simon, 0883; Opinions on League of Nations, 0885; Role in Creation of World Crisis, 0882

Stock Market: Analysis, (1929–1933), 1650; Crash (1929), Literature, 3285

Stockton, California: Cannery Strike, (1937), 2349; Port Construction Project, 4890

Stokes, Thomas L., Impressions of the New Deal, 2760

Stone, Edward D., and the International Style in America (1930s), 3180

Stone, Harlan F., 7036–7039

Stone, I. F., Life and Career, 3967

Stored Program Concept, Development (1943–1946), 4998

Straton, Hillyer, His Critique of *Middle Town*, 6581

Stritch, Samuel, And Milwaukee Catholicism, (1930–1940), 4440

Strong, Anna L.: Biography, 6303; Communist Apologist, 6312

Stryker, Roy: and the Farm Security Administration Photography project, 2833, 2883

Student Activism at the University of Florida, (1936–1939), 4399

Student Demonstrations (1930s to the 1960s), 4358

Student Employment at the University of Kansas, (1934–1943), 4410

Student Opposition to War (1930s), 8001

Student Peace Movement in the U.S. (1930–1941), 8011

Sturges, Preston: Analysis of his Writing Technique, 3757; Screenwriter and Director (1940s), 3741

Stuyvesant Town Controversy, New York, (1943), 1786

Su, Lin, First Panda Brought to the United States from China, 7460

Sugar Act (1934), Economic and Diplomatic Effects, 2542

Sugar Beet Workers and the Federal Government (1930s), 5689

Sugar Hill, A Black Neighborhood in New York City, 5488

Sullens, Frederick, A Southern Editor Views the National Scene (1930s), 4082

Sullivan, Anna, Career, 2470

Sullivan, Mark: As Critic of the New Deal, 7078; His Friendship with Herbert C. Hoover, 7126

Sun Rise Colony, (1933–1936), 4666, 5779

Supreme Court: and Racial Exclusion Cases (1935–1960), 5572; Cases Involving Civil Rights (1940), 5391; Justices, Nominations (1789–1974), 6968

Sustained-Yield Forest Management Act (1944), 8141

Swabeck, Arne, Interviews Leon Trotyski (1933), 6342

Swanson, Claude A., Biography, 0664

Swanson, Robert, Criminal Activities, 4712

Swedish-Americans and the Depression Years (1929–1932), 4772

Sweezy, Paul M., Activities as a Socialist Intellectual (1920s–1980s), 6344

Swing Music in New York City (1930s), 3561

Swing, Raymond Gram, Career as Radio New Commentator (1930s), 3884; Radio News Commentaries, (1939–1945), 3919

Swisher, Perry, Childhood Experiences during the Great Depression, 1713

Sykes, Eugene O., His Impact on the Development of the Broadcasting Industry, 3905

Synthetic Fuel Industry, Failure to Develop in the Untied States, 4855

Synthetic Rubber, Invented during World War II, 4895

Szilard, Leo, And the Manhattan Project, 4887

T-Formation, Origins, 4594

Table Rock Dam, Development, 1459

Taft, Robert A., Foreign Policy Views, 1262–1265

Tales from the 30s, 1681

Talmadge, Eugene F., and the Georgia Textile Strike (1934), 2102; And the University System of Georgia (1941–1942), 8426; Attempts to Purge the University of Georgia of "Communists", 6416; Depression Era Activities, 7076; Dispute with Walter Cocking, 1209, 1211; Dominates Georgia Politics, (1927–1946), 1212; Political Career, 1208; Speaking Ability, 1210

Tamiment Playhouse, (1931–1960), 3231

Tampa, Florida, Labor Organizers Kidnaped and Flogged, (1935), 4723

Tansill, Charles C., Revisionist Historian, 9747

Tarbell, Ida M., Her Public Speaking Career (1905–1941), 6017

Tarzan Films (1930s), 3797

Tate, Allan, Agrarian Period, (1926–1938), 3307

Tatsuguchi, Paul N., His Attu Diary (1943), 5729

Taylor, "School Boy" Johnny, Pitches No hitter against Satchel Paige (1937), 4602

Taylor, Glen H., Political Career, 6847

Taylor Grazing Act (1934), Impact, 1515

Taylor, Myron C.: Appointment as Minister to the Vatican, 0889; As American Emissary to the Vatican (1939–1945), 4520; As Roosevelt's Emissary to the Vatican During World War II, 4494; Mission to the Vatican, (1940–1950), 0887, 0888

Teachers Union in Saint Louis, Origins, 2182, 2183

Teamsters: Efforts to Organize in Sioux Falls, South Dakota, (1930s), 2358; Organized in Sioux City, Iowa, (1933–1938), 2356

Teheran Conference, 8591, 8597, 8600, 8619, 8623, 8625, 8626, 8634

Technocracy Inc., Failure, 4673

Technocracy Movement: 4908; (1932), 6823; (1900–1941), 4810

Technological Change in the Pulp and Paper Industry, (1915–1940), 2510

Technological Problems in Switching from Silent Movies to the "Talkies," 3758

Technological Trends and National Policy (1937), 4909

Technology and the Domestic Market (1930s), 4835

Telephones, Declining Use in Rural America (1920–1940), 4872

Televised Sports, Early Years, (1937–1947), 3872

Television: in Los Angeles, Early History, (1931–1952), 3922, 3927, 3931

Tenancy, Its Role in the South (1930s), 5293

Tenant Farming: Decline, 1346; Decline of in the South, 1324; History, 1355

Tenant Unions in NYC, (1933–1949), 1816

Tennessee Churches (1930s), 4504

Tennessee Valley Authority: Analysis, 2683; and Grass Roots Democracy, 4670; As a Social and Educational Enterprise, (1933–1953), 3125; and Southern Agrarians, 3130; As Symbol of a Democratic Society, 2910; Background, 2909; Benefits of Flood Control Projects, 3101; Changing Nature, 2671; Conservative Critique by Donald Davidson, 3129; Development (1943), 3123; Electric Home and Farm Authority Project, 3095; Grave Relocation Project, (1933–1936), 3116; History, (1933–1973), 3131; History, (1933–1983), 3120; Impact of Regional Planning on Blacks, 5400; Impact on Farmers in Tishomingo, Mississippi (1934–1950), 5280; Impact on Governmental Institutions in the South, 3124; Impact on Memphis, 3083; Impact on Ordinary Farmers, 3092; Impact on the Environment, 3127; Internal Debates over Power Distribution, 3090; Non-Power Activities, 3087; Origins, 3103, 3139; Records, 9662; Resettlement Program, 3117; Role in the Development of the Tennessee Valley, 3091; Shift to Steam and Nuclear Power Electricity Production, 3114; Stimulates Regional Growth, (1933–1953), 2918; versus Private Enterprise, (1933–1939), 3115; versus Private Power Industry, (1934–1939), 3085; Water Management Policies, 3128; Wendell Willkie's connection, 0766

Tenney, Jack B.: And Anti-Communist Legislation in California (1940–1949), 6130; Political Career in California (1940–1949), 6693

Terrell, Mary Eliza Church, Biography, 5972

Tetton County, Wyoming, Transformation from an Isolated Mountain Region to a Modern Vacation land, 5239

Texas Agricultural Experiment Station, Amarillo, 1487

Texas: and Labor Discrimination, (1940–1944), 4173; and the Mexican Labor Question (1942–1947), 9056; Attitudes toward Relief, 1648; Church Humor (1940s), 4117; Congressional Delegation (1933–1938), 6651; Folklorists and the Emergence of a Post-Regional

Consciousness, 3425; Newspapers and Internationalism, (1944–1945), 4013; Origins of Negro Peace Officer Association (1935), 5367; Panhandle, World War II Era Photographs, 3641; Politics (1938–1957), 6524; Politics, Far Right Wing (1930s to 1960s), 6118; Radicals during the Great Depression, 1722; University, and its Football Program (1930s), 4596

Textbooks of the 1930s, Treatment of the Depression, Roosevelt, and the Rise of Fascism, 4411

Textile Industry in the South, Worker Interviews, (1880–1940), 2538

Textile Workers Sit Down Strike, Covington, Virginia, (1937), 2206

Textile Workers Union of America: Activities in Henderson, North Carolina, (1943–1958), 2160; in the South, (1937–1945), 2347

The City (1939), Its Focus on the Urban Crises (1930s), 3761

The Outlaw (1943), Discussion, 3815

The Party Organizer, Communist Periodical (1927–1937), 6346

The River, Critical Study, 5093

Theater: Analysis (1930), 3202; as Cultural Indicator, (1920s–1930s), 3205; Federal Involvement, (1939–1965), 3191; Guild, (1928–1939), 3261

Theatrical Workers, Unionization (1939), 2230

Theoretical Physics in the United States (1920–1950), 4986

Thiry, Paul, And Emergence of Modernism in Northwest Architecture (1930s), 3163

Thomas, Elbert D., Foreign Policy Influence, 1062

Thomas, J. Parnell, 0520

Thomas, Norman: and Arkansas Sharecroppers, 3136; And the Failure of the Socialist Party in America, 6321; And the Socialist Party of America, 6239, 6288; And the Townsend Convention (1936), 6349; Criticizes Agricultural Adjustment Act, 2950; His Anti-War Speeches (1939–1941), 8503; His Role in the Socialist Party (1912–1948), 6317; Political Career, 6261; Political Leadership, 6331; Social Theory, 6332

Thomason, Eugene Healan, His Artistic Portrayal of the Inhabitants of Rural North Carolina, 3658

Thompsen, Hans, and German-American Relations (1938–1941), 7284

Thurber, James: and the Great Depression, 3277; His Little Man Characters (1930s), 3280; Relations with Harold Wallace Ross, 4092

Timber Management Program in the New Deal, Development, 1428

Timberline Lodge, Oregon, History, 5240, 5243

Tinker Air Force Base, Oklahoma City, Origins, 1880

Tire Industry, and Structural Change (1920–1937), 2529

Tittle, Ernest F., As Critic of the American Social Order, 4556

Tobin, Maurice J.: 0764; and the Decline of Bossism in Boston, 6583; New Deal Democratic in Boston, 6582

Tojo and the Coming of War, 7493

Tokunosuke, Abe, Efforts to Develop a Tuna Fleet in San Diego, 5715

Tokyo Rose, 8496

Toledo: Auto-Lite Strike, (1934), 2271; Chevrolet Strike, (1935), 2196; City Council Elections (1934–1949), 6408; Industrial Peace Board (Part V), 3050; Industrial Peace Board (Parts I and II), 3048; Industrial Peace Board (Parts III and IV), 3049

Toll Road Movement, Origins, 1870

Tolley, Howard, New Deal Career, 1564

Tomorrow, A Film About Southern Life, 3720

Tool and Die Markers Strike, (1933), 2197

Topical Satire and the Temper of the Early 1930s, 3996

Tortilla Flat (1935), Analysis, 3273

Tough Guy Writers (1930s), 3362, 3412

Touring California during the Great Depression, 1704

Townsend Movement: 6833; Analysis (1936), 7169; Evaluation, 6444; Origins, 7110

Toys and Sex Roles in America (1920–1940), 4686

Tractors: Ownership during the Great Depression, 1385; Growth of their Use in California (1930s and 1940s), 4818; Prices, (1923–1933), 1383

Tracy, Dick, Reflects American Social History, 4065

Trade Policy, Twentieth Century changes, 1836

Trade Union Growth in the US, (1900–1960), 2107

Trammel Park, Political Biography, 6567

Trans-Canadian, Alaskan, and Western Railways, 1928

Transiency in New York State, 1660, 2650, 2651; in the U.S., 2649; in Texas, 1723

Transport Workers Union: Activities, (1934–1944), 2301; of New York City, (1933–1948), 2204

Transportation Act (1940), Opposition, 1855

Traylor, Bill, Street Artist in Montgomery, Alabama, (1930s), 3703

Treasure of Victoria Peak, 1684

Treasury Section of Fine Arts: Murals Project, 5141; Mural Projects in the South, 5273; Post Office Murals, 5080; Post Office Mural Project in Michigan, 5219, 5220

Tree Planting on the Great Plains, 1443

Trilling, Lionel: Critical Thought and Social Commentary (1930s and 1940s), 4793; Recalls His Youth (1930s), 3490

Trotskyites, Eliminated from Teamsters Union (1941), 2255

Trotsky, Leon: Trial (1937), 6353; His Letters Housed at Yale University, 6192

Trucking Industry, Emergence of Federal Regulation, 1858, 1859

Truman Committee, Activities, 6098

Truman, Harry S.: As U.S. Senator, 0612; As Vice President, 0609, 0610; Biography, 0606; Chair of Senate Committee to Investigate National Defense Program, 0615; Concern for Blacks, 0605; Early Political Career, 0600; Election to the U.S. Senate (1934), 0603, 0613; Path to Power, 0608; Political Beliefs, 0614; Relationship to Pendergast, 0601, 0607, 0611; Relationship with Senator Josiah Bailey of North Carolina, 0604; Review of the Literature (1979), 9767; Senate Voting Record, 0602

Tucker, Lorenzo, Stage and Screen Career, 3216

Tucson-Phoenix High School Football Game, and Violence (1937), 4591

Tugwell, Rexford G.: and City Planning in New York, 0714; As Governor of Puerto Rico, 0718; As Prime Mover of Greenbelt Town Plan, 0715; Biographical Sketch, 0712; Memoir, 0717; New Deal Ideology, 0716; Views on Municipal Planning, 0713; Writings, 5052

Tureaud, Alexander P., Legal Career, 5593

Turkish-American Relations: (1930s), 7404; in the Inter War Period, 7402, 7403

Tuskegee Flight Training Program (1934–1942), 5617

Twentieth Century Farm Strikes, Comment, 1540

Twining, Nathan F., Biography, 0961

Tydings, Millard E., Opposed by Roosevelt for Reelection (1938), 1266

Tyler, Ralph W., Career of a Progressive Educator, 4347

Typewriter as an Agent of Change (1867–1954), 4844

Twentieth Century American Radicalism, Bibliography, 9599

U.S.S. *Panay*, Sinking, 9387

Ultra, 9277

Ultra-Conservative Thought in the United States (1920s and 1930s), 6124

Ulysses, Ruled not to be Obscene in Court, (1933), 4740

Underclass, Rise as a Permanent Group, 4224

Underwood, Felix J., and the Mississippi State Board of Health, (1924–1958), 4194

Unemployed Citizens League in Seattle (1931–1932), 7138

Unemployed, Inc. of Minneapolis, (1932–1935), 2484

Unemployed Leagues, (1932–1936), 2480

Unemployed Worker's Movement, (1930s), 2485

Unemployment: (1929–1933), and Radical Response, 2479; among Professionals during the Early Depression, 2482; during the Great Depression, 2472, 2475, 2476, 2477; Historical Analysis, 2487; in Denver during the Great Depression, 2478; in Hawaii during the Great Depression, 2481; in the 1920s and 1930s Compared, 1657; Reform in America, Origins, 2489; Relief before the New Deal, 2483

Unemployment Insurance: at the State Level (1930s), 6407; History, 1973, 2857, 2858

Union Activity: in Austin, Minnesota, (1933–1937), 2162; in Chicago, 1930s, 2399; Impact, (1930s–1940s), 2308

Union: Attitudes toward Government in Industrial Relations, (1900–1948), 2184; Avoidance Strategy in the Rubber Industry, 1930s, 2318; Development in Voluntary Social Work, (1930–1950), 2101; Growth in America, (1880–1960), 2386; Leaders in General Electric and Westinghouse, (1933–1937), 2363; Membership, Growth in the South, (1939–1953), 2389; Officialdom during the

New Deal, Collective Evaluation, 2417, 2418; Organization Suppressed in Nevada County, California, 1938, 2120; Rivalry in Detroit during World War II, 2364

Union Parish, Louisiana Conspiracy (1933), 5586

Union Party: (1932–1936), 6816; Activities (1936), 6826; Origins, (1936), 2121, 6844, 6845

Union Township, New Jersey Schools and the Depression (1929–1938), 4279

Unionism: and Work Related Safety in the Bituminous Coal Industry, (1898–1945), 2158; in Gadsden, Alabama, (1930–1943), 2292; in the full-Fashioned Hosiery Industry, Reading, Pennsylvania, (1936–1937), 2268; in the Alaskan Canned Salmon Industry, 2293

Unionization: Among Domestic Workers, (1870–1940), 2392, 2393; at New York Ship, Federal Ship, and Fore River, (1898–1945), 2334; Impact on San Francisco Longshoremen, 2261; Impact on Wages in the Transit industry, (1920–1948), 2288

Unions: and Politics in Washington State, (1885–1935), 2172; and the Growth of Workers' Organizations in the United States (1930s), 2220

United Auto Workers: and Communism, 2269; and Michigan State Politics, (1930s–1970s), 2149; and Polish Workers in Detroit, 2256; and Women, (1935–1955), 2208; Case Study, (1935–1948), 2200;Communist Influence, 2263; Communists and Factionalism, (1937–1939), 2265; Decline of Communist Influence in during World War II, 2264; Development of Local 287, Muncie, Indiana, 2165; Education Program, (1936–1959), 2285; Early History, 2246 Factionalism, (1937–1941), 2141; Failure of Left-Center Coalition, (1937–1955), 2310; in Hamtramck, Michigan, (1936–1939), 2205; Origins, (1933–1935), 2195; Sit Down Strike in Atlanta, (1936), 2233

United Cannery, Agricultural, Packing, and Allied Workers of America: Organizing Activities in Texas, (1935–1950), 2326; Origins, 2325

United Congo Improvement Association, Efforts to Establish a Colony in Alaska (1935–1938), 5501

United Electrical and Radio Workers of America: Internal Discord, (1933–1949), 2189; Origins, (1933–1937), 2190

United Farmer's League of South Dakota, 1546

United Mine Workers of America: and the Election (1934), 2163; Development, (1932–1933), 2259; District 11 of Indiana (1930–1940), 2203; History, (1890–1939), 2297; in Horlon County, Kentucky, (1931–1939), 2384; Legislative Policies, (1933–1947), 2188; Reorganization in Pennsylvania during the New Deal, 2258

United Nations: and Cultural Relations, 9459; and the Presbyterian Church, 9461; and the State Department, 9456; and U.S. Policy (1944–1945), 9453, 9454; and Unfulfilled Expectations, 9462; Charter, 9455; Founding, 9451, 9457

United States Armed Forces: Desegregation (1933–1953), 5606, 5608; Desegregation during World War II, 5619; Problems of Racism and Segregation (1940–1950), 5618

United States Army: Condition (1919–1941), 5013; (1930s), 4955; History of War College (1901–1940), 4820; Maneuvers in Tennessee (1941), 4850; Maneuvers in Wisconsin (1940s), 4861; Political Rivalry with the Marines before World War II, 4957; Recruiting Activities Between the Wars, 4956; Training Maneuvers in Louisiana (1941), 4839

United States Children's Bureau, Health Services, (1935–1953), 4197

United States Congress, Conservative Coalition (1933–1980), 6133

United States Department of Agriculture, and the Navajo (1930s), 5877

United States Film Service, History, 5158

United States: Aid to France (1938–1940), 8696; Air Power (1941), 9304; and Agricultural Assistance to Bolivia (1941–1974), 9036; and Aid to China (1941–1942), 8897; and Aid to China, (1941–1946), 8895; and Aid to the Chinese Nationalist Air Force (1931–1949), 8914; and Argentina (1943–1948), 7655; and Arms Inspections, (1926–1946), 9255; and Aviation Diplomacy in Brazil (1939–1941), 7659; and Aviation Diplomacy in Colombia (1939–1940), 7664; and Bolivia (1941–1946), 9035; and Brazilian Alliance, 9041; and Brazilian Relations, 7657 9042, 9043; and British, 8727, 8741, 8754, 8762; Business and the Coming of World War II (1935–1941), 8057; and Canadian Defense Cooperation, 8676; and Canadian Military Relations (1939–1945), 8673 and Canadian Mutual Defense Agreement, 8672; and Caribbean Policy (1939–1945), 9045; Center of Military History, Publications (1977–1978), 9691 and China (1938–1945), 8901, 8908, 8913, 8921; and Colombia (1938–1942), 7662; and Colonial Sub-Sahara-Africa (1939–1945), 8661; and Cuba (1933–1945), 7672; and Cuba during the New Deal Era, 7667; and Education in Haiti (1915–1934), 7683, 7684; and El Salvador (1930s), 7678; and Fascism (1936–1945), 9063; and French Aircraft Purchases, 8693, 8694; and French Guiana, 9049; and French North Africa (1940–1942), 8705; and Guatemala (1933–1956), 7679; and Haiti (1902–1934), 7685; and Hemispheric Solidarity (1939–1941), 7642; and India (1940–1955), 8940, 8941; and India and Pakistan, Historiographical Essay (1987), 9744; and Indo-China (1942–1945), 8948; and Indonesian Independence (1944–1947), 8954; and Iran (1941–1947), 8976, 8977, 8979 and Ireland (1941), 8781; and Italy (1943–1946), 8782, 8783, 8785; and Japan Commercial Disputes (1930s), 7540; and Japan, 7502, 7509,7516, 7521, 7528, 7532, 7544, 7561 7584, 7586, 7589, 7596, 7604, 7858, 7893, 8949, 9771; and Jewish Refugees (1934–1945), 9075; and Labor Organization, (1937), 2561; and Latin America, 7627, 7646, 7653, 9010, and Liberia, 7247, 7248 7249, 8662, 8663, 8664; and Mexico, 7686, 7690, 7692, 9050; and Military Preparedness (1938–1940), 9311; and Naval Arms Limitation

(1921–1938), 7537; and Palestine, 9006; and Panama, 7694, 7696, 7697, 7698, 7699; and Peace Movements Before Munich, Historiography (1969), 9762; and Philippine Independence Policy (1926–1941), 7615; and Plans for a Post War Pro-Western Bulgaria, 8802; and Poland (1941–1945), 8811; and Portugal Relations (1945), 8787; and Power Politics in the Middle East (1941–1947), 8973; and relations with Canada and Great Britain (1932–1942), 7252; and Russia, 8820, 8830; and Saudi Arabia, 7624, 8986, 8990; and Slovakia during World War II, 8812; and Syria (1941–1949), 8987; and the Anglo-American Statement on Palestine (1943), 9005; and the Anglo-Iraqi Crisis (1940–1941), 8975; and the Australian-New Zealand Agreement (1944), 8670; and the Balkan Crisis (1940–1941), 8798; and the Berlin Olympics (1936), 7851; and the Break Down of Naval Arms Limitations (1933–1939), 9243; and the British Economy (1938–1939), 8758; and the British International Finance Crisis (1940–1941), 8749; and the Caribbean (1914–1941), 7700; and the Chinese Revolution, 8912, 8925; and the Cold War (1943–1954), 8801; and the Coming of Constitutional Government in Thailand, 8961; and the Crisis in Iran (1941–1947), 8978; and the Crusade in China (1938–1945), 8922; and the Cuban Revolution (1933), 7668; and Cultural Relations with China (1942–1945), 8910; and the Decision to assist Greece, 8774; and the Defense of Shanghai, (1931–1941), 8911; and the Defense of Singapore, 8960; and the Dominican Republic (1930–1940), 7677; and the Dominican Republic during the Roosevelt Era, 7675;and the Economic Development of Puerto Rico during the 1930s and World War II, 7707; and the Emergence of Pakistan (1940–1947), 8957; and the Failure of Collective Security in (1930s), 7934; and the Far Eastern Crisis (1933–1938), 7853; and the Fate of European Jews (1933–1945), 9087; and the Forced Repatriation of Soviet Citizens (1944–1947), 8832; and the Grand Alliance, 8649, 8651, 8652, 8654, 8657; and the Holocaust, 9070; and the Indian Crisis (1941–1943), 8938; and the Indian Political Crisis (1942), 8943; and the Iranian Oil Crisis (1944), 8874; and the Mexican Oil Controversy (1938–1943), 9057; and the Mexican Treaty (1944), 9052; and the Middle East during World War II, 8972; and the Middle East (1919–1945), 8969; and the Naval Arms Limitation Movement, 8035; and the Netherlands East Indies (1942), 8953; and the Neutrality Question (1940), 7888; and the Origins of the United Nations, 9460; and the Palestine Problem (1917–1939), 8993; and the Palestinian Refugee Problem (1939–1956), 8999; and the Panama Canal (1938–1947), 7693; and Peru, (1942–1943), 9062; and the Philippines (1929–1946), 8959; and the Portugese Wolfram Embargo (1944), 8789; and the Promotion of Hemispheric Democracy, 7633; and the Recognition of the Czechoslovak Republic (1939–1943), 8805; and the Reoccupation of the

Netherlands East Indies (1945), 8955; and the Russo-Finnish War, 8879, 8880; and the Special Relationship with Israel, 7621; and the Transfer of Economic Power from Britain (1933–1944), 8763; and the Turkish Republic before World War II, 7401 and the Viet-Minh (1945), 8947; and the World Court (1920–1966), 7971; and Trade with Guatemala (1933–1936), 7680; and Venezuela (1928–1948), 7708; and Vichy France, 8697, 8699, 8701, 8707, 8708; And the Argentine Proposal for Non-Belligerency, 9030; Anti-Drug Policy in Latin America (1930–1945), 7649; and USSR (1940–1941), 8843; and USSR and Lend Lease, 8844; and USSR during World War II, 8819; Argentine Relations, 7656, 8666, 8667,8869, 8671, 9027, 9029, 9031; Canadian Diplomatic Relations, 7253; China Policy and Pubic Opinion (1941–1951), 8917; Chinese Relations (1942–1948), 8898, 8916; Colombian Trade Treaty (1933), 7663; Commercial Struggles with Germany in Latin America (1934–1939), 7658;Constitution Compared to Philippine Constitution, 7609; Costa Rica (1940–1949), 9048; Cultural Relations with the USSR (1917–1958), 8873; Czechoslovakia Relations (1938–1945), 8804, 8806; Defense Site Negotiations (1946–1948), 9446; Diplomacy (1933–1938), 7946; Diplomatic Relations with China, 7548, 7549; Diplomats and Soviet Diplomacy (1934–1939), 8861; Diplomats and the Origins of the Cold War, 8828; Diplomats in Europe, (1919–1941), 7844, 7845; Diplomats in Moscow (1934–1939), 8859; Disputes with Britain over Palestine (1942–1947), 9009; Economic Policy and Japan (1931–1941), 7518; Economic Policy toward Latin America (1940s), 7628; Far Eastern Policy, 7553, 7566, 7585; Finnish Relations (1919–1941), 8709; Foreign Relations, Historiographical Survey (1957–1971), 9800; French Relations,8711, 8713; French Relations and the Munich Crisis, 8695; French Relations and the OSS (1942–1945), 8710; French Relations and the Political Role of the French Army (1943–1945), 8700; French Relations during World War II, 8691, 8706; German Relations (1933–1941), 7847; Historiography since the New Deal, Oral History Research Prospects (1976), 9853; History, (1915–1945), 2555; History (1920s to the 1930s), 6082; Government, Changing Role in Science and Technology, 4976; Image in Venezuela (1901–1948), 7709; in Venezuela (1908–1948), 7710; in World Affairs (1929–1941), Historiographical Survey (1961), 9723; in World War II, 8650, 8658; Intelligence (1939–1941), 9261; Interest in Latin America (1930s), 7640; Interpretation of Soviet Policy (1928–1947), 8863; Investment in Mexico (1930s and 1940s), 7688; Journalists in China (1930s and 1940s), 8906; Military and Higher Education, 4258; Military Assistance to Latin America during the First Half of the 20th Century, 7625; Military History, Bibliography, 9613; Military, Level of Readiness (1938–1941), 8311; Military Strategy and

China (1941–1944), 8902; Missionaries in Japan and U.S. Foreign Policy (1870–1941), 7590; Moroccan Relations during World War II, 8665; Naval Relations with the USSR (1930s), 8860; Neutrality Policy and the Paris Press (1935–1939), 7870; Newsmen in China (1941–1945), 8927; Occupation of Haiti, (1929–1934), 7681; Occupation of Tonga, (1942–1945), 8967; Oil Policy and the Coming of War in the Pacific (1940–1941), 7504; Participation in Inter-American Conferences (1933, 1936, 1938), 7641; Perceptions of Latin America (1933–1945), 7647; Periodicals and the Palestine Question (1936–1947), 8997; Proposal to Lease Destroyers to Brazil (1937), 7650; Public Opinion and Nazi Germany (1930s and early 1940s), 7882; Public Opinion and the Soviet Union (1935–1945), 8854; Refugees and U.S. Diplomacy (1938–1939), 9134; Refugee Policy, (1933–1940), 4177; Role in Indian Independence (1940–1947), 8939; Strategic Interest in the West Indies (1918–1938), 7661; Strategic Planning for Latin America (1930–1945), 7630; Strategic Thought in Latin America (1936–1940), 7639; Trade Policy, (1930s–1970s), 1821; Vice Counsels in North Africa (1941–1943), 8683; Withdrawal from Haiti (1929–1934), 7682; Yiddish Press and the Rise of Nazism (1930–1933), 9064

United States Army: Advisory System in Latin America (1922–1941), 7645; Airplane Inventory (1940), 4838; and Civil Defense, 4851; and Louisiana Maneuvers (1941), 9287, 9379; Records, 9647

United States Congress: and the Coming of War (1939–1940), 7861, 7862; as Viewed by the British Foreign Office during World War II, 8738

United States Foreign Policy: and Diplomacy (1935–1945), 7993; and European Integration during World War II, 8679; and Finland (1941–1945), 8681; and Japan (1931–1941), 7512; and Latin American Regimes (1933–1960), 9013; and Middle East Oil (1941–1948), 8989; and Palestine during World War II, 8992; and Palestine (1933–1948), 8995; and Public Opinion (1939–1941), 7867; and Public Opinion in Chicago (1939–1941), 7877, 7878; and Saudi Arabian Oil (1933–1945), 8988; and the Emergence of Communist Bulgaria (1943–1947), 8803; and the Loss of Eastern Europe (1938–1946), 8799; and the Netherlands East Indies (1937–1945), 8956; and the Organization of American States (1940s and 1950s), 7631; and the Peace Movement (1934–1938), 7962; and the Persian Corridor Project (1942), 8823; and the Question of Neutrality (1941–1956), 7866; and the Sino-Japanese War (1937), 7583; and the Soviet Union (1943–1945), 8822; and the Status of Puerto Rico (1936–1968), 7704; and the Zionist Lobby, 7865; and Yugoslavia (1941–1949), 8814; before World War II, 7915; Documents (1941–1949), 9686, 9694; Diplomatic Papers (1940–1943), 9670; in China (1937–1941), 8888; in Latin America (1900–1945), 7632,

7636, 7644; in Panama (1940–1977), 9061; in Southeast Asia (1940–1950), 8883; in the Middle East (1932–1949), 7619; toward Argentina (1941–1945), 9033; toward India, 8936, 8937; toward Iran (1941–1946), 8981; toward Japan (1941), 7559 toward Korea, (1941–1950), 8950, 8951, 8952; toward Latin America (1940–1948), 9014, 9022; toward Lebanon (1943–1976), 8983; toward Palestine (1948–1949), 9008

United States Immigration Policy: 9086; and German Refugees (1933–1940), 9161; and Jewish Intellectuals, 9149; and Jewish Refugees (1933–1945), 9081, 9082, 9131, 9132; and the Holocaust, 9099; (1930s), 4178

United States Navy: and American Foreign Policy Relative to Japan (1936–1941), 7520; and British Royal Navy, Development between the Two World Wars Compared, 4941; and Far Eastern Policy (1930–1939), 7568; and Jim Crow (1798–1941), 5615; and the Caribbean Sea, (1941–1941), 5031; and the Capital Ship Program (1934–1945), 9375; and the Oil Embargo (1940–1941), 7519; and the Role of Women (1917–1953), 9289; and Efforts to Develop an Intelligence System (1919–1945), 9276; Compared to British Navy and Japanese Navy between the Wars, 4903; Development of War College (1919–1941), 4919; in the Aleutians before World War II, 9395; Integration (1941–1978), 5614; Operating Expenditures (1932–1941), 4901; Partnership with California Cities, 4937; Plans for War (1937–1941), 7977; Plans for War in the Pacific (1919–1941), 5019; Spending Patterns (1921–1941), 4902; Strategic Interest in Pacific Islands, (1934–1942), 4900; the Treaty Period (1919–1937), 4980; The Two-Ocean Concept (1933–1941), 4977

United States Office of War Information: and the Polish Question (1943–1945), 8809; Influence over the Content and Presentation of Hollywood Movies, 3785

United States Senate: and the Conservative Coalition, 6125, 6123; and the Shaping of Foreign Policy (1921–1941), 7859; and Voting Alignments (1933–1944), 6065; Voting Patterns (1938–1952), 6075, 6076

United States State Department: Efforts to Promote the Importation of Argentine Meat and Paraguayan Tea, 7651; Failure to Coordinate War Plans and Diplomacy with the Military (1919–1939), 8593

United States Supreme Court: Activities, 6910, 6911, 6928; an Analysis of the *Erie Railway* v. *Tomkin's Case* (1938), 6917; and Administrative Law, (1932–1952), 6944; and Civil Rights (before 1937), 6906; and Constitutional Reform (1929–1940), 6956; and Internal Security (1935–1980), 6904; and Judicial Activism, 6922; and Judicial Review, 6903; and Public Opinion, 6926; and Religious Issues in the Public Schools (1940–1987), 6916; and Religious Liberty in Education (1930–1980), 6907; and Shifting Social Philosophy, 6900; and States' Economic Power (1932–1937), 6908; and the *Case of Humphrey's Executor* v. *The United States*, 6923; and the

Case of *The United States* v. *Curtiss-Wright* (1936), 6924; and the Case of *West Virginia Board of Education* v. *Barnett*, 6925; and the Commerce Clause (1937–1968), 6902; and the Court Packing Scheme, 6947–6966; and the Nazi Saboteur Case, 6901; and the Politics of Nominations, 6940; and the Press (1930s), 6912; and the Probability of Vacancies, 6913; and the Rise of Dissents and Concurring Opinions (after 1941), 6945 ; and Wagner Act Cases (1935–1937), 6909; and the Wagner Act (1937–1941), 6919; And Presidential Appointments, 6938; And the Case of *United States* v. *Belmont* (1937), 6929; Appointments (1937–1972), 6969; Attempts to Redefine its Place in American Government (1937–1955), 6920; Biographical essays on the Justices of the Hughes Court, 6933; Biographies of the New Deal Justices, 6905; Break up of the Roosevelt Court (1930s), 6918; Civil Rights and World War II, 6915; Conflicts with Roosevelt and Certain New Deal Legislation, 6921; Discord on the Roosevelt Court, 6970; Dynamics and Determinates of Change (1933–1982), 6932; Finding its Place in the Political Revolution of the New Deal Period (1933–1937), 6927; in the Twentieth Century, 6930; Interpretive Development of the Constitution (1918–1969), 6931; Nominations and Presidential Cronyism, 6937; Politics and Values (1937–1947), 6936; Roosevelt Court becomes the Truman Court, 6943; Statistical Analysis of Behavior (1941–1945), 6939; The Justices' Differing Opinions on Major Issues during the Roosevelt Era, 6935; Voting Behavior of the Justices (1931–1940), 6934; *United States* versus *Northern Pacific Railroad Company*, Final Settlement of Land Grant Case, (1924–1941), 1910

United Textile Workers of America, Strike in Alabama, (1934), 2237

Universal Production Company, History, 3207

University of Chicago, Efforts to Reform Liberal Arts Instruction (1929–1941), 4364

University of Idaho, Southern Branch Students Protest Roosevelt's Domestic and Foreign Policy, 4418

University of Maryland, Desegregation, 5640

University of North Carolina, Controversy over Jewish Student Quota, (1933), 5765

Upper Midwest Response to New Deal Tariff Policy, (1934–1940), 1824

Upper Mississippi River Region, Population, (1890–1945), 1508

Urban Fiscal Crisis of the Inter-War Years, (1915–1945), 6533

Urban History, Methodology, 9801

Urban, Joseph, Career, 3157

Urban League, Activities (1941–1946), 5489

Urban Planning: in Philadelphia, (1942–1945), 1783; Origins (1877–1935), 4640

Urban Reconstruction (1930s), 1807

Urban Renewal, Origins, 1780

USS Astoria, Visit to Japan (1939), 7501

Utah, and the Battle for Repeal of Prohibition, 4751

Van Devanter, Willis: 7048, 7049

Van Dusen, Henry P., Interventionist Views, 4565

Vandenberg, Arthur H.: Changes Concept of America's Role in World Affairs, 1273; Conversion to Internationalism, 1270; Favors Neutrality (1939), 1272; Isolationist Views, 1276; Private Papers, 1277; Supports Bipartisan Foreign Policy, 1271, 1274, 1275; Supports Formation of the United Nations, 1267, 1269; Views on the Polish Question, 1268

Vanderbilt, Arthur T., And Court Reform in New Jersey (1930–1947), 6485

Vanderbilt Agrarians, As Critics of the New Deal, 7089

Vanity Fair, History, (1914–1936), 4097

Vann, Robert Lee, And National Politics (1932–1940), 5650

Vassar Class (1935), 5932

Vatican Influence U.S. Foreign Policy During World War II, 4433

Vaudeville, Last Days in Los Angeles, 3258

Velvet Project (1942), 8856

Vendovi Island, Father Devine's Paradise in the Pacific, 4524

Venereal Disease in Baltimore, (1930s–1940s), 4201

Veterans' Pensions and the Rise of Social Security, 4186

Veto Power, Analysis of its Use (1889–1985), 6066

Vic and Sade, Popular Radio Program, (1932–1936), As an Artifact of Folklore History, 3917

Vice Presidents, and their Wives, 0563

Vidor, King: Autobiography, 3260: His Film *Our Daily Bread* (1934), Analyzed, 3803

Vigilante Activities in the South (1930s), 4720

Villard, Oswald Garrison, As a Link Between Progressivism and the New Deal (1918–1932), 6156

Vincent, Fred, And the Post War British Loan, 8743

Vincent, John Carter, As U.S. Representative in China (1924–1953), 8909

Vinson, Carl, Promotes Naval Expansion, 1106

Vinson, Fred M.: 7061, 7062

Vinson-Tramell, Naval Ship Replacement Act (1934), Significance, 4867

Virginia: Black Leaders (1930–1945), 5388; Efforts to Promote Reading (1920s and 1930s), 3265; Evolution of Jim Crow Laws in the Twentieth Century, 5598; Interpretations of 20th Century History (1986), 9743; Racial Discrimination in Jury Selection (1933–1965), 5568; Voters and Foreign Affairs (1933–1941), 6663

Vivas, Eliseo, Influence Upon Him of His Philosophy Professors at the University of Wisconsin (1930s), 4429

Vladeck Housing Development, New York, (1930–1940), 1785

Voice of America: (1940–1962), 9392; (1942–1982), 9381

Volunteer Army, Inter-War History (1919–1940), 4885

Volunteers in Social Welfare during the Depression, 1682

Vorse, Mary Heaton, Labor Journalist and Lecturer, 4089

Vorys, Congressman John M.: and Foreign Policy (1939–1958), 6121; and the Arms Embargo (1939), 7953

Voting Alignments in the House of Representatives in the Post New Deal Era, 6045

Waburn, New Jersey as an Example of the Garden City Movement, 4664

Wadsworth, Congressman James W. Jr.: And the Origins of the Peace Time Draft (1940), 8314; As Critic of the New Deal, 7103

Wage and Hour Legislation, Drafting, (1937), 2863

Wage Rigidity during the Great Depression, 2021

Wagner Act: Analysis, 2764; Impact on the Coal Industry, 2815 Written of by Leon Keyserling, 2678

Wagner-Hatfield Amendment to Federal Communications Commission Act (1934), Discussion, 3902

Wagner, Robert F.: Contributions to Social Reform, 1278; Fights for Passage of National Labor Relations Act, 1280; Supports Far Reaching Social Legislation, 1279

Wagner-Steagall Act (1937), Origins, 1788

Walker, Frank, New Deal Career, 0719

Walker, Kirby, As Superintendent of the Black School System in Jackson, Mississippi (1937–1969), 5638

Wall Street Investigation, (1933–1934), 2598

Wall Street Journal Coverage of the New Deal and World War II, 4100

Wallace, Henry A.: As Secretary of Agriculture, 0579, 0582, 0587; As Vice President, 0588; Biographical and Psychological Sketch, 0569; Biographical Sketch, 0581; Career as Farm Editor, 0580; Compared to Ezra Taft Benson, 1375; Complex Personality, 0575; Diary (1942–1946), 0598; Duties as Vice President, 0572; Economic Ideas, 0585; Foreign Policy Views, 0597; Helping Farmers Fight the Depression, 0571; Ideas and Beliefs, 0578, 0589; Interest in Hybrid Corn, 0570; Liberal Views, 0583; Management Skill, 0586; Not Re-Nominated for Vice President (1944), 0594; Political Career, 0599; Political Philosophy, 0590, 0591, 0592; Promoting Iowa Farmers, 0576; Reasons for Supporting the New Deal, 0577; Relationship with Milo Reno, 0593; Relationship with Nicholas Roerich, 0596; Role as Intellectual and Political Leader of American Agriculture, 0595; Speaking Ability, 0574; Sponsoring Organized Corn Husking Matches, 0573; Views Farming as a Male Occupation, 0584; Writings, 5052

Waller, Fats, Career in Harlem (1920s and 1930s), 3519, 3549

Walsh Amendment (1940), 7891

Walsh Brothers Dairy Farm in Nome, Alaska, 1402

Walsh, James J.,Life and Career, 4211

Walsh, Thomas J., Biography, 1063

Walt Disney Studio during World War II, 3841

Walters, Theodore A., As Assistant Secretary of Interior (1933–1937), 6678

Wanger, Walter and Independent Film Production in Hollywood, (1939–1949), 3723

War Debt Question (1917–1924), 7225

War Department: and Disarmament (1926–1935), 7241; and the Planning and Directing of Civil Affairs, (1940–1943), 4829; Reorganization (1931–1942), 4894

War Films, Characteristics, (1939–1970), 3840

War Motif on Broadway, (1933–1941), 3217

War of the Worlds (1938): Analysis, 3907; Brief Description, 3910; Causes Widespread Panic, 3906; National Newspaper Editorial Reactions, 3933

War Plan Orange, 7565

War Plays as Lasting Dramatic Literature, 3238

War Production Board: and Industrial Regulation, 8132; As Portrayed by Historians it Employed, 8091; Removes Controls on Business (1944–1946), 8108

War Referendum Movement: (1914–1941), 8000, 8023

War Refugee Board and U.S. Refugee Policies, 9115

Ward, Angus, And the Recovery of American Artifacts in Petrograd, 7434

Ward, Harry F., As Founder of the Methodist Federation for Social Service, 4525

Waring, J. Walters, Biography, 5599

Warm Springs, Oregon Indian Reservation (1855–1955), 5909

Warner Brothers: Crusade Against the Nazis, (1933–1941), 3737; Film Production System, (1930–1949), 3765; Musical Films, (1927–1980), 3770

Warren, Robert Penn: Analysis of His *All the King's Men*, (1946), 3387; Claims He Did Not Intend Willie Stark to Resemble Huey Long in *All the King's Men*, 3449

Wars, How they Start, 7236

Warsaw Uprising (1944): 8810; and the American Press, 8510

Wartime Technology and commercial Aviation, 1895

Washington and Casablanca Conferences, Documents, 9689

Washington and Quebec Conferences, Documents, 9690

Washington Commonwealth Federation: (1935–1945), 6404, 6186

Washington, DC Economics Industry, (1938), 2621

Washington Naval Treaty, Failure (1921–1935), 4914

Washington State Labor Politics during World War II, 2171

Water Rights Dispute on the North Platte River, (1934), 1458

Waterfront Workers and Militant Unionism Among, (1930s), 2316

Weather Bureau, Development (1870–1941), 5021

Weaver, Richard M., Changing Views, 6136

Weaver, Robert C., Career, 0720

Webb, Margot, Life and Times, 3532

Webb, Walter P., Impact on the Formulation on Federal Policy (1930s, 1940s, and 1950s), 4663, 9749

Weddell, Alexander W., As American Ambassador to Spain (1939–1942), 7369

Wedemeyer, General Albert C.: Claims the Politicians had Imprecise Warnings, 9436; Papers and Letters, 0962; Recalls his Experiences in China, 8932

Wehle, Louis B., Autobiography, 0765

Welfare: Administration in California, (1930–1945), 4215; Crises in the Northeast, (1935), 1581; Ideal of the 1930s, Contrasted with Consumerist Individualism of the 1920s, 4238; Policy and Expenditure in the United States, Analysis, (1929–1979), 2657; Relief in Pennsylvania, 1316

Welfare Capitalism as Used by Union Leaders, 2201

Welles, Sumner: And Cuba (1933), 7674; Diplomatic Career, (1933–1943), 0890; His View of New Deal Diplomacy (1944), 7237; Mission to Cuba (1933), 7665

Wells, Orson, Collaborates with Gregg Toland on *Citizen Kane*, (1940–1941), 3733

Welty, Eudora, As a Photographer for the Works Progress Administration (1930s), 3705

Wesely, Charles H., Biography, 5409

West Coast Teamsters and Longshoremen's Unions in the Twentieth Century, 2170

West, Helen Hunt, Advocate of the Equal Rights Amendment, 5980

West, Nathanael: Analysis of his Fiction, 5776; Analysis of His Novel *A Cool Million* (1934), 3482; His Comic Strip Novel *Miss Lonelyhearts* (1933) as an Attack on Popular Culture, 4137; Life and Work, 3857

West Texas Oil Boom, (1930s–1950s), 1748

West Virginia: and Factional Conflict in the Democratic Party (1941), 6599; and Moonshining Activities (1930s), 4711; Great Depression, (1932–1933), 2659

West Virginia Pulp and Paper Company, Organization, 2413

Western Farmers, Failures, 1367

Western Frontier, Myth in American Dance and Drama, (1930–1943), 3220

Western Massachusetts, and the 1932 Presidential Election, 6749

Western Movies, Evolution, (1930–1946), 3807

Western Swing, Development, 3537

Westway Highway Plan in New York City, 6658

Weyerheuser Lumber Workers Oppose Bedaux Speedup System, Willapa Harbor, Washington Mills, (1933–1935), 2181

Wharton, Edith, *The Buccaneers* (1938) Compared to Her Earlier Novels, 3499

Wheat Acreage Program, Impact, (1934–1968), 1479

Wheat Conference (1933) and Recognition of the Soviet Union, 7415

Wheat Farmers and Federal Support Programs (1939–1964), 8163

Wheat Farming in the Big Bend of Washington, 1486

Wheeler, Burton K.: And Montana Politics, 6680; Friendship with Hiram Johnson, 1065; Not a Reactionary, 1066; Public Career, 1064

Wherry, Kenneth S.: and Nebraska Politics, 6470; Political Career, 1067

White Collar Unionism, (1940–1950), 2296

White, George, As Governor of Ohio (1931–1935), 6672

White House: Conferences on Children, 4675; Organization and Management, 0378; Staff, 0376

White, Hugh L.: As Governor of Mississippi (1930s), 6461; Promotes Industrialization in Mississippi (1936), 6462

White Motor Company, History, 2546

White Schooling in the South, (1880–1940), 4308

White Southern Racial Liberalism (1920–1950), 6177

White, Theodore H., Recalls his Experiences in China, 8933

White, William A.: And the 1932 Gubernatorial Election in Kansas, 6451; As Critic of the New Deal, 7165; Debates with Verne Marshall, 7988; His Political Views (1930s and 1940s), 4011; His Resignation from the Committee to Defend America by Aiding the Allies Explained, 7978, 7989; His Views on the New Deal, 7083

Whitehead, Ennis C., Biographical Account of Long Career in the U.S. Air Force, 0963

Whitman, Walt, Reputation among Radical Writers during the Depression, 3588

Who's Who in America, Black Entries (1936–1955), 5301

Wickard, Claude, Career, 0665

Wilkins, Roy, Life and Civil Rights Career, 5341

Williams, Aubrey W.: Nominated as Rural Electrification Administration Administrator (1945), 0722; Post New Deal Career, 0723

Williams, Claude and Joyce, Southern Reformers, 5499

Williams, David R., Avant-garde Architect and Community Planner (1919–1962), 4672

Williams, George A., Political Career in Nebraska, 6727

Williams, James Robert, His *Out Our Way* Cartoons Memorialized the Humor of the West, 4119

Williams, Michael, and the Founding of *Commonweal*, (1922), 3965

Williamsburg Restoration, (1936–1942), 3186

Willkie, Wendell: and the 1940 Presidential Campaign, 6340, 6790; and Campaign Buttons (1940), 6798; Biography, 0770; Campaign Speeches, 0771; Presidential Nomination (1940), 0767, 0772; Republican Party Leader, 0769; Speaking Ability, 0768

Wilson (1944), Discussion, 3784

Wilson, Edmund: Analysis of his Writings, 9732; His Political Thought (1930s), 6226; His Political Writings (late 20's and early 30's), 6225; His Views on America from the 1920s to the Viet Nam War, 3973; Political Transition (1930s), 3494; Political Views, 6271

Wilson, Frank, Biographical Essay, 4491

Wilson, Hugh R.: and American Relations with the League of Nations, (1927–1937), 0891; Last Pre-War U.S. Ambassador to Germany, 7320

Wilson, M. L.: and the Campaign for Domestic Allotments, 2748; and the economic ideas of Tugwell, Rexford, Warren, George, and Myers, William, 2052; as Undersecretary of Agriculture, 0773; New Deal Career, 1563; Views on Planned Agricultural Production, 1567

Wilson, Robert R., His Experiences at Los Alamos (1943), 5026

Wilson, S. Davis, As Mayor of Philadelphia (1935–1939), 6679

Winant, John G.: Ambassador to the Court of Saint James, 0892, 0895, 8870; Career of, 0893, 0894

Windmills in Wyoming, 1739

Winet, John G., and New Hampshire Politics (1930s), 6574

Wingfield, George: and Nevada Politics (1907–1940), 6488; Comeback from Bankruptcy in the Great Depression, 2528; Political Influence in Nevada (1906–1935), 6675

Winograd, Leonard, American Jew as Prisoner of War (1944–1945), 9175

Winrod, Gerald B.: Fundamentalist Evangelist, 6546; Influence on Kansas Mennonites, 4512; Spokesmen for the Radical Right, 6394

Winter in Iowa, (1935–1936), 1740

Wisconsin: Combating the Depression, 1450; Dairy Farmers on Strike, 1354; Life on its Farms and in its Towns (1940), 4257; Milk Strikes, (1933), 2252; Progressive Party (1934), 6834; School for Workers, (1930s), 2366; State Government, Role in Labor Relations, (1937–1939), 2241; State Historical Society, Labor Manuscripts, 9612

Withlacoochee Land Use Project, Photograph Essay, 1528

Wolfe, Thomas: As a Southern Writer, 3332; Death, 1938, 4222; Disputes with the Vanderbilt Agrarians, 3492; His Method of Writing Short Novels in the 1930s, 4003; Western Trip (1938), 3218

Women: and Industrial Unionism (1930s), 2378; and Machinery on Iowa Farms (1930s), 5966; and Pacifism in the United States (1915–1941), 8043; and Protective Legislation in Ohio between the Wars, 5924; and Social Reform in Philadelphia, (1920–1945), 5987; and the Pennsylvania Railroad during World War II, 5992; And their Sexual Fantasies in Montgomery, Alabama (1930s), 5967; and Working Class Activism (1920–1945), 5996; Appointees in the Roosevelt and Truman Administrations, 5939; Army Auxiliary Corp and the News Media, 8198; as Lawyers in America (1920s and 1930s), 5928; as Pilots (WASP) during World War II, 5969; as Portrayed in American Film (1940–1950), 3798, 6021; as Portrayed in American Film during World War II, 3826; as Pilots (1927–1940), 5930; as Portrayed in the *Saturday Evening Post*, (1931–1936), 5961; as seen in American Fiction (1930s), 3305; as Portrayed on the American Stage (1930s), 3195; as Radio Pioneers (1920s and 1930s), 5954; as Transients and Tramps, 6024; as Writers in Hollywood's Golden Age, (1930–1950), 3860; Discrimination in the American Work Place, 5994; Garment Workers in St. Louis (1930s), 5929; in Connecticut Politics (1915–1945), 5993; in Military Service during World War II, 5950; in Modern America, (1930s to 1945), 5914; in Northwestern Missouri and Northeastern Kansas, (1920s, 1930s, and 1940s), 3352; Politics in Florida in the Wake of the 19th Amendment, 5989; in Politics in New Mexico (1900–1940), 5968; in Professional Rodeo, (1929–1947), 4606; in Roosevelt's

Life, 5933; in Popular Fiction (1940s), 5962; in the Texas International Ladies Garment Workers Union (1933–1950), 5959; in the United Auto Workers at the Ternstedt General Motors Plant, (1936–1950), 2303; in the Work Place during World War II, 5986; on the Great Plains Farms (1910–1940), 5965; Their Political Roles in the United States and Great Britain Compared, 5941; Their Role as portrayed in *Gone with the Wind* (1939), 3806; Their Role in American Fiction (1864–1933), 6004; Their Role in Sustaining the Social Reform Agenda from the Progressive Era to the New Deal, 5990; Their Role in the Family (1920–1940), 5922; Their Role in the Labor Market and Economic Structure during the Great Depression, 5964; Their Role on Nebraska and South Dakota Farms (1930s), 6009

Women's Bureau: and U.S. Latin American Relations, 6012; Efforts to end Gender Discrimination in the Work Place (1920–1970), 5977; History (1920–1950), 6013

Women's Films at Warner Brothers, (1939–1950), 3869

Women's International League for Peace and Freedom: 8015; American Section, 6842; and American Neutrality (1935–1939), 5997; in North Newton, Kansas, (1936), 6007

Women's Labor Union Membership in Minneapolis, (1929–1946), 2187

Women's Literature on Obligations to World War II Veterans, 5952

Women's Organizations: Activities (1919–1941), 5913; during World War II, 5951

Women's Peace Union (1921–1932), 7997

Women's Proletarian Fiction of the 1930s, Evaluated, 5999

Women's Revolutionary Novels (1930s), 6000

Women's Roles: (1900–1980), 6019; (1920–1940), 6022; in Montana Agriculture during the first Half of the 20th Century, 5981; in Society as Portrayed in the Comic Book Character Lois Lane, 6025

Women's Social Movements in 20th Century Minnesota, 5998

Women's Work, As Redefined in the Auto Industry during World War II, 5983

Wong, Jade Snow, Autobiography, 5671

Wood, John S., Military Career, 0964

Wood, Robert E., His Association with Conservative Organizations, 6116

Woodring, Harry H.: As Secretary of War, 0666; Dispute with Louis Johnson, 0668; Early Career in Kansas, 0667; Political Biography of, 0669

Woodruff, Hale, Life and Career, 3633

Woodrum, Clifton A.: Changes from Supporter to Opponent of New Deal, 1108; Political Career, 1107

Woodson, Carter G.: And the Movement to Promote Black History, 5394; Biography, 5535

Woodward, C. Vann, Modifies his Views of the South (1930s), 9779

Woodward, Ellen S.: And Women's Relief in the New Deal, 5159; As New Deal Administrator, 5160

Woodward, William E., And the Writing of Biography, 9712

Words as Political Symbols, 6062

Workers' Education Program at the University of California, (1921–1941), 4293

Workers' Film and Photo League, Records Worker Unrest during the Great Depression, 3752; Workers' Letters About Life on the Job (1930s), 2080

Workers' Theater and the American Labor Movement (1930s), 3224

Workers, Supply and Demand during the Great Depression, 1589

Working Class: Bibliography on the Great Depression and World War II Eras, 9608; Consciousness, Origins, (1930–1946), 2343; Discontent in America, (1929–1937), 1693; Militancy in the 1940s, 2222; Political Behavior (1870–1940), 6091; Sociability in Connecticut, (1850–1940), 2068

Workmen's Compensation, Challenged during the New Deal and World War II, 4188

Works Progress Administration: and Aid to Public Libraries, 3073; and Hawaiian Preparedness, (1935–1940), 5209; and Kentucky Politics (1935), 6592; and the Election of 1936 in North Carolina, 6608; Arts and Crafts Program, 5129; Art Programs, 5036; Art Project as a Humanist Experience, 5073; Artist and the Communist Party, 5085; Arts Project, 5083; Church Survey, 5249; City School Curriculum Project in San Diego, 5259; Dyess Colony Resettlement Project in Arkansas, 3064; Evaluation of Slave Narratives, 2771; Family History Project in Louisiana, 5177; Historical Records Survey, 2897; in Alaska, 5210; in the Southeast, 3097; in Mississippi, 5232; in Nashville, (1935–1943), 3043; in New York City, 2786, 3039; in Pennsylvania, (1935–1940), 2937; Murals Project, 5040; Nursery Schools in Boston, (1934–1943), 5250; Photographs of Virginia, 2915; Programs in Cleveland, (1935–1937), 3054; Project at Port Judith, Rhode Island, 3059; Project S-149, Interviews with early Oklahoma Settlers, 5907; Projects in Texas, 3029; Samples of State Guides, 2969; Sewing Projects in Hillsborough County, Florida, 3079; State Wide Library Project in Texas, 5218; Strike in Minneapolis and Saint Paul, (1939), 3055; Timberline Lodge Project, Mount Hood, Oregon, 3082; Writers Project, Interviews with Participants, 5039

World Conference of Christian Youth, (1939), 4571

World Court Question (1935), 6825

World Economic Conference: (1933), 1833, 7216

World Labor Athletic Carnival in New York City (1936), 4623

World Today, Analysis of Documentary Film Series, 3717

World War Humor, 4115

World War I Films, 1930–1938, Analysis, 3773

World War II: 7177; Administrative Problems, 8578; Aims and Goals of the United Nations, 8571; America as the Arsenal of Democracy, 8078; America on the Verge of War (1941), 8073; American Diplomacy, 7848; American Life under the Stress of War, 8070; American Military Leaders, 0896; American Strategy in the War with Japan (1933–1945), 8561; An Intelligence Leak on the Battle of Midway, 9358; and "Rosie the Riveter", 8210, 8222; and Africa's Strategic Minerals, 8660; and Air Craft Production, 8139; and Alabama Women, 8240, 8241, 8242; and Allied Strategy 8627, 8628, 9235; and Allied Strategy in the Balkans, 8760; and American Air Strategy in China, 9412; and American Armed Forces in Europe, 9352; and American Blacks in England, 9299; and American Citizens in the Canadian Royal Air Force (1939–1942), 8675; and American Diplomacy, 8579; and American Diplomatic Relations with the Vatican, 8586; and American Economic Aid to France, 8686; and American Fear of Soviet Expansion, 8581; and American Influence on British Policy in the Middle East, 8721; and American Propaganda in Argentina, 8537; and American Psychiatry, 8287; and American Slovaks, 8300; and American Steel Makers, 8147; and American Strategic Thought, 9438; and American Women as Portrayed in Film and Fiction, 8229; and American Women, Historiographical Survey (1987), 9766; and American Women Writers, 8230; and American Zionist Reaction to the Holocaust, 9076; and Amphibious Operations in the Pacific, 9278; and Anglo-American Cooperation, 8745, 9428; and Anglo-American Cooperation in Asia, 8769; and Anglo-American Defense Relations, 8719; and Anglo-American Indo-China Policy, 8768; and Anglo-American Naval Diplomacy, 8718; and Anglo-American Operations in North Africa, 9322; and Anglo-American Planning for the Invasion of Italy (1943), 9263; and Anglo-American Policy toward Yugoslavia, 8815; and Anglo-American Relations, 8716; and Anglo-American Relations in the Far East, 8765; and Anglo-American Relations with Iran (1942–1944), 8980; and Anglo-American Relations with Turkey, 8794; and Anglo-American War Aims, 8878; and Anglo-American Wheat Negotiations (1941–1942), 8723; and Army Morale (1941), 8323; and Asia, 8887; and Black American Soldiers in the Caribbean, 9388; and Black Protest, 5378; and Black Soldiers in Great Britain, 8737; and Black Women Workers, 8252; and British Airman in Detroit (1943–1945), 9266; and British Efforts against Japan, 8722; and British Intervention in Greece, 8730; and British Mediterranean Strategy, 9426; and Camp Kallan, San Diego, 8319; and Censorship, 8526; and Child Labor, 8254; and City Planning, 8173, 8190; and Coalition Warfare, 9425; and Code Breaking, 9331, 9348, 9349, 9406; and Command Decisions, 8568; and Conscientious Objectors, 8014, 8286, 8317, 8324; and Consumer Advertising, 8548; and Consumer Rationing in Lucas County, Ohio, 8186; and Cooperation between the U.S. and Soviet Air Forces, 9248; and Counter Intelligence Operations, 9257; and Cross Channel Attack

Proposals (1942), 8582; and Deferment as a Solution to
Industrial Manpower Problems, 8261; and Divided
Command in the Pacific, 9268; and Economic
Mobilization, 8140; and Economic Policy, 8168; and
Employment for Women in San Francisco, 8223; and
Farm Labor, 8144; and Female Workers in Knoxville,
Tennessee, 8218; and French Opposition to Allied
Landings in North Africa, 8685; and Gasoline Rationing,
8193; and Gender Discrimination, 8208; and Gender
Politics, 8205; and Gender Roles, 8215; and Government
Controls over the Iron and Steel Industries, 8164;and
Government Policy toward Civilian Women, 8236, 8237;
and Government Propaganda in Public Radio, 8528; and
Grand Strategy, 9233; and Grand Strategy in the Pacific
(1941–1943), 9370; and Great Military Decisions, 9362;
and Greek American Activity in the Office of Strategic
Services, 8584; and Hawaii National Park as a Bombing
Range, 9326; and Hemispheric Defense, 9021; and
Historical Record Keeping, 9730; and Historical
Revisionism, 9786; and Hollywood Feature Films as
Propaganda, 8494; and Hollywood War Films, 8504; and
Industrial Management, 8273; and Industrial
Mobilization, 8116; and Industrial Production, 8318; and
Industrial Production in Minnesota, 8119; and Inflation,
8155; and Intelligence, 9330; and Intelligence Gathering
in North Africa, 9382; and Inter-American Relations,
7913; and "Intrepid," 9420; and Irish Neutrality, 8780;
and Its Documents, 9385; and Japanese Bomb Carrying
Balloons, 9364; and Japanese War Balloons in South
Dakota, 9344; and Joint Tax Returns, 8219; and Labor,
8263, 8267, 8268; and Leaflet Propaganda, 8511; and
Lend Lease Air Craft to the Soviet Union (1941–1942),
8858; and Life on the Pittsburgh Home Front, 8302; and
Lord Allan Brooke, 8731; and Malta, 9351; and Man
Power Strategy, 9232; and Maritime Strategy, 9400; and
Mexican Labor in the Pacific Northwest, 8280; and
Mexican Migration to Washington State, 8281; and
Mexican Workers in Wyoming, 8292; and Military
Civilian Liaison, 9431; and Military Justice in Hawaii,
9325; and Milwaukee Labor, 8312; and Mountain Troops,
9242; and Natural Resource Management, 8187; and
Naval Intelligence in the Pacific, 9253, 9312, 9318, 9319,
9374; and News Management, 8546; and Nisei
Intelligence Agents, 9237; and Nuclear Secrets, 9292;
and Office of War Information Activities in Australia,
New Zealand, and South Africa, 8538; and Operation
Overlord, 9307, 9347; and Organized Labor, 8272, 8298;
and Organized Labors' Role in Governmental Agencies,
8321; and Pilot Training, 9335; and Pre-War Propaganda,
8500; and Pre-Yalta Policies on the Liberation of Europe,
8585; and Price Controls, 8194, 8196; and Prisoners of
War in the Philippines, 8255; and Private Sector
Propaganda, 8505; and Pro-War Propaganda in America,
8549; and Propaganda, 8543; and Propaganda Films,
8506; and Propaganda Posters in Virginia, 8487; and

Psychiatrists, 8284; and Psychological Warfare in Europe,
9281; and Psychological Warfare in the Pacific, 9421;
and Radio Communications in the Field, 9346; and Radio
Propaganda, 8491; and Radio Propaganda, 8545; and
Railroad Transportation, 8245; and Rationing Programs,
8195; and Real Wages, 8315; and Recruitment
Propaganda, 8514, 8515; and Refugees in Alaska, 9077;
and Rent Control, 8148; and a Review of Historical
Interpretations of American Entry (1981), 9740; and
Secular Conscientious Objectors, 8282; and Selective
Service, 9386; and Service Women, 8262; and Seward,
Alaska, 9310; and Ship Building by the Dravo
Corporation, 9432; and Small State Diplomacy, 8653;
and Soviet Japanese Neutrality, 9306; and Soviet
Japanese Relations, 8852; and Spain, 7358; and Special
Forces in Europe, 9390; and Stalin's Foreign Policy,
8836; and Stilwell's Command Problems, 8918; and
Stilwell's Mission to China, 8919; and Strategic
Bombing, 9327; and Strategy in the Pacific, 9329; and
Strikes in the Auto Industry, 8143; and Submarine Action
Against Japan, 9247; and Tactical Air Support
(1944–1945), 9328; and the G. I. Bill of Rights, 8433;
and Thailand, 8965; and the "Deal with Darlan", 8689;
and the 3rd Air Division (1943–1945), 9442; and the 8th
Air Force, 9441; and the Absence of an Analysis of
Nazism in American Literature, 8430; and the Accidental
Bombing of Switzerland, 9313; and the Allied Command,
9393; and the Allied Decision to Forgo Chemical
Warfare, 9367; and the Allied Unity of Command, 8704;
and the American Conscience on Bombing, 9321; and the
American Contacts with the French Resistance,
(1940–1943), 8688; and the American Mass Media, 8509;
and the American Occupation of Iceland (1941–1946),
9323; and the American Surrender to the Japanese in the
Philippines (1942), 9337; and the Anglo-American
Alliance, 8726, 9366; and the Anglo-American
Controversy over the Italian Campaign, 8744; and the
Anglo-American Debate over the Trusteship Issue, 8766;
and the Anglo-American Grand Strategy Conferences,
8605; and the Anglo-American Invasion of North Africa,
9286; and the Anglo-American Oil Agreement, 8729,
8767; and the Anglo-Soviet Balkan Agreement, 8775; and
the Army Air Force Body Armor Program, 9365; and the
Army Airwaves Communication System, 9402, 9422; and
the Army Chemical Warfare Service, 9251; and the Army
Rangers, 9317; and the Battle of Alaska, 9380; and the
Battle of Midway, 9240; and the Birth of the Synthetic
Rubber Industry, 8180; and the Bombing of Dresden,
9419; and the Bombing of German Civilians, 9411; and
the Bracero Program, 8279; and the Brazilian Air Force,
9038; and the British Intelligence Center in New York
City, 9324; and the British Joint Staff Mission in
Washington, 8759; and the Bureau of Motion Pictures,
8524; and the Canadian Oil Pipeline, 9332, 9384; and the
Chemical Industry in Latin America (1942–1944), 9020;

and the Civilian Pilot Training Program, 8434; and the Clark-Darlan Agreement (1942), 8687; and the Concept of Strategic Bombing, 9282; and the Concept of Total War, 8562; and the Construction of the Greater Cincinnati Airport, 8250; and the Controversy over the Use of Air Power during the Normandy Invasion, 9444; and the Creation of Guerrilla Organizations in Oregon (1942), 9279; and the Creation of the Office of War Information, 9439; and the Cross Channel Invasion, 8569, 9305; and the Decision not to Bomb Auschwitz, 9447; and the Decline of German Scholarship, 8429; and the Decoding of German and Japanese Communications, 9274; and the Defense of the Aleutian Islands (1940–1943), 9308; and the Defense of the Western Hemisphere, 9267; and the Development of a Long Range Escort Fighter, 9250; and the Development of American Studies, 8428; and the Development of Cartography, 9403; and the Development of Landing Craft, 9371; and the Development of National Policy for Foreign Oil, 8176; and the Development of Strategy Making Policy, 9361; and the Development of the Atomic Bomb, 9296, 9376, 9414; and the Diplomacy of Global War, 8636; and the Doctrine of Unconditional Surrender, 8557, 8566, 8583, 8590; and the Education of Black Soldiers, 8435; and the Emergency Farm Labor Program in Arkansas and Mississippi, 8325; and the Employment of Prison Inmates, 8293; and the Employment of Women in Defense Production, 8285; and the End of Japanese Control in China, 8920; and the Enlisted Man, 8277; and the Evolution of Strategic Planning in the Pacific, (1940–1941), 9343; and the Excess Profit Tax Law, 8177; and the Failure of the French and British Armies to End it (1939), 9336; and the Failure of the Second London Naval Conference, 7572; and the Female Labor Force, 8232; and the Finance Department, 8316; and the Formation of a Military Political Policy (1941–1943), 8606; and the Frankfurt School, 9333; and the Gathering of Enemy Scientific Literature, 9401; and the Gender Gap in Earnings, 8197; and the General Electric Naval Ordinance Manufacturing Program, 8117; and the Good Neighbor Policy, 9015; and the Grand Alliance, 8747; and the Greek American Community, 8556; and the High School Victory Corps, 8440; and the Historical Role of Libraries, 8539; and the Historiography of Military Intelligence, 9798; and the History of U.S. Naval Operations, 9369; and the Holy See Documents, 9637; and the Housing Shortage in Utah, 8185; and the Hughes HK-1, 8157; and the Humanitarian Efforts of the Mennonite Central Committee, 8742; and the Illinois Hemp Project, 8154; and the Image of Women in Film, 8201; and the Impact of Allied Air Power on the German War Economy (1944–1945), 9363; and the Impact of Government Pressure on Movie Studios, 8525; and the Independence of Thailand, 8962; and the Indians of Virginia, 8303; and the Inter-American Military System, 9259; and the Inter-American System

(1939–1945), 9017; and the Internment of Japanese Americans, 9314; and the Invasion of Europe, 9280; and the Irish Economy, 8761; and the Japanese Merchant Marine, 7571; and the Japanese Peace Maneuver (1944), 8564; and the Japanese Surrender, 8559, 9418; and the Joints Chiefs of Staff, 9309; and the Katyn Forrest Massacre, 9429; and the Landing in Southern France, 9315; and the Liberation of Paris, 8684; and the Major Strategic Conferences (1941–1943), 8592; and the Manhattan Project, 9339; and the Manpower Dilemma, 8258; and the Manufacture of Atomic Bomb Parts in Pocatello, Idaho, 8274; and the Mennonite Church, 8016; and the Misuse of the Battleship, 9373; and the Mobilization of American Psychologists, 8305; and the Mobilization of Black Support, 8523; and the Mobilization of Manpower in Columbus, Ohio, 8297; and the Mobilization of the Economy, 8146, 8295, 8296; and the Mobilization of the Media, 8521; and the Model Air Craft Project, 9450; and the National War Service Controversy, 8301; and the Nazi Sabotage Program in America, 9397; and the Need to Unite Military and Political Command, 8573; and the No Strike Pledge, 8299; and the North Atlantic Convoy System, 9229; and the Occupation of Austria, 8680; and the Office of Strategic Services, 9295, 9420; and the Office of War Information, 8488, 8520, 8522, 8529, 8554, 9246; and the Origins of Nuclear Research, 9342; and the Origins of the Civil Rights Movement, 5356; and the Origins of the Joint Chiefs of Staff, 9430; and the Origins of the Office of War Information, 8489; and the Origins of the Selective Service System, 8307; and the Planning of Operation Overlord, 9368; and the Poetry of Marianne Moore, 8231; and the Political Indoctrination Program, 9389; and the Political Influence of American Catholics, 8734; and the Politics of Surrender, 9334; and the Politics of the Second Front (1941–1944), 9427; and the Port Chicago Disaster, 8251; and the Preparation of Officers at Ft. Leavenworth, 8306; and the Prisoner of War Experience in Germany, 8271, 8278; and the Procurement of Merchant Vessels, 8246; and the Promotion of the Anglo-American Alliance, 8542; and the Propaganda Film, 8517; and the Propaganda Film *Victory through Air Power* (1943), 8493; and the Protection and Salvage of Artistic and Historic Monuments, 9300; and the Protection of War Essential Facilities in Maryland, 8265; and the Quest for a National Policy on Foreign Oil, 8991; and the Question of Currency Management, 9409; and the Question of Universal Military Training, 8266; and the Railroads, 8248; and the Regulation of the Labor Supply, 8276; and the Relief of Wake Island, 9294; and the Republican Party as Loyal Opposition, 8530; and the Role of the Arts in the U.S. and Germany Compared, 8436; and the Roosevelt Coalition in Connecticut, 8519; and the Sale of War Bonds in Oklahoma, 8551; and the Saving of Fine

Arts, 9302, 9303, 9340; and the Second Front Question, 8641, 8842; and the Secrets of Lake Michigan, 9252; and the Shaping of the American Army, 9437; and the Sino-American Cooperation Association, 9413; and the Special Deferment for Farmers, 8259; and the Status of Women in the Puget Sound Area, 8199; and the Strategic Bombing of Germany, 9440; and the Strategic Bombing of Urban Areas, 9269; and the Strategic Bombing Offensive in Europe, 9434; and the Strategic Bombing Survey, 9353, 9354, 9355; and the Struggle for East Asia's Rim Lands, 9357; and the Struggle for Rubber, 8188; and the Struggle for Turkish Chrome, 8795; and the Summit Conferences, 8613; and the Training of Civil Affairs Officers, 9449; and the Treatment of Battle Fatigue, 9258; and the U.S. Air lift to China, 8903; and the U.S. Alliance with New Zealand, 8678; and the U.S. Army, 9394; and the U.S. Army Air Force, Bibliography, 9631; and the U.S. Army Air Force, 9271; and the U.S. Army Finance Corps, 9408; and the U.S. Canadian Oil Project, 8674; and the U.S. Economy, 8181; and the U.S. Military Presence in Trinidad, 9448; and the U.S. Soviet Alliance, 8846; and the Ultra Secret, 9275; and the Use of Bomb-Laden Aircraft as Missiles, 9270; and the Use of Popular Culture as Propaganda, 8513; and the Use of Radio Intelligence in the Atlantic, 9404; and the Use of the Atomic Bomb, 9316; and the Use of the Draft, 8260; and the Use of Ultra Intelligence in the Atlantic, 9338; and the Uses of Manpower, 8270; and the War Department Scientific Intelligence Mission (1943–1945), 9356; and the War Hawks, 8490; and the Washington Treaty Navy, 9320; and the WAVES, 9290; and the Weakness of American Tactical Leadership, 9391; and the Women's Air Force Service Pilots, 8294; and the Writers' War Board as a Propaganda Agency, 8516; and Trailer Housing in San Francisco, 8189; and U.S. Agricultural Trade Policy, 8655; and U.S. Aid to China, 8915; and U.S. Aid to the Soviet Air Force, 8855; and U.S. Aid to the Soviet Union, 8848, 8850, 8857; and U.S. Air Bases in Latin America, 9023; and U.S. Appraisal of Japanese Strength, 9241; and U.S. Army Air Corps Bases in Brazil, 9040; and U.S.-Brazilian Relations, 9039; and U.S.-British-Yugoslav Policy toward Greece, 8817; and U.S.-Chinese Relationships, 8931; and U.S. Diplomacy in the Caribbean, 9046; and U.S.-Irish Relations, 8776, 8777, 8778; and U.S. Knowledge of Japanese Submarine Operations in the Pacific, 9249; and U.S.-Mexican Cooperation on the West Coast, 9054; and U.S.-Mexican Military Collaboration, 9051; and U.S.-Mexican Relations, 9058, 9059, 9060; and U.S. Military Bases in Brazil, 9044; and U.S. Nuclear Policy, 9415; and U.S. Objectives in Latin America, 9011; and U.S. Oil Diplomacy in Latin America, 9018; and U.S. Plans for the Conquest of Taiwan, 9291; and U.S. Policy in Egypt, 8717 and U.S. Policy in Latin America, 9012; and U.S. Policy in the Caribbean, 9047; and U.S. Policy toward

Eastern Europe, 8797, 8800; and U.S.-Portugese Relations, 8786, 8788, 8790; and U.S. Relations with Argentina and Chili, 9025; and U.S. Relations with Argentina and Brazil Compared, 9026; and U.S. Relations with Greece, 8772, 8773; and U.S.-Soviet Negotiations, 8826; and U.S.-Soviet Relations, 8835, 8837, 8841, 8851, 8872, 8882; and U.S.-Spanish Relations, 8791; and U.S. Strategic Planning, 8624; and U.S.-Thai Relations, 8963, 8964, 8966; and U.S. Troops in New Zealand, 8677; and U.S. Vice Counsels in North Africa, (1941–1942), 9383; and U.S.-Vatican Relations, 8796; and Universal Military Training, 8142; and USO Camp Shows, 8291; and Wage Stabilization, 8152; and Wage Stabilization in Agriculture, 8153; and War Information Centers, 8508; and War Propaganda, 8497 and Wives of Conscientious Objectors, 8211; and Women in American Shipyards, 8234; and Women in the Aircraft Industry, 8213; and Women in the Civilian Labor Force, 8217, 8238; and Women in the Military, 8243; and Women in the Ship Building Industry, 8216; and Women in the Shipyard, 8200; and Women in the Workplace, 8227, 8244; and Women Shipyard Workers in Portland and Vancouver, 8221; and Women Workers in Michigan, 8206; and Women Workers in the Auto and Electrical Industries, 8225; and Women's Home Front Roles, 8203, 8204; and Women's Work Experiences, 8212; and Working Class Women, 8220; and Working Women, 8235; and Yugoslavian Resistance, 8813; And Domestic Economic Legislation, 8122; And Efforts to Prevent Profiteering, 8129; And Farm Price Support Programs, 8130; And Industrial Mobilization, 8125; And Industrial Unionism, 8128; And Martial Law in Hawaii, 8090; And Penicillin Allocation on the Home Front, 8184; And Price Controls, 8124; And Racial Violence in the South, 5328; And Small Manufacturers, 8133; And the Automobile Industry, 8107; And the Business Community, 8137; And the Development of Penicillin, 8136; And the Gloucester Fishing Industry, 8123; And the Great Lakes Shipbuilding Industry, 8106; And the Increase in Industrial Production, 8131; And the Michigan Farmer, 8113; And the Origins of the Civil Rights Movement, 5351; And the Revival of Welfare Capitalism, 8127; and the Shaping of American Identity, 4246; And U.S. Economic Policy, 8121; And War Industry in Utah, 8102, 8103; And War Production in Indiana, 8109; Army and Navy Nurses as Prisoners, 8209; as an Historical Problem, 9748; As a "Good War", 8086; As Seen through the Eyes of Hollywood, 8531; at Sea, Bibliography, 9630; before Pearl Harbor, 7508; Bibliography,9622, 9624 9628, 9632; Causes and Consequences, 7192; Causes, 7300; Comparative Analysis of German and American Newsreel Coverage on the Eastern Front (1941–1942), 8512; Conflict between Civilian and Military Policy Makers, 9283; Construction and Repair of Railroad Cars in Pocatello, Idaho, 8247; Debate over Intervention (1939–1941),

7873; Diplomacy, Bibliography, 9629; Discussion of Documents, 9672; Discussion of Sources, 9667, 9671; Documents, 9638, 9640; Documents on Policy and Strategy, 9653; Documents Related to Major Issues, 9651; Economic and Political Impact on the Sun Belt, 8101; Economic and Social Impact on America Life, 8085; Economic Causes of American Entry, 7319; Efforts to Promote American Society and Values, 8527; Evaluation of American Strategy, 8567; General Discussion of the American Experience, 8563; German and American Propaganda on Women Workers Compared, 8228; Government and Organized Labor, 8304; Great Myths, 7226; Historical Appraisal of American Entry, 9722; Historical Documents (1938–1955), 9656; Historiographical Essay on the Home Front (1971), 9742; Historiography (1971), 9734; Historiography, 9704; Historiography of American Entry (1979), 9725; Historiography of Diplomacy (1981), 9761, 9796; History, 8752, 9254; Impact of Americans in Morocco, 8560; Impact of Wage and Price Controls on Big Business, 8170; Impact of War Worker Migration on the Public Schools of Richmond, California, 8424; Impact on Agricultural Labor, 8151;Impact on American Business and Industry, 8104; Impact on American Culture and Society, 8064, 8065; Impact on American Society, 8167; Impact on Arkansas, 8320; Impact on Banking Policy, 8165; Impact on Black America, 5384, 5472, 5487, 5554, 5631; Impact on Black Colleges, 8425; Impact on Black Families in Texas, 5326; Impact on Black Music, 5523; Impact on Charleston, South Carolina, 8083; Impact on Chicago, 8071; Impact on Civil Liberties, 8088; Impact on Connecticut Politics, 6557; Impact on Denver, 8150; Impact on Economic Activity in Texas, 8095; Impact on Female Employment, 8207; Impact on Florida, 8061, 8171; Impact on Higher Education (1940–1942), 8438, 8439; Impact on Homestead Steel Works, 8160; Impact on Illinois, 8100; Impact on Indiana, 8068; Impact on Iowa, 8062; Impact on Kirkland, Washington, 8156; Impact on Las Vegas, Nevada, 8161; Impact on Liberal Arts Education in the United States, 4424; Impact on Los Angeles, 8322; Impact on Lowell, Massachusetts, 8158; Impact on Martin, Tennessee, 8081; Impact on Michigan, 8069, 8112; Impact on Mississippi, 8063; Impact on Mobile, Alabama, 8097; Impact on Odessa, Texas, 8084; Impact on Omaha Urban League, 5485; Impact on Pocatello, Idaho, 8096, 8178; Impact on Portland, Oregon, 8183; Impact on Race Relations, 5369; Impact on Race Relations in Seattle, 5364; Impact on San Diego, 8179; Impact on San Francisco's Black Community, 5324; Impact on Centenary Collage, Shreveport, Louisiana, 8427; Impact on Society and Economy in Michigan, 8114; Impact on South Dakota, 8191; Impact on Teenagers in Indianapolis, 8441, 8442; Impact on the American People, 8172; Impact on the American

Working Class, 8079; Impact on the Black Press, 5377; Impact on the Chattanooga School System, 8423; Impact on the Citizen Solider, 8288; Impact on the Far East, 8884; Impact on the Greek Community in Atlanta, 8072; Impact on the Lumber Industry in Coos Bay, Oregon, 8169; Impact on the Medical Profession, 8275; Impact on the Pacific Northwest, 8175; Impact on the Portland, Oregon School System, 8431; Impact on the South, 8118; Impact on the Textile Industry, 8192; Impact on Virginia Politics, 8555; Impact on Washington D.C., 8066; Impact on Working Women in Mobile, Alabama, 8289; in the Far East, 9265; in the Mediterranean, Historiographical Essay (1970), 9745; in the Pacific, 9396; Introduction to the Sources (1974), 9807; Its Great Mistakes, 8558; Japanese and Chinese Documents (1937–1949), 9642; Lack of Historical Studies (1962), 9772; List of Federal Records, 9692; Literature on the Involvement of Women (1981), 9739; Lowell, Massacuhetts, 8082; Mediterranean Strategies, 8572; Military History, 9264; Military Humor, 4134; Mobilization of Men and Machines, 8257; Naval Policy and Strategy, 8575; Naval Records, 9643; New Left Interpretation of U.S. Diplomacy, 8574; Official Studies of (1948), 9770; Origins, 7211, 7218, 7219, 7235; Origins of the American Japanese Phase, 7579; Politics and Strategy of the Belligerent Powers, 8565; Posters, Compared to World War I Posters, 8540; Pre-1960 Writings, 9718; Prompts Efforts to Find Use for Surplus Agricultural Products, 8126; Protecting Enemy Diplomats, 8076; Replacement Practices of the U.S. and German Armies Compared, 9445; Response of the American People (1941–1942), 8074; Revisionism Compared to World War I Revisionism, 9790; Revisionist Literature, 3463; Secret History, 7227; Selected Bibliography, 9606; Socio-Sexual History, 4198; Strategic Dimensions, 9405; Studies (1968–1969), 9773; The Army Specialized Training Program and the Navy Training Program in Virginia, 8432; The Home Front, 8067, 8080, 8087, 8089, 8094, 8098, 8149, The Italian Campaign, 9341; The Literature of Code Breaking, 9719; U.S. and German Intelligence Services Compared, 9377; U.S. and German Mobility Compared, 9398; Why the United States Fought Germany, 7278

World Wars, Official Histories, 9627
Wright, Cleo, Lynching (January 5, 1942), 5334
Wright, Ernest, Community Organizer in New Orleans, 5479
Wright, Fielding, Political Career in Mississippi, 6543
Wright, Frank Lloyd: Activities, (1931–1941), 3170; and the Idea of Planned Communities, 4671; Visits Moscow, (June, 1937), 3171
Wright, Howard T., His Flight Across America (1942), 5029
Wright, Richard: and Langston Hughes, Analysis of their Literary and Political Ideas, 3360; Analysis of his Novel *Black Boy* (1945), 3487; and the Chicago Renaissance, 3618; and the Communist Party, 3440; Historical Background on His *Native Son*, 1940, 3399

Wright, Willard Huntington, Analysis of His Novel *The Dragon Murder Case* (1933), 3491

Wyoming, Drainage Districts during the Great Depression, 1436

Y.M.C.A. Graduate School, Nashville, (1919–1936), 4262

Yachting (1930s), 4610

Yakima Valley, Press Coverage of Japanese-Americans, (1920s–1930s), 4000

Yakusa, Japanese Crime Syndicate in Los Angeles (1930s), 4707

Yale University, Unionization (1931–1985), 4335

Yalta Conference: 0802, 8594, 8598, 8599, 8600, 8601, 8602, 8609, 8612, 8618, 8629, 8632, 8637, 8638, 8643, 8646; As Evaluated in Indiana Newspapers, 8633; Historiography, 9806; Impact on Chinese Domestic Politics, 8648; Impact on Polish Americans, 8642

Yearling, The (1945), Problems in Filming it, 3844

Yee, Quin War, Challenges the Oakland, California Chinese Laundry Ordinance, 5673

Yosemite National Park, Construction of Facilities, 1499

Young, Arthur N., As Financial Advisor to China (1929–1947), 8934

Young Socialist Movement in America (1905–1940), 6308

Young Women in the West, Values and Attitudes (1943), 5926

Young Women's Christian Association, Efforts to Achieve Racial Understanding in the South (1920–1944), 5561

Yugoslav Emergency Council in New York (1941), 8060

YWCA in Cincinnati, (1920–1940), 1776

Zangara, Giuseppi: Attempts to Assassinate Roosevelt, (1933), 4734, 4739

Zanuck, Daryl F., And the Failure of *One World* (1939–1945), 3865

Zeppelins, 9231

Zionism: Differing Views, 9156; in America, 9007

Zionist Movement: American Critics of (1917–1941), 5773; and Liberal Jews in America (1917–1941), 5772

Zon, Raphael, Career, 1510

Zook, George F., Analysis of his Contributions to American Education, 4276

Zoot-Suit: and Service Men in Los Angeles (1943), 5698; and Style Warfare during World War II, 4703; Riots during World War II, 5699

Zuck, Mary, Role in Detroit Meat Strike (1936), 2365

Zugsmith, Leane, And the Social Novel (1930s), 3392